OF

D1422418

THE ART OF CREATING POWER

BENEDICT WILKINSON
JAMES GOW
(*Editors*)

The Art of Creating Power

Freedman on Strategy

OXFORD
UNIVERSITY PRESS

Oxford University Press is a department of the
University of Oxford. It furthers the University's objective
of excellence in research, scholarship, and education
by publishing worldwide.

Oxford   New York
Auckland   Cape Town   Dar es Salaam   Hong Kong   Karachi
Kuala Lumpur   Madrid   Melbourne   Mexico City   Nairobi
New Delhi   Shanghai   Taipei   Toronto

With offices in
Argentina   Austria   Brazil   Chile   Czech Republic   France   Greece
Guatemala   Hungary   Italy   Japan   Poland   Portugal   Singapore
South Korea   Switzerland   Thailand   Turkey   Ukraine   Vietnam

Oxford is a registered trade mark of Oxford University Press
in the UK and certain other countries.

Published in the United States of America by
Oxford University Press
198 Madison Avenue, New York, NY 10016

Library of Congress Cataloging-in-Publication Data is available
Benedict Wilkinson and James Gow.
The Art of Creating Power: Freedman on Strategy.
ISBN: 9780190851163

Printed in Great Britain by Bell and Bain Ltd, Glasgow

CONTENTS

CONTENTS

PREFACE

One of the key points in Lawrence Freedman's *Strategy: A History* is that strategy relies on scripts to set agendas and help transform ideas, theories and aims into practical achievement. However, unlike the dramatist's script which dictates the middle and end, as well as the start, the strategist's script is a starting point or an opening gambit, susceptible to social processes—interaction, construction, constitution—in which an opponent's script or the fates challenge and, indeed, almost certainly alter the initial script. Scripts therefore need almost constant shaping and reshaping to ensure that they and the strategies they underpin remain viable and prevail.

The same might well apply, at least to some extent, to the experience of producing this book. We came together on the project at a relatively late stage, when Ben, just completing his PhD as one of Lawrence Freedman's last research students, volunteered to assist James. He quickly became a colleague and ever more involved in all aspects of a project for which James had sketched the first script about Freedman's intellectual approach and the need to explore it coherently and critically as he approached his sixtieth birthday. As we write this, he has already passed the 65-year mark and is heading towards his seventieth in 2018. A core script has remained—the purpose of bringing out the theoretical and methodological 'glue' that has made Freedman one of the great intellectual figures in the canon of international politics, strategy and war, and yet that 'glue' was seemingly both unnoticed and lacking in definition.

The seeds of that purpose were sown in various conversations around the world in which James was welcomed with approbation as being from King's and part of the Freedman 'school', as well as for his own work in a similar vein. There was always a sense that there was a mass of 'good stuff', but nothing beyond the names of King's and Freedman that bound it together and made sense of it. Yet, personally, the sense grew that there was a considerable sum to all the parts. The seeds swiftly grew into shoots in September 2008, during one week of intense work exchanging emails around the clock, as Sir Lawrence developed the proposal that would become the Research Councils UK Global Uncertainties Fellowship, in which the idea of 'strategic scripts' emerged and from which *Strategy* was a major outcome. That week made the need to take stock of Freedman's thought, work and influence an imperative—the mission to bring out the theoretical and methodological glue in that oeuvre, the core script. While the core script has remained, the narrative, the complex pattern of interactions it experienced with other scripts, other protagonists and events, inevitably took different directions. This collection of research essays is the interim conclusion of an unfinished narrative.

Some individuals have been especially important in the genesis of this project. Rob Ayson and Jeff Michaels were passionate in their support for the project and would doubtless have been co-editors but for the practicalities of life. Nevertheless, in spirit, we see them as co-editors: both separately conceived the idea to produce a book of reflections on Freedman's work and the four of us discussed the book part of this project together in its infancy; both also contributed to the project by reading some of the material at an early stage. In addition to Rob and Jeff, Srinath Raghavan and James also had several conversations about a project of this kind. Sadly, personal circumstances meant that Srinath could neither participate in the research conference we held nor make a written contribution. We are, nonetheless, extremely grateful to him for the time he invested in thinking about and planning the project at earlier stages and certainly regard him as part of this venture. Phil Sabin and John Gearson took active parts in the research conference and made important critical contributions. Phil's place in the Freedman project deserves, and has, our fullest appreciation, though he did not contribute to the present volume. Although John did not present a paper at the conference, his substantial written reflections are included in the volume. Similarly, David Dunn and Ned

Lebow were both completely committed to the project, even though previous engagements meant they were unable to attend the conference. Nevertheless, their valuable written contributions appear in this volume. Ned also deserves our thanks for his immediate, positive support for the project, and the moments when he was particularly helpful and happily—and swiftly—changed course in a way that really facilitated the book.

Several of our colleagues and of Freedman's at King's College London deserve thanks as well. Vivienne Jabri was a very willing and critical mainstay of intellectual support in discussing theoretical aspects of this project and would surely have contributed, had her precious time not already begun to be devoured by the contemporary bureaucratic Gargantua of British academic life that is the 'research excellence exercise', where, for the sin of her eminence, she was appointed a member of the all-consuming sub-panel for politics and international studies. Theo Farrell, at the time, head of department in succession to Freedman, was unhesitating and generous in his support, both at the conference and in the background. On the practical side, Ernst Dijxhoorn was an invaluable crutch on which to lean for many things, as he has been on other occasions, and gladly contributed editorial and research assistance. In addition, Brad Robinson, Susanne Krieg and Helen Bhandari made management of the conference and the project as a whole easy. Away from King's, on the editorial and publishing side, our thanks for their commitment and support go to Jonathan Derrick, Michael Dwyer, Jon de Peyer, Daisy Leitch and David McBride, as well as to Cambridge University Press for permission to use and present an edited and revised version of Lawrence Freedman's 'Confessions of a Premature Constructivist', published in its original form in *Review of International Studies*. Acknowledgement is also due to those who gave permission to use the images in Jan Willem Honig's contribution (for which full acknowledgment is expressed in the chapter): François Robichon; the Toledo Museum; the Musée du Louvre; and the Service Historique de la Défense, Vincennes.

Finally, we cannot express sufficient thanks and gratitude in any form we recognize to those without whom the whole project would not have been possible: Karen Colvard and the Harry Frank Guggenheim Foundation, and Lawrence Freedman himself. The 'Freedman project' that results in the present volume would not have been possible without either. Both are committed to the aspiration to use the very best research possible on conflict and violence to work for a real and beneficial difference in the world. This is no doubt one aspect behind Karen's support for this project as Program Director of the Foundation, as well as the support of the Foundation more broadly. Karen made everything possible, from her initial discussion over lunch in New York with James about a research project of this kind and her advice on shaping its proposed agenda (graciously accommodating James's thirteenth-hour proposal drafting) to her support to make the Foundation Research Conference possible and her active engagement in the conference itself. In all of this, she proved herself, once again, to be adept at strategic scripting, as well as a warm and engaging intellectual presence— qualities shared with Lawrence Freedman.

For those qualities, as well, our final enormous acknowledgement of personal and intellectual debt goes to Lawrence Freedman himself, along with thanks for all his support and encouragement—an acknowledgement that all those who have known him and worked in his wake will share (and one which those who have benefited from his contribution without knowing it would share, surely, if only they knew). However, that acknowledgement must be expressed in a specific and immediate version for the way in which he readily, if uncomfortably, engaged fully with the difficult enterprise of 'being researched' and having his thought and work critically interrogated, so long as (with his typical humility) it was not a 'vanity project', but something with intellectual substance. The volume has been discussed with him beyond his own contribution to it. The book might well not be what some readers would expect. It is not a Festschrift—at least not in any conventional sense (aside from a reference to the work that Freedman himself edited in honour of Sir Michael Howard). Our subject made it clear that he would only enjoy and cooperate in the enterprise if it were a serious research project book exploring his 'school of thought' (including whether such a thing could be said to exist) and the scope of his work, spanning strategy, military and political history, policy and practice— as might obviously be expected—and also his lifelong engagement with sociological, theoretical and ethical aspects of war, international politics and life. We hope that the book reflects something of the serious enterprise he sought—and that others, if looking for a different book, will understand and appreciate the nature of our undertaking. If they read it fairly we trust that they will. We believe the intellectual substance is evident in the richness of the chapters that follow—even if this and Michael Howard's Foreword to the volume will make him blush awkwardly.

James Gow and Benedict Wilkinson   *London, January 2017*

FOREWORD

Sir Michael Howard

When the Department of War Studies was established half a century ago, the Cold War was at its height. Our main concern then was not fighting wars: it was deterring them. Much of our time was spent reading, digesting and interpreting the massive tomes about 'deterrence' and 'limited war' by pundits such as Kissinger, Kahn, Schelling, Brodie and Osgood that were pouring across the Atlantic. Most of these are now relegated to the most remote shelves in our libraries, but there is now no need to consult them: all we need do is read *The Evolution of Nuclear Strategy* by Lawrence Freedman. And anyone who seeks to know how the subject has broadened and developed over the past fifty years need only consult his numerous, authoritative and wonderfully accessible works.

When we first began to think how war studies might be further developed, I have to admit that, as a historian with all the limitations and prejudices of the profession, I myself had in mind only a spectrum extending from the legitimized and limited conflicts of the 'Westphalian' era to the massively destructive wars of the twentieth century; a range defined by the Clausewitzian distinction between 'limited' and 'total' war. But I quickly learned that Clausewitz, genius though he was, was a very culture-bound guide. He wrote about war as it had been understood and practised in Europe, and would be until the mid-twentieth century. But the conflicts of the 1960s were not fought in Europe; nor were they waged between 'states' of the kind with which Clausewitz and his disciples were familiar. They were termed, by those who waged them, 'people's wars'. A few decades earlier they had been dismissed as 'imperial policing'. Later they would acquire a certain respectability as 'counterinsurgency'. But to understand them one had to read not Clausewitz but Mao Zedong. These were 'asymmetric' conflicts between sophisticated professional armies and highly motivated groups, initially equipped with little more than fanatical enthusiasm but also, if they were successful, the support of the peoples among whom they were fighting. Until we understood the dynamics of this kind of warfare, we would never be able to fight, let alone win, such wars.

It was the conflict in Vietnam that taught the West its first, hard lessons about 'war among the people'. It also revealed the problems involved in fighting other people's wars for them and, more generally, 'wars of intervention'. By the beginning of the twenty-first century these had become our primary concern. When was intervention in other people's conflicts 'legitimate'? What limits should be set on it? How could it be justified in terms of international law? These problems were initially forced on our attention by conflicts in a region with whose troubles Europeans were only too wearisomely familiar— the Balkans. But these in their turn were to be dwarfed by the appalling event now termed '9/11': the destruction, by a handful of suicidal fanatics, of the World Trade Center building in New York on 11 September 2001.

What this gruesome massacre made clear was that 'counterinsurgency' was no longer just a local affair of 'winning hearts and minds'. The insurgents were now global in their reach, and could fight back with weapons quite as destructive in their way as any that we possessed. Further, they might well have allies within our own population. Was this, as President George W. Bush initially termed it, a 'Global War on Terror'? If so, how should it be waged? What rights did it carry of intervention—forcible or covert—in the affairs of other countries? What would it involve in terms of control over our own populations? Above all, how would we know when it was over—or did we now live in a Hobbesian condition of universal and permanent war of which specific conflicts were only manifestations? Would war now multiply itself throughout the world like a malignant cancer?

These are huge and terrifying questions. All fall, for better or worse, within the remit of war studies. As the scope of the subject has expanded, so has the range of Lawrence Freedman's expertise and that of his colleagues and pupils who now teach war studies all over the world. Of their work this volume in his honour can provide only a tiny example. But it provides some indication of the quality and range of the scholars who are proud to think of themselves as his friends, his admirers and his disciples.

ABOUT THE CONTRIBUTORS

Robert Ayson has been Professor of Strategic Studies at Victoria University in Wellington since 2010. He completed his PhD in war studies at King's College London in 1996 under Lawrence Freedman's supervision. He has held academic positions at the University of Waikato and Massey University in New Zealand and at the Australian National University. Ayson has also worked as a New Zealand government official, is a former Senior Research Associate with the University of Oxford's Centre for International Studies, and is an Adjunct Professor with the ANU's Strategic and Defence Studies Centre and an Honorary Professor at the New Zealand Defence Force Command and Staff College. His writings include *Thomas Schelling and the Nuclear Age* (Frank Cass, 2004), *Hedley Bull and the Accommodation of Power* (Palgrave Macmillan, 2012), and *Asia's Security* (Palgrave Macmillan, 2015).

Mats Berdal is Professor of Security and Development at the Department of War Studies, King's College London, where he is also the Programme Director for the MA in Conflict, Security and Development. He joined the department in 2003, having previously been Director of Studies at the International Institute for Strategic Studies (IISS) in London from 2000 to 2003. He is Visiting Professor at the Norwegian Defence University College and was a Consulting Senior Fellow at the IISS from 2009 to 2011, responsible for the institute's Economics and Conflict Resolution Programme. Berdal is a member of the Academia Europaea and directs the Conflict, Security and Development Research Group. His publications include *Building Peace After War* and the jointly edited volumes *Ending Wars*; *Consolidating*

Peace: Economic Perspectives; *The Peace in Between: Post-War Violence and Peacebuilding*; and *The Political Economy of Peacebuilding: Power after Peace*. Berdal completed a multi-year research project on post-war violence and peacebuilding together with Astri Suhrke (CMI, Bergen), and another with Dominik Zaum of Reading University, supported by the Carnegie Corporation of New York, on the 'Political Economy of Post-Conflict Peacebuilding'. Berdal's other principal research interest is the UN and the end of the Cold War, in particular the UN's involvement in the mitigation, containment and resolution of civil wars. Recent writings have focused on developments at the UN since the start of the war in Iraq in 2003, NATO, and the political economy of armed conflict. Other research interests include violence in post-conflict societies, the changing character of war, the evolution of NATO, developments in UN peacekeeping and Philip Windsor's contribution to the study of international relations, in particular his ideas on strategy and war. In addition to this, he retains a longstanding interest in the history of the Cold War and Nordic security. From 2015 to 2016, Berdal served on the Commission of Inquiry set up by the Norwegian Government in 2014 to examine Norway's military, humanitarian and development contributions to allied operations in Afghanistan between 2001 and 2014.

Philip Bobbitt is Herbert Wechsler Professor of Federal Jurisprudence and Director of the Center for National Security at Columbia University, and Distinguished Senior Lecturer at the University of Texas. His previous positions span academia and public service. Bobbitt is a former member of the Oxford University Modern History Faculty and the Department of War Studies at King's College London. Previous visiting positions include James Barr Ames Visiting Professor of Law at Harvard Law School and Florence Rogatz Visiting Professor of Law at the Yale Law School. Bobbitt has served as Associate Counsel to the President, the Counselor on International Law at the State Department, Legal Counsel to the Senate Iran-Contra Committee, and Director for Intelligence, Senior Director for Critical Infrastructure and Senior Director for Strategic Planning at the National Security Council. He has published nine books: *Tragic Choices* (with G. Calabresi); *Constitutional Fate*; *Democracy and Deterrence*; *U.S. Nuclear Strategy* (with L.D. Freedman and G.F. Treverton); *Constitutional*

Interpretation; *The Shield of Achilles: War, Peace and the Course of History*; *Terror and Consent*; *The Garments of Court and Palace: Machiavelli and the World He Made* and in 2015 *The Ages of American Law* (2d ed. with G. Gilmore). He is a member of the American Academy of Arts & Sciences and currently serves as a member of the External Advisory Board of the CIA.

Richard Caplan is Professor of International Relations and an Official Fellow of Linacre College, Oxford. His books include *Europe and the Recognition of New States in Yugoslavia* (Cambridge University Press); *International Governance of War-Torn Territories: Rule and Reconstruction* (Oxford University Press); *Europe's New Nationalism: States and Minorities in Conflict* (Oxford University Press); *Exit Strategies and State Building* (Oxford University Press), and, *The Measure of Peace* (forthcoming). Caplan holds degrees in political theory and international relations from McGill University (BA Hons), the University of Cambridge (MPhil), and King's College London (PhD), where he was supervised by Lawrence Freedman.

David Dunn is Professor in International Relations at the University of Birmingham, where he is Director of Internationalisation for the College of Social Sciences. Between 2012–16 he was Head of the Department of Political Science and International Studies at UB. Since 2000 he has also been chairman of the West Midlands Military Education Committee. His research focuses on US foreign and security policy, and diplomacy and statecraft. He is currently the holder of three research grants from the Economic and Social Research Council (ESRC), the Open Society Foundation (OSF) and the Gerda Henkel Foundation on different aspects of drone warfare. He is the previous holder of both a NATO Fellowship and a Fulbright Fellowship. His books include *The Politics of Threat: ICBM Vulnerability in American National Security Policy*; *American National Security Policy after the Cold War: Beyond Containment*; *Diplomacy at the Highest Level: The Evolution of International Summitry*; and *Poland: a New Power in Transatlantic Security*. He holds degrees in Political Theory and Institutions from Liverpool University (BA Hons), International Studies from the University of Southampton (MSc), and War Studies from King's College London (PhD), where he was supervised by Lawrence Freedman.

The Honorable Richard A. Falkenrath, CISSP, PhD is Chief Security Officer of Bridgewater Associates, the world's largest hedge fund. He is also the Shelby Cullom and Kathryn W. Davis Adjunct Senior Fellow at the Council on Foreign Relations as well as a member of the Aspen Strategy Group and the Trilateral Commission. Previously he was Deputy Commissioner for Counterterrorism of the New York City Police Department; Stephen and Barbara Friedman Senior Fellow at The Brookings Institution; Deputy Assistant to the President and Deputy Homeland Security Advisor under President George W. Bush; and Assistant Professor of Public Policy at Harvard University's John F. Kennedy School of Government. He is a *summa cum laude* graduate of Occidental College, with degrees in economics and international relations. A British Marshall Scholar, he received a PhD from the Department of War Studies at King's College London at age of 23 under the tutelage of Lawrence Freedman.

Sir Lawrence Freedman KCMG CBE is Emeritus Professor of War Studies at King's College London, where he held the Chair of War Studies 1982 to 2014 and was Vice-Principal from 2003 to 2013. He was educated at Whitley Bay Grammar School and the universities of Manchester, York and Oxford. Before joining King's he held research appointments at Nuffield College Oxford, IISS and the Royal Institute of International Affairs. In 1996, he was appointed Official Historian of the Falklands Campaign and in June 2009 he was appointed to serve as a member of the official inquiry into Britain and the 2003 Iraq War.

Lawrence Freedman has written extensively on nuclear strategy and the Cold War, as well as commentating regularly on contemporary security issues. Among his books are *Kennedy's Wars: Berlin, Cuba, Laos and Vietnam* (2000), *The Evolution of Nuclear Strategy* (3rd edition 2004), *Deterrence* (2005), the two volume *Official History of the Falklands Campaign* (second edition 2007) and an Adelphi Paper on 'The Transformation in Strategic Affairs' (2004). *A Choice of Enemies: America confronts the Middle East*, won the 2009 Lionel Gelber Prize and Duke of Westminster Medal for Military Literature. *Strategy: A History* (2013) was awarded the W J McKenzie Book Prize by the Political Studies association. His latest book is *The Future of War: A History* (2017).

ABOUT THE CONTRIBUTORS

Mervyn Frost is Professor of International Relations at the Department of War Studies, King's College London. He was educated at the University of Stellenbosch and subsequently, as a Rhodes Scholar, read Politics at Oxford. He held lectureships at the University of Cape Town and at Rhodes University before being appointed to the Chair of Politics and Head of Department at the University of Natal in Durban. In 1996 he was appointed Professor of International Relations at the University of Kent in Canterbury. He is author of numerous publications, including *Ethics in International Relations* and *Global Ethics*. He has been President of the South African Political Studies Association and editor of its journal *Politikon*, as well as serving on the Executive Committee of the International Studies Association (ISA), where he was chairman of the International Ethics Section until 2008. Frost joined King's in 2003 as Professor of International Relations in the Centre for International Relations. He served for six years as Head of the Department of War Studies from 2007 to 2013.

John Gearson is Professor of National Security Studies and Director of the Centre for Defence Studies at King's College London. From 2002 to 2007, he was seconded to the UK House of Commons as the principal defence policy adviser to the Defence Select Committee and as a Parliamentary Clerk to the Constitutional Affairs Select Committee. While at Parliament, he was responsible for inquiries into Defence and Security of the UK, the Iraq War, the 'New Chapter' to the Strategic Defence Review, the 2003 Defence White Paper, and the Freedom of Information Act. Subsequently, he acted as a senior adviser to the UK Ministry of Defence study into the military role in counter-terrorism and contributed to background work for the 2010 UK Strategic Defence and Security Review. Previously, he was Director of the MA in Defence Studies at the Joint Services Command and Staff College at the UK Defence Academy, a management consultant, and a special adviser to the City of London Corporation on the terrorist threat to the City. He also held research positions on the Nuclear History Project and at the German Historical Institute, London. He was editor of *World Defence Systems* from 2008 to 2013 and is a member of the editorial board of *Studies in Conflict and Terrorism*. His publications include *The Nature of Modern Terrorism*; *Britain and the Berlin Wall Crisis, 1958–1962*; and *The Duty of Care in Insecure Environments*.

ABOUT THE CONTRIBUTORS

James Gow is Professor of International Peace and Security and Co-Director of the War Crimes Research Group and Director of the International Peace and Security Programme at King's College London, as well as a non-resident scholar with the Liechtenstein Institute, Princeton University, and previously lectured in European studies at the University of Hatfield. He has served as an expert adviser and an expert witness for the Office of the Prosecutor at the UN International Criminal Tribunal for the former Yugoslavia, where he was the first-ever witness at an international criminal tribunal, and as an Expert Adviser to the UK Secretary of State for Defence. Gow has held visiting positions at the University of Sheffield, the Woodrow Wilson International Center for Scholars in Washington D.C., Columbia University and Princeton University. His numerous publications include *War and War Crimes*; *Prosecuting War Crimes: Lessons and Legacies of the International Criminal Tribunal for the former Yugoslavia*; *Security, Democracy and War Crimes* (as co-author), all in 2013, and *War, Law and Technology* (2017, as co-author). In 2013, Gow won a Leverhulme Trust Major Research Fellowship to research and write on the trial of General Ratko Mladić.

Matthew Harries is Managing Editor of *Survival* and a Research Fellow for Transatlantic Affairs at the International Institute for Strategic Studies (IISS). Prior to joining the IISS, he was a postdoctoral Research Associate at the Centre for Science and Security Studies (CSSS) in the Department of War Studies at King's College London, working on deterrence issues. His PhD research, on the Nuclear Non-Proliferation Treaty, was funded by the Economic and Social Research Council's 'Global Uncertainties' programme, forming part of Professor Sir Lawrence Freedman's fellowship on 'Strategic Scripts'. He also holds a First Class degree in modern history and politics from Christ Church, Oxford.

Beatrice Heuser holds the Chair of International Relations at the University of Reading. Previous positions include Director of Research at the Military History Research Office of the Bundeswehr (Germany), Chair in International and Strategic Studies at King's College London, and a visiting position at NATO Headquarters. She holds a BA (History) and an MA (International History) from the University of London, and a DPhil (Political Science) from the University of Oxford; also a Higher

Doctorate (Habilitation) from the Philipp University of Marburg. Heuser's books include *The Evolution of Strategy*, several works on nuclear strategy and on small wars as well as *The Strategy Makers* and *Strategy before Clausewitz*. Heuser is a member of advisory boards of the Institute of Strategy Research of the Ecole militaire of France, of the Institut français des Relations internationales, and the German Stiftung Haus der Geschichte; an editor of *Cold War History*; and a member of the editorial boards of *The Journal of Strategic Studies*, and of *Aussen und Sicherheitspolitik*. She has also taught in France (Universities of Reims, Paris IV, Paris VIII; Graduate School of Journalism in Lille) and in Germany (Universities of Potsdam and of the Bundeswehr/Munich).

Jan Willem Honig is Senior Lecturer in War Studies, King's College London. He received degrees in history and medieval history from the University of Amsterdam and holds a PhD, supervised by Lawrence Freedman and Michael Dockrill, in war studies from the University of London. Between 2007 and 2011, he was on loan from the Department of War Studies to the Swedish National Defence College in Stockholm, where he was the first holder of the chair in military strategy. He remains a visiting professor there and also holds a visiting position at the Department of Peace and Conflict Research at Uppsala University. He taught for many years at the Royal College for Defence Studies in London and offered a postgraduate course on 'Contemporary War and the Liberal Conscience' at the Maxwell School for Citizenship and Public Affairs at Syracuse University. He has held visiting positions at the Remarque Institute, New York University, and the Center of International Studies at Princeton University. Earlier in his career, he held a John D. and Catherine T. MacArthur Postdoctoral Fellowship and taught at the University of Utrecht and New York University. Between 1990 and 1992, Honig was a Research Associate at the Institute for East-West Security Studies in New York. He is author of *Srebrenica: Record of a War Crime*, and is currently writing a book for Cambridge University Press which seeks to uncover what we in the West have come to understand by 'winning wars' and how we think the use of force generates desired political effects.

Sir Michael Eliot Howard, OM, CH, CBE, MC (born 29 November 1922) is a retired British military historian, formerly Chichele

Professor of the History of War and Regius Professor of Modern History at Oxford University, Robert A. Lovett Professor of Military and Naval History at Yale University, and Professor of War Studies, King's College London, where he founded the department. Sir Michael was educated at Wellington College and Christ Church, Oxford (with service in the Second World War in-between). He is best known for expanding military history beyond the traditional campaign and battle accounts to include wider discussions about the sociological significance of war. In his account of the Franco-German War of 1870–1, Howard looked at how the Prussian and French armies reflected the social structure of the two nations. He has also been the leading interpreter of the writings of Karl von Clausewitz in the late twentieth century. Howard helped found the Department of War Studies in 1963 and the Liddell Hart Centre for Military Archives at King's College London. He is currently president emeritus of the International Institute for Strategic Studies, which he also helped to establish, and a fellow of the British Academy. Sir Michael was knighted in 1986 and was appointed to the Order of the Companions of Honour in 2002 and the Order of Merit in 2005. After Oxford, Howard began his teaching career at King's College London, where he created the Department of War Studies. From his position at King's he was one of the Britons most influential in developing strategic studies as a discipline that brought together government, military and academia to think about defence and national security more broadly and deeply than had been done before. He was one of the founders of the International Institute for Strategic Studies. From his family, education, and service in the Guards he had extensive connections at the higher levels of British society, and he worked them astutely to further his intellectual goals. He had close connections in the Labour Party but was also employed as an adviser by Margaret Thatcher. During the Second World War, Howard was commissioned in the Coldstream Guards and fought in the Italian Campaign. He was twice wounded and won a Military Cross at Salerno.

Richard Ned Lebow is Professor of International Political Theory in the Department of War Studies, King's College London, and James O. Freedman Presidential Professor Emeritus at Dartmouth College.

He is also a Bye-Fellow of Pembroke College Cambridge. He previously taught strategy at the US National and Naval War Colleges and served as a scholar-in-residence in the Central Intelligence Agency during the Carter administration. He has held visiting appointments at the University of Lund, Sciences Po, Paris I (Sorbonne), the University of Cambridge, the Austrian Diplomatic Academy in Vienna, the London School of Economics and Political Science, the Australian National University, the University of California at Irvine, the University of Milan, the University of Munich and the Frankfurt Peace Research Institute. He is the author and editor of 35 books and over 250 peer reviewed articles and chapters. His recent publications include *Causation in International Relations, Return of the Theorists: Dialogues with Dead Thinkers, National Identities and International Relations, Conflict Management and Resolution, and Max Weber and International Relations*.

Jeffrey H. Michaels is a Senior Lecturer in Defence Studies at King's College London. Previously he worked as a Research Associate in the Department of War Studies and has also held visiting fellowships at the Changing Character of War Programme in Oxford and at the Egmont Institute in Brussels. Earlier experience included serving as an intelligence officer attached to the US European Command and the Pentagon's Joint Staff. He completed his PhD in War Studies at King's in 2009, under the supervision of Lawrence Freedman, focusing on contemporary US political-military discourse. He is currently working on a revised fourth edition of Freedman's *The Evolution of Nuclear Strategy*.

Patrick M. Morgan is the Tierney Chair, Peace and Conflict and Professor of Political Science in the Department of Political Science at the University of California, Irvine. He received his first degree from Harpur College and his PhD from Yale University, and was previously at Washington State University. Morgan has held visiting positions and fellowships at the Woodrow Wilson International Center for Scholars in Washington; the University of Washington; the Catholic University of Leuven as Fulbright Scholar; the Rockefeller Center, Bellagio; the Department of War Studies, King's College London; the College of Europe, Bruges; and the East-West

Center, Honolulu, where he held the POSCO Fellowship. In 1988–9, he was Vice President of the International Studies Association. He is author of *Deterrence Now* and co-author of *Security Studies Today*. He has concentrated his research primarily on national and international security matters: deterrence theory, strategic surprise attack, arms control, and related subjects. He has also had a longstanding interest in theoretical approaches to the study of international politics. Currently he is involved in projects on the theory and practice of deterrence in the post-Cold War era, security strategies for global security management, and security in North East Asia.

Sir David Omand is Visiting Professor in the Department of War Studies, King's College London. He joined the department in 2005, after retiring from government service. He was previously the first UK Security and Intelligence Coordinator, responsible to the Prime Minister for the professional health of the intelligence community, national counterterrorism strategy and 'homeland security'. He served for seven years on the Joint Intelligence Committee. He was Permanent Secretary of the Home Office from 1997 to 2000, and before that Director of GCHQ (the UK Sigint Agency). Previously, in the Ministry of Defence as Deputy Under-Secretary of State for Policy, he was particularly concerned with long-term strategy, with the British military contribution in restoring peace in the former Yugoslavia, and with the recasting of British nuclear deterrence policy at the end of the Cold War. He was Principal Private Secretary to the Defence Secretary during the Falklands conflict, and served for three years in NATO Brussels as the UK Defence Counsellor. He has been a visiting Professor in the Department of War Studies since 2005/6. He is a member of the editorial board of *Intelligence and National Security*, is responsible for delivering training to government intelligence analysts, and lectures in intelligence studies.

Major General Julian Thompson, CB, OBE is a Visiting Professor at King's College London and previously served in the Royal Marines for 34 years in the Near Middle East, the Far East, Europe and Northern Ireland. He commanded 40 Commando Royal Marines for two and a half years and the 3rd Commando Brigade for two years. The latter period of command included the Falklands War of 1982. He is a graduate of the British Army Staff College, and later instructed there. He graduated from the Royal College of Defence Studies in 1980. He retired from the armed services in 1986 and began life as a military historian, conducting research on logistics and armed conflict under a grant from the Leverhulme Trust in the Department of War Studies, King's College London, where he also lectures. His publications include *No Picnic: 3 Commando Brigade in the Falklands* (three editions); *Ready for Anything: The Parachute Regiment at War 1940–82*; *The Lifeblood of War: Logistics in Armed Conflict*; *The IWM Book of Victory in Europe: North-West Europe 1944–45*; *The IWM Book of the War at Sea: The Royal Navy in the Second World War*; *The IWM Book of the War Behind Enemy Lines: British Special Forces 1940–1945*; *The Royal Marines: From Sea Soldiers to a Special Force*; *The IWM Book of Modern Warfare: The British Experience since 1945*; *The IWM Book of the War in Burma*; *The IWM Book of the War at Sea 1914–1918*; *The Victory in Europe Experience*; and *1916: Verdun and the Somme*.

Dr Benedict Wilkinson is a Senior Research Fellow in the Policy Institute at King's where he focuses mainly on British defence, security and foreign policy. He completed his PhD, which was funded as part of the Economic and Social Research Council's 'Global Uncertainties' programme, on the strategies of terrorist organizations in the Middle East, under the supervision of Lawrence Freedman in 2013. Upon completing his PhD, he joined the Policy Institute first as a Research Associate (2013), and then Research Fellow (2014), before being appointed as a Senior Research Fellow in 2015. From 2013 to 2015, he also held a Lectureship in Defence Studies at the Royal College of Defence Studies. From 2010 to 2011, he was Head of Security and Counter-Terrorism at the Royal United Services Institute. He was made a Fellow of the Royal Society of Arts in 2014 and also holds Associate Fellowships at the International Centre for the Study of Radicalisation and the Royal United Services Institute. In a previous incarnation, he studied Classics at Jesus College, Cambridge, at both undergraduate and postgraduate level, before taking a second Masters degree in Terrorism Studies at King's College London. He also holds a Diploma in Arabic from the School of Oriental and African Studies.

INTRODUCTION

James Gow and *Benedict Wilkinson*

Lawrence Freedman has been a major academic and public intellectual figure in the UK, the US and around the world since the 1970s. His contributions to scholarship, teaching and policymaking are universally accepted as outstanding—even among those who provide a critique.[1] He is without doubt a figure worthy of investigation and also celebration.[2] As an individual, he has produced an immense bibliography of influential work and has been one of only a very small handful of non-American scholars to 'break' the US intellectual, security policy and book markets.[3] Unlike most of that handful of others who gained reputations beyond a narrow sphere in those worlds—Michael Howard, Colin Gray, David Holloway and Paul Kennedy spring to mind—Freedman did not move to prestigious US institutions along the way.[4] He steadfastly maintained and built his base in London where he gave opportunities to others and nurtured and developed their work. Both he and those working with him have become recognized for the excellence and impact of their work on problems of peace and security. Through his own work and his talent for developing others, he was responsible for putting King's College London very firmly on the global security studies map and establishing it as the biggest and, on some measures at least, the leading centre of such studies in the world.[5]

While Freedman is acknowledged as a figure of unique standing, there are different versions, perhaps unavoidably, of what makes him unique.[6] There is the dominant figure in national (or international) security studies and nuclear deterrence, where an introduction to his explorations of ethics and humanitarian intervention might be met with responses of 'What has this to do with Freedman?' Yet, for others, perhaps less aware of his early career work on nuclear strategy, it is precisely his work on humanitarian intervention—and his contribution to UK Prime Minister Tony Blair's seminal Chicago speech, handed down as the 'Blair Doctrine'—for which he is renowned and perhaps castigated equally (especially outside academia), and that is also the reason why students were most likely to seek his mentoring in the decade and a half before he took emeritus status.[7] For others, Freedman is the historian of British and US foreign and security policymaking—the award-winning author of studies of the Falklands War, the Kennedy presidency and US policy in the Middle East.[8] For yet others, he is known less for the distinction of his work—though this is surely assumed—than for his impact, whether in the policy world or in education—and the latter divides into academic enterprise and defence education. In the later stages of his career, for many—including the crowds who did not know his work previously—it is his monumental and commercially successful *Strategy: A History* that simply *is* Freedman, with its wide-ranging scholarship from the Bible to business studies and its mix and critique of social, political and international relations theory, as well as its introduction of his scriptural approach to strategy, study and policy.

Freedman's work is wide-ranging, spanning nuclear deterrence, transnational terrorism and humanitarian intervention, through armed conflicts in the South Atlantic, south-eastern Europe, the Middle East, South East Asia and Africa. Crucially, his record also spans both theory and practice, reflecting and informed by his experience of strategy, but extending beyond strategic studies as such. It is work that meets the demands of both practitioner and theorist. Where theory and practice are often seemingly at odds in the world of foreign and security policy, Freedman's work sits comfortably in both. Freedman's success in blending theory and practice to bridge the academic–policy divide is significant. Indeed, for us, this could be one of the characteristics that contribute to Freedman's distinctive standing as an intellectual figure.

It might well be a part of something that makes him more than just a very good scholar whose various eclectic pieces of work have been recognized in his lifetime.[9] Practitioners frequently find the theoretically driven work of scholars to be irrelevant to the needs of 'real world' problems, while academic theorists tend to regard the problems that beset those who engage with the practical as secondary at best. This holds true, above all, in the realm of international relations, where the field has largely become a philosophical battle between different schools of thought, each reflecting its disciples' values and prejudices, each reifying the views of the other. Freedman stands apart, both between polarized positions and outside them, producing, the record would suggest, outstanding work and, at one and the same time, having great influence on the policy world.[10]

Freedman, then, is clearly a figure of significant distinction; one who has had real world influence, yet whose theoretical depth and development have been largely overlooked. In the beginning, this was James Gow's starting point. He asked whether there was anything distinctive in Freedman's approach, a way of working, a methodology, or even the roots of a school of thought. How can we make sense of the extensive and diverse record? Is it possible to bring coherence to it? Is there a common theoretical or methodological thread running through it? How far does this work of great impact have theoretical weight? Is there something more than chance and personality involved—a way of working, with which academics can have real impact on issues of peace and security, and produce intellectually meaningful work at the same time? How can we make sense of this record of conducting and supporting research that makes a difference in a way that also suggests coherence and a scholarly identity? Has a distinctive working method—a school of thought—emerged around 'war studies', without actually being given a name, under the leading influence of Professor Sir Lawrence Freedman for thirty years (succeeding the founder of war studies, Sir Michael Howard)?

Freedman's approach and the Freedman project

These questions informed the research project underpinning this volume, as did the more particular question of whether the concept of 'constructivist realism' captured the essence of the Freedman approach and provided linking coherence for a school of thought (as discussed below). The spur for this was Freedman's own perspective. The project was born in conversations between Freedman and Gow as they discussed the major funding proposal from which *Strategy: A History* would emerge. Those conversations were about methods and approaches, and how to characterize the approach taken, as well as blending theory and practice. This included the possible link in Freedman's work between his avowedly constructivist approach and his recognition of the impetus of political realism as a theory. These were not completely uncharted waters: Peter Katzenstein had once called Freedman a 'realist constructivist', and Freedman himself had written an article about his early involvement with constructivist theory and had mused how, had he realized that an approach he regarded as 'normal' would later be seen as having revolutionary significance in the field of international relations, he might have formed a school of thought.[11] (Instead, rather than writing about constructivism, he simply got on with using it.)

However, constructivism alone would not have been sufficient. As the Katzenstein comment (and the parallel exploration by Gow) indicated, there appeared to be a conjunction of constructivism with realism in the Freedman approach. The project proposed, therefore, was to explore the potential and the limits of constructivist realism as a theoretical prism for social researchers engaged with tangible problems of war and peace. Its mission was to investigate, test, expand and develop the constructivist realist approach, and also its potential as a school of thought and its merits as a distinctive intellectual (combined with practical) contribution. Did Freedman's own sense of constructivism and realism blended constitute a comprehensive methodology? Did it capture and reflect the Freedman, or 'war studies', approach? Did this amount to a school of thought?

There seemed to be sound reasons to adopt this line of inquiry—aside from Freedman's own inclination. The dominant abstractions of political realism, on one side, and idealism-liberalism, on the other, suffered from being unrealistic and lacking contact with the empirical.[12] Constructivism was adopted on the liberal and 'critical' side of this theoretical divide as a way to challenge realism. However, the Freedman approach seemed to suggest that this was mistaken and raised the possibility that there could be real value in using the constructivist approach not so much in opposition to realism, but as a complement to it, albeit one quite possibly tempering theoretical extremes. This means understanding that questions of peace and security, and the conduct of human groups around them, involve social processes. These processes are based on interactions, in which the behaviour of one group necessarily impacts on the understanding and behaviour of another. The analytical strength of constructivism is that it can explain processes and the dominant interpretations of them. How far is allying this understanding of processes with notions of necessity and power—that is, an approach that recognizes that some things, whether material or values, matter to the actors in any situation and are not mere abstractions—a promising approach?

While the inquiry started with the aim of investigating whether or not constructivist realism held the key to the Freedman way of working—including, it should be stressed, both the possibility that it did not and the supplementary question whether there might be an alternative—Freedman's work on strategic scripts emerged part way through the project in his totemic *Strategy: A History*. That book had been maturing as part of the (successful) major funding proposal that Gow and Freedman had been discussing at the time the present Freedman project was conceived. The conversations between the two focused on Freedman's methods and approaches, and how to characterize his approach and blend of theory and practice; in particular, they considered whether 'constructivist realism' captured that approach and might be said to provide linking coherence to a school of thought. The idea of scripts relied on the same elements of social theory as the realist-constructivist notion. As time passed and Freedman's new work began to see the light of day, it became clear that the notion of strategic scripts also needed to be considered in our project.

In this sense, the research agenda was open and we did not impose a single perspective on those invited to participate. This openness was beneficial in allowing us to embrace Freedman's scriptural approach as it emerged. As well as the mission to explore constructivist realism as a leading theoretical element in Freedman's work, the project embraced a complementary second mission to investigate, test, expand and develop the scriptural approach, and also the potential this approach held for theoretically underpinning a school of thought and providing a distinctive intellectual (combined with practical) contribution to scholarship and society.

In the end, having begun with questions about constructivist realism and having later supplemented those with questions about strategic scripturalism, we are left with the overarching question that set the whole inquiry going plus three more specific questions, all of which are addressed in one way or another in this volume. First, to what extent does constructivist realism constitute a theoretical prism that gives coherence to Freedman's and the war studies approach to questions of peace and security, and also defines a school of thought? Secondly, to what extent does strategic scripturalism offer a sustainable theoretical framework that captures the Freedman and war studies approach and thus underpin a school of thought? Is there some other theoretical approach that can be said to characterize Freedman's approach? Finally, the overarching question, which each of these others addresses: is there a cohesive school of thought that originates with Freedman, is evident in his approach, and combines theoretical strength and scholarly recognition with tangible impact on the real world aspects of peace and security?

This is the significant challenge, then, that we have undertaken in the present volume: to explore different aspects of Freedman's scholarship with a view to seeing if it could add up to more than the sum of its parts. The task we have set ourselves is to discover if we can identify in Freedman's work a cohesive pattern of thought or approach, which is not only oriented towards having tangible impact on the practical aspects of peace and security, but is also underpinned by sufficiently robust theory to allow for full recognition by other academics. Indeed, this challenge is linked more broadly to those associated with the Department of War Studies at King's College London, founded by Howard and transformed into a global leader in the field under Freedman.

Thus the purpose of the volume and the project from which it arises is to explore the thread between theory and practice found in Freedman's work, and to test the theoretical and scholarly coherence in it. To do this, we bring leading academics together to ask whether there are elements of a school of thought in Freedman's writing that bind and unite his work. In short, is there an identity that goes beyond the individual parts? We considered a variety of approaches to complete this task, but, true to Freedman's own preference, we opted for a volume that is not bound by subject or region, topic or theoretical approach. Rather, we have sought to bring together a collection of chapters that embody the very approach that Freedman advocated in his intellectual career: providing theoretically robust, academically rigorous research that has, at the least, implications for practitioners. Inevitably, much of this touches on areas on which he has focused throughout his career. However, where clear gaps emerged, we sought to fill them—the chapters by Gearson, Omand and Thompson, as well as the second chapter by Gow, were recruited in response to critical peer review, which identified gaps in the initial approach, and were deemed necessary for a sufficiently comprehensive examination of Freedman's work.

Investigating Freedman's diverse work at the frontiers of security studies scholarship and the borders of the policymaking world was conceived as a research exercise. Yet, in focusing on his work and career, even while offering critical investigation and exposition of it, the collection takes on something of the character of a Freedman festival. The book was decidedly not intended as a Festschrift. It represented personal commitment to undertaking a research project rather than a fawning ego-massage, as well as Freedman's own expressed preference in response to various suggestions that he might merit a volume of that kind. Inevitably, however, in focusing on the quality and essence of his work, the project serves contingently as a celebration, an aspect that peer reviewers noted—prompting us to include recognition of this aspect of the book and warmly to assert that if anyone is deserving of being feted, it is Lawrence Freedman.

The authors, including the editors, were not bound by any sense that a particular formula is needed to explain, justify or bring coherence to Freedman's rich body of work. Each contributor was free to determine his or her topic and the approach taken (although we did specifically ask some authors to write on, or in relation to, particular aspects of Freedman's oeuvre while we ourselves took responsibility for the two main areas of constructivist realism and strategic scripts). We determined that the best way to investigate, test, critique, develop and extend Freedman's opus, and that of those working in his wake, was to follow the example set by our subject—allowing each problem to be addressed on its own merits, providing the material with which to explore provisionally the potential scope of something approaching a school of thought. This was a wood that might emerge from the trees of open research. If Freedman could be judged a figure of great intellectual distinction, rather than just the author of many important studies, this should be discerned from the various contributions to the project. As will be seen, several authors respond to both the constructivist realism and strategic script themes, suggesting some coalescence, while others do not or do not do so explicitly. However, we judge (and trust that those reading it fairly will agree) that the book as a whole provides signposts to, and markers of, a distinctive approach that embraces method, disposition and the application of knowledge and understanding in the practical and empirical world—all testimony to a distinguished intellectual figure.

The book

The contributions in the present volume reflect the way in which the horizons of Freedman's scholarly world, and thus of war studies, expanded from the platform Michael Howard created. This is true, even where the authors are not based at King's—indeed, one of the important ambitions in this project was to avoid what could have been (and have been seen to be) a 'King's love-in', even while the project sought to acknowledge Freedman's significance. The pieces come from younger and older academics, from those who have crossed the practitioner–policy–scholar boundaries (Philip Bobbitt on the left of US politics, Richard Falkenrath on the right,[13] David Omand from the centre of the UK policy bureaucracies, and Julian Thompson from the British military), as well as those whom Freedman taught formally (Jan Willem Honig, David Dunn, Robert Ayson, Richard Caplan, John Gearson, Jeffrey Michaels, Matthew Harries and Benedict Wilkinson) and those influenced by him in their careers (Pat Morgan, Beatrice Heuser, Mats Berdal, Mervyn Frost, Ned Lebow and, of course, Gow)—and all of them influenced Freedman himself, along the way.

Each of these contributions addresses an aspect of Freedman's work, in some cases challenging it, filling gaps or bringing to light new aspects, in others developing understanding in relation to the more obvious themes. The sections that structure them in the book show this—though, evidently, they overlap in some cases. In the first section, the authors explore Freedman's writing on strategy in relation to intellectual projects in international relations, the conduct of war, and the changing policy environment—key concerns of his that run throughout his writing. Ayson and Honig examine understandings of strategy in the ways Freedman led them to discover as students, linking them to the intellectual worlds to which Freedman's work relates, whether in international relations theory and philosophy or in the history of warfare—both informed by the Freedman approach that is underpinned by social theory. Morgan and Falkenrath respond to the challenge of deterrence in the twenty-first century, taking Freedman's seminal work in this field as a cue to explore both relevance and application in a globalized world. The former investigates the ways in which theory developed for the Cold War world, framed by superpower nuclear standoff, can at all be related to a world of flux and change where transnational and subnational actors present challenges but where the tenets developed for a purely state-based world do not fit. 'With great difficulty' is the answer. It is an answer taken up by Falkenrath, who, as Special Assistant to the President and Senior Director for Policy and Plans within the Office of Homeland Security and, then, Deputy Assistant to the President and Deputy Homeland Security Advisor in the administrations of George W. Bush, had to confront the challenges of deterrence and change as a practitioner. He traces the change from deterrence based on punishment to deterrence based on denial. This is a sharp shift from a position, as in the Cold War, where the point of deterrence is that consequences will follow if an opponent acts in a threatening way, to one in which some form of action will be taken anyway because the threat is assumed to be constant and, so, the levels of communication are qualitatively different. It is in this world that the sophisticated intellectual frameworks espoused by Ayson and Honig, and the abstract theory considered by Morgan, become paramount. This is a realm of analysis that not only stems from Freedman's work, but in which he would happily engage.

Similarly, the section on ethics and humanitarian intervention is one that not only relates to Freedman and his work, but also develops in ways that would challenge and encourage him. This set of research essays is stimulated by Freedman's work on humanitarian intervention and just war, notably his seminal note for the Chicago speech by Tony Blair. Again, this is a world where rapid international change presents challenges and where values are seen and felt to be paramount, not merely the size of armed forces or the throw-weight of nuclear warheads (of course, values were always relevant, as the authors and Freedman would hold). For Frost, extending Freedman's work both on humanitarian intervention in this changing world and on combating international terrorism in the wake of the revolution in strategic affairs that Freedman described, victory can only come from values. If these are forgotten or betrayed, the social impact on support for opponents, or the withering of support among those supposedly being protected, will be decisive. In a sense, although this is not Frost's purpose, he is addressing the question that might arise from Heuser's chapter on the heritage underpinning the Chicago speech (although this is beyond the scope of her contribution): what about that which some might see as the fallout from the speech—the problematic international encounters in Iraq and Libya, or Syria? That heritage underpins not only Freedman's thinking, in the way it was intended, but also the chapters by Caplan and Berdal, both of which address the challenges that humanitarian intervention faced, in practice, in the post-Cold War era—as well as noting that the Chicago speech was subsequent to some of the major interventions. While Caplan charts a problematic contemporary history for a concept and practice Freedman certainly espoused, Berdal engages with the way in which this problematic sphere reflects perhaps an implicit tension in Freedman's strategic thought and practice in relation to these questions—the tussle between liberal values and an 'unsentimental temper'. This is the central dilemma of humanitarian intervention—balancing one version of 'doing the right thing' with another: saving lives and alleviating suffering, but not attempting the impossible, making things worse or harming one's self. This section of essays, in effect, coheres around this dilemma, as does Freedman's extensive work on interventions, in practice.

The third section of the book encompasses a blend of the major—and key—historical and policy topics that Freedman has tackled, all focused on the two countries with which he has shown commanding expertise, the US and the UK. Michaels uses new empirical research to fill what is all but a gap in Freedman's study of the Kennedy presidency by addressing the 1963 coup in South Vietnam, which occurred a few weeks before Kennedy's assassination, and to point to the indecision defining US policy. Dunn focuses on a different kind of hesitancy fifty years later under President Barack Obama about Syria, where 'the United States was reluctant to take a decisive position of even limited active intervention on either side in [the] conflict'. He judges that this 'risk aversion' on using armed force jeopardized US and global security, and was caused, in his view, by an 'Iraq syndrome' even more profound than the version of it labelled thus by Freedman. Thompson and Gearson address British questions. The former takes Freedman's *Official History of the Falklands Campaign* and its observation that it was an example of the kind of war for which Britain had not planned to fight, and how the initial operational legacy, the creation of both structures and processes for such a contingency, has been reduced to the real legacy: very little. Gearson expansively covers the British reinterpretation of security from the Cold War to the second decade of the twenty-first century in which Freedman was central, charting not only the broadening of the concept and the widening of frameworks, but also the development and expansion with it of the academic delivery of military education, which Freedman pioneered—perhaps one of his most remarkable accomplishments.

In the fourth section, Lebow, Gow, Bobbitt and, Freedman's last PhD students, Harries and Wilkinson all address more philosophical, abstract and theoretical issues in their subject's intellectual harvest. These chapters draw out an aspect of Freedman's work not always recognized by observers, his lifelong reflection on, and engagement with, theory—often the work is so successful that its theoretical approach is not noticed. Yet, in many respects, this is the Freedman it is most important to know—the one who, in the message gently suffusing Bobbitt's piece about Freedman on Machiavelli, understands and also uses theory and applies it (virtuously, of course, as would the Italian master, Bobbitt would remind us). The other chapters draw out the importance of theory in Freedman's analysis, in particular the place of a grounded, practical, even, sober form of constructivism, tempered by a strong sense of reality—including the reality that strategic positions and relationships are constructed and, his great insight, depend on scripts. The scriptural theory is crucial, expounded by Harries and Wilkinson with regard to the field in which Freedman initially made his name—nuclear security—but also exemplified in the other two chapters, as Lebow shows the value of scripts, while Gow explores the mechanisms at work.

The final part of the book includes three contemplations of Freedman's work and career, including the final reflection in this book, on the endeavour that underpinned his work and on Freedman and his scholarship. The chapter by Omand looks at the relationship between Whitehall and the academy, the relationship fostered by and with Freedman, between not only him and government, but also between government and the wider security policy family at King's College London. This is the perspective of the senior mandarin who has worked both from inside government with King's and others, and from King's with some of those who succeeded him. He astutely points out that where government benefits from outside input is in the provision of that which government does not have, or cannot do, itself—longer-term research, knowledge and understanding of phenomena springing up, or how to provide an academic education to practitioners, for example—something that Freedman, ever the astute judge and strate-gic master of the practical, always understood: how to be useful, not irrelevant or an irritant. Freedman's reflection on his own theoretical perspective and on intellectuals and policy confirms this, as well as the importance of this theory in his approach. In the final contribution to this section, Gow offers wider reflections on the scope and variety of Freedman's work, introducing sceptical perspectives on it, which point to some of its limitations—an aspect otherwise largely absent in the book, in which (perhaps not surprisingly) authors have broadly positive dispositions towards their subject.

After the final section, we offer a brief conclusion. This considers the book as a whole and the Freedman project overall, pointing to the integrating ways in which the research essays in the book engage with their subject's thought and considering the way in which this and the scope of war studies as developed by and beyond Freedman move towards the identification of a discrete school of thought. We conclude, as editors, that there is the necessary intellectual distinction in

Freedman's scholarship and approach to warrant the elevation of his work into the ranks of 'significant thinkers', and that there is a distinctive coherence around notions such as constructivist realism, strategic scripts and the understanding of social interaction and processes that define a body of work related to making a difference in the world which has done just that.

PART 1

STRATEGY AND DETERRENCE

1

STRATEGIC THEORY AS AN INTELLECTUAL SYSTEM

Robert Ayson

Lawrence Freedman devotes about as much space in his magisterial *Strategy: A History* to the thinking of the American theorist Thomas Schelling as he does to the work of Karl von Clausewitz.[1] In early writing Freedman names Schelling among the 'major theorists of the nuclear age', as 'the most imaginative and influential of them all',[2] and Freedman's doctoral supervisor, Sir Michael Howard, also had a high regard for Schelling. I investigated Schelling's work as the eventual topic of my doctorate (under Freedman's supervision).[3] But the original topic had been a much broader study of stability as a strategic concept. And before I decided to focus my attention on Schelling, inspiration came from something my supervisor had written in a now rather obscure piece from the late Cold War years: that the

> idea of stability was derived from systems theory. This was in vogue among
> social scientists at the time, having in turn been adopted from biological
> theories. It stressed the inter-relatedness of human behaviour, and encour-
> aged analysis from the perspective of the system as a whole rather than
> from that of an individual actor within the system.[4]

17

It seemed to me then, and it still does now, that good strategic thinking recognizes that strategic actors are part of a system where their actions and expectations are interrelated, and that the best analysis is able to explain this system as a whole. This chapter suggests that Freedman's strategic theory, developed over several decades, is itself evocative of a system: an intellectual system which places particular ideas and actions in a wider context in which other related parts need to be taken into consideration.

In saying this, I am aware that systems theory per se reached its heyday some time ago, indeed about the time that Freedman was completing his doctoral studies in the first half of the 1970s. Systems theory was part of the noble but overly ambitious quest for a general theory of the social sciences, and Freedman's undergraduate student days had left him wary of such approaches. Instead of the systems theorists, Freedman's favourite sociologist had been C. Wright Mills. In his essay 'Confessions of a Premature Constructivist', Freedman writes admiringly of the attack by Mills on what he saw to be two false paths of mainstream sociology: 'On the one hand was Grand Theory, whose self-importance he famously deflated with translations of pages of the obscurantist prose of Talcott Parsons into a few lines, and on the other there was Abstracted Empiricism, full of microscopic studies that remained marginal to the big questions of the day'.[5]

On the second of these problems, I think it can be accurately said that Freedman's interest in the big issues, and not the marginal ones, stands out across his scholarship. But on the first problem I would argue that the idea of the system is to be found in a good deal of what he has to say. One reason is that systems theory reflects a multidisciplinary approach to academic work. This fits with the intellectual curiosity and eclecticism that help make Freedman's work, and that of many of the others who have influenced him, so appealing. It is there in *Strategy: A History*, where he considers the way that business leaders as well as military and political leaders think about ends and means. What they are doing, and the obstacles they face, including the gap between intentions and outcomes, is not so different as to make their conceptions of strategy mutually unintelligible.[6] We also find this breadth in the variety of social settings that Freedman uses to illustrate the meaning and functioning of deterrence.[7]

The interdependence of strategic actors

But more important is the emphasis within systems thinking on inter-relatedness such as exists between factors in a natural system and between actors in a social system. The close awareness that strategy is about interrelated features and decision-makers is something one very definitely sees frequently in the Freedman oeuvre. We can start with the more obvious point that strategy consists of much more than a relation between military means and political ends considered in a national context, and is found in the interaction between purposeful actors whose respective ends may not converge. 'All strategy', Freedman says in one prominent study, 'is concerned with the relation-ship between ends and means, but military strategy is also about the relationship between two or more opposing forces'.[8]

This gives rise to some of the most interesting aspects of the subject. In fact strategy would be a thoroughly boring affair if one's moves were unaffected by the moves of another actor who might not always wish us well. This dynamic is what makes the subject worth studying and is captured in Freedman's citation of Schelling's theory that 'in games of strategy … "Each player's best choice depends on the action he expects the other to take, which he knows depends, in turn, on the other's expectations of his own"'.[9] Accordingly, Freedman himself tells us that 'it is the interdependence of choice that provides the essence of strat-egy and diverts it from being mere long-term planning or the mechani-cal connection of available means to ends'.[10]

This helps explain Freedman's comment in his big book on *Strategy* that he was attracted to the subject of strategy because it is about choice.[11] How one chooses to respond to, or anticipate, the choices of others is precisely what makes strategy the riveting subject it is. Personally I continue to find it amazing how many definitions of the subject emphasize the links between ends and means without bringing in the wider strategic world in which the really big strategic choices have to be made by more than one purposeful actor. The interaction of these choices is the crux of strategy, supplying Freedman with much of his best material. For example, some of Freedman's most interesting writings have been on the concept of escalation and thus are really a study of the dynamics of strategic interdependence. But unlike the purists, he departs from convention by treating escalation as a metaphor. Interdependence still occurs, and two actors can end up in difficulty as each responds to the other. But escalation is not as automatic as the metaphor might suggest. In one of these essays, readers are warned

> against being mesmerized by prophecies of rapid and uncontrollable escalation once any hostilities anywhere begin. Talk of escalators and quagmires—of relentless, independent processes—encourages the view that after a point, considered strategic judgements which weigh available military means against desirable political ends become irrelevant.[12]

Political agency

So what was Freedman's alternative to this perception? Here is his answer as he continues the same passage: 'I want to reassert political responsibility for the higher conduct of war'. If military engagements are 'shaped by the logic of political commitment, then it must be government decisions, however flawed and misinformed, that are crucial when it comes to altering the scope and intensity of conflicts'.[13] We still have a system of interdependent parts, but it is an *open* system. The wider environmental context in which that interdependence of decision has to operate consists of the political direction given to conflict. The notion of the relationship between military forces as somehow hermetically separable from political influence draws Freedman's criticism on many occasions. For example, in his assessment that Stephen Biddle's well-known work on military power offers a 'theory of battle not of war', we get the argument:

> Conceiving of battle as two regular forces operating as part of a self-contained system can produce a powerful model but it is bound to be limited. Battles are part of a wider system of war which is in itself part of a wider system of international relations. Politics pervades the activity at all levels, and even when individual engagements appear to be governed by purely military factors, and civilians and irregulars are not intruding, they make little sense until they are related to the broader course of a war.[14]

Out of similar concerns comes Freedman's argument that we should be interested in the potential for transformation of strategic affairs, not of a strictly military arena, which was too often viewed in isolation from its wider political context. His two elegant Adelphi Papers devoted to this theme reward close reading. In the first of these, published in 1998, he argued that: 'In practice, the revolution in strategic affairs is driven less by the pace of technological change than by uncertainties in political conditions'.[15] He continued this train of thinking nearly a decade later in the second, observing: 'The reasons for suggesting that a transformation of strategy is now underway reflect the demilitarisation of inter-state relations, particularly among the great powers, and the expansion of the state system as a result of decolonisation, which has resulted in many new states that are also internally unstable'.[16]

This was a long-standing view. When his initial opus, *The Evolution of Nuclear Strategy*, was first released in the early 1980s, Freedman could be seen criticizing the Albert Wohlstetter style of systems analysis for 'a tendency, which gradually became more acute, to place an extremely sophisticated technical analysis within a crude political framework'.[17] Even earlier, in 1979, Freedman was already complaining that 'the most cursory glance at the contemporary literature reveals a succession of crude political assumptions and assertions, and a preoccupation with the properties of new weapons systems at various stages in their life cycles'.[18]

But this train of thinking is evident earlier still. In some of his earliest published work, Freedman was demanding a rich and broad understanding of what politics is and what politics does. In 1975 he had presented an offshoot of his doctoral research as his first conference paper for the British International Studies Association (BISA). In the version that was published in the following year, we see Freedman take aim squarely at the bureaucratic politics models of Graham Allison and Morton Halperin. These involved, the young Freedman argued, a spurious separation between rational logic on the one hand and politics on the other. The latter was much more than 'the intrusion of the parochial preoccupations of ambitious bureaucrats, suspicious military men and electioneering Presidents, and something broader than the attempts within the establishment to strike bargains that satisfy these divergent preoccupations'.[19]

Instead, Freedman speaks of a 'hierarchy of power … a power structure … a limited set of groups and individuals', or what C. Wright Mills once famously called a power elite. And this is not a fly-by-night affair. 'Domination within a power structure' means 'the capacity to designate the broad objectives of policy and organise the process so as to create a reasonable degree of certainty that individual results will conform to basic objectives'. In ignoring this power structure, he argues, Allison's *Essence of Decision* and Halperin's *Bureaucratic Politics* missed the wood for the trees: they did not see 'that the random clashes of fragmented, selfishly motivated actors are, in fact, reasonably patterned and linked to conceptions of the national interest'.[20]

The next sentence, which finishes this 1976 article, is worth replaying in full: 'The structure and patterns', the 27-year-old Freedman argues, 'can only be discerned by standing back from the immediate battles with a long-term rather than a short-term perspective, examining those things that the participants take for granted: the shared images, assumptions and beliefs and the "rules of the game"'.[21]

At least two things can be taken from these excerpts. First, the need for a long-term perspective rhymes with the historical dimension, which features in a great deal of Freedman's work: the need to put things into perspective, if only to indicate when people are trying to reinvent strategic wheels. The second is a strong belief in political agency. The essay on escalation and quagmires includes one of the all-time best lines from Clausewitz, that 'war is an act of force, and there is no logical limit to the application of that force'. 'Each side, therefore, 'compels its opponents to follow suit: a reciprocal action is started which must lead, in theory, to extremes'.[22] The American theorist Schelling was in agreement a century and a half later: 'Like Clausewitz', we are told in *Strategy: A History*, 'Schelling saw how raw and angry passions could also undermine restraint'.[23]

Expressions of Freedman's own agreement with this possibility include a passage in an article in *Survival* from the late 1990s where he notes: 'Wars create their own political stakes—including a reputation for staying power and determination—that can quickly take belligerents beyond their immediate concerns'.[24] But Clausewitz also insists elsewhere that even the most chaotic, heated and passionate situation can be made subject to a degree of political influence. 'Within the paradoxical trinity', Freedman writes of Clausewitz's thinking, 'violence and chance could still be subordinated to politics and the application of reason'.[25]

Strategy and power

This is Freedman's own view as well. Strategy would not be strategy were it not for a belief that by doing a certain thing we have a chance of changing the environment, of making a difference, although we might not readily get quite the change we originally look for. Strategy and power are in this sense hopelessly interlinked: 'A strategic view of power', Freedman says in an essay on terrorism published three decades after his penetrating critique of the bureaucratic politics model, 'is about the sources of advantage in political relationships, the process of turning capacity into effects'.[26] And the type of effect that strategy produces is itself inherently political: 'strategy tends to have a transformational quality', Freedman says later on in his terrorism article, 'that is, it is geared to either sustaining a position within a political structure or causing it to change, rather than to second- and third-order issues'.[27]

The idea that strategy is about inducing political effects raises some important questions about how we understand Freedman's contribution to our subject. In his inaugural lecture as Professor of War Studies at King's College London, which he delivered in November 1983, Freedman argued 'that strategic studies must reintegrate politics into its analytical framework'.[28] That strikes me as the core of his message all along, but it also requires us to take on the rich and deep understanding of politics—and especially of power—that has animated his work. This means accepting that organized politics makes a difference, and that power structures and power elites also factor in. I do not think it is any coincidence, for example, that Freedman's main book about the conflicts that challenged the United States in the 1960s is entitled *Kennedy's Wars*. Decision-makers matter because their choices count. The opening pages not only feature Freedman's assessment that 'Kennedy can be said to have succeeded' in his 'first priority' in making the Cold War less dangerous.[29] They also include a three-page list of dramatis personae, the political and policy elite who made and shaped the big choices.[30] Similarly, I doubt we would have seen books on the Falklands, the Gulf War and other conflicts in the Middle East if only the military interactions themselves were important and interesting, as opposed to the political contexts in which they occurred.

There is a connection between historical studies, where a long-term approach can allow for the overall patterns of decision-making to become clear, on the one hand, and appreciating the international political environment in which those choices are made, on the other. This is reflected in the newly appointed Freedman's suggestion as to what a Department of War Studies at King's College actually does: 'The sort of strategic studies I have in mind', he said, 'must return to its roots in military history and international relations, to the sort of work that for the past three decades has been the business of the Department of War Studies at King's College London'.[31] But I think this comment may have undersold in advance the sort of strategic studies that he would be part of. It seems to me that Freedman's strategic studies are the place where strategic history—as opposed to military history per se—meets and intermingles with international strategy, as opposed to international relations. If there is a shorthand for this approach, it comes from Bernard Brodie, the influential American strategic thinker, who argued at one point that 'strategic theory is a theory for action'.[32] That is more forward-looking than the approach we sometimes get from military history and less theoretically trapped than the work we can so often see in international relations.

Avoiding pigeonholes

What then of the notion, encouraged by a comment from Peter Katzenstein, that we might understand Lawrence Freedman as a constructivist realist? This automatically describes his work as a hybrid of two of the pigeonholes of international relations, denying the possibility that strategic studies is a sister subject rather than a subordinate discipline.[33] If we must use an 'ism' to depict Freedman's approach, there is nothing wrong with pluralism, something that I think also sums up the style of Hedley Bull, whose work and style he also admires. There may be an understandable appeal to the realist tag, given Freedman's argument that 'strategy is the art of creating power', a point he makes in concluding his essay in honour of Michael Howard,[34] and repeats early on in his *Strategy*.[35] Yet Freedman's definition of power as 'the capacity to produce effects that are more advantageous than would otherwise have been the case'[36] does not evoke the decisive, authoritative view of power that appears to sit in the realist world. And would a realist really have written the following lines from the last paragraph of his first book, a revised version of his Oxford DPhil thesis on American official perceptions of Russia's military power? 'Judgements on the "threat" depend not only on estimates of what the Soviet Union is attempting to do, but also on a sense of the vulnerabilities in the US military position, understood by reference to broader perspectives on the character and sources of strategic thought in the modern world'.[37] Those broader perspectives are part of the intellectual system that I believe Freedman sees in strategy. Slightly earlier in the same early study, he argues that strategic knowledge does not derive from clinical assessments of the external environment. Those who write intelligence estimates, he says, 'do not work in "ivory towers" but in a community with its own political structure'. They find themselves 'amongst colleagues who share a political adversary image and come, perhaps subconsciously, to adopt this image as their own'.[38]

Some will interpret this point as evidence of a view, already clear in Freedman's earliest work, that knowledge is socially constructed. That is clearly the case, although to deny that ideas (and thus strategies and policies) can be understood without some consideration of the context in which they have emerged would seem to be a denial of academic common sense. At the 2005 BISA conference, Freedman observed that 'constructivism describes how I have always tended to approach issues'.[39] But in the sentence that concludes the same paragraph he says, 'The approach, however, came rather naturally to anyone who had studied sociology over that period'.[40] This opens up the possibility that, as happens to all approaches, constructivism's star will wane while people who believe that there is a socio-political context for theory and action will continue to do their good work.

We may not need such a label as 'realist constructivist' to remind us of the importance of the style of work that is evident in Freedman's analysis. All the 'isms' are just like the 'patterns of political relationships' that he refers to in his article on the bureaucratic politics model. These are, he says, 'transitory and conditional'.[41] By comparison, there is a much more permanent aspect to good strategic studies, which examines the full political context in which decisions are made about the use of force. This, it seems to me, is just what Freedman's thinking and writing have continued to do.

Conclusion: an intellectual system of many levels

What then of the intellectual system that, in my view, lives in the work of Sir Lawrence Freedman? I think there are at least three levels in which this system can be said to operate. First, strategy is an intellectual system in the sense that it is composed of interrelated parts. There is the relationship between ends and means, recognized in most of the standard depictions of strategy. Freedman does not contest this view, but he draws particular attention to the interrelatedness that also exists between strategic actors. Each of these actors has their own ends-and-means relationship to manage, but it is the interdependent relationship between these actors that contributes much more to the nature of the system. In this connection, it is perhaps a little risky for Freedman to use the idea of a script as a metaphor for strategy. Rather like a narrative, on which it is meant to be an improvement, a script can operate autonomously in its own closed world. 'The dramatist', Freedman observes, 'controls the plot, manipulating the behaviour of all parties'; … '[a]ll the main characters are under her control'. And, '[s]he can decide how they meet and interact'.[42] By contrast, 'the strategist has to cope with the choices of others while remaining relatively ignorant of what they might be'.[43] The question this leaves me with, however, is how easy it is to conceive a set of interacting scripts, each shaping the other, which is what strategy involves.

Secondly, strategy is an open system. The choices involving the use and potential use of force are not made in some sort of closed, albeit interactive, universe. Political conditions are the wider (and pervasive) environment in which strategic decisions are made. It may seem odd to have to make this point since nearly every strategic theorist has heard of Clausewitz. But a good deal of strategic theory seems to be unaware of the political sociology of strategic action, which is an inherent part of the Freedman intellectual system. This is why so much of his writing attacks temporarily popular but politically naive views of strategy which promise to bypass the obstacles that all strategic theory has to deal with. In his contribution to the Festschrift for Michael Howard, Freedman opens with the following passage from his supervisor's essay on 'The Strategic Approach to International Relations':

> The 'strategic approach' … is one which takes account of the part played by force, or the threat of force in the international system. It is descriptive in so far as it analyses the extent to which political units have the capacity to use, or to threaten the use of, armed force to impose their will on other units; whether to compel them to do some things, to deter them from doing others, or if need be to destroy them as independent communities altogether. It is prescriptive in so far as it recommends policies which will

enable such units to operate in an international system which is subject to such conditions and constraints.[44]

It is the politics of that international system in which force is used, threatened and restrained that accounts for so many of those 'conditions and constraints'.

Thirdly, the strategic system is a dynamic one. Important change certainly can and does occur in the military dimension of strategy, and this may have a direct effect on political conditions. In one essay published in the very early 1990s, Freedman looks back on the management of US–Soviet strategic relations during much of their long nuclear competition: 'Arms control is relevant', he argues, 'if it is assumed that the state of the military relationship will be a decisive factor in whether or not a crisis might transform a cold into a hot war'.[45] But normally it was the other way around: it was the change in political circumstances that mattered the most strategically and conditioned the military aspect. In earlier comments in the same essay, Freedman noted 'that the strategic nuclear focus has encouraged arms control theory to concentrate on standards of stability within a bipolar military relationship', and complained that 'this has been to the detriment of our understanding of conventional arms control, which has always been shaped by complex political relations. We lacked, he thought, 'a theory for a period of political transition'.[46]

But that leads to a fourth aspect of this intellectual system: strategy does not operate in a world where those changing political conditions automatically set the context in an automatic or preordained manner. Strategy is often about an attempt to achieve a political transition, even if this fulsome product of the art of creating power is rarely achievable. This is the big reminder that the strategic system favours the impact of purposeful actors over the impact of environmental factors. Towards the end of his *Strategy*, Freedman insists that

> when we look forward to the future we have little choice but to identify a way forward dependent upon human agency which might lead to a good outcome. It is all well to avoid illusions of control, but in the end all we can do is act if we can influence events. To do otherwise is to succumb to fatalism.[47]

If our choices were already made for us by impersonal forces and constraints, the rationale for understanding strategic theory as an intellectual system would disappear. Strategic thought would just be a case of aligning oneself with the inevitable, not working through the options—our own, the options of other actors in the relationship in question, and how these influence one another. In fact, it would hardly be strategic thinking at all, in any autonomous sense. In the second chapter of the same big book, Freedman looks at the biblical world's interaction with the original creator of power. In considering the philosophical problem of free will, he argues that 'if the players in this drama', who included Moses and Pharaoh, 'were merely acting out a preordained script from which no deviation was permitted, then the only strategist at work here was God'.[48] The rest of *Strategy:A History* is about the thinking of human beings who, as political actors of one sort or another, have been seeking to create some power of their own. Whether we regard that history of human strategy as misguided rebellion or necessary independence, the intellectual system detectable in Freedman's work is a sure guide to the socio-political contexts in which strategy always occurs.

2

UNCOMFORTABLE VISIONS

THE RISE AND DECLINE OF THE IDEA OF LIMITED WAR

Jan Willem Honig

Describing certain visions of war as 'uncomfortable' (and others, by implication, as 'comfortable') could be considered highly inappropriate: surely all wars are extremely unpleasant for participants and witnesses?[1] Yet certain visions of a disagreeable phenomenon can be deemed 'uncomfortable' if they question the familiar, and therefore 'comfortable', notions that govern the understanding of that phenomenon and the ways of dealing with it. The topic explored in this chapter is the tension—the clash, even—between two constructs of war and warfare, one invented in the mid-nineteenth century, which has shown remarkable tenacity and endurance, and another, constructed in the mid-twentieth century, which seemed to answer an acute need (a need that actually continues to exist), and showed much promise. That second construct had clever people and clever theory, and squarely faced real issues, but nonetheless failed to make much headway. The older construct, I argue here, proved more successful because it provided a more 'comfortable' vision of war, one that corresponded more closely with prevailing notions of what war, however gruesome and abhorrent, was believed and supposed to be. The more modern construct, however admirable in its aim of making war more finely tuned, humane and limited, failed because it threatened to take war's established construct out of its comfort zone. Failure was not a simple question of impracticality, of ends and means that could not be brought into balance and made to work; in addition, as I hope to explain, limited war raised disturbing questions of an intellectual and moral nature. First, it questioned what war is and what makes war work by throwing into doubt the centrality of the active agent (or regulative principle) that was believed to win wars; secondly, it questioned the nature of the object of attention in war, the enemy, and to what treatment he should be entitled.

These issues retain great pertinence. The consistently unhappy experience of twenty-five years of Western interventions and small wars since the end of the Cold War has unsurprisingly led to renewed and persistent inquiries into the question whether war has changed. Much of the contemporary debate, however, concentrates on questions of changing actors and motives, and tends to see effective responses mostly as a matter of adaptation in organization and technique. Only rarely are questions raised about what, intellectually and morally, we believe the deeper nature of war to be and how this might determine the ways in which wars are conducted. The possibility—to paraphrase a well-known description of a popular theory of international relations—that war is what we, and our militaries, make of it is perhaps a notion that deserves more attention.

What follows could be termed an exercise in Freedmanesque constructivist realism. I will not engage too explicitly with Lawrence Freedman's work, but to those familiar with his work, the debt to him should be obvious;[2] this chapter, I believe, is also very much a product of the tradition of the King's College London Department of War Studies. I seek to address an issue of significant contemporary relevance through an interdisciplinary approach aiming to be deeply mindful of the moral issues arising from the study and practice of war, on the basis of a careful study of the past that has produced us, our ideas and our practices.

The invention of modern 'comfortable' war

Three historic paintings illustrate the construction of a vision of war and warfare that was, two centuries ago, novel or indeed revolutionary, but became associated with a practice of war that seemed so natural that it could be called 'comfortable war'. First, there is the painting of the Battle of Lodi (see Plate 1), which was created in 1797—that is, within a year of the actual battle between Napoleon and the Austrians. Its creator was Napoleon's 'geographical engineer', Louis-Albert-Ghislain Bacler d'Albe (1761–1824). When Napoleon was on campaign, Bacler d'Albe was said to be the person he saw last before he went to bed and first when he woke; he was the keeper (and maker) of the maps that informed and guided Napoleon's campaign designs and the man with whom he stuck pins in these maps to track the movements of his army.[3] He was one of Napoleon's longest-serving associates. They had met right at the start of Napoleon's steep ascent to power and fame at the siege of Toulon in 1793, and Bacler d'Albe only retired from his service, because of ill health, in 1814. Mapmaking and painting were more than associated arts at the time: they were one and the same. The Lodi painting was part of a project to 'map' the great general's achievements.[4] It is, of course, propaganda. But it is also a construction of reality that was considered 'real': the work was based on observed and carefully studied practice and, when committed to canvas, it was designed to inform and guide future successful practice. Napoleon and his generals, in short, would have regarded the painting as true. It can therefore be taken authoritatively to illustrate certain vital elements of a radically new idea of what war is about and how it should be conducted and decided. Significantly, however, it is only half modern.

What is modern is that the painting encapsulates a view of war that centres on battle and decision, a view of war concentrated in time and place. That message is new in the 1790s and it is thus also conveyed in a new way. There was no style of battle or war painting like this before that period. It is realistic in that it deliberately sets out to be faithful to local geography and to the events that took place within it. Bacler d'Albe planted his easel (or sat down with his sketchbook) on the battlefield so as to represent accurately the actual terrain, and he carefully researched the events that had taken place in order to identify the 'real' decisive moment that was worthy of being frozen for all time on

Plate 1: Louis-Albert-Ghislain Bacler d'Albe (1761–1824), 'Battle of Lodi, 10 May 1796', 1797 (65.5 x 43 cm), Service Historique de la Défense, Vincennes, Cat.no. B160 © Ministère de la Défense, France

canvas. The painting also envelops the viewer in the action, it is demo-cratic: there is no more bird's-eye view, no viewing of human activity from some exalted, distant and divine height. The complicated meta-phors and allegories that litter the earlier tradition of paintings of war scenes are absent—except perhaps for little Napoleon in the lower left hand corner, who might appear as a latter-day Bourbon king, but even so he and his staff, in terms of position, action and dress, are directly relevant to and integrated within the overall scene in a way that dis-plays the great general's immediate commanding power over battle. The viewer is thus given a direct sense of what matters in war and also, by implication, what generalship is about and how it relates to all involved in the event. The didactic element should not be underrated: war is meant to be understood as being about achieving a decision on the battlefield, and this painting shows you how that could and should actually be done.

However, and here the lack of modernity shows up, the painting is not about 'fighting'. War and warfare are not primarily seen to revolve around 'fighting' as killing. The relative unimportance of fighting is illustrated by the placing of the product that we associate with it: death. Death and killing are treated in traditional fashion: as ornamen-tal. The decision on the battlefield, and by implication in war also, is not achieved by meting out death, but instead through movement. At the centre of the painting stands the French army's crossing of the bridge over the river Adda—where Bacler d'Albe allows himself artis-tic licence by lengthening the bridge to underscore the monumental sweep of the soldiers storming across. And then there is the real deci-sive movement which requires the viewer to look twice, and which conveys the main military lesson of the painting: the surprise move-ment of the French cavalry crossing the river in the background. It was this flanking manoeuvre that was considered to have won the day against the Austrians.

It is the role of death in war that slowly but radically changes, lead-ing to the idea that decisiveness can be enhanced and compressed fur-ther in time and place, into the one grand decisive battle that decides war, completely and finally, by permanently removing the enemy's armed forces from this world. The Lodi painting is part of a series that treats the very substantial number of Napoleonic battles as coequal

events. War is still seen as an endless progression of unceasing movements that converge from time to time on a battlefield where enemies
continue to move on and around each other in close proximity. Battles
build a series of momentary decisions that have the potential to move
war forward towards some ultimate but ill-defined and distant conclusion. For Bacler d'Albe and his master, decisiveness is a tactical
moment and not yet a clear-cut strategic one. There is no expectation,
or even intention, of finally deciding war in a day's bloody work.[5] That
idea emerges only once battle comes to centre on physical annihilation.
As a result, the idea of war and the practice of war change radically.
Modern war, or war as we know it and think we understand it, comes
into being only then.

The process by which movement ceded pride of place to killing can
be seen advancing under Napoleon, but it does not find its completion
until well after his enforced retirement. An example of 'progress' is a
painting made a decade after Lodi by another soldier, so entangled in
the Napoleonic establishment that he is said to have come 'closest to
being in everything but name [Napoleon's] official war painter'.[6]
Colonel Antoine-Jean Gros's 1808 painting of 'Napoléon visitant le
champ de bataille d'Eylau le 9 février 1807' is a five-by-eight-metre
monstrosity that still greets visitors in one of the main monumental
halls of that greatest of state museums, the Louvre (see Plate 2).
Technically not a battle painting since it depicts the day after the two-
day battle, it nonetheless illustrates how the place of death in warfare
is changing. It was painted for a competition that the Napoleonic
regime organized soon after the battle to commemorate—or should
one say celebrate?—what had been a particularly bloody event, fought
over two days in blinding snowstorms in the remote wastelands of
eastern Prussia, which modern accounts claim caused some 40,000
casualties, including one in three of the Russian soldiers present.[7]

What struck visitors to the Salon of 1808—the annual exhibition of
the best in government-sponsored modern art—was the foreground, a
tangle of dead and dying men. The ground the dead occupy takes up a
third of the painting. That was novel. Their reserved place was usually a
small ornamental band, as in the Lodi painting. Also the realism was
striking. It is tempting (especially for us today) to read the painting simply (to quote the website of the art museum in the United States that

Plate 2: Antoine-Jean Gros (1771–1835), 'Napoleon on the Battlefield of Eylau, 9 February 1807', 1808 (5.21 x 7.84 m), Musée du Louvre, Inv. 5067
© RMN-Grand Palais (Musée du Louvre)/Daniel Arnaudet

owns a study for the final design) as 'a horrifically realistic depiction of the bloody costs of war' which reinforced this central point, in ironic or even bitingly sarcastic fashion, through its juxtaposition with the saintly and obviously hypocritical presence of Napoleon.[8] That would not be quite right. The painting won the competition prize that year and Gros had the Légion d'honneur pinned on his chest by the great man himself in an act of such memorable theatricality that Gros sketched out the event in oils.[9] The key thing for us is that death is still treated as a by-product of war—useful only in the sense that it permitted a presentation of Napoleon dispensing succour to the defeated by letting loose a swarm of seven doctors (including his chief surgeon) to tend the enemy wounded[10]—but a by-product nonetheless. The decisive action takes pride of place in the background where the French army is seen sweeping across the battlefield, usefully driven along by the clearing skies. Movement is still depicted as the main active ingredient in war, of what defines the conduct of war and battle. This was even clearer in Gros's first major design of Eylau, which more emphatically highlighted the grand onward movement of the French army (see Plate 3).

War, to repeat, is not yet about 'fighting' as killing: war is seen to produce its effects through movement; death is a by-product and not what makes war a politically effective instrument. This changes in the forty years after 1815. Across Europe, killing is put at the centre of war in both military theory and practice. The infliction of death now becomes a deliberate tactical and strategic activity in war. One sees that in military theory, where the watershed event is the posthumous publication in 1832 of Clausewitz's *On War*, in which the author expressed the hope—which contemporary reviewers across Europe all picked up—that it would cause 'a revolution' in theory.[11] One can see it in the increasingly formalized teaching of strategy at the new military academies that sprang up across Europe. One can also see it in the bureaucratizing war-planning processes, and in weapons design and training: it is only in this period that soldiers begin to be systematically trained to shoot to kill in dedicated '*écoles de tir*'.[12] By the 1860s, when the European 'great wars' resume, death securely occupies the centre stage in war. War is now understood to achieve its useful tactical and strategic effect through the infliction of death. To paraphrase Clausewitz, imposing one's political will is seen to be best achieved by making the

Plate 3: Antoine-Jean Gros (1771–1835), 'Napoleon on the Battlefield of Eylau', 1807, oil on canvas, 104.9 x 145.1 cm, Toledo Museum of Art (Toledo, Ohio), Purchased with funds from the Libbey Endowment, Gift of Edward Drummond Libbey, 1988.54. Photo Credit: Photography Incorporated, Toledo.

enemy defenceless through the physical destruction of his armed forces. That idea is summarized in a painting of 1870, entitled simply 'Un coup de mitrailleuse', or 'A burst of machine-gun fire', which shows at centre stage a group of Germans (Saxon light infantry, apparently) machine-gunned to death (see Plate 4). It would be a mistake, as with Gros, to see this picture as a critique of war. Yes, viewers were struck by the horror, but equally by its veracity, its deeper truth, its depiction of what war necessarily was and had to be. The painting is by another establishment figure, close to the military, Édouard Detaille (1848–1912). Detaille made a very successful career out of painting military scenes. He had served in the Franco-Prussian War and observed the scene with the line of dead German soldiers. Most tellingly, despite losing two brothers to the war, Detaille embraced the idea that war proper, at its dark heart, was about meting out death.[13]

Detaille depicts the outcome of a process that in intellectual, educational and doctrinal terms was completed in the decade or so before the outbreak of the Franco-Prussian War in 1870. A fundamentally different place and value were now accorded to the presence of death in war. Death, of course, had been hard to miss on the Napoleonic or earlier battlefields, but it came to be seen differently. It should be noted also that this new vision of what war was and how it should be conducted constitutes a form of war that could be described as limited. War is conducted by a special category of people (uniformed soldiers) in a certain delimited place (the battlefield) and, on the whole, for political aims that also are limited. However, no such term as 'limited war' as yet exists. The process of defining war in the decades of peace after 1815 is marked by a strong inclination to view war as a unitary phenomenon. Both in theory and practice, this permits a grand and unprecedented attempt to 'regularize' war. The underlying unity that war possesses is built on the new understanding of war as a phenomenon regulated by the application of force and the belief that the pre-eminent medium for the efficient application of force is the decisive battle. Clausewitz's theory offers the foremost example of this process. His categorization of 'absolute' war (that is, war in theory) and 'real' war exemplifies the attempt to elucidate war as a single, regular phenomenon. Even though he recognized that political ambitions could dramatically moderate the intensity of war (hence his late introduction

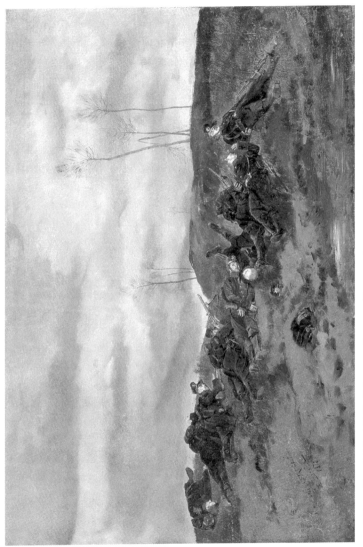

Plate 4: Édouard Detaille (1848–1912), 'Un coup de mitrailleuse—à mon ami Albert Goupil', 1870, Private Collection François Robichon. Reproduced with permission.

within real wars of a subcategory of wars with limited aims), Clausewitz denied that this in any way altered the nature of war and urged that moderation in war should be used with the utmost caution.[14] When in his younger years he taught the course on 'small war' at the Berlin military academy, he also presented this form as an integral, indissoluble part—together with its complement, 'great war'—of one and the same phenomenon, one that was ultimately regulated by the judicious meting out of death. As small wars become a staple of military activity in nineteenth-century colonial warfare, that remains the case. At the very end of the century, the noted British theorist Colonel C.E. Callwell, for example, conceded that small war might be a special form of war, but it was not a separate category. 'The object', he wrote, remained 'to fight, not to manoeuvre', because 'the battle-field decides, and on the battle-field the advantage passes over to the regular army'. 'The enemy', Callwell insisted, 'must be brought to battle, and in such manner as to make his defeat decisive'.[15]

The invention, rise and decline of limited war

If war was regulated by violence, then the party that could deploy the most violence was most likely to emerge victorious. Theory thus provided a justification for deploying as many people with deadly weapons as possible in war. The concern with maximizing means expressed itself in the spread of universal conscription and the development of ever more lethal weaponry in the nineteenth century. This, in turn, gave rise to the question whether such a mobilization of human and material resources could be justified politically. Why would the people offer themselves up for death on the battlefield? Death might serve the strategic aim of attaining absolute mastery of the battlefield, but what overarching political purpose did battlefield mastery serve? A powerful current of politico-military thinking justified the sacrifice demanded by developing a political analogy to the intellectual construct that had come to guide the understanding of war: just as nature had defined war as violence, so too it had marked out the international system as a struggle for survival among nations. Thus the violent nature of war was brought into balance with the presumed violent nature of politics, and individual sacrifice was justified by the highest, most precious goal of national survival. This vision meant that war spilled beyond the borders of the traditional battlefield and traditional military timekeeping. Fighting the 'Great War' demonstrated that an unremittingly murderous front line could extend for years from the English Channel to Switzerland, across the Alps and over parts of the Middle East. The sharp end of war, moreover, was underpinned by an equally important and sprawling home front. That meant that the perception of who constituted a legitimate target in war also changed. The application of violence was no longer limited to uniformed soldiers, but extended to whole nations. The necessary involvement of the people in war led to a refinement—if one could call it that—in the theory of war which was completed in the 1930s. By then it became known, with lasting effect, under a new epithet: 'total war'.[16]

Total war held out the prospect of breaching all limits. Where would it end? Holocaust was one option, but not attractive to all and sundry. Pessimism was widespread, however, and it was among those who doubted, with regret, that modern war could be restrained that the term 'limited war' seems to have first emerged. It is employed to mark the stark contrast between modern total war and a long-lost era of warfare that could readily be described as limited. As far as I can see, the historian of the French Revolution, R.R. Palmer, employs the term first in his contribution on 'Frederick the Great, Guibert, Bülow: From Dynastic to National War' to the famous and often reprinted 1943 edition of *Makers of Modern Strategy*.[17] For Palmer, the term and the associated idea made sense within a teleological worldview which postulated that modern national, or total, war had relegated *ancien régime* dynastic, or limited, war to a past that was lost for ever. The contrast thus encompasses a critique of current practices and an essentially nostalgic yearning for a more civilized and gallant form of warfare that was believed to have existed before the French Revolution. Yet it represents a view that resigns itself, however unhappily, to the fate wrought by unstoppable politically, industrially and militarily driven 'progress'.[18]

There were, however, examples of practical men who tried to devise practical ways of countering the trend. Liberal and conservative military thinkers alike searched for methods of finer distinction, of finding points of attack—critical vulnerabilities, one might also call them—whose selective destruction would bring the socio-political edifice of the enemy down and render him defenceless. While seeking to bypass or short-circuit the requirement of wholesale slaughter, they did not disavow the idea that war must in principle revolve around violence, death and destruction, but they believed there must exist more efficient or more clever ways of war. This approach was not straightforwardly connected with emerging notions of limited war, however. The logic of war, and now total war, posed a particular challenge for those who regarded war as abnormal or wrong in principle and who were repelled by the enormous blood-letting that seemed to be required. To them, war made little moral or productive social and economic sense.

The obviousness of these facts reinforced a sense that, given a chance, normal people would surely choose peace over war. This suggested that war was a phenomenon started by a peculiar kind of people or political order. To contend with these 'aggressors', 'realistic' (as opposed to pacifist) liberals accepted that wars had to be fought occasionally.[19] Such wars should only be a last resort fought purely out of self-defence against the evildoers who brought it into the world. But what should be the fate of those who started wars of aggression and the agents who fought it on their behalf? Should they be shown the error of their ways and offered a chance to repent? Or should they be considered beyond the pale and punished by death, even after unconditional surrender? Should the firmly established paradigm that war was in essence about killing and destruction remain intact and be brought into line with an uncompromising political agenda, or should warfare take on a more argumentative, reformational and corrective quality? Did liberal 'limited' war just require a finer, more precisely targeted application of violence than total war, while remaining equally uncompromising vis-à-vis the enemies it singled out? Or should it be marked by some process of careful calibration of factors beyond violence alone and make war a process of compromise and, possibly, compromise outcomes?

An early exemplar who struggled with these questions was the British military thinker Basil Liddell Hart (1895–1970). The agenda he set himself, and the fundamental tension that came with it, were summed up well by Michael Howard: 'War was hell, but mere wishing would not prevent its recurrence. Somebody had to consider how, if it did occur, it could be fought more cleanly, more decisively, and above all more intelligently'.[20] In searching for 'decisive' warfare Liddell Hart never abandoned the fundamental tenet of the classic nineteenth-century tradition of strategic thought. However much his ideas and theories were informed by liberal convictions and attempts to limit the effects of modern destructive war, some of his early strategic recipes have a surprisingly brutal quality about them. They advocate gassing the enemy capital's civilian population as a way to quick and relatively bloodless victory.[21] They also lead him, without a trace of irony, to label the US Civil War general William T. Sherman as 'the first modern general' and laud his decisive march through Georgia, which deliberately targeted civilians and their possessions.[22] As he matured, Liddell Hart abandoned advocacy of the 'hard' targeting of civilians and instead sought decision through the psychological 'dislocation' of the enemy's regular armed forces. He summed up this idea in a theory he labelled the strategy of 'indirect approach', by which he achieved great fame. While he sought to soften across various editions the association with more traditional concepts of 'decisive battle', the indirect approach differed little, in ends and means, from the direct approach he railed against, except perhaps in the amount of blood spilt and in the more intelligent use of force. The 1929 book that launched the theory was tellingly entitled *The Decisive Wars of History*. That title was not a misnomer.[23] The author maintained that 'the perfection of strategy would be … to produce a decision—the destruction of the enemy's armed forces through their unarming by surrender—without any serious fighting'.[24] Later, expanded editions from 1941 onwards changed the title to *Strategy: The Indirect Approach* and, among numerous subtle changes, removed from the passage just quoted the phrase explaining the nature of a decision. Liddell Hart himself may have believed that he was developing not just a more humane theory of warfare but one of liberal, limited war, as Azar Gat claims, though it is questionable whether this fully registered with his many readers, whether resident in liberal democracies or in more autocratic and even totalitarian states. They had little difficulty in associating Liddell Hart's theory of clever, less bloody warfare with highly decisive results that disarmed an opponent and thus paved the way for an imposition of peace—which need not be limited. In effect, his theory could be read (and his many historical examples reinforced this) as propounding a more efficient and economical form of warfare in which the enemy's psychological breakdown was still achieved by (to use recent popular terminology) a shocking and overawing application of force. In short, the indirect approach fitted within the comfortable paradigm of warfare.

Liddell Hart's fascination with decisiveness sat uneasily with his earnest and deeply felt concerns with the pursuit of limited strategic and political aims.[25] He did not help his case by appearing to be a politically naive and nostalgic idealist regarding the latter aims. His persistent advocacy of small professional armed forces and compromise peace seemed dangerously out of touch with the totalitarian threat emanating from Germany and Japan. Liddell Hart's influence on policy and strategy unsurprisingly took a nosedive during the Second World War. That he made a comeback after the war was mainly due to two reasons. One is that his ideas on decisive warfare benefited from the addition of one more compelling recent example: German *Blitzkrieg*.[26] The second reason was that international politics changed dramatically. With the introduction of nuclear weapons into a political environment marked by a state of absolute enmity between 'superpowers', the practice of total war now stood a real risk of becoming identical with absolute war. Force of circumstance produced an unprecedented interest in limited means and limited aims.[27] Liddell Hart now began, soon after the end of the Second World War, to use the term 'limited war'.[28] While his direct engagement with these debates was mostly concerned with reiterating his earlier prognostications that total war made no sense, the peculiarities of a developing nuclear stalemate gave them a force that they had not possessed before. Liddell Hart was less clear on what limited war in practice looked like.

It was the influence of nuclear weapons that made 'limited war' a household term during the 1950s and brought forth a concerted effort to create a theory. However, it proved very difficult to get away from an idea that in political terms, liberal-democratic states should aim at the overthrow of the opposing communist-totalitarian political system. Moreover, even if they chose not to pursue such an objective, the enemy's clearly stated aim was the end of the capitalist order. So the debate and the object of theorizing moved quickly to a focus on limitation of means as the way of reducing the risk of escalation resulting in mutual annihilation.[29] Yet, even here uncertainty was so great that, in practical political terms, it seemed safer to avoid superpower war altogether and accept a situation of 'peaceful coexistence' anchored in nuclear deterrence. That conclusion also meant that in preparations for possible war, necessary to make deterrence credible, ideas very close to total war continued to prevail—even though, strategically, both sides wanted to discriminate in their targeting: the US desiring out of principle to save the good Russian people and only destroy the oppressive communist system, and the Soviet Union meaning to destroy the capitalist system while saving the oppressed working class. Indiscriminate, total targeting made little sense for 'real' war, but it did make sense in preventing war.

But avoidance of superpower war did not banish war among proxies. This seemed the perfect stamping ground for limited war to show its true mettle. Could force be used in theatres far removed from the superpowers in a way that avoided lighting the proverbial powder trail to all-out nuclear war? Advertising plainly that such wars would only involve the use of non-nuclear, conventional weaponry did not, however, answer the questions of how, how much, and to what strategic and political end those 'limited' weapons should be used. Theory converged on a sense that limited force had to be calibrated carefully in support of limited ends. Limited war thus became a theory of graduated responses, coercion and signalling. To recall the title of what many regard as the summation of the theory, 'arms' were to be used as a means of obtaining 'influence'.[30] However, such an approach to war conjured up uncomfortable visions. For liberal democracies, war had become a very special zone of danger. If it was fought (and fought it had to be, as that was war's nature), war must be undertaken only for exceptional ends and must lead to a successful, uncompromising conclusion. How could a resort to the evil of war and deadly violence otherwise be justified?

A vignette may illustrate the issues. The precise date is a little unclear, but in late 1964 or early 1965 the US Assistant Secretary of Defense, John T. McNaughton, had a meeting with the eminent strategic theorist (and later Nobel Prize winner) Thomas C. Schelling. At the time, the Johnson administration was busily looking for ways to make a recalcitrant North Vietnamese regime more sensitive to US demands while avoiding the risk of widening the conflict to include other, nuclear-armed superpowers. Schelling, who had made a name for himself as an imaginative thinker on strategic bargaining (and who had usefully briefed McNaughton before on how to approach arms control negotiations), was an obvious person to call in for advice on devising a plan for what was called 'graduated action' within the corridors of power. However, in the only publicly available account we seem to have of the meeting, a caustic judgement is offered of Schelling's performance: 'Tom Schelling, when faced with a real-life "limited war", was stumped, had no idea where to begin'.[31]

Freedman gallantly leapt to his intellectual hero's defence in a 1996 article claiming that 'Schelling's theories had not been developed for this kind of occasion' and adding that 'there was not, and could not then have been, a suitable theoretical framework for South Vietnam, for scant consideration had been given in theories of strategic coercion to the problem of shoring up a rotten regime against a resolute opponent'.[32] For Schelling, limited war was an integral part of the larger superpower conflict. As he had written in 1961: 'a main consequence of limited war, and the main reason for engaging in it, is to raise the risks of general war'.[33] That was not a game that the Johnson administration dared play in Vietnam. McNaughton, in Freedman's words, became a 'disillusioned strategist' who could not see a way of dealing effectively, and honourably, with the incorrigibly disappointing character and behaviour of his Vietnamese opponents and allies alike. Disillusionment also struck his interlocutor. Schelling turned away almost entirely from politico-military strategic analysis soon after this foray into actual strategy-making. His 1966 book, *Arms and Influence*, was his last major word on the matter. As Robert Ayson diplomatically put it in his biography of Schelling, there was 'a correlation between the relative frequency of Schelling's publications dealing with strategy in the nuclear age and US fortunes in the Vietnam War'.[34]

But reasons, arguably, went deeper than the practical complexities of real war defeating theoretical sophistication. Intellectually, the theories of limited war as they emerged in the 1950s threatened the unitary character of war and the purity of means that was so closely associated with it. Violence became just another element within a range of means employed for wheeling and dealing with an enemy. Impurity of means in turn undermined the treasured simplicity of traditional ends, in which violence produced defenceless enemies, defenceless enemies conceded victory, and with victory came peace. Tinkering with this logic led to the prosecution of 'half-hearted' war, as Clausewitz had already feared.[35] The result would be messy compromise outcomes or, worse, defeat. Critically, however, limited war went against the commanding liberal notion that war was something extraordinary, whose violent, morally questionable means could only be justified comfortably by having it applied by a special category of 'professional' military against a singularly exceptional category of 'enemies'. Limited war, not unlike total war, threatened to make war escape from the battlefield and turn it from a special instrument into a normal part of politics. War would no longer really be war. That created an uncomfortable moral hazard.

As Schelling moved away from limited war, the theory's popularity waned and the older paradigm of war reasserted itself. Although since the end of the Cold War pressures have re-emerged to conduct war in a way that limits the emphasis on violence and seeks compromise with the enemies that litter the globe, limited war theory has not made much of an officially sanctioned comeback. Western militaries have resisted it. Politicians and their electorates feel uncomfortable with it. Pressures to apply violence more precisely have not abated, but once the cross hairs are trained on the enemy, force is used uncompromisingly. Counterinsurgency doctrine, for example, for all its emphasis on 'winning hearts and minds', is pretty clear about its primary function. To quote the famous 2006 US *Counterinsurgency Field Manual*: a supportive population helps to 'displace enemy networks, which forces enemies out in the open, letting military forces seize the initiative and destroy the insurgents'.[36] Violence and war retain their special battlefield place. Real war's comfort zone is still believed to lie where it was put in the middle of the nineteenth century.

3

REFLECTIONS ON LAWRENCE FREEDMAN'S 'DETERRENCE'

Patrick M. Morgan

Lawrence Freedman's concise and impressive book *Deterrence*, published in 2004, describes how deterrence in international politics might work differently, which involves probing how the character of deterrence itself can be altered. In turn, that invites consideration of how this new approach to deterrence could contribute to and reinforce an expanded, more elevated level of global community.

I start with remarks about deterrence in the Cold War, briefly reprise portions of *Deterrence* that convey its conception of possible ways to change the impact of deterrence, and conclude by surveying major characteristics of today's international system and assessing the relevance of Freedman's concept in that environment.

Deterrence in the ColdWar era

Deterrence is an old practice, utilized in many societies in a variety of social situations involving or pertaining to crime, child-rearing, business, politics and other activities. It has a long history in relations among states and societies, being employed in military and other security activities to avoid being attacked or otherwise seriously harmed and, by using force, to discourage others from inflicting harm in the future. States have also used deterrence more broadly to configure and maintain relevant aspects of the international security environment to their satisfaction.

In *Deterrence* Freedman offers a simple definition: 'deterrence is concerned with deliberate attempts to manipulate the behaviour of others through conditional threats'.[1] In international politics those deliberate attempts are mounted by states, alliances and other actors (such as terrorists, drug cartels and insurgents), typically to manipulate the behaviour of others who might inflict harm on the deterrer or those whom the deterrer wants to protect. While 'deterrence' is applied via threats to do *significant* harm, particularly by using force, it is also practised by threats of sanctions, shunning and isolation, trials of individuals in international or domestic courts, freezing of assets, and other means.

In international politics deterrence had long been standard and as such was straightforward, not carefully studied or elaborately designed. Then it was abruptly elevated to great prominence, starting in a limited way in the 1930s but really in response to the Second World War and the development and use of nuclear weapons and the prospects this generated about future wars. It became a crucial component in the strategic postures and thinking of the most powerful governments soon thereafter. As Bernard Brodie wrote about deterrence, 'Thus far, the chief purpose of our military establishment has been to win wars. From now on its chief purpose must be to avert them'.[2] Thus it began to be seriously examined by analysts in governments, armed forces, think tanks and academic institutions.

Actually, seeing deterrence as critical for dealing with the problem of war was long overdue—almost criminally so. The First World War had demonstrated, as Woodrow Wilson pointed out, that war was becoming too awful to tolerate, and the fundamental design of the League of Nations rested on deterrence by means of the threat that any member attacking another would be attacked by the rest of the members, in response. The Second World War and nuclear weapons just made the point more starkly.

But using deterrence, including nuclear deterrence, during the Cold War to prevent another world war—and prevent lesser wars because they might escalate or spread—never had overwhelming approval. After all, it coped with the problem of war by threatening war, it seldom settled serious quarrels and often even stood in the way of settling them, and it seemed much too risky and expensive. Deterrence with nuclear weapons in particular could readily be labelled a cure worse than the disease. Preparing to do dreadful things was a very crude way of keeping safe. One way of putting all this at the time was that mutual nuclear deterrence was like getting drivers to avoid car accidents by requiring that they tie their children to the car bumpers. Many people insisted that just studying deterrence was idiotic, even criminal, to say nothing of using it.

Nevertheless, once deterrence became prominent in military planning, analysts assiduously investigated it. The resulting body of theory would eventually be described by observers and participants as the most influential ever produced by the social sciences, one of the most distinctive features of the Cold War, and largely responsible for the fact that we all survived it.

However crude, deterrence turned out to be complicated both to employ and in its effects. Rational decision analysis depicted an opponent facing a deterrence threat as doing a careful cost-benefit analysis in reaction, then not attacking if the costs outweighed the benefits. But the threat might readily provoke an emotional response as well, or be misinterpreted as a threat to attack instead. Being threatened can make people bristle, become highly resentful, frustrated at being restrained, or afraid that giving in will just invite more threats, and thus strongly disinclined to accept being deterred; or the threat can produce determination that, even if they comply with it, they will work very hard to design around it. Thus deterrence can work badly precisely because it involves a threat.

Two points about Cold War deterrence deserve emphasis here. Firstly, theorizing about deterrence and how best to use it was intended to provide an abstract, rational guide for states and statesmen. The goal was maximizing chances of states and their citizens surviving the nuclear age through imposing on an intense political conflict a theory that would shape the opponents' behaviour. But the times greatly shaped deterrence in turn, making an impact on the theory and how it was applied and causing serious departures from what strategists, analysts and decision-makers had sought. Deterrence in practice often reflected its environment, making it a creation not just of analysts, but of the international system, military preoccupations and domestic politics. This was evident from early in the Korean War onwards, in

- the scale of superpower nuclear arsenals. They were soon vastly larger than the US and USSR needed to deter each other and anyone else, incomprehensible in the scale of death and destruction to be inflicted if 'necessary'. This was alongside the unprecedented levels of peacetime conventional forces of the superpowers and their allies.
- the gross caricatures each side generated of the other in justifying that destructive capability.
- the misapplication of numerous measurements used by each side to assess how deterrence was doing.
- the pursuit of policies that often contradicted the best analysis and evidence provided by deterrence theory.
- the endless list of things deemed critical to maintain the credibility supposed to be necessary to make deterrence threats work.

The resulting deterrence structure could readily have had catastrophic consequences if a conflict and resulting war went astray. It was a structure that itself intensified the Cold War, providing a vastly greater destructive potential than necessary at greater expense than necessary with greater risks than necessary, including risks of grievous harm from accidents, misperceptions, escalation, emotional misjudgements, and even insanity in high places or low. It was a structure so elaborate, so deeply embedded, that almost twenty-five years since the Cold War there is no prospect of its finally being completely disassembled despite widespread indications that it is obsolete, lacks a mission, is virtually unusable, remains too expensive, and sets a bad example.

Why did we do this? Ultimately, because of recently experienced wars that killed in massive numbers, indiscriminately, with indiscriminate damage to match. We were used to expecting that from enemies and used to doing it ourselves—used to being very good at it. Hence we readily detected certain new people eager to do that to us again or worse—we were certain they hated us so much; people who would not hesitate to attack given the opportunity, who could only be stopped by either planning to do that to them first or scaring them out of it. Either a pre-emptive/preventive war or deterrence seemed the available choices, and the planning proceeded accordingly. We still live with the after-effects of this. Remnants of Cold War deterrence arrangements remain, operating in a far different context but with clear roots in the Cold War era, testimony to how potent environment can be in shaping deterrence.

Another legacy that shaped the Cold War and Cold War deterrence is geographical in nature. Its impact was initially greatest on the main Cold War protagonists, particularly the United States. The world wars, especially the Second World War, generated a perceived necessity to think on a global scale about security. European great powers had long been absorbed in operating globally through their empires and their security; they had global interests to pursue and protect. But, joined by Japan, they finally fought a war in which for some states the objective was collective global domination and not just global reach.

After the war the US and USSR absorbed this perspective; each announced that the Cold War was ultimately about global domination, making their security interests and concerns, above all their perceived security threats, global as well. The Cold War was therefore a global contest, conducted worldwide on the assumption that the whole world was at stake. The other members of the system never operated on that basis, but many felt that the global-level outcome of the Cold War could readily affect their security deeply, starting of course with the potential effects of nuclear war. Managing global security was for a few states to do, some others to contribute to, and many other states to worry about.

In anticipation of this, efforts had been made to transfer the core responsibility for global security management to the permanent members of the Security Council, but the Cold War undermined that, sharply circumscribing the UN contribution. Other international groups were formed to try to exercise at least some influence, but with modest results. That left global security management largely to the major Cold War actors through their competition and rivalry.

This brings me to my second point about that period: those doing the intellectual spadework in shaping our understanding of deterrence, and eventually the leaders largely responsible for global security management, discovered that to use deterrence reliably under Cold War circumstances the major states had to cooperate in important ways with each other, both despite and because of their conflicts.

The intellectual analysis began by observing that deterrence threats in a crisis (immediate deterrence) had to have the opponent's cooperation; if deterrence was to work, the opponent had to agree to comply. It also became clear that, with major states living in a highly conflictual relationship in the nuclear age, deterrence would be operating all the time (general deterrence). Fears of all sorts, especially of a nuclear war, then made it imperative that in both general and immediate deterrence situations deterrence remained stable, not collapsing into warfare. Thus the main objective of cooperation among the opponents would be to keep deterrence stable roughly all the time. That would require cooperation across the Cold War divide and also among the participants on each side of it. Relatively soon, some states outside the Cold War felt pressure to join in a number of those cooperative efforts. After all, they had a big stake in successful deterrence for global security management. In fact, the more intensive the conflict and the more states involved, the more elaborate the cooperation had to be.

Analysts set out to sell all this to policymakers, military leaders and others, and that turned out to be difficult—not the idea of the parties talking with each other, but the idea that they would exchange large amounts of sensitive information and often take steps to accommodate the 'enemy'.

The most important result of cooperation was the development of significant norms and agreements for governing deterrence and other security-related aspects of conducting the Cold War. As norms are statements of acceptable, usually desirable, behaviour, deterrence-related (and Cold War-related) norms provided guidelines (formal and informal) for how the parties should cooperate within their overall antagonism. They set constraints on the core military–political antagonism, some of its spinoffs, and the intense military competition (particularly the arms race) in order to help stabilize deterrence. Some norms and agreements pertained primarily to the US–Soviet relationship, some to the inter-bloc relationship, and others—like the non-proliferation regime—concerned the stability and security of the entire system.

This has important implications for the last section of this chapter. Normally, deterrence is coercive, resting on fear: 'You cooperate with our demand that you not attack (or do related things we don't like) or we will seriously hurt you'. That is the equivalent of the Godfather's 'I'll make him an offer he can't refuse'. Cooperation in Cold War deterrence pursued stability by evolving fairly early on into cooperation around norms, understandings or accepted practices, not just threats.

Thus the analysts' greatest contribution was to work out not only the dynamics of Cold War deterrence as a threat system but also its dynamics as a cooperation system. The latter was more innovative, surprising and difficult to understand and thus harder to institute politically. What was soon called 'arms control' was, in theory and practice, a greater contribution than deterrence. Deterrence has typically been considered the dominant phenomenon and arms control largely its handmaiden—a supplement that helps make deterrence viable. But, conceptually, arms control is the master concept. It is best defined as deliberate steps taken to contain the costs and other harmful consequences of the continued existence of arms. Deterrence is one of those deliberate steps and is thus a form of arms control, making deterrence theory a subset of arms control theory. And efforts to contain the costs and other harmful consequences arising from deterrence had to be pursued largely by means of cooperation, which is a central feature of arms control.

This perspective clashed with the common notion that security via cooperation, for example through international institutions or norms or negotiations, required abandoning deterrence in favour of creating relationships in which it would be irrelevant. The basic premise of arms control during the Cold War and down to the present has been that this is unrealistic. Major conflicts will continue between and within states, and so arms are not about to disappear and will inevitably be used.[3] Thus deterrence remains unavoidable and makes a necessary contribution but must, like other arms control efforts, work safely and be stable. This requires a notable element of cooperation.

Internalized deterrence

With this in mind, we can turn to the concept of internalized deterrence. This was offered by Freedman to help us properly appreciate and better shape the contributions that deterrence can make now and in the future in managing international security.

His argument in *Deterrence* is straightforward. He notes that while debates about deterrence are similar in strategic studies and criminology, the two communities of scholarship rarely draw on each other's findings and accumulated experience—though they should. He concludes that studies of deterrence dealing with crime confirm that deterrence can and does work, albeit inconsistently, but that it works better through instilling certain psychological effects in the target than by just posing threats of serious harm and inflicting it on those who fail to comply. He calls the emphasis on threats an 'interest-based' approach[4] to the understanding and use of deterrence. The other approach reflects the fact that deterrence works best when it leads or contributes to the target's beginning or continuing to internalize norms widely seen as embodying proper social behaviour. This 'norms-based' approach seeks to reinforce certain values 'to the point where it is well understood that they must not be violated', so that what results is 'actors internalizing a sense of the appropriate limits on their actions'.[5] Punishment can help as well but is less important than getting the target to understand that what he has been doing, or thinking about doing, is wrong, unacceptable. When that happens, such behaviour begins to seem shameful and others' condemnation of it looks more and more correct:

> …when the deterrer and the deterred are working within a sufficiently shared normative framework … it is possible to inculcate a sense of appropriate behaviour in defined situations that can be reinforced by a combination of social pressures and a sense of fair and effective punishment. Out of this comes a view that criminal deterrence might work through the complex interaction between a government seeking to encourage the idea that certain behaviour is anti-social and elements in society that are sympathetic to this idea. Those otherwise inclined to act improperly are therefore deterred not only by the prospect of punishment, but also the disapproval of their friends and neighbours when their crime becomes known. The deterrent effect becomes less necessary as they come to share this definition of what is anti-social.[6]

This is why, in other studies, findings suggest that the nature of the punishment threatened or applied to someone who has done something wrong is less important than a very high probability that he or she will be punished—especially if the punishment seems appropriate to the target. Successful deterrence is really about inculcating norms that lead to the target's rejection of the anti-social behaviour concerned. The target gradually learns to deter himself, accepting the constraints of proper social behaviour, gaining the benefits of being seen as behaving properly and avoiding disapproval for behaving otherwise. In effect, deterrence shifts away from simply threatening toward including, somewhat indirectly, teaching as well.

Turning to international relations, Freedman cites the English school and the constructivist perspective (I think the liberal internationalist perspective belongs on that list as well) as helping us understand why a similar phenomenon can work there. They stress that interactions among states, especially in today's world, press them towards generating and adopting shared values, giving international politics aspects of being a society.

> This framework lends itself to the consideration of the development of norms, because that is exactly the process that helps bind the society of states together … This has encouraged a growing focus on the role of norms, defined by Katzenstein as 'the standard of appropriate behaviour for actors with a given identity'.[7] They can both set limits on and encourage distinctive types of behaviour … and can also be constitutive in shaping how actors think about themselves. They are bound up with notions of legitimacy, a key ingredient for any action that depends on the support and approbation of others, and which can be found at an intersection close to legality, morality and social acceptability. There is therefore a potentially supportive environment for making an assessment of whether there are circumstances in which the processes of censure, shame and stigma that work at the national level might also work at the international level.[8]

Freedman is talking at least partly about actors learning from their social interactions about what is and is not acceptable within a difficult, competitive environment. It is the legitimacy involved that helps shape that learning and makes the deterrence effect itself more like learning.

The development of norms of appropriate behaviour that have legitimacy can lead to states or others actually shaping their behaviour around such norms because of the way they would be characterized and treated otherwise. He adds that this process is bolstered when powerful 'interests' in international politics—leading states or major international organizations (IOs)—are behind the norms in question, because they often play a significant role in shaping those norms and supplying enforcement to uphold them. We can add that this should lead to greater adherence to the norms by powerful states too, because of their stake in having sponsored them—something that did a good deal to make arms control efforts successful during the Cold War.

Doubts

Critical responses to this approach readily spring to mind, some of which Freedman surveys. We recognize how such a pattern of behaviour emerges in a domestic society, but has it been widely characteristic of international politics? After all, internalized deterrence does not fit the nature, behaviour and history of the actors. And if deterrence is something that one party implicitly or explicitly does to another, how can it be said to arise within the target? The threat has to be external; the history of international politics and its actors' behaviour indicates that deterrence has to generate much more than self-regret.

Secondly, it can be said that states do not internalize in such a fashion. They are not like individuals. If they internalize, it is through policies adopted in decision-making processes or through standing bureaucratic practices, reflecting extensive experience or bureaucratic routine. Or the internalization emerges from elements drawn from a domestic culture or a religious perspective. Or their behaviour is ultimately dictated by leaders reflecting primarily domestic considerations, especially on domestic security, and is thus apt to reflect international norms only marginally.

Another negative reaction would be the typical realist one. A norm cannot readily be internalized as Freedman suggests because states are rational actors, weighing options against available resources and interests. State interests take precedence.[9] Being deterred is complying with a threat from outside because it is in the state's interest or cost-benefit calculations to do so. This reflects the self-centred nature of states, making associations dispensable, principles flexible and norms dispensable when interests dictate. The outside deterrence threat is not internalized; what has been internalized is this general way of dealing with threats. They are accommodated or not depending on what the state or its leaders see as valuable.

But Freedman's position on what is possible cannot readily be dismissed. To begin with, deterrence is never unilateral. As noted earlier, the target allows itself to be deterred—it must decide to cooperate with the threat—and Freedman makes this point himself.[10] Thus, when it works, deterrence is always internalized to that extent. Freedman is describing how the target can come to convert that decision from an undesirable but, under the circumstances, acceptable action to a decision that is acceptable or desirable without outside threats of physical coercion, or not just because of them.

An alternative view of how internalized deterrence can work would be that a social imperative is rather like a foreign threat in its impact; the actor is not 'free' and acting 'freely', especially when what has to be done to meet society's standards is quite unattractive—uncomfortable or unwanted—no matter how proper it is. To adhere to a social imperative is to be deterred to some degree, in the way the term 'deterrence' is usually used. The desire to go through with a desired action is partly externally and partly internally deterred.

As to whether states learn from deterrence encounters over time, Elli Lieberman's book *Reconceptualizing Deterrence* shows how one might probe for evidence that a state, or a group like Hezbollah, can come to internalize deterrence out of repeated confrontations, including outright fighting, with foreign opponents. His detailed investigation of the effects of deterrence covers the serial deterrence encounters of Israel with Egypt and Hezbollah over an extended period, and he found that the lesson learnt was not that it was wrong to attack Israel, but that a regional situation including Israel was tolerable and more acceptable than continued fighting.[11]

Other interesting and relevant work challenges rational actor approaches. Jonathan Mercer has a notable approach treating emotion as an unavoidable element in decision-making by individual officials and in a state's collective decisions in international politics.[12] Drawing on recent findings in cognitive psychology, he contends that states' officials, like people in other circumstances, can be sensitive to what others think of them, or what they think others think of them, or what they think others will think of them when selecting a course of action. This makes Freedman's position on the impact of norms still more worthy of consideration.

The standard opposition to the Freedman approach would be that international politics, as it has been classically described, forces states and statesmen to do what would otherwise be seen as unacceptable to sustain the state within a vigorously competitive environment. International politics is not like domestic society and cannot be. When the national interest requires, internalized deterrence will be ignored or set aside. Thus international politics cannot provide a congenial environment of the sort Freedman describes as needed for the internalization of deterrence.

As noted above, Freedman sees the international system as capable of promoting not only relatively realist behaviour but also behaviour characteristic of a society. In fact, his analysis was based on the rapid adjustments in that direction which international politics made in the first decade after the Cold War. Thus the next step in these reflections is to outline, first, the nature of the post-Cold War international system as it initially emerged, and then the relevant aspects of the system today and its prospects. The goal is to see how internalized deterrence fits into today's system—or not. This is in line with the earlier point that the international environment shapes deterrence—the role it plays and how it works.

Deterrence and the post-Cold War world

After the Cold War the system shifted markedly, becoming significantly more compatible with the Freedman perspective. This is something that Freedman understood. His discussion in *Deterrence* reflects his appreciation of it. What were some of the more important indicators?

As we know, after the Cold War we moved into an extended period of hegemony in international politics. Often called American hegemony, it is more properly termed Western hegemony—'Western' not only in a geographical sense but referring to a cultural–ideological–political cluster of closely associated governments and societies that encompasses Japan, South Korea, Australia, Israel and others, plus some associates that do not embody and are not attracted to Western values and behaviour (Saudi Arabia and the smaller Gulf states are examples). American prominence economically, militarily, and politically largely sustains the group's cohesion. Most of the group has given preference to Western norms and efforts, to press them vigorously on others. Hegemony also enables individuals and groups in Western societies to have far more influence on their own in advancing Western norms and values, and this extends to holding Western governments' feet to the fire about adhering to those norms and values.

A striking example of the results is the contemporary preoccupation with sharply reducing casualties and damage from military engagements. This was initially instigated by the demonstration in the 1991 Gulf War that Western forces could win with considerably limited harm not only to allied forces but also to the other side. Since then Western uses of force have been expected to virtually eliminate civilian casualties and damage, to win by crippling opponents' military capabilities, communications and transportation systems, avoiding harm to civilians and minimally killing even the opponents' military. This has largely become a norm of contemporary 'modern' warfare, and there have been strong pressures to have the same restrictions apply to warfare by others, as in Syria today; it has also been readily extended to warfare by drones or selective assassination. All this reinforces the norm of war as unacceptable—something to be minimized. It is an invitation to internalize deterrence, to treat using force, going to war, as a last resort at best.

The major result was to stimulate a broad international effort to reduce warfare, including an expansion in forceful interventions to back up deterrence threats in response to a wide range of—mostly intrastate—violent conflicts. Various analysts eventually pointed out that, collectively, the international system had begun winning the war on war. After the initial post-Cold War years interstate wars declined significantly; intrastate wars, flourishing initially, also declined; deaths from war worldwide declined; the number of nuclear powers remained lower than anticipated; the number of nuclear weapons dropped sharply; the number of refugees from wars declined.

This was fertile ground for progress on the internalization of deterrence. Freedman's design is quite in keeping with what I have just described. Internalized deterrence could readily be seen, without being regularly cited as such, as a key objective of a good deal of this activity. The results reflected greatly expanded studies and experience in making deterrence more effective *inside* societies and nations, *within* communities. The surge in attention to norms bearing on the curbing of warfare was surely a sign of a further developing global community—limited and fragmented, yet already a distinct change from traditional international politics. Chances of progress along the lines Freedman suggested were certainly much better than in the past.

One of the most important developments along these lines was, with the Cold War collapsing, the hugely successful transformation of virtually all of Europe into a pluralistic security community, including the suppression of vicious warfare in Bosnia and Kosovo, motivated both by deeply felt humanitarian reactions and by a battery of emerging norms pertaining to elimination of violent conflict, in an elaborately collective application of deterrence. All this represented a major enlargement of the impact of norms that emerged first to help support, and then were reflected in and enhanced by, the development of the European Union.

At the top of the broader international system after the Cold War there were significant frictions among the most powerful states at times, but nothing like an intense conflict or competition. They no longer saw each other as constantly posing significant threats to attack. This was reflected in the way major states and many others turned to lower levels of military spending, a significant drop in arms sales, smaller arsenals including smaller nuclear arsenals, and lower readiness levels for smaller military forces. Political-economic competition continued, as did jockeying for prestige and influence, but not with Cold War-like military postures. This was more like a transformation than a shift. Nuclear deterrence for most of the states with nuclear arsenals was relegated to the background. The range of amicable relations among major states expanded. Where did this sharp shift in the environment leave deterrence?

Among major powers, the most dangerous relationship is the Sino-American one. Each side focuses largely on the other's military capabilities and their evolution, each thinks of its security in terms of a possible future military confrontation or conflict, but with no immediate prospect of a military clash. Among major states only the US has significant conventional forces on relatively high alert, but it is on a much smaller scale than during the Cold War. The other prominent deterrence dyads are well known: the two Koreas, the US and North Korea, India–Pakistan, the two Sudans, Israel and Iran, and the US and Iran.

More common are violent internal conflicts, which, at lower levels of fighting, often display extensive serial deterrence through fighting. But some conflicts involve casualties and destruction reaching near-catastrophic proportions. Violent internal conflicts came to be often treated as so important that the system's members would consider, or actually undertake, issuing deterrence threats and, fairly often, implementation of such threats.

Deterrence resources used on behalf of internal security management include non-military capabilities (sanctions for example) as well as military ones, and the deterrence sought is often aimed not just at a particular present target, but also at influencing others in the future. A number of these deterrence threats have been made by or under the auspices of international organizations against particular governments or non-state elements within states (as in the Congo).

As noted earlier, driving many international conflicts today are norms, bearing on conflicts both within and, less frequently, between states and societies, intended to embody acceptable behaviour. A number of these norms are long established; many are relatively new.[13] Norms play a much larger role in the international system today than in the past in shaping conceptualizations of conflict situations, the acceptability of various courses of action, and the justifications for taking action.

While ideological pressures of a political nature are less prominent, intense religious commitments and ethnic conflicts have fuelled or aggravated military and other conflicts in numerous parts of the world. In many cases, the deaths and destruction, refugees, survival and health problems, and the loss of social and political cohesion often involved, are considered serious threats to international security.

To a considerable extent, this has been instigated by a major inflation of the concept of security on humanitarian grounds, especially by means of the concept of human security. This is another facet of the emergence of norms into greater salience and prominence. The result is that the conception of stability in international politics has been much enlarged as well. Both human security and stability and the stability of security in international politics are now readily seen as encompassing domestic conditions and situations. As a consequence, the events and activities with which deterrence must contend are much more numerous.

Freedman's interest in how internalizing deterrence can operate includes stress on how norms can be quite powerful in gradually replacing the familiar heavier-handed forms of deterrence, diminishing the need for them. This suggests that the increased impact of norms is a central feature of today's international politics, which should sharply alter the nature of deterrence and its impact.

Very prominent is the surge in Western efforts to promote norms through, or linked to, the spreading of democracy, free enterprise and other Western values. There was a pent-up demand for pushing such values resulting in the huge expansion in attempts by Western states, state-sponsored private entities and private entities on their own to spread democracy, in what may best be described as a crusade.

Where fighting has been suppressed, much of the resulting 'peace-building' has included efforts to instil democratic practices. The underlying rationale is the belief that democratic entities do not go to war with each other, that this is apparent with states, and that, properly instituted, the coming of democracy can make it the case within societies too (something that has been far more difficult to achieve and then sustain). In fact, democratic peace theory is, to date, the most elaborate analytical and practical expression of the idea that ultimately deterrence should be and can be internalized.

Also making a big impact was the terrific increase in international interactions on virtually all levels after the Cold War, especially as a result of the explosion in communications, transportation, trade, and other interaction capabilities, all continuing to develop at a frantic pace. They require the burgeoning of facilitative cooperation arrangements, formal and informal, promoting a wide variety of efforts to provide them. Particularly important is that this has vastly escalated interest in the promotion of norms and their application, not just by states and international organizations, but also by domestic and international private entities and NGOs (of which there are now roughly 65,000), a phenomenon typically referred to as the emergence of international civil society.

Interest is focused not only on new norms but also on more and better use of existing ones, re-examining the latter with an eye to refinement, adjustment or repair. Of special importance for deterrence are norms associated with banning particularly dangerous weapons or their further spread, protecting civilians from attack by military weapons and forces, and rejecting anything like genocide and other actions that create large refugee flows. An example of refining a standing norm very pertinent to deterrence is the emergence of the principle that a government must uphold its citizens' welfare, that when it does not, and particularly when it contributes to their harm, sovereignty can be breached to protect the citizens from atrocities or other egregious harm. Efforts to suppress behaviour violating this norm have risen sharply; numerous NGOs are involved alongside IGOs and governments in calling attention to serious violations and generating intense pressure to do something.

With respect to deterrence, these efforts range from expanding aid to greatly enlarged numbers of people working abroad on human welfare to military interventions against excessive violence, occasional outright takeovers of states and their societies, plus elaborate peace-building and nation-building efforts. At times international judicial proceedings against regimes and officials for violating the norms in question are involved.

There are other steps that prepare the way for the enlargement of or directly enlarge the international community, and have implications for the further development of deterrence. There have been many more, and more penetrating, efforts to sustain and improve security within and between societies. These include efforts at agreements to end or suppress fighting through peacekeeping, peace enforcement, peace imposition and peace-building undertaken by IOs, alliances, temporary associations of convenience, and individual states. Variants of deterrence are often involved, seeking not only to halt serious violence but to deter people from undertaking it again.

Particularly interesting is the expansion in IO involvement in coping with war and other extreme forms of violence. Freedman argues that legitimacy is important to the impact of norms in internalizing deterrence, and this makes it vital to link norms on violence to international organizations. After the Cold War the legitimacy of IOs—particularly the UN—improved considerably. Governments turned to them much more readily, joining in collective efforts under the aegis of the UN and others on many peacekeeping, peace enforcement and peace-building enterprises. This has typically been in response to failures of deterrence efforts, but in some cases it has been in trying to head off a possible catastrophe in the making.

Along the same lines the United States added important additional international capabilities for deterrence and security management. After the Cold War this effort emerged from a sizable expansion of US alliances (formal and informal), the serious reluctance of the allies and the US to see an American retreat from that network politically or with its forces, and therefore the need to find the network things to do lest it atrophy. One outcome was the retention of the alliances and a significant part of the network of bases for US forces, as well as much of the logistical and supply networks, in addition to strengthening of the emerging US Combatant Command network.

Another outcome was that the basic functions of the alliances were significantly adjusted, largely at US insistence. This shifted the alliance network from the existing preoccupation with protecting the allies to reorienting the allies towards joining the US in using deterrence in the management of global security affairs. American forces abroad are no longer primarily prepared for helping to protect allies. They are now trained and prepared for going anywhere they are needed. The allies now have primary responsibility for their national security, and are also to be to some extent prepared to support US forces elsewhere. This reflects the fact that global management of security is required, and the US and the allies have the most impressive military capabilities. Various allies have high-level agreements with the US, referring to these 'strategic' alliances to signal the shift in allies' functions and responsibilities.

The resulting global intervention capability on behalf of security concerns is, in effect, a substitute for the permanent UN forces that were envisioned by the UN Charter, but never created, though with a considerably greater military punch. Essentially this can create the kind of intervention forces generated for the Korean War. The force assembled for the Gulf War was a preliminary version; the force that assembled to halt the war in Bosnia a model of how it would normally work at its best. Available to support UN resolutions, it represents also, in effect, a capacity to act when the Security Council cannot.

People certainly take note of the actions of this force (in Afghanistan, for instance) but have only a vague conception of how it works. It consists of:

- US Combatant Command organization of military exercises, training, conferences and other meetings with the allies on a continuing basis, which serve as the administrative and communications structure of the network;
- major US arms sales to allies and associates (at times more like donations);
- joint financial and technical support in developing new weapons;
- integrated missile defence development and missile defences;
- American logistical support for allied efforts, not only on joint military efforts but on individual ally operations;
- shared intelligence, especially sharing of American intelligence on major joint operations.

Today and tomorrow

Global security management is as important as ever, and now more complicated. More complicated because more states are moving towards becoming significant players in international politics, rapidly increasing their capabilities and involvement. More important because we are racing (and tumbling) towards an ever more interdependent and interconnected world—politically, economically, militarily, socially—which heightens the potential effects everywhere of dangerous and harmful developments anywhere. The Western world took the lead in attempting to build security management around its interests, preferences and values, deeming them fundamentally universal. This included efforts to build an effective deterrence regime to contain interstate and intrastate conflicts and threats, in reaction to, and further advancing, the continuing development of global norms. Freedman has suggested that in the developing global society deterrence could become significantly internalized, achieving a more sophisticated degree of conflict management.

However, it should come as no surprise that this chapter ends on a sober note. There is another side to how we have been doing since the Cold War. To summarize, the security management that emerged rapidly, though incompletely, after the Cold War is receding in effectiveness and is in danger of collapse. There are various reasons for this, some quite fundamental.

To begin with, the central difficulty posed by the enhanced salience of norms in international politics is that the norms in question deliberately apply well beyond international politics. As with any emerging community, the pertinent norms often extend to the better conduct of domestic affairs as well. The international community, the West in particular, now cares much more deeply about: the degree of democracy in political systems; the treatment of women in societies; the treatment of minorities; the well-being of people—health and healthcare, living conditions, poverty, the environment; and religious liberty. The international community is (more or less) committed to trying to improve these matters, and Western governments in particular are not shy about saying so—a prominent aspect of international affairs now. International civil society elements are particularly active and intense. Western governments face significant domestic political pressure domestically, as well as more pressure from each other and other governments, to propel progress on these matters—meaning offers of more assistance plus threats and force as needed.

This Western effort is, in effect, an assault on many governments' legitimacy, seemingly inviting major regime, societal and economic change, whether there is a deliberate intervention to bring it about or not.[14] It is simultaneously a threat to many societies and to central aspects of their cultures. This is particularly true of American relations with others, because the US is often the major participant in interventions linked to such norms or in providing or facilitating interventions by IOs, other states and NGOs.

Thus many governments are deeply wary of Western-endorsed norms and eager to champion norms—notably sovereignty—that protect them from outside intervention. There is strong resistance to central elements of Western democracy by religious fundamentalists, and there is a frequent charge that the US is an empire pursuing classic imperial ambitions or that the West is bent on dominating the international system.

Norms can be unforgiving, very rigid. The contemporary international system is roiled by serious clashes over norms that inhibit international cooperation. This erodes the capacity of norms to promote the internalization of deterrence and inhibits international cooperation even in the face of serious interstate and intrastate conflicts, as happens frequently at the Security Council and other venues.

In addition, the West's efforts at management have lost a good deal of the cohesion needed to sustain them at a consistently high level. That has been one cause of the uneven Western record of military interventions. In cases like Rwanda or Darfur there was little Western appetite for intervention despite classic human security depredations. There was the failure in and hasty departure from Somalia. There was the complete Western disarray about initiating war with Iraq, especially the Bush administration's arrogance about proceeding unilaterally and its certainty about why Iraq's military capabilities posed such a grave threat. What ensued was the abject failure to produce a workable society, economy and democracy in Iraq or even a suitable justification for the war, as well as the likelihood that Afghanistan will continue as a failed state.

Iraq and Afghanistan added to the accumulating evidence that the Western world cannot consistently create Western-style nations, societies and cultures in keeping with its international norms. Some analysts say the West does not know how to do it. Others increasingly suspect that it cannot consistently be done—Western efforts are bound to be too resented to really take hold; non-Western societies must make the transition on their own or else will not do it at all because of deep attachments to their own societies and cultures or ferocious fundamentalist or ethnic opposition to change. Some analysts suggest the entire endeavour has been basically propelled by Western arrogance and insensitivity.

Various Western academic and other analysis insists that democracy and related Western norms have stopped advancing, citing a recent decline in the number of recognized democracies, the erosion of democracy in Russia, its lack of real progress in China, and so forth. This tendency is exacerbated by the outcomes of the Arab Spring revolutions.

The great recession has been a devastating Western-generated problem, followed by its prolongation due to the lack of a Western consensus on what to do about it. This has downgraded the West's image and its legitimacy, particularly in regard to its management capabilities, in the rest of the world. All this has eroded public support in the Western world for interventions, above all military intervention, and the West is now inclined to retreat from its other efforts to manage the international system. There is little public support for upholding global security management. Simultaneous lack of success in economic, political and military matters has afflicted not only the West's prestige abroad but its self-confidence at home also.

The rise of deterrence in the Cold War led to a realization that security in international politics, and thus a good deal of international affairs in general, needed management, and this continued to shape American and Western behaviour after the Cold War dissolved. But that has become a contentious, often unpopular view with the bitter aftertaste of the wars in the Middle East, the frustrations of dealing with Africa, and the broad context provided by the Great Recession.

Much of this adverse reaction is familiar. The American reaction to the First World War was very similar, and Roosevelt predicted something similar for the US after the Second World War—it took the Cold War and the outbreak of the Korean War to block it. Americans and others felt similarly disenchanted after the Vietnam War, leading Kissinger and Nixon to publicly announce that the US would shrink its responsibilities and involvements. Less familiar is the reinforcement of such sentiments by a massive recession—the only prior parallel in modern history is the impact of the Depression on American unwillingness to take responsibility for international security management. The current situation has an eerie resemblance to what democracies faced in the 1930s with the rise of Fascism. Even in the US there is the same litany of reservations and explanations: 'Why does the US have to lead everywhere?' 'US interests are not at stake'. 'Why spend money on foreigners with such huge problems at home?' 'Even modest involvement will lead to a much bigger one'. 'Those societies are in such disarray, nothing we do will really help in the long run'.

Such views are widespread today in the West. Absent is a solid grasp of the importance of global security management because democratic electorates hate the costs, non-democratic regimes and non-modern societies fear the consequences, and major norms advanced for the system have nothing like universal support when it comes to implementing them. Freedman has outlined an important objective for an emerging global international community—moving towards a situation where deterrence becomes largely internalized. Clearly we cannot get there by abandoning security management. But we are close to adopting the operating principle that conflict and a security management response to it should be taken seriously only if the problem is small enough and dealing with it will not cost much.

As a result, we are seeing, or will shortly see, even more setbacks in promoting democracy and weaker international effort when it comes to managing security. One result will be a widening interest in arms spending beyond the West, something already under way in India, Brazil, Russia and China. The arms control situation will remain frozen or even deteriorate.

Conclusion

Careful study of deterrence helped promote the idea of actively managing international security on the basis of alliances and other cooperation with supporters, as well as even cooperation with opponents on the stabilizing of deterrence and its effects. Deterrence today remains the spine of any serious security management regime. It is fine to promote the development of a global community, and the outline of one is rapidly emerging from our ever greater interdependence and interaction in almost every aspect of life. In that community, deterrence today is a central recourse within a distinctive environment—Western dominance with an emphasis on promoting Western norms and preferences. That makes for a different kind of deterrence within a significantly intrusive management. But the necessary Western cohesion has faded; so have public support, respect for the West, and the global sense of community needed to support and legitimize security management and its deterrence component. All this is evident in reactions to the Syrian civil war, but not just there. There is a nasty confluence of past dreadful mistakes and notable insensitivity (past and present), the reverberating security effects of the Great Recession, and rising expressions of neo-isolationist sentiments. We are in danger of becoming much too tolerant again of ignoring the plight of people far away about whom we know little.

This is very disturbing because there is no viable alternative to Western leadership in global security management. Certainly there is no alternative state or group of states that would be able to gain the necessary acceptability and legitimacy, none that would have the requisite experience or resources, and none that aspires to take on the burdens and pay the costs anytime soon.

The academic world contributed greatly to grasping the need for management from early on in the Cold War, but it retreated from closely monitoring deterrence with the end of the Cold War, producing reduced guidance and creative advice on adjusting deterrence to the world we have now. Attention to deterrence only revived in response to the developments flowing, to some extent, from the West's failures—new kinds of threats from new kinds of opponents, new constraints on using force, continuing proliferation threats.

Obviously, we don't want a recurrence of the sorts of failure in managing international security that occurred after the First World War, after the Second World War, and after the Cold War. And deterrence is a relatively primitive way to manage security in a global community and can be quite dangerous in operation. It is a fundamental back–up, but hardly ideal. We must help ensure it is applied in sophisticated ways. Lawrence Freedman has outlined a central component of the way to proceed, encouraging development of constraints that reduce the necessity to use deterrence in the traditional fashion. And that will require steadily instilling a higher level of community. We need a renewed energizing of and dedication to global security management along these lines.

4

DETERRENCE AND DEMOCRACY

REFLECTIONS ON AMERICAN POST-9/11 HOMELAND SECURITY

Richard A. Falkenrath

On 18 September 2001, just days after the atrocities of 9/11, President George W. Bush signed the Authorization for the Use of Military Force (AUMF). The terrible violence of 9/11 had demanded rapid and uncompromising retribution and the AUMF provided for such an unequivocal response by permitting the President to 'use all necessary and appropriate force against those nations, organizations, or persons he determines planned, authorized, committed, or aided the terrorist attacks that occurred on September 11, 2001, in order to prevent any future acts of international terrorism against the United States'.[1]

The AUMF was—and remains—one of the most unusual authorizations of force in the history of the US. Whilst it was primarily a de facto and immediate declaration of war against al-Qa'ida, it was also a much more open-ended legal construction that authorized the President to use force in an extraordinarily broad set of circumstances with no end date set on the use of force, nor restrictions laid on the geographical locations or nationality of the targets.[2] Indeed, the AUMF required only two criteria to be fulfilled: first, that the President must determine that the targets played some part in 9/11 and, secondly, that force must be used to prevent further acts of terrorism against the US.

As the AUMF has no expiry date and, at the time of writing, has not been repealed, the US is, in a legal and official sense, still at war, and the Global War on Terror rumbles on. And yet, as I will argue in this chapter, the nature of that war has shifted, at least in terms of strategy—something familiar to any scholar of strategy and certainly to one educated by Lawrence Freedman. At the outset of the Global War on Terror (as, for convenience, I shall term it here despite the fact it is now an increasingly unpopular term), the US adopted a traditional Cold War deterrence 'by punishment' posture. Over time, that has shifted to one of deterrence 'by denial'.[3] In the context of nuclear weapons, the former involved making threats against an enemy, which were sufficiently credible and coercive to deter them from undertaking particular forms of action that one would find undesirable. Or, as Richard Ned Lebow puts it, deterrence by punishment is a way of preventing 'an undesired behavior by convincing the party who may be contemplating it that the cost [of that behaviour] will exceed any possible gain'.[4] Deterrence 'by denial' is rather different. Here, one can limit or even remove the choices of others by having the capabilities to prevent them from taking particular actions (for example, the ability to prevent others from acquiring nuclear materials, or the capacity to intercept nuclear weapons, without risk to oneself).

After 9/11, these two strategic visions were taken out of their Cold War context and applied to US Homeland Security strategy. The 'punishment' strategy involved making threats of resolute military retribution against terrorists, which rendered attacks so costly (in terms of the likely loss of resources, personnel and safe havens) that terrorist aggressors considering such action recognized that the costs outweighed the benefits. In essence, this involved threatening the use of military force against the countries that harboured, shielded, or supported terrorists as well as against the terrorists and their networks themselves. The 'denial' strategy, by contrast, involved strengthening the defence of likely targets and infrastructure, on the one hand, and implementing security policies which increased the likelihood of terrorists getting caught, on the other. The purpose of this 'by denial' strategy was to render terrorist aggression so likely to be interdicted, or so unlikely to cause sufficient deaths, mayhem, or fear, that terrorist adversaries would perceive it as an unworkable option and dismiss it out of hand.

While some have acknowledged the fact of the strategic shift in the War on Terror from deterrence 'by punishment' to deterrence 'by denial', few have examined the reasons that underpin it. This chapter is, therefore, an attempt to explore the reasons behind the shift, drawing on and underpinned by Lawrence Freedman's work on deterrence.[5] The chapter begins with the deterrence by punishment posture adopted at the beginning of the War on Terror. The second section will explore the shift to deterrence by denial and the underlying strategic motives for this shift, before the third and concluding section identifies some problems on the horizon for US Homeland Security strategy posed by technological developments such as drones and cyber warfare.

Deterrence by punishment and US Homeland Security

At its most basic, the AUMF was a signal of America's intent to deploy military action against al-Qa'ida and to remove the threat it posed to US national interests, both at home and abroad. In this respect, it was a clear statement of a 'scorched earth' or 'salt the land' policy towards al-Qa'ida—a resolute declaration of a war whose key objective was to eradicate those who had perpetrated (or had helped to perpetrate) the attacks of 9/11. In this sense, the primary objective of the AUMF and the War on Terror which ensued was to secure the US and its interests from an immediate terrorist threat in the form of al-Qa'ida and its decentralized, dispersed networks.

In addition, the AUMF overtly delineated a longer-term vision that went beyond the immediate need to eradicate the threat posed by al-Qa'ida to the US. This strategic and deterrent element was to be found in a key, but often overlooked, phrase in the AUMF—that the objective of military force was 'to prevent any future acts of international terrorism against the United States'. Here, the crucial point was that military force authorized under the auspices of the AUMF was not simply about eradicating the threat posed by al-Qa'ida, but also about deterring future aggressive behaviour, whether perpetrated by al-Qa'ida or by other terrorist organizations. From this perspective, the AUMF drew a line in the sand: the US had been attacked, but the ferocity of the response would construct a credible threat of force that would dissuade others from emulating al-Qa'ida's tactics. The AUMF therefore fitted into a conventional deterrent framework: credible threats of significant military reprisals were made against would-be aggressors with the aim of dissuading them from their actions by persuading them that the costs of such actions would outrank the perceived benefits. Under this logic the threat of resolute military action, bolstered in terms of credibility by the extent of US operations in Afghanistan, meant that, in the future, terrorist actors assessing whether to attack the US would calculate that the likely response of the US to such action would cost the organization more than it could gain from terrorist action.

It is important to note that the success or failure of America's deterrence 'by punishment' strategy, encapsulated in the AUMF, rested on (at least) three factors. First, the threats made by the US had to be credible, and this relied, at least in part, on the initial military response to al-Qa'ida in Afghanistan and later in Iraq; if military action authorized under the AUMF was to deter future aggressors, then the US military response to al-Qa'ida had to be sufficiently uncompromising, rapid and ferocious that future aggressors contemplating terrorist action against the US would calculate that they would be on the receiving end of considerable force. Secondly, the deterrence by punishment strategy relied on the adversary being what Wyn Q. Bowen terms 'a cost-benefit calculator'—that is, a rational actor who assessed strategic options in terms of costs and benefits rather than through some other kind of framework.[6] Thirdly, it relied on being able to identify an appropriate target, that is, a target which could both be threatened with punishment in the form of military force and be sent deterrent messages in order to influence its cost-benefit calculations and thus its decisions.

The unique nature of terrorism, however, posed a number of problems for deterrence by punishment in the context of US Homeland Security. As Lawrence Freedman wrote in his 2007 article 'Terrorism as a Strategy', terrorism is a challenging problem in strategy because it is

> a purposive activity that generally fails to meet its purposes. Strategy comes into play as soon as there are choices, and the art of strategy is to

shape the choices of others, friends and supporters as well as enemies and rivals. Because terrorism only has one method to influence choice it lacks variety and flexibility. If particular targets do not respond to attacks then there are no other options, or if there are they require a move away from terrorism.[7]

It is hard to disagree with this. Since 9/11 few, if any, terrorist activities have succeeded in achieving their long-term political objectives, though some have gained their more short-term ambitions of drawing the attention of the public and the media; even al-Qa'ida, across its various offshoots, has been very far from achieving its purposes in any meaningful way.

But why, if terrorism is a predominantly unsuccessful strategy, does it still persist? At least part of the reason can be ascribed to the internal dynamics of terrorist groups and their desire to maintain group cohesion. Academics such as Mark Sageman and Jerrold Post, for example, have explained that internal group dynamics are central to the process of radicalization and the path to violence. Post suggests that embryonic terrorist organizations are characterized by 'fragmented psychosocial identities', which are held to varying extents by members of the group.[8] Over time, he argues, groups become increasingly close-knit as members internalize a privileged, valued 'self' and externalize a negative, demonized 'other' in a process that not only justifies violence but also makes it an obligation.[9] By contrast, Sageman describes an 'in-group love' model in which, he argues, self-forming cliques (which he later termed 'Bunches of Guys') undergo three non-linear stages in radicalization: (a) friendship and discipleship lead to an association with *jihadi* ideology; (b) 'one-upmanship' leads to group intensification of extremist beliefs; and (c) contact with an individual outside the group facilitates a semi-formal acceptance into the *jihad*.[10]

The importance of internal group dynamics to terrorist behaviour presented a number of difficulties for the US Homeland Security strategy of deterrence by punishment—specifically with regards to the notion of deploying the power of the state to attack terrorist groups directly and discourage their formation in future. In the first place, though it was possible to threaten terrorists as a broad category with retributive violence, the problem was precisely whom to threaten to punish. While it might be tempting to target the leaders of terrorist organizations, they

77

were (and are) frequently difficult to identify, locate and isolate from the population. Moreover, as in the case of al-Qa'ida, these leaders might have decision-making authority in the organization but no involvement in the actual execution of attacks, with the corollary that operational members—often even more secretive and difficult to locate—also had to be targeted. Still further issues, largely ethical, were raised by those who are on the fringes of terrorist movements and provide valuable support in the form of shelter, supplies and logistics. The difficulty, put frankly, is that we often lacked what Trager and Zagorcheva refer to as a 'return address'—that is, an easily identifiable target toward which we might direct force: on the one hand, it was often not clear against whom retaliation must be conducted and, on the other, it was difficult to locate the key leaders and isolate them from those who played no part in terrorist activity.[11] The effect was that the threat of force, central to the deterrence by punishment strategic posture, lost a degree of credibility and, with it, a degree of coercive leverage.

The second and related 'credibility problem' was that, even if we had been able to easily identify appropriate targets (whether they were decision-makers or in more operational roles), it seemed unlikely that threats of retributive force actually deterred al-Qa'ida from directing terrorist action against the US. The difficulty was that, for deterrence by punishment to be successful, the target had to evaluate potential courses of action in terms of the costs and benefits of those actions; the threat of punishment was designed to upset the balance between cost and benefit, tilting it in favour of costs and rendering the action less likely to achieve desired outcomes—and more likely to end in failure. The problem with al-Qa'ida, particularly in comparison with other more 'conventional' terrorist organizations, was that they calculated costs and benefits according to different metrics. The fact that they seemed to value our deaths more than they valued their own lives, for example, meant that our threats did not render their courses of action more costly than beneficial. Indeed, in some senses, we actually felt that the threat (or use) of force as punishment for certain actions seemed to play into al-Qa'ida's hands by lending them a certain kudos in the minds of their adherents and, simultaneously, providing them with valuable publicity. Once again, the threat of force suffered in terms of credibility—even if we could identify appropriate targets of military action, the threat of force did not seem to render actions costly in terms of our reprisal.

Deterrence by denial in Homeland Security

> In principle, denial is a more reliable strategy than punishment … With punishment, the target is left to decide how much more to take. With denial the choice is removed.[12]

The two 'credibility' issues I outlined in the previous section—the lack of a 'return to sender address' and the unconventional nature of terrorists as cost-benefit calculators—are not simply inherent in deterrence by punishment in the Homeland Security context, but they also pervade deterrence by punishment in a more general sense. This is because those issues stem from a single and crucial facet of the strategy: that, as Freedman has pointed out, for all the threats one makes and for all the coercive leverage that those threats generate, the target retains choice about how to act. The corollary is that, if the strategy is to be successful, it must be sufficiently (and perhaps even continuously) coercive—threats must always be constantly making the costs of undesirable forms of action greater than the benefits.

This difficulty became apparent in the final months of 2001 and throughout 2002 with the consequence that, by late 2003, there had been a definite and conscious shift in strategy. My own time in the White House and then the NYPD (which, to a certain degree, filled the void left by the lack of a US domestic intelligence service like MI5) saw a rather different strategy emerging, one which was rooted in both deterrence and risk theory, but differed from the 'deterrence by punishment' posture that had been adopted immediately after 9/11. The key assumption underpinning the strategy was that New York City was not the only target in the US, but was probably the most attractive one for terrorists. Under the deterrence 'by denial' strategy, we sought to 'harden' the city and to communicate this to the potential attackers to the greatest extent we could, doing it quite openly, visibly, sometimes exaggerating and playing up the degree of readiness and preparedness and the degree of intelligence penetration into these groups and their community associations.[13] The purpose of this was to shift the risk of terrorism away from New York and toward targets that would be far less attractive to terrorists in terms of symbolic value, population density and so on. In this sense, deterrence 'by denial' also had an element of misinformation: we constantly sought to plant in the mind of extremists or potential extremists who might have been connected to those groups the seeds of a thought that New York City was uniquely hard to attack.

The short-term purpose of this strategy was to adjust the terrorists' perceived probability of success in attacking New York, with the aim of getting them to attack somewhere else. There are not too many things at NYPD that I can say had a Freedmanesque logic to it, but this was one of them. In the longer term, however, we wanted to 'internalize' this (to use Freedman's language) in terrorist strategic decision-making: we wanted New York City to have the reputation of being so difficult to attack that no terrorist would even bother to consider the option, dismissing it without even contemplating it because it was so unlikely to work or difficult to implement with any success. The key advantage of such a strategy is that it renders courses of action unappealing and choices are removed from the target.

Into the future: emergent technology and US counterterrorism strategy

The gravest threat the US faces is at the crossroads of radicalism and technology.[14] In 2002, the US National Security Strategy predicted that al-Qa'ida would seek ever more innovative and technologically advanced methods to wreak destruction and, in so doing, to pursue their political ambitions. As yet, this is more of an appearance than a reality, though there is evidence that al-Qa'ida and other terrorist organizations have considered forms of cyber warfare as well as using different explosives such as TATP and PETN to avoid detection. By way of conclusion, it is worth looking to the future and examining how some technological developments might affect the strategy of the US. For the purposes of this chapter, I will focus on drones and electronic surveillance, in part because there is something slightly unusual and special about both technologies and in part because they both continue to dominate the headlines.

Drones have perhaps the greatest capacity to alter the nature of counterterrorism and counterinsurgency strategy. In the first place, they have, of course, changed the experience of warfare: drones have the potential to remove the soldier from the proximity of war—or what John Keegan described as the 'face of battle'. Now, serving military officers can operate a drone in some foreign battlefield before going home that night, dropping into the kids' baseball game and inviting friends round to a family barbecue. In the second place, the US currently has something of a monopoly on drones, at least in their ability to be so precise and global. This monopoly has given the President of the United States options which he has never had before. It offered President Obama, for instance, the relatively unique opportunity to kill Anwar al-Awlaki despite the fact that he was in Yemen, which was not a formal war zone or battlefield in the way that Iraq or Afghanistan were. Thirdly, and most important for the present purpose, drones present the possibility of a return to deterrence by punishment. Previously, terrorists like Anwar al-Awlaki would have been dealt with by the criminal justice system. Drones, however, provide even liberal presidents like Obama (who was, let us not forget, a professor of constitutional law) with the opportunity to pinpoint terrorist threats and to eliminate those threats without the significant costs and risks of boots in the sand. This, in theory at any rate, allows us to mitigate the first of our problems with deterrence by punishment—that it was difficult to know whom to threaten and still more difficult to locate and isolate them to carry out those threats. Drones remove this by giving an unprecedented, near-immediate and highly accurate method of targeting terrorists. In time, this is very likely to render our threats all the more credible—and deterrence by punishment all the more effective.

However, the hardest part of countering terrorism through 'punishment' is likely to centre on the difficulties of identifying and locating those who are threats in the first place—and much of this will depend on electronic surveillance. Since 9/11, and since the US has become preoccupied with global counterinsurgency and counterterrorism, the importance of electronic surveillance (and its value to virtually every other intelligence collection technique) has risen dramatically. The rise of electronic surveillance has proceeded in parallel with—and accentuated the issues of—cyber security and offensive information warfare. As our capabilities in this field become ever more advanced, our capacity to identify and locate threats—and ultimately to use military force against them—will bolster the threats we are able to make in a deterrence-by-punishment strategy. However, electronic surveillance also presents one of the most profound conundrums for a democracy that values free speech, for which the internet economy is one of the most dynamic sectors in society. This is an issue that is not going away. It will be with us for quite some time and is actually central to the future of counterterrorism.

PART 2

ETHICS AND PRINCIPLES

5

ETHICS IN ASYMMETRICAL WAR

Mervyn Frost

Strategy is perhaps the major area of Lawrence Freedman's expertise. He built his reputation by writing about the strategy of nuclear deterrence, which was an essential component of the bipolar order during the Cold War.[1] As he approached formal retirement, he published his prize-winning book on the history of strategic thinking.[2] In doing so, unlike many focused on military matters and strategy in the Cold War, Freedman's work was always informed by ethics and values—good strategy has good ethics. In the present chapter, I shall develop this point, arguing that this aspect of international relations[3] will become increasingly significant for the development of strategy in the early twenty-first century: the role of ethics in strategic thinking in a time of asymmetrical warfare is vital.[4]

Recent wars have been wars of choice.[5] They include military interventions undertaken for humanitarian reasons.[6] These are asymmetric wars—it seems to be a necessary feature of such wars. They are fought between a state (or alliance of states), with overwhelming military, economic and technical superiority, on the one hand, and states or other groups whose capabilities are significantly inferior, on the other.[7] The weak party in such wars is weak in all the dimensions usually measured by political scientists, which include military muscle, economic clout, population size, levels of industrialization, levels of education, and so on. Yet the weak, as measured in these conventional terms, have exerted considerable power over the strong states. By 'power' I mean the ability to get an actor to do something that the actor would not otherwise have done.[8] We have seen this happen in Afghanistan and Iraq where the superpower and its allies have failed to achieve the objectives they initially set for themselves and have had to retreat on a number of different fronts.

The wars that fall into the category of 'asymmetric wars' are not all of a piece. Yet there are some general questions one can ask about them as a group. Key among these is the question: what is the source of power of the 'weak' party in such wars, and how is it that such parties, with their limited resources, turn out to wield international power sufficient to move even a superpower to change its conduct?[9] If the source of their power is not properly understood, whatever strategy is devised to counter them will fail. This is an important question for everyone involved in world politics.

There are a number of ways in which one might set about tackling this question. One might examine the kinds of attacks that these groups have launched, the kinds of weapons they have used (hijacked aircraft, improvised explosive devices, suicide bombers), the kinds of ideologies used to justify their campaigns (for the most part religious ones), the communication methods used (these include all the modern social media including Facebook, Twitter, Tumblr and others), and the military strategies that they follow. One could examine the ways in which such belligerents have recruited fighters from around the world (thus internationalizing the conflicts) and the ways in which some citizens in democratic states have been sufficiently radicalized to volunteer as fighters for these groups.[10] Similarly one might examine the modes of organization used by transnational networks of belligerents. A key feature of these is that they do not depend on centralized, top-down command structures; instead they are characterized by a maximum degree of devolution that almost borders on anarchy. All these directions of inquiry are focused on the operational level. They ask: Who does the fighting? How are they organized? And what means of fighting do they use? The underlying goal of these inquiries is to develop ways of fighting back, that is, ways of fighting enemies that are geographically dispersed and hidden within the general population worldwide.

The planning of an appropriate response to such enemies produces a host of ethical problems that have become well known. Key among these are the following: What might democracies legitimately do to combat such belligerents? To what extent is 'conventional just war' thinking applicable to such conflicts?[11] How should captured fighters (terrorists) be treated—as criminals, unlawful combatants, or prisoners of war?[12] This is a difficult question that depends on fine interpretations of the laws of armed conflict. What means might be used in intelligence gathering?[13] This is related to the question about the legitimacy of torture to extract intelligence.[14] There are also difficult questions about what modifications might be contemplated to some countries' existing legal procedures to facilitate the gaining of intelligence that could lead to the capture of such fighters. A typical question here is: what kind of surveillance ought to be accepted in democratic states with a view to preventing terrorist attacks?[15] What limitations might properly be put on civil rights when seeking to prevent such things?

Overall, at the heart of these questions about the enemy in asymmetric war is this one: How might they be prevented from doing harm? What makes this so difficult is the problem of identifying who 'they' are. Once they have been identified, the problem then becomes that of determining what 'they' are planning to do. Then there are further difficult operational and ethical questions relating to the problem of preemption and even preventive action against such enemies. Are we entitled to deprive people of their human rights on the grounds that we have profiles of them suggesting that they might in future be susceptible to radicalization?[16]

After seeking answers to the questions outlined above, the major powers have deployed a number of techniques for waging asymmetric war. These have included the use of special forces, private intelligence-gathering companies, and specialist technologies (including technologies of surveillance and, of course, new technologies for delivering lethal force, with drones for example). They have also put considerable effort into the development of techniques of mass surveillance, including those which allow for the tapping globally of telephone conversations, broadband linkages, email traffic, cell-phone traffic, and so on.[17]

A central feature in such asymmetric wars is that, in the early phases of these conflicts, the weaker party (measured in conventional terms) recruits, trains, secures weapons, develops strategies, and so on, in secret. These activities then elicit countermeasures that are themselves often conducted in secret, away from scrutiny by the general public.

In metaphorical terms the whole fight against global terrorism (both within states and internationally) is conceived in terms of the 'needle in the haystack' metaphor. The problem is understood to be that of finding the terrorist 'needles' in the international 'haystack' and to do this without burning it down. While it is of the utmost importance that those planning terrorist attacks be found and prevented from carrying them out, in what follows I wish to make the case that our preoccupation with the hunt for the needles in the hay has distracted us from investigating a more fundamental aspect of this kind of war. It has led us to overlook the source of power that the weak rely on in such asymmetrical wars. It has allowed us to overlook elements without which they would be powerless. My contention is that without a proper understanding of the power on which these small groups rely, all efforts to fight these asymmetric wars successfully will be in vain. The question then is: where does the power of the 'weak' come from in these asymmetric wars?

One possible answer can be dismissed right away. To say that the power derives from the sowing of terror among the population at large is patently wrong. The 'terror' attacks that have taken place did not succeed in creating a global terror that incapacitated governments and peoples. This was true in the US in 2001, in Madrid in 2004, in London in 2005, and remains true after the attacks in Kenya in 2013. While these attacks (and many others) brought about short-term local panic, in the longer term, far from bringing about a generalized and incapacitating global terror working to the advantage of the perpetrators, such attacks brought about a determination to stand firm against such atrocities. If the source of power does not reside in the sowing of terror, in what then does it?

A better explanation for the political power deployed by these small actors lies in their use of ethical leverage within the practices of global politics. They come to use this in the following way. The terrorist groups (such as al-Qa'ida, al-Nusra, al-Shabab, the Taliban and many others) committed deeds that, when measured against widely accepted international ethical standards, are judged by most of humankind to be obnoxious. They flew hijacked aeroplanes into the Twin Towers in New York, they carried out a series of bombings in London and Madrid, they sent suicide bombers into public places in Afghanistan, Iraq, Israel, Algeria, India, Pakistan, Yemen and Egypt. Such attacks were made by different groups, which gave different justifications for what they did. Internationally, though, there was widespread recognition that they had committed significant human rights abuses—they committed what the vast majority of people worldwide considered to be ethical wrongs. None of these deeds caused significant damage to the states within which they took place, when 'significant' is measured by criteria used to assess damage in conventional wars, nor did they succeed in spreading global terror. Instead, by these acts, al-Qa'ida and the others, intentionally or unintentionally, provoked ('bounced') the superpower and its allies into a set of righteous responses to the wrongs to which they had been subjected. It is what happened next that is crucial to understanding the power that accrued to the weaker parties in these asymmetrical confrontations.

The initial reaction to the wrongdoing by the terrorists was followed by an overreaction in which some of the ethical constraints normally observed by participants within the practice of states were undermined. In other words, the minnows provoked the pikes into committing a series of wrongs that undermined their own ethical standing, prestige and legitimacy, and finally their influence and power internationally. For example, the initial bombing of the Twin Towers in 2001 led to the invasion of Afghanistan and then of Iraq (both of which could plausibly be construed as occupations, which is an ethical wrongdoing in contemporary international affairs); the institution of a new type of interrogation perilously close to torture (which flouts a widely held international ethical norm against torture, embodied in an international convention); the introduction of a new category of prisoner, 'the unlawful combatant', who is neither a prisoner of war nor a criminal (which can plausibly be construed as departing from an established set of ethical and legal constraints governing the treatment of prisoners captured during war); the introduction of the procedures of rendition (which can easily be interpreted as a means of circumventing widely accepted ethical and legal norms against torture); the resort to previously outlawed methods of assassination, often extending into the sovereign territory of neighbouring states (which may be interpreted as flouting ethical norms to do with due process, at the very least); and so on.

Within the wider international community, many of these actions were interpreted as gross affronts to core ethical values embedded in both the society of sovereign states and global civil society. These ethical criticisms have been telling and have had widespread effects globally. One effect has been to inspire many young people from a wide range of countries to consider supporting al-Qa'ida and its allies, either directly by volunteering for active service in some conflict zone (Afghanistan and Syria) or indirectly by providing material and political support to their preferred group. Another was to give many citizens within the US and its allied states good reason to oppose their own governments. In both the US and the UK this opposition made itself felt in subsequent elections, resulting in setbacks for the Republicans in the US and the Labour Party in the UK. In general, these ethical criticisms dealt a substantial blow to the ethical standing of the superpower and its allies within the international domain. This in turn affected their political power on the international stage and increased the power and the influence of their adversaries.

Let me repeat the rudiments of the ethical leverage I have described. It involves a small terrorist group carrying out actions that offend against widely held international ethical norms, the most important of these being the norm against the killing of innocent people. These actions then provoke a series of unethical actions by the superpower and its allies, which then afford the initial wrongdoers an opportunity to move towards the ethical high ground in order to mobilize international opinion against the great powers.[18]

Somewhat frivolously one may compare this manoeuvre to one that sometimes takes place in games like soccer, rugby, water polo, ice hockey and boxing. Here, sporting 'terrorists' have been known to reap advantage by committing a wrong to provoke a worse one by the opponent. One typical method is to mutter racist, nationalist, or religious insults at the opponent out of earshot of the referee, to provoke the opponent to commit a foul that results in a penalty which can be used to win the match.

In both international relations and sport, such uses of unethical conduct to leverage ethical advantage, which may then be translated into political advantage, can only be understood against the backdrop of the 'rules of the game', which themselves encapsulate the ethical values central to the sport in question. The constitutive rules of these sporting practices specify a whole range of things that are not to be done to competitors on the opposing side. Flouting these not only brings on a loss of ethical standing for the player thus charged, but at the limit can bring about exclusion from the game itself. In like manner, our international practices are made up of elaborate systems of laws, rules, principles and ways of doing things that are underpinned by widely accepted ethical values. Where these are flouted, participants lose power and status.

So what are the global practices referred to here? Before answering this, let me make a few quick points about social practices in general. I am not referring here to recurrent patterns of behaviour that may be studied, as it were, from some external point of view, in order to detect regular correlations between specified variables with a view to developing covering laws to predict future behaviour.[19] Instead, I am referring to social practices which must be understood from the internal point of view—the point of view of participants who understand themselves to be participating in a social forum that requires following certain well-established rules.[20] How does one know that a social object of inquiry is a practice that needs to be studied from this internal point of view? One knows this when one encounters a group of people who demand and expect of one another that they behave in conformity with certain rules, and when they criticize those who fail to do this. What is vital here is that these demands, expectations and criticisms are reciprocally recognized among the participants. An example of the point made here is the practice of speaking English. In this practice speakers demand, expect and criticize one another's use of the language according to well-known rules of grammar and meaning. There can be no doubt that international practices exist, for we find globally that people make claims upon one another, have expectations about how they should act, and criticize fellow participants for mistakes they may make, in ways that indicate the existence of such practices.[21]

So, what are the key global social practices within which terrorist organizations come to deploy ethical leverage? Firstly, there is the social practice within which sovereign states are constituted as the key participants. This is a practice of practices: the key participants are states, but each state is itself a sub-practice within which the key participants are citizens. In the macro-practice of states, there is an elaborate set of rules of recognition that determines which social entities are to be considered sovereign states and as such accorded the right to participate in this practice. The rules that determine this are contained in the corpus of international law. Within this body of law there are many ongoing disputes about aspects of recognition, but there is a firmly settled core of laws and norms defining statehood.[22] What is to count as a sovereign state is determined by the practice of states themselves.[23]

The central ethical norm embodied in the practice of sovereign states is that the participant states are entitled to a domain of freedom internally and non-intervention externally. This is the content of sovereignty. Again, there are many areas of dispute, but the core understanding of sovereignty is well understood. In this practice states are entitled, when all else fails, to defend their sovereignty against aggression by force of arms. According to the core values, which are served by the settled laws and norms of this global practice, states are constituted as free, and the body of free states makes possible diversity among them. Each sovereign state is accorded the freedom to pursue its own chosen policies internally and externally, provided that in doing this it does not curtail the freedom of other states to do the same. By using their freedom some states configure themselves on Islamic principles, others have established Christian churches, others are secular, some are communist and others social democratic.[24]

The second great global practice of our time is global civil society. This is the global society in which individual men and women recognize one another as the holders of first-generation rights. Again, not everything is settled in this practice; there are disputes about what rights ought to be on the central list. However, there is widespread acceptance of a core set of fundamental rights. These include the standard liberties to do with safety of the person, freedom of movement, freedom of contract, freedom of conscience, academic freedom, the right to own property, and so on. These are often referred to as negative liberties. The values that are nurtured by this set of norms are similar to the values preserved by the society of states, except that in this case the values of freedom and diversity made possible in this arrangement pertain to individual men and women rather than to the collective individuals we know as sovereign states.

Given that all men and women everywhere are participants in both the society of sovereign states and global civil society, it is of fundamental importance that they are able to participate in both simultaneously. By doing this they are able to make real the values of freedom and diversity for individuals and for states. The only way in which the norms, rules, principles and values of these two practices can be made to harmonize is through acceptance that each sovereign state is required to nurture and protect that portion of global civil society which falls within its territory. This is not to suggest that this is what, in fact, happens in every one of the 193 states in the practice today, but it is what is required of them internationally.

To return to the nub of the present argument about leveraging power through ethical criticism: in order not to undermine their own standing within the practices within which they are constituted as free actors, there are a number of things that sovereign states and rights holding individuals ought not to do if they wish to maintain their ethical standing and the associated influence and power that go with it. When confronted with wrongdoing by terrorists, states must devise counter-strategies that do not undermine the core values of freedom and diversity in either of these global practices. For example, if consideration is being given to sending troops into a sovereign state in order to prevent gross human rights abuses taking place there (the classic reason for embarking on humanitarian intervention), every care must be taken to avoid any action that could plausibly be interpreted as a wrongful act of aggression against a sovereign state by an imperial power—as an act that deprives the target state of its freedom. It is important to note that this cannot be done by simply asserting that the military intervention is not an occupation, not an imperial action. Stipulating what an act is does not necessarily make it so.[25] Other conditions also need to be satisfied. The key one would have to be that the military intervention is seen to have widespread support within the practice of sovereign states as a whole—that it is widely understood, for example, to be an act of humanitarian intervention in pursuance of the principle of the Responsibility to Protect (R2P). The primary manifestation of this kind of support would be provided if the Security Council of the United Nations were to endorse it. If, on the contrary, there is division within the practice of states about whether or not the intervention was an imperial act, then the assumption would have to be that a military intervention would not be justified.

Another key criterion to be satisfied relates to global civil society. Some indication would have to be available that the majority of people in the target area would welcome such a military intervention on ethical grounds. If there were widespread disagreement within the area about the justifiability of military intervention, a question mark would hang over it. During the ongoing civil war in Syria there has been no clear agreement amongst the states in the region or among the population about the justifiability of an international military intervention. This suggests that intervention in this case would not be justified.

In both of these practices, that is, in both the global society of sovereign states and global civil society, it is essential that actors considering becoming involved in an asymmetric war of choice take the utmost care not to flout the constitutive norms of the global practices in which they are participating. For it is the flouting of these norms that provides the only source of international power for the weaker party in such wars, whether that party be a state or a terrorist group. Although groups deploying terrorist methods may achieve significant local power within a specific region by terrorizing the local population,[26] this kind of terrorism cannot work on a global scale in which there are 194 sovereign states operating in a steady and successful fashion year after year, upholding the norms that are embedded in their practice. Here, it is only by provoking actions by their opponents that run contrary to the embedded norms in these two global practices that terrorist groups gain any global power and influence at all. To fight asymmetric wars successfully, free states and free men and women everywhere must defeat their opponents in that sort of war by denying them ethical leverage. This requires that they do not do certain things—that they do not undertake actions that undermine the values of freedom and diversity embedded in the two primary global practices that constitute them (and us) as who we value ourselves to be. The greatest power we have over such terrorist actors is to refrain from unethical conduct.

Avoiding a range of unethical acts will ensure that these weak actors do not come to wield disproportionate power in global affairs. When the major actors in international relations do not undermine their (and our) ethical standing, they will be able to work together to combat states and groups which, through their own wrongdoing, seek to provoke reactions that give them ethical leverage. If international actors succeed in constraining themselves in the ways I have mentioned, it will then be relatively easy to classify these groups properly as what they are—as small, fanatical and unethical, and opposed to the order and values made possible in our highly stable international practices. Having thus denied them undeserved international power, it will then be easier to develop long-term strategies to oppose them.[27]

6

THE RISE, FALL AND RESURGENCE OF 'JUST WAR' THINKING FROM CICERO TO CHICAGO

Beatrice Heuser

On 22 April 1999,[1] British Prime Minister Tony Blair addressed the Economic Club of Chicago, a gathering of leading US businessmen, in a speech that would publicize the Blair Doctrine (which evokes other famous pronouncements on war and peace such as the Truman Doctrine or the Weinberger Doctrine). Blair presented a series of conditions that should be fulfilled for his (or any) government to decide to resort to the use of force in international relations.[2] It transpired soon that the key passage setting out the conditions was a verbatim transcription of a paper written for the British government by Lawrence Freedman, while he held the Chair in War Studies at King's College London.[3] While Tony Blair has long been out of government, and his own record of applying what should be called the Freedman Doctrine is much debated, the doctrine lives on, rightly so, as we shall see. This paper seeks to contextualise it in the larger tradition of thinking about just war.

Judicialization of war?

In the context of the Russian–Georgian war of 2008 and the Ukrainian crisis that broke out in 2014, Western criticism of Russian behaviour as contrary to international law and non-approved by the United Nations Security Council was shrugged off in Moscow with the reproach that other states had equally ignored international law when NATO intervened against Serbia on behalf of Kosovo in 1999, or when a US-led coalition went to war against Saddam Hussein's Iraq in 2003.[4] In each of these events, all sides invoked just war arguments for their own resort to the use of force, the *jus ad bellum*. Both Russia and the US react with irritation to external legal constraints placed on their sovereign decision to use force, but both use them to criticise the other when the opportunity arises.

Since the end of the Cold War, other Western governments have generally sought to secure the permission of the Security Council before embarking on military operations other than in direct self-defence. As such permission was rarely, if ever, forthcoming during the Cold War because the Permanent Five (P5) members with their veto power came from the different camps of that ideological schism, it was common for the very same P5 to take action where they saw fit without the UN's blessing. The end of the Cold War made way for P5 consensus on intervention in several cases, despite continuing differences in other areas. As this consensus now seems attainable in principle, great efforts have been made to attain it, some successful, as those preceding the intervention in the Libyan civil war in 2011 (Operation United Protector) and in Mali in 2013 (Operation Serval). When one of the P5 has taken action without approval by the Security Council, it has never been without a negative blowback.

Just war arguments are also invoked with regard to the way a war is fought, as the *jus in bello*. Soldiers in turn complain increasingly that their actions are restricted by rules of engagement and references to the laws of war in unprecedented ways. They talk, with some irritation, of the 'judicialization of war'. They see this as problematic, as legal constraints more often than not will limit military options, indeed frequently eliminating the technically most effective ones. Soldiers complain that they have to fight with one hand tied behind their backs.

The poignancy of this tendency was highlighted by the conviction on 7 December 2012 of three French officers who believed they were merely following orders when they took action in 2005 leading to the death of a wounded rebel leader, Firmin Mahé, in the Ivory Coast, while their commanding officer was acquitted. The situation was based on a political-strategic judgement: there was a good chance that his supporters would try to free him, and had the rebel leader been freed by his supporters, it was deemed likely that it would have refuelled the ongoing civil war which the French expeditionary force Licorne was supposed to help pacify. A French military court pronounced the colonel and two NCOs guilty, while recognizing the difficulties they were facing in Ivory Coast.[5]

In a similarly complex political context, a German colonel in September 2009 had misjudged a situation in Afghanistan, under political pressure both from local leaders and from his own government to act more violently against the Taliban in his area of operations. He ordered the bombing of two fuel trucks which had been hijacked by the Taliban but ended up stuck in the mud while fording a river. Unable to extract them, the Taliban invited civilians to help themselves to fuel, and in the middle of the night people of all ages were swarming around the tankers to fill their jerrycans and other containers. The colonel was eventually acquitted by a German court, but the episode led to the resignation of the German Generalinspekteur (chairman of the Chiefs of Staff) and eventually of the Minister of Defence.

In both cases, the pursuit of strategic aims seemed to suggest a course of action in conflict with the laws of war—in the first case, the rule that a wounded prisoner must be afforded medical aid, as quickly and extensively as possible and, in the second, that all due care must be taken to distinguish between civilian and military targets. While both actions seemed to have—at least at first—strategically desirable effects, eventually both turned important elements of public opinion against the counterinsurgency forces that had carried them out. In other words, the larger political effects resulting from the injustice of the measures trumped the narrower (but still political) considerations that had led to them. The context of this is one where unjust acts—acts deviating from self-imposed and openly proclaimed, or multilaterally accepted, norms—are seen as undermining the moral stance in the conflict of their perpetrators.

This may not be a universal view—there are cultures, most notably that of militant Islamism, in which sweeping aside constraints on violence and cruelty is seen as an act of virile bravado or a sign of moral strength (not weakness) and admirable determination in the pursuit of a great cause. Yet emphasis on acting within the rules of war is not confined to our times only. The following sections will track examples of considerations about restraints on when to go to war and on how to act in war throughout recorded European history. Questions arise, such as whether, even here, there were periods and cultures where restraints were absent or by contrast taken very seriously; whether proclaimed restraints were honoured in practice or only by lip service; and whether self-imposed restraints were at all times the luxury which only a superior power could afford.

Roots of the 'just war' tradition: 'jus ad bellum'

There is widely scattered evidence that the roots of our just war tradition can be found in ancient Greece. In his pronouncements attributed to his teacher Socrates, Plato gave a pragmatic hint about the reasons one should provide for fighting: one might usefully claim to be 'victims of deceit or violence, or spoliation'.[6] Plato's own disciple Aristotle went further and listed 'arguments for making war on somebody'. These were:

> That we have been wronged in the past, and now that opportunity offers ought to punish the wrongdoers; or, that we are being wronged now, and ought to go to war in our own defence—or in defence of our kinsmen or our benefactors; or, that our allies are being wronged and we ought to go to their help; or, that it is to the advantage of the state in respect of glory or wealth or power and the like.[7]

Subsequently, in Roman times, the last argument—that one went to war for glory or the enrichment of one's own polity—was often applied in practice, but was no longer acceptable in theory, if we can believe Cicero.

The Greeks also established some basic rules about which authority could legitimize the resort to war. Where the political system was not a tyranny, it was the *ekklesia*—the assembly of the citizens—that was the proper authority. But even tyrants, as well as 'democracies' and oligarchies, would consult an even higher authority: the gods. Thus, sending somebody out to consult an oracle was 'an opportunity for a society to glean whether the gods would endorse the proposed war'.[8]

Towards the end of the Roman Republican period, Cicero—our main source on just war theory—wrote as if he was merely reflecting Roman theory and practice in his time, though in his work snippets of earlier texts to which he refers can be found. Cicero wrote that war could only be just if its aim was to establish a just peace, that is, a peace that meted out justice to both sides, and that the defeated side could recognize as just.[9] Only two causes justified the resort to war: the need to defend oneself, or blatantly unjust actions on the part of the enemy.[10] For such criteria to apply, however, Cicero noted certain conditions: namely, that both sides should be what we might call states ('republics', in his words), with a senate, a treasury and an established consensus among citizens on the cause of the war.[11] Actions against criminal bands (he spoke of pirates) would not fall in the category of war and were thus subject to fewer (if any) restraints.

Other, earlier Roman writings suggest that war had to be the last resort and that one might only take recourse to the use of force once persuasion had been tried and failed.[12] A ritual had to be followed that would culminate in a formal declaration of war, but only after the enemy had been encouraged formally, for a last time, to right the wrongs he had committed.[13]

One does not have to accuse the Romans of cynicism when they identified the link between one's just cause and the morale of one's soldiers. Writing in the century after Cicero, during the early Principate, Onosander wrote:

> The causes of war ... should be marshalled with the greatest care; it should be evident to all that one fights on the side of justice. For then the gods also, kindly disposed, become comrades in arms to the soldiers, and men are more eager to make their stand against the foe. For with the knowledge that they are not fighting an aggressive but a defensive war, with consciences free from evil designs, they contribute a courage that is complete; while those who believe an unjust war is displeasing to heaven ['the gods'], because of this very opinion enter the war with fear, even if they are not about to face danger at the hands of the enemy. On this account the general must first announce, by speeches and through embassies, what he wishes to obtain and what he is not willing to concede, in

order that it may appear that, because the enemy will not agree his reasonable demands, it is of necessity, not by his own preference, that he is taking the field.

Even the concept of the just intention is fully articulated here: the general 'should call heaven to witness that he is entering upon war without offence, since he has not failed to consider the dangers that fall to the lot of combatants, and is not deliberately seeking, in every possible manner, to ruin the enemy'.[14]

To sum up, most of the criteria we now associate with just war predate any Christian writings on the subject and can be traced back to Greek and Roman sources. This is not unimportant, as Cian O'Driscoll rightly explains: 'The characterization of the just war tradition as a product of Christian political thought exaggerates its distinctiveness … This impedes the possibility of inter-communal dialogue on the norms of war'.[15]

Just war criteria identified in pagan antiquity can be summarized as follows. To be on the side of justice, a party to a war needed:

- a just cause (self-defence against an attack, or some wrong suffered at the hands of an adversary);
- the right intention of enforcing justice, for the sake of establishing peace with justice, not wanton destruction or unwarranted enrichment;
- a sense of proportionality—the destruction and suffering resulting from the war must not exceed the wrong to be righted;
- for war to be the last resort, if parlays have led to nothing;
- for only the legitimate authority—the *ekklesia* or, initially in Rome, the Senate and the *comitia centuriata*, later the emperor—to declare war;
- for war to be initiated with a formal declaration.

Cynics will not be surprised to hear that practice diverged from theory. Polybius remarked that there were notable differences between the pretexts given for going to war and the real reasons. One can turn this example around, however, and use it to illustrate that the Romans were well aware of the moral difference between pretext and actual intention. Seneca and Lucan thus bluntly denounced Alexander the Great's expansionist strategy as that of a 'robber', as no just cause underlay his wars.[16]

Famously, St Augustine of Hippo, writing in the early fifth century, as the Western Roman Empire was beset by attacks by Goths and Vandals, fused this classical Roman thinking with Christianity, and passed on the thinking of Cicero and his civilisation to later generations. Augustine was thus not the 'father' of these ideas, as Catholic scholars have liked to claim, but was merely the channel through which these classical enlightened thoughts were preserved for later generations. Augustine's scattered pronouncements on the subject were put in some order in the Decretals of Gratian of the twelfth century, in the work of St Thomas Aquinas in the thirteenth century, and in the writings on just war during the Enlightenment, notably the *Encyclopedia* of Diderot and d'Alembert.

Roots of the just war tradition: 'jus in bello'

The just war tradition also dealt with how wars were to be fought. Plato had commented that soldiers fighting in wars should have the right sort of intentions. They should not be acting from a lust for destruction, or from a perverse desire to see dead and mutilated bodies. Soldiers should behave with discipline, ready to fight bitterly against enemies, but, as a guard dog would, doing no harm to the master's friends.[17] This simile would be echoed by European writers of the Middle Ages and in early modern times.[18]

The ancient Greeks had fairly systematic thoughts about who and what should be protected against violence in war. This did not include only noncombatants in general such as women and children, but also priests (and all forms of sanctuaries, and those who sought sanctuary there), heralds, those on their way to consult an oracle, and those on their way to ceremonial sporting events such as the Olympics. Indeed, war was not to take place during the time of such games.[19]

The Romans equally developed a set of restraints during the centuries of the Republic. We have no proper Roman government source that lists these and only know them through their echoes in the writings of individuals, but Cicero for one had held high government offices and was well acquainted with Roman law. For Cicero, the aim of establishing a good peace had to be intrinsic not only to the intention to go to war, but also to the conduct of war.[20]

If Cicero's view of the world is reflective of more than his own views, even the Romans, representing the hegemon in Europe and the Mediterranean world, saw Rome not as a power to dictate the law to the rest of the world, but as part of a larger 'human society' united by laws.[21] For Christian thinkers of classical antiquity and the Middle Ages, such a unity of humanity only concerned Christianity, the *universitas Christianorum*, to which Roman law was applicable. This included Christianised areas that had never been part of the Roman Empire through the construct of the *translatio imperii*, the claim that the Roman Emperor Constantine had in fact bestowed the whole Empire on the Pope as God's representative on earth. But the imagined civilised world also included areas which had previously been part of the Christian Roman Empire of late antiquity, even if in the meantime they had been conquered by Muslims and parts of the previously Christian populations had been converted to Islam.

The concept of an area of law and order—the Pax Romana or the Christian world—and an area where it did not apply, paradoxically coexisted since antiquity alongside another construct: the idea that different peoples throughout the world were united by a commonly held type of law, the law of peoples or *jus gentium*, a concept which we know particularly from the works of the Roman jurist Gaius (fl. c.150–180 CE),[22] and in the Digests and Pandects of the Emperor Justinian.[23] In the West, after the fall of the Roman Empire, we find both views permeating the conduct of war. On the one hand, there is a pattern of generally applied rules and restrictions, founded on the generally recognized humanity of the adversary. More prevalent was a pattern of differentiation: one form of war was waged by Europeans against those they saw as legitimate and equal adversaries, but quite another against 'pagans', and also against 'heretics' and insurgents in their own societies.[24]

Either way, within the Christian universe, we find a tendency usually led by the Christian Church to place restraints on warfare for the protection of certain categories of noncombatants. Echoing ancient Greek customs, the Second Lateran Council of 1139 stipulated that clerics, pilgrims, merchants and peasants should be spared throughout Christendom in times of war.[25] This ruling is also reflected in Gratian's Decretals of 1150.[26] Eight such categories of noncombatants are listed by Pope Gregory IX in his late twelfth-century *De treuga et pace* and later in the papal decretals of 1234.[27] This did not mean that these restraints were always followed: John Gillingham has shown that the enslavement of enemy civilians (especially women) after a victory continued well into the second millennium, despite the condemnation of such practices by the Church.[28]

Nevertheless, rulings against such practices would be repeated, and we find them considerably elaborated in the works of the Bolognese jurist Giovanni da Legnano (c.1320–1383) and the otherwise rather bloodthirsty French cleric Honoré Bouvet or Bonet (c.1340/5–c.1410).[29] Christian compassion and ideals of medieval chivalry merged in the writings of Christine de Pizan (c.1364–c.1431), a French writer of Italian origin, who articulated the concern for protecting the common people from the sufferings caused by wars.[30] The same arguments for the protection of women, children and clergymen would be found in the writings of Francisco de Vitoria (1492–1546), professor of law at the University of Salamanca.

In addition to this list of people who were to be spared, we find another concept, namely, that the enemy, collectively, must not be made to suffer disproportionately for the wrong he has done, for which he was being punished.[31] But Vitoria interestingly inserted a clause that would echo throughout the laws of war until the present: namely, a deviation from such rules had to be permitted if it was necessary for the achievement of the higher (or, we might say, strategic) purpose of war.[32]

As 'Roman law' and rules imposed by the Roman Church were assumed to apply throughout Christianity, there was no need to restate them in the form of any agreed document. Jurists like Giovanni da Legnano would merely remind their readers of the existence of these rules.[33] By contrast, monarchs and their generals would deem it necessary to instruct their own forces about these rules, in 'ordinances' or 'articles of war'—what today would be called rules of conduct and rules of engagement. We find these going back well into the High Middle Ages, as increasingly monarchs, secular rulers, took the place of the Church in disciplining their own armies. This implied setting out rules and the publication and proclamation of such sets of ordinances and articles of war. While earlier examples are likely to exist, such unilateral proclamations of ordinances are extant from around 900 at least. We can find examples throughout the following centuries, usually unilaterally adopted and occasionally adopted by allies in a war. Take the example of the treaty between the United States and Prussia of 1785: both parties to this bound themselves in wars against third parties to provide for the free passage of ships under third party flags, except where contraband was concerned. It gave merchants nine months to settle their business before leaving the country. It allowed 'all women and children, scholars of every faculty, cultivators of the earth, artisans, manufacturers, and fishermen unarmed, and inhabiting unfortified towns, villages or places in general and others whose occupations are for the common substance and benefit of mankind … to continue their respective employments, … nor shall their houses or goods be burnt or otherwise destroyed nor their fields wasted by the armed forces of the enemy into whose power by the events of war they may happen to fall …'[34]

It is only from the late nineteenth century that such rules on the conduct of war were codified in multilateral treaties binding upon all their signatories, who might at a future date find themselves at war with each other. As we have seen, this does not mean that *jus in bello* did not exist previously—indeed, in addition to the self-denying ordinances, there was a common assumption, reflected in these late–nineteenth- and early twentieth-century treaty texts, that there were universal rules that were customarily followed.

The decoupling of the conditions for going to war and the just conduct of war

For Cicero, Augustine and the subsequent medieval and Renaissance authors cited above, the *jus in bello* and the *jus ad bellum* were intimately linked. To be acting according to God's will, one must not only behave with mercy and restraint in war, but also have a just cause for going to war and do so only if all else failed. But in modern times, the two sides of the just war tradition have become uncoupled.

This came about little by little and with the best of intentions. It began with the realization that it is at times very difficult to ascertain which side has a just cause. Moreover, as princes struggled to monopolize the use of force in their own countries and to stop their nobles from taking justice into their own hands, they also insisted that no other prince could interfere in their realm. The kings of France, England and the various Iberian realms rejected any claim of the Holy Roman Emperor to override them and settle their disputes—with other princes or with their own subjects. 'The king of France is emperor in his realm' was the tenet that summed up this stance (or, more precisely, 'the king of France is the prince in his realm and does not recognize any secular superior').[35] Emperors, in turn, clashed with popes over who had the last say on matters temporal. The Reformation put an end more generally to the acceptance of the pope as arbiter, let alone judge, among Christian princes. Who was now to judge the justice of a cause?

This problem had already been recognized during the frequent and long quarrels between popes and emperors by Giovanni da Legnano in his treatise of 1360. He came to the conclusion that war could be seen as a duel, which he described as an institution of Germanic (Langobardian) origin designed to settle a dispute in the absence of a judge whose verdict both sides were prepared to obey.[36] We find the idea of war as a duel taken up again by Francisco de Vitoria, and after him by many others, such as the French Calvinist theologian Bertrand de Loque, but also Catholic Balthasar de Ayala in Antwerp, who stated bluntly that a war could be subjectively believed to be just by both sides.[37] In England in the early seventeenth century, William Fulbecke wrote in his *Pandectes* that *bellum* was also called *duellum*.[38] War could also be seen as a means of punishment by one of the other, if no impartial judge was there to impose such a punishment. Again, this made war a tribunal without a judge, as Francisco Suárez opined at roughly the same time.[39] Still in the same century, Samuel von Pufendorf wrote:

> The belligerents at the outset made an agreement to rest their case with the fortune of battle. This is understood to be the case … when the revenge for the injuries and the securing of their claims … are left to *the arbitrament of Mars*, and both sides enter the conflict with the thought, 'Either I will revenge my right or injury in war, or else I will lose still more'.[40]

In the Age of the Enlightenment, it was no more than an oft-stated truism that war was a sort of duel. Emmerich de Vattel in his *Law of Nations* (1758) spoke of war as the means to obtain one's rights by force.[41] Frederick II of Prussia asked his lawyers to come up with good legal pretexts, once he had decided to go to war. At the beginning of the following century, after the rise and fall of Napoleon, August Rühle von Lilienstern wrote in his field manual for Prussian officers, 'War is the means of settling through chance and the use of force the quarrels of the peoples. Or: it is the pursuit of peace or for a legal agreement by States with violent means'.[42]

So when Rühle, and after him Carl von Clausewitz, wrote of war as a duel, the idea was a commonplace. But if war was a duel and any sovereign prince wielding legitimate authority could engage in it as he saw fit, there was no need any longer for a just cause. One might say that Clausewitz's writings buried the just war tradition, as, for him, war was nothing more than 'a duel on a larger scale' and 'an act of violence meant to force the enemy to do our will'.[43]

From the writings of Clausewitz onwards, there is an almost total absence of references to just war on the part of any military authors. Military strategists only pondered how to achieve military victory and wasted no time or ink on the question of what the situation after a war should look like—and, thus, on how the political aims governing strategy could be realized above and beyond the clash of arms. After Napoleon, it was accepted on all sides that sovereign powers could go to war when they pleased, and that reasons listed for a declaration of war were window dressing at best.[44] Amos Hershey in his 1906 history of the Russo-Japanese War wrote:

> International law, as such, … does not consider the justice or injustice of a war. From the purely legal standpoint, all wars are equally just or unjust; or, properly speaking, they are neither just nor unjust. International Law merely takes cognizance of the existence of war as a fact, and prescribes certain rules and regulations which affect the rights and duties of neutrals and belligerents during that continuance. The justice of war in general or of a certain war in particular are questions of the gravest importance and of the most vital interest, but they belong to the domain of international ethics and morality rather than to that of International Law.[45]

Moreover, it was accepted until 1919 that the victor could impose any punishment and demands for reparations he saw fit, as Napoleon had done in his peace treaties, which were to set the precedent followed by the Treaty of Frankfurt imposed by Prussia on France in 1871, and in turn by France and her allies on Germany at Versailles in 1919.

If non-military writers and thinkers of the nineteenth century tried to lessen the pain of war, they concentrated almost exclusively on regulating the conduct of war, that is, the *jus in bello*. Efforts made during that century, such as the founding of the Red Cross and the creation of the Lieber Code in the US, sought mainly to alleviate the suffering of the soldier, not of civilians caught up in the war. The well-meant outlawing of the confiscation of ships (previously an acceptable measure of retaliation) had the grim effect that from then on navies preferred to sink these ships, including merchant ships flying the enemy state's flag, rather than burdening themselves with providing safe conduct to ports for their passengers and sailors.[46]

The year 1864 saw the signing of the Geneva Convention on the treatment of prisoners of war and of wounded combatants, which was reformulated in 1906, again in Geneva. In 1868 Alexander II, the Russian tsar, hosted the Conference of St Petersburg, which produced a convention that outlawed specific ordnance, a list of outlawed weapons to which dumdum bullets were added later.[47] In 1874, at a conference in Brussels, again convened by Alexander II, the great powers agreed not to treat prisoners of war as criminals but as legitimate adversaries, subordinate to an enemy government, who should not be subjected to violence or any form of punishment.[48]

It was only in 1899 at the Hague Conference that lawyers again considered the fate of noncombatants. As part of a corpus of laws agreed by the participating parties, the Russian lawyer Fedor Fedorovich Martens drew up an additional clause that would become known under his name, which included the following text:

> Until a perfectly complete code of the laws of war is issued, the Conference thinks it right to declare that in cases not included in the present arrangement, populations and belligerents remain under the protection and empire of the principles of international law, as they result from the usages established between civilized nations, from the laws of humanity, and the requirements of the public conscience.[49]

In his study of this subject area, Geoffrey Best found that these commitments were often ignored by the signatories. Even several prominent jurists of the time, like the infamous German Karl Lueder (1834–1895), thought legal engagements were likely to be brushed aside for the war-time equivalent of *Staatsräson* (literally, reasons of state, the contemporary equivalent of what the Americans would later call 'national interest'), namely *Kriegsräson*. Lueder pontificated that 'the true instructions to be given by a State to its generals are: "Succeed— by war according to its laws, if you can—but in all events and in any way, succeed."'[50] This approach was widespread and reflected the postulates of the early German Realists (who might also be termed sovereigntists, defending the sovereign right of any state to pursue its state or national[51] interests against the interests of others, whatever the cost to the latter).[52] Until the middle of the twentieth century, such statements were commonplace: many strategists from Lueder's contemporaries to those of the interwar years, like the Italian air-power strategist Giulio Douhet or Lord Trenchard, one of the founding fathers of the Royal Air Force, subscribed to the view that in wartime such treaties were not worth the paper they were written on—mainly, they tended to add slyly, because the wicked enemy would not respect them.[53] This attitude would change only with the war crimes trials of Nuremberg and Tokyo.

The rediscovery of 'just war'

Stephen Neff has argued that the first step towards the resuscitation of general interest in the *jus ad bellum* was curiously made with the Versailles Peace Treaty with Germany after the First World War. The lawyers representing the victorious powers did not want to prosecute Germany for crimes committed in law according to the *jus in bello* at the time, for fear that the Germans would turn around and accuse the Entente Powers of having committed the same or similar crimes (the invocation of the rule *quoque tu*, that is, 'you too have committed these crimes'). For that reason they based their rationale on the accusation that Germany and her allies were responsible for the First World War, which was enshrined in Versailles Peace Treaty, clause 231: 'The Allied and Associated Governments affirm and Germany accepts the responsibility of Germany and her allies for causing all the loss and damage to which the Allied and Associated Governments and their nationals have been subjected as a consequence of the war imposed upon them by the aggression of Germany and her allies'.

Meanwhile, Article 228 of the Versailles Treaty provided for trials of Central Power soldiers for war crimes proper. It provided that the accused parties be handed over to the Entente Powers for trial before military tribunals. In the event, for political reasons, the Entente Powers left it to the Germans themselves to prosecute their own forces for crimes committed in war at the War Crimes Trials held in Leipzig in 1921, which were pursued but feebly: only twelve individuals were brought to trial.[54]

Neff notes that in previous centuries it was quite normal to impose harsh payments ('indemnities') on the vanquished party. Napoleon made the states he crushed pay heavily, and throughout the nineteenth century there were many examples of peace treaties imposing payments to the victor which engaged generations not yet born (notably the treaty ending the Franco-Prussian War).[55] Especially in the seventeenth and eighteenth centuries, peace treaties also included an amnesty or a clause of 'oblivion', which wiped out any potentially incriminating actions of the defeated side, whether these be crimes committed in times of war or the act of going to war for what might arguably be seen as unjust causes in the first place. This was a reflection of the view of war as a duel, which settled a cause once and for all, bringing it to an honourable end for both sides. Even the treaties of the nineteenth century had not attempted to apportion responsibilities for the war. Contrary to the perceptions of later generations, it was thus not the reparations imposed on Germany at Versailles but the war guilt *clause* which rankled particularly. It rocked the very foundations of the Realist worldview that had so firmly established itself particularly in the late nineteenth century, namely, that any sovereign state by definition had the right to go to war for *Staatsräson* or 'national interest', as this was an inherent right derived from its sovereignty, indeed from the very definition of sovereignty, as traceable to Jean Bodin in the sixteenth century.

Subsequently, the creation of the League of Nations continued this revival of the *jus ad bellum* side of the just war tradition. The League had as its aim to keep the peace established by the Versailles Peace Treaty, and its Covenant committed its members to 'undertake to respect and preserve as against external aggression the territorial integrity and existing political independence of all Members of the League. In case of any such aggression or in case of any threat or danger of such aggression the Council shall advise upon the means by which this obligation shall be fulfilled'.[56] As in Roman times, self-defence against aggression was thus seen as an intrinsic right, while aggressive war was not.

The creation of the League, pioneered by US President Wilson but then not supported by US membership, was followed astonishingly quickly (given the usual snail's pace in the change of international law) in 1928 by the Briand-Kellogg Pact ('the Paris Pact'), a text drawn up jointly by the French and American foreign ministers Aristide Briand and Frank Kellogg, which was later signed by the representatives of 53 states. The contracting parties to this pact 'solemnly declare in the names of their respective peoples that they condemn recourse to war for the solution of international controversies, and renounce it, as an instrument of national policy in their relations with one another'.[57] The realist view of war as an instrument of state politics, irrespective of the cause or aim, was thus branded illegitimate by an overwhelming international consensus.

This did not prevent Hitler and Mussolini or, indeed, the Japanese from following the earlier Realist thinking, resorting to aggressive war and extolling the interests of their nation (or race) above those of all others. (Bizarrely, even Hitler felt the need to create a fiction of self-defence in the strange staged incident of a supposed Polish attack on the German radio station at Gleiwitz to justify his attack on Poland.) After the shock of the Second World War, which served to overcome remaining resistance to change in international law, the successor organization to the weak and heavily flawed League of Nations, the United Nations (UN), enshrined the just war *jus ad bellum* in its Charter. Only self-defence, or else action to preserve or restore the peace (with a flexible definition of what constitutes a threat to peace) as approved by the UN Security Council, was henceforth acknowledged by international law as fully legal.[58]

Few if any wars have been declared or otherwise engaged in since then that are not in some way presented by the parties involved as self-defence, or as the defence of another party that has been attacked, or as action requested by the Security Council in response to a threat to international peace and security, as stated in Chapter VII of the Charter. Chapter VII does not have any guidelines defining the circumstances in which the Security Council should authorize such action. After several decades during which the Permanent Five members of the Security

Council were on mutually hostile sides of the great Cold War ideological divide, paralyzing Security Council decision-making by vetoes, the end of the Cold War revived the UN's role and the possibility of using this instrument to legitimize military action.

In the Middle Ages and early modern times, one finds expressions of the responsibility of Christian princes to protect their co-religionists against violence or other repression by other princes, even within their territories.[59] In the 1990s this idea was reinvented in a new secular shape. First referred to as the 'droit d'ingérence'—the right to intervene—it was subsequently called Responsibility to Protect, in acute cases of state-perpetrated atrocities, including against sections of the state's own population—what Rudolph Rummel has called 'democide'.[60] The debate of the 1990s concerned the question of whether one needed UN Security Council approval for action under this new-old concept or whether, to act faster to prevent large-scale atrocities, a state might unilaterally intervene to stop a state-condoned or state-sanctioned butchery of its own subjects. The case of Rwanda, where such massacres were not stopped by outside intervention, is an *acte manqué* haunting the Western powers to this day. Arguably, the Responsibility to Protect could come to constitute another exception to the UN Charter's Article 2(4),[61] added to that of self-defence.

It was only in the early 2000s that guidelines were developed to determine when to identify a 'threat to the peace, breach of the peace, or act of aggression'.[62] Then UN Secretary General, Kofi Annan, charged a High Level Panel of elder statesmen and women from different parts of the globe, different cultures and religions, to develop such guidelines in their document of December 2004, under the title of 'A More Secure World: Our Shared Responsibility'. Here we find the old just war *jus ad bellum* criteria.

In considering whether to authorize or endorse the use of military force, the Security Council should always address—whatever other considerations it may take into account—at least the following five basic criteria of legitimacy:

(a) Seriousness of threat

Is the threatened harm to State or human security of a kind, and sufficiently clear and serious, to justify prima facie the use of military force? In the case of internal threats, does it involve genocide and other large-scale killing, ethnic cleansing or serious violations of international humanitarian law, actual or imminently apprehended?

(b) *Proper purpose*

Is it clear that the primary purpose of the proposed military action is to halt or avert the threat in question, whatever other purposes or motives may be involved?

(c) *Last resort*

Has every non-military option for meeting the threat in question been explored, with reasonable grounds for believing that other measures will not succeed?

(d) *Proportional means*

Are the scale, duration and intensity of the proposed military action the minimum necessary to meet the threat in question?

(e) *Balance of consequences*

Is there a reasonable chance of the military action being successful in meeting the threat in question, with the consequences of action not likely to be worse than the consequences of inaction?[63]

Those criteria, articulated through the UN and the work of the High Level Panel that set them out, had been prompted by Tony Blair's 1999 Chicago Speech, itself inspired by Freedman.[64] It listed 'five major considerations' to be pondered before resorting to war. 'First, are we sure of our case?' This is a restatement of the principle of the need for a just cause. 'Second, have we exhausted all diplomatic options?' This is a restatement of the principle of last resort. 'Third, on the basis of a practical assessment of the situation, are there military operations we can sensibly and prudently undertake?' This implies that the outcome of the military operations, and the situation afterwards, must be better than the (admittedly unsatisfactory) status quo. The fourth consideration has no older precedent that I can find, but is drawn from 'lessons learnt' from the conflicts of the second half of the twentieth century.

> Fourth, are we prepared for the long term? In the past we talked too much of exit strategies. But having made a commitment we cannot simply walk away once the fight is over; better to stay with moderate numbers of troops than return for repeat performances with large numbers.

The final consideration named by Blair, 'Do we have national interests involved?', is a bow to self-interest, which has presumably always been a factor in the practice of strategy-making. This passage of the Blair speech, seemingly couched in the selfishly nationalist terminology of realism, was counterbalanced by this qualification: 'If we want a world ruled by law and by international co-operation', the Chicago speech continued, 'then we have to support the UN as its central pillar. But we need to find a new way to make the UN and its Security Council work, if we are not to return to the deadlock that undermined the effectiveness of the Security Council during the Cold War'.[65] Thus significantly, if the UK, the US and other states choose a world 'ruled by law and international co-operation' (which Blair could assume the businessmen in his audience would agree with), self-interest dictates that the authority and ability of the only supra-state organ of the world, the UN, to take action should be enhanced. By contrast, the sovereigntists' insistence on the state as ultimate legitimate actor can only undermine it.

Back to the future

The Chicago speech does not mark the end of an evolution in thinking about just war, but arguably it marks the full rediscovery of older traditions of just war thinking and its explicit reintroduction as the basis of strategy-making. In short, in many respects we have come full circle and rediscovered that it is in our interest to subject warfare and strategy to laws, and to subject our own freedom of action to restraints applying to all sides, just as society itself is widely recognized as working better if all sides surrender the right to use force to a legitimate authority to exercise this on our behalf, in our defence.

Along with this resurrection of the *jus ad bellum* criteria, we find a new wave, since the end of the Cold War, of preoccupation with the fate of noncombatants in wars (in the context of the *jus in bello*), together with an unprecedented growth of international humanitarian law, on the basis of the human rights that were first articulated in the revolutions of the eighteenth century but became linked with international institutions through the UN Universal Declaration of Human Rights of 1948.

While international law as it has evolved since the mid-nineteenth century has tried to distinguish between any discussion of the *jus ad bel-*

lum and the *jus in bello*, prior to the eighteenth century this distinction was not always made categorically. Even though international humanitarian law tries to concentrate on the *jus in bello*, the distinction is increasingly difficult to maintain, and it is again being challenged today.[66]

The judicialization of war was well under way in Roman times. But then the insistence on every state's independence from any higher authority was born in the High Middle Ages when rulers of kingdoms which had sprung up outside the confines of the Roman Empire's medieval successor insisted that they were sovereign and not bound by the authority of pope or emperor. This partly reversed the process of self-limitation which had commenced in pre-Christian Roman times. The self-limitation was further abandoned with the adulation of the state, which we find in French and German political philosophy of the seventeenth to nineteenth centuries, as the centrality of the sovereign prince of old was replaced by the sovereign state. When coupled with nationalism—as opposed to a humanist reference system embracing all of mankind—this led to a rejection of the restraints on the right to go to war. Nevertheless, the late nineteenth century also saw efforts to universalize by multilateral treaties constraints on the way war was fought, turning unilaterally formulated ('self-denying') ordinances into treaty-based universal norms. The First World War marked the slow revival of constraints based on the right to go to war, which would later become enshrined in the UN Charter.

The struggle to gain universal application for them is, however, far from over. It is only states where there is agreement that, above all, they 'want a world ruled by law and by international co-operation' that are committed to this set of constraints. The challenge to them is how to persuade others—both those without roots in the Roman tradition and those who are too strong at present to think they have to care—that such self-limiting rules are ultimately in everybody's interest. One means of persuasion has to be that of good example, including in all military actions abroad—even if the price to pay may be the perceived and, at times, irritating 'judicialization of warfare' and 'fighting with one hand tied behind one's back'. As for the Blair (Freedman) Doctrine, governments the world over should heed its principles and take seriously its call to strengthen the UN, in order to contain the bloody anarchy produced by a world of selfish but proudly sovereign states that reject the limitations of the laws of war.

7

HUMANITARIAN INTERVENTION

LESSONS FROM THE PAST FEW DECADES

Richard Caplan

The two decades either side of the second millennium witnessed an extraordinary number of interventions for humanitarian purposes. This was a significant feature of Lawrence Freedman's oeuvre in the 1990s, especially—and, as in so many other areas, he was at the forefront of academic policy discussions.[1] We have to be clear, of course, about what we mean by 'interventions of a humanitarian nature', as the term has various meanings. I am using the term fairly liberally to refer to the threat or use of force by a state or group of states for the purpose—but not necessarily the sole purpose—of preventing, mitigating, or putting an end to widespread and grave violations of human rights and humanitarian suffering without the consent of the state that is the target of the intervention. So motive is important; I am less interested in cases where states act primarily for non-humanitarian reasons even if these actions produce positive humanitarian outcomes, as was the case with India in East Pakistan, Tanzania in Uganda, and Vietnam in Cambodia during the Cold War era, or arguably the United States and Britain in Iraq more recently. But I accept that motivations are almost always mixed—Libya is a good example—and that requiring a humanitarian intervention to be motivated exclusively by ethical values sets too high a standard, which few if any actions would in fact be able to meet.

Definitional precision is not too important, however, because by almost any measure the past few decades have witnessed a remarkable number of humanitarian interventions—more, arguably, than any other time in the past hundred years. If it is agreed that there is or, until now at least, has been an all-time high, what lessons can we draw? 'Lessons of what kind?' and 'lessons for whom?' one might ask. Often 'lesson-learning' exercises have as their objective the identification of measures that, if adopted, might improve performance: they provide recommendations to policymakers for doing things better. This chapter, however, is less concerned with how to get things right than with what this heightened humanitarian activism tells us about whether, and to what extent, international politics and policy can be said to be undergoing a fundamental shift of any kind.

The basic argument I want to make is that the sea changes we are witnessing are in some important respects more apparent than real. This is not to underestimate the changes that underpin this humanitarian activism; on the contrary, I would argue that the changes are even greater than a narrow focus on humanitarian intervention would suggest. The interventions, many of them at least, are part of a larger trend that has seen states giving increased weight to human rights and humanitarian norms as matters of *international* concern—to the extent that the Security Council may now choose, and frequently has chosen in the recent past, to characterize these concerns as threats to international peace that may justify enforcement measures under Chapter VII of the UN Charter. This is not entirely unprecedented—Security Council-mandated sanctions against the racist regimes of South Africa and Rhodesia in the 1960s and 1970s were adopted on the basis of Chapter VII as well;[2] but those were isolated cases, and the practice became much more widespread in the 1990s. It is not only through enforcement action that humanitarian norms have achieved increased prominence; the international community has also taken important steps in this period to give greater substance to humanitarian law. The establishment of two ad hoc international war crimes tribunals (for the former Yugoslavia and for Rwanda) and three hybrid or international-ized war crimes courts (for Sierra Leone, Cambodia and East Timor); the creation of a permanent International Criminal Court (ICC) with jurisdiction over war crimes, genocide, and crimes against humanity; the indictment and arrest abroad of former heads of state for human rights crimes committed in their own countries (notably Chile's Augusto Pinochet and Liberia's Charles Taylor); and the adoption of the Responsibility to Protect norm by heads of state and government gath-ered at the World Summit in New York in September 2005—all this attests to the increased importance of human rights and humanitarian norms in international relations.

Kosovo and the search for international criteria for humanitarian intervention

All these are indeed significant developments, but when one examines state practice more closely one sees the need to make important quali-fications. To begin with, and notwithstanding very substantial interna-tional support for effective humanitarian action, we cannot say that there now exists a right of humanitarian intervention. In many respects Kosovo in 1999 was thought to mark a turning point—at the very least, to have provoked certain doubts about the continuing salience of the UN Charter provisions governing the use of force when the Security Council, in the face of an actual or impending humanitarian emergency, is unable to agree on a common course of action. Some saw state support for NATO's war over Kosovo as evidence of the emergence of a customary law of humanitarian intervention. Christopher Greenwood, then a professor of public international law, now a judge of the International Court of Justice, was one of them.[3] But while the war enjoyed the support of all NATO member states, and several other states as well, the position taken by most states in the world was, and remains, that NATO's actions were illegal and that there is no legal basis in the UN Charter or in the provisions of the principles of general international law for unilateral military action. Anyone who has any doubts about this preponderance of international opinion need only conduct a cursory review of the General Assembly debate in September

1999 where states, with very few exceptions, reaffirmed the cardinal importance of Security Council authorization for any military operations, whether based on humanitarian grounds or not. The persistent objections of so many states to unilateral interventions can hardly be said to offer evidence of a customary legal basis for a right of humanitarian intervention.

In the wake of the Kosovo crisis, some states sought to find a way to reconcile the need for effectiveness in defence of human rights and humanitarian law with the need for legitimacy of process. The British government, under Tony Blair, took a leading role (but without much fanfare) in efforts to forge a *political* consensus among the five permanent members of the Security Council and the Group of 77—that is, the bloc of developing countries at the United Nations—in support of, in Blair's words, 'agreed principles on when we should use force, limited in scope, and proportionate in scale to the humanitarian objective of preventing major loss of civilian life'.[4] A global consensus on the criteria for humanitarian intervention, it was thought, would ensure that any such interventions would be governed by shared or, at the very least, predictable expectations of behaviour, thus helping to minimize the tensions that could arise over such action. It was also thought that agreed policy guidelines would help to curb abuses on the part of interveners. But these efforts were not successful. The UK after Kosovo may not have been best placed to carry such an initiative forward. Moreover, Blair's description of Kosovo as a 'just war' that was 'based on values' made many in the Global South rather uneasy. After all, the Crusades and colonialism were based on values too. Further efforts were made by the Canadian government-supported International Commission on Intervention and State Sovereignty—ICISS for short—and the UN Secretary-General's High-Level Panel on Threats, Challenges and Change, both of which offered specific recommendations for guidelines governing the use of force for humanitarian purposes.[5] But as it was realized that the political winds were not favourable, these particular recommendations were not among those put forward by UN Secretary-General Kofi Annan to the heads of state and government who convened in New York for the World Summit in September 2005.[6] So, not only have states rejected any notion of a right of humanitarian intervention, but an important opportunity was lost as well, perhaps unavoidably, for building a 'second-best' political consensus on the substantive and procedural requirements for humanitarian intervention.

The Responsibility to Protect

But what about the Responsibility to Protect doctrine itself, which was adopted at the World Summit?[7] Some maintain that it represents the introduction of a right of humanitarian intervention through the back door. It is true that the heads of state and government meeting in New York at the World Summit accepted that every state has a responsibility to protect its population from genocide, war crimes, ethnic cleansing and crimes against humanity. And they also agreed that the international community may act, if necessary, through the United Nations to take collective action to protect populations at grave risk when national authorities are manifestly unable or unwilling to do so. But while coercive action certainly figures as an available option in the Outcome Document that was adopted unanimously at the summit, it is clearly understood to be a measure of last resort, only to be considered in extreme cases—when all other efforts have been exhausted—and only with the Security Council's approval in accordance with the UN Charter. This is a far cry from a right of humanitarian intervention. In this regard, the World Summit Outcome Document in effect codifies what has been the broadly accepted ad hoc legal practice ever since the Security Council was seized with its first primarily humanitarian crisis, in Somalia in 1992.

Indeed, the virtue—but also the limitation—of the Responsibility to Protect doctrine is that it recognizes the primary responsibility for protecting a state's people from large-scale human rights violations as residing with that state itself. In this sense the Responsibility to Protect constitutes an *affirmation of sovereignty*, not an assault on it. This is very important. Only if states are unable or unwilling to provide that protection does responsibility shift to the wider international community of states. And, even then, the role that other states are expected to play in the first instance is to support, assist and persuade. As already emphasized, only in extreme cases is it anticipated that resort may be made to coercive military intervention, and, in addition, the use of military force is highly circumscribed. This reorientation of focus—from a right to intervene to a responsibility to protect—is what has made acceptance among states so widespread. And, by any reasonable measure, this represents a major accomplishment. But this acceptance has been achieved at a price: the sidelining of efforts to achieve clarity and consensus on the principles governing humanitarian intervention, which, however, have always been and can perhaps be expected to remain elusive, given the seriousness of the impasse.

While the Responsibility to Protect principle was adopted unanimously by the UN General Assembly in 2005, and reaffirmed by the vast majority of states in an intense General Assembly debate in July 2009,[8] it is important not to overstate the depth of support for the norm. Many states remain concerned that humanitarianism can be used too easily as a pretext for major power interventions, as with Russia's invocation of the Responsibility to Protect to legitimize its use of force against Georgia in 2008. Or they remain reluctant to adopt more robust measures should diplomacy fail, as was shown in the reaction of a number of states—China foremost among them—to Sudan's conduct in Darfur. What is frequently hailed as early evidence of the Responsibility to Protect at work is the international mediation in Kenya in 2008, which successfully defused an incipient ethnic conflict—a conflict that could have turned very quickly into a conflagration. It is worth examining this case closely for what it reveals about the prospects for humanitarian intervention at the sharp end.

Kenya held presidential elections in December 2007, the results of which were disputed. After violence broke out and 1,500 people were killed and another 300,000 were displaced, the African Union responded by dispatching—with the consent of the Kenyan government—a diplomatic troika headed by the former UN Secretary-General Kofi Annan, which was able to persuade the Kenyan President, Mwai Kibaki, and his main opponent, Raila Odinga, to conclude a power-sharing agreement and to bring pressure to bear on their supporters to put an end to the violence. Soon after his mediation, Annan made the following statement:

> I saw the crisis in the R2P [Responsibility to Protect] prism with a Kenyan government unable to contain the situation or protect its people. I knew that if the international community did not intervene, things would go

hopelessly wrong. The problem is when we say 'intervention', people think military, when in fact that's a last resort. Kenya is a successful example of R2P at work.[9]

The then UN Secretary-General, Ban Ki-moon, also invoked the Responsibility to Protect in his characterization of the situation and used it to remind Kenya's leaders of their responsibilities. What better evidence can there be, one might think, of the salience of the responsibility to protect norm and of the norm's effectiveness?

But the question arises: how was Annan's mediation any different from the use of what is called the 'good offices' of the UN Secretary-General, which have been employed on numerous occasions in the UN's history—stretching back for decades—to alleviate situations of gross violations of human rights and humanitarian law?[10] In other words, has anything really changed apart from the terminology? It is just as easy to imagine diplomatic mediation of this kind in Kenya taking place without explicit reference to the Responsibility to Protect—as it has done so many times in the past. When states and multilateral organizations have been inclined to work towards resolution of a crisis, they have availed themselves of a range of existing tools—conceptual as well as applied—for effective action. The problem generally, in other words, has not been the paucity of useful instruments but the disposition of states. In this regard, the Responsibility to Protect appears to be one more tool for the diplomatic toolkit.

A catalyst to action

But is it just one more tool? Up to a point its champions are right to say it is more. Gareth Evans, co-chair of the ICISS commission, has referred to the Responsibility to Protect as a 'political game-changer'.[11] He means that it has made it possible to overcome historical hurdles to intervention—to bridge the chasm between ardent defenders of sovereignty traditionally construed and proponents of more relaxed rules for international intervention: not by inventing an entirely new idea but by rearticulating the issues in such a way as to produce resonance with states that earlier notions did not and could not achieve. The same sort of outcome was produced in the 1980s, Evans points out, with the notion of 'sustainable development'. But one would go even further and say that it is a political game-changer because, unlike many existing tools, the Responsibility to Protect actually has the potential to serve as a catalyst for action because of the rights and obligations that are constitutive of its meaning. This makes the Responsibility to Protect relatively unique. In contrast to the Secretary-General's 'good offices', it has the potential to serve as a factor of influence over national and international behaviour because it carries with it certain expectations: the expectation that states will refrain from major violations of human rights and humanitarian law and the expectation that states may (and indeed should) take action to prevent, mitigate, or put an end to such violations when they threaten. So while it is very doubtful that Kofi Annan needed the Responsibility to Protect norm to inspire him to mediate in the Kenyan dispute—existing tools and concepts were more than satisfactory for that purpose—it is possible to imagine that the norm is having the effect of altering states' expectations, which in turn could influence, or is already influencing, states' behaviour.

But is there any evidence of this? If we go back to the Kenyan episode, the evidence there is actually not very compelling. On the 'demand side' of the equation, if it may be called so, we do not know whether the Responsibility to Protect had any particular bearing on the decision of Kenya's President Kibaki and Raila Odinga to find a political solution and take action to end the violence, but it seems unlikely in the light of what we know about the 'supply side' of the equation, about which Alex Bellamy, an Australia-based scholar, has written with great insight.[12] Bellamy observes, first of all, that it was not so much the Responsibility to Protect but the African Union's emerging Peace and Security architecture—another existing tool, by the way, which predates the Responsibility to Protect—that provided the basis for the AU's mediation in the conflict. The AU chairperson, Jean Ping, even questioned the appropriateness of the Responsibility to Protect principle in this case, because the killing, in his view, had been relatively small in scale. And while the AU's actions were perfectly consistent with the Responsibility to Protect norm, it does not seem—according to Bellamy—that the AU was prepared to take more robust measures (including humanitarian intervention) had the diplomatic mediation not succeeded. Support for such measures, among African leaders, has been and remains very weak indeed. All of this calls into question the salience of the Responsibility to Protect norm in the behaviour of many of the key protagonists—on both the demand and supply sides—in this particular case. It is true, as noted earlier, that Ban Ki-moon invoked that norm in his characterization of the situation; moreover, the Security Council issued a Presidential Statement reminding the leaders of 'their responsibility to engage fully in finding a sustainable political solution and taking action to immediately end violence'.[13] But while the vocabulary may be different, the responses are what one could have reasonably expected from the Secretary-General and the Security Council 15 or 20 years ago.

What about elsewhere? Of course, it is early days for the Responsibility to Protect norm—less than twelve years since its adoption by the UN World Summit—and it is therefore rather difficult to establish the influence, if any, of the norm on the behaviour of states or of non-state actors (notably belligerents). Indeed, even with a larger time frame it will always be difficult to isolate the norm's influence—and to distinguish its effect from that of distinct but closely related factors, such as the threat of prosecution by the International Criminal Court. But, again, Bellamy has conducted some very interesting preliminary analysis in this regard, based on conflict trends. He notes that the Uppsala Conflict Data Program recorded a sharp reduction in the number of fatalities caused by one-sided violence between 2004 and 2008, while his own survey of episodes of mass killing involving the intentionally caused deaths of more than 5,000 civilians shows an equally sharp decline, with no new episodes after 2005. (His research was conducted before the outbreak of civil war in Syria, which, of course, bucks the trend.) So Syria aside, there has been a downward trend in relation to attacks on civilians. This trend is particularly important, Bellamy observes, because it coincides with an increase in the number of armed conflicts overall between 2004 and 2008, suggesting that armed belligerents are generally less likely to resort to atrocities than they were previously.

Taken together, the data suggest that the period since the adoption of the Responsibility to Protect has been associated with a general decline in mass atrocities—although we would, as already noted, need to qualify this claim in the light of government attacks on civilians in Syria. But concentrating on the relative decline, one cannot conclude from these trends that the Responsibility to Protect caused this effect. As Bellamy observes, there are three reasons for this: firstly, each of the trends was already in evidence prior to 2005, when the Responsibility to Protect was adopted; secondly, it is unclear whether it was international activism, local factors, or anything else for that matter that encouraged actors to refrain from mass atrocities; and, thirdly, to the extent that international activism may have been a factor in accounting for the decline, it is impossible to know from global figures alone whether that activism was prompted specifically by the Responsibility to Protect principle.[14]

Indeed, even claims about the centrality of that principle in the decision to intervene in Libya would appear to have exaggerated its importance, as Marie-Eve Loiselle demonstrates in her analysis of the Libyan case. 'A striking feature of [UNSC] resolutions 1970 and 1973', she finds, 'is the lack of any reference to the responsibility of the international community to protect the population of Libya'.[15] Rather, the resolutions underline the responsibility of the Libyan authorities, not the international community, to protect the Libyan population. In the debates leading up to the adoption of resolutions 1970 and 1973, only one state (France) referred to the Responsibility to Protect: all other states referred either to the threat to international peace and security or to the protection of civilians—a related and well-accepted humanitarian norm but one that is distinct from the Responsibility to Protect.

Conclusion

So, although we have been witnessing dramatic changes within the domain of humanitarian action in the past two decades, including changes relating to humanitarian intervention, in some important respects these changes are more apparent than real. The nub of the problem is an unalterable fact of international relations: we inhabit an international system that relies ultimately on the voluntary support and cooperation of states to achieve many of the very laudable goals to which states commit themselves, including the Responsibility to Protect. And mobilizing international support to respond more effectively to humanitarian crises, even in those cases where there are reasonable prospects for success, can often be extremely difficult. The

Responsibility to Protect may prove to be a catalyst for change, but the evidence is that it has had only limited effect to date. Indeed, even Gareth Evans, one of the strongest and most eloquent proponents of the norm, has expressed concern that emphasizing the preventive aspects of the Responsibility to Protect—the assistance, support and persuasion components mentioned above—may well have the effect of diluting the real value-added of the norm, which was originally intended to serve, in Evans's words, as a 'rallying cry for effective international action when things really start getting out of hand'.[16]

To conclude: when future generations look back on the past 20 years—the early post-Cold War period—they will probably be struck by the heightened international concern for human rights and humanitarian norms, underpinned by shifting notions of sovereignty and a relaxation of constraints on humanitarian intervention. But in some important respects the promise inherent in the Responsibility to Protect norm, as originally conceived, remains unfulfilled. Indeed, in a curious and almost perverse way, the norm has refocused attention on entirely worthy but distinctly different approaches to the challenge of preventing mass atrocities. Whether and to what extent it can also serve as a fulcrum to leverage effective action to save civilian populations from their own governments when these other approaches are found to be wanting remains to be seen.

8

'REALISM AS AN UNSENTIMENTAL INTELLECTUAL TEMPER'

LAWRENCE FREEDMAN AND THE NEW INTERVENTIONISM

Mats Berdal

Lawrence Freedman's unique contribution to the study of international relations and strategic thought covers one of the most striking features of the period of international relations that falls between Security Council Resolution 688 of April 1991, which provided the basis for the establishment of a safe haven for Iraqi Kurds in northern Iraq, and Security Council Resolution 1973, which in March 2011 authorized 'all necessary measures to help protect civilians' in Libya from attack by forces loyal to Muammar Gaddafi.[1] That feature is a growing tendency over this period for the use and threat of use of military force in international relations to be justified, whether wholly or in part, on humanitarian grounds and in defence of liberal and solidarist values. It is a tendency that is especially striking if we subsume under it, as I propose to do in this chapter, the employment of military force not

merely in a coercive capacity to address gross human rights violations—that is, humanitarian intervention proper—but also in actions
that began as consent-based operations in response to internal conflicts
with a significant humanitarian dimension. Every UN field operation
since 1990 has included a human rights component and nearly every
one of more than a dozen missions launched by the Council since the
late 1990s has been explicitly mandated under Chapter VII of the UN
Charter to 'afford protection to civilians' caught up in armed conflict.[2]
I shall refer to this tendency as the New Interventionism in international relations after the Cold War, though other terms and phrases—
the 'humanitarian impulse', the 'humanitarian imperative', even
'humanitarian war'—have been used to capture aspects of the same
general phenomenon.[3]

Now, the actual record of using military force, whether in a coercive
or a consent-based way, for avowedly humanitarian purposes has raised
and continues to raise a number of profound issues for scholars and
practitioners alike. These range from the way norms evolve and are
disseminated and internalized within international society to questions
regarding the utility of force in advancing humanitarian objectives, the
changing character of war, and the evolving role of armed forces in
Western society. Through his scholarly work and, on occasion, more
direct input into the policy process, Freedman has made a significant
contribution to what is an ongoing debate in each of these areas.
Plainly, it is not possible to do justice to the full range of his contributions within the span of a single essay. My concern in the present chapter is confined to three sets of closely connected issues.

The first of these concerns the drivers behind the New Interventionism and, in particular, the question whether the phenomenon is
best understood as a function of a distinct era and a distinct set of
geopolitical circumstances, or whether it is more properly viewed, in
the words of Andrew Hurrell, as part of 'a much longer term change
in the normative ambition of international society'.[4] Freedman's own
work—by reference to which I shall explore the growth and some of
the implications of the New Interventionism—suggests that these are
not mutually exclusive categories. It is nonetheless appropriate to ask,
at the end of the period bookended by Security Council resolutions
688 and 1973, whether the New Interventionism has been decisively

weakened by the fallout from Western-led wars in Iraq, Afghanistan and Libya; by a much-diminished will and capacity on the part of Western powers to project (also for humanitarian purposes) power and influence in far-flung places; by the return of great power politics at the UN and in other international forums; and by mounting resistance on the part of so-called emerging powers—India, Brazil and South Africa—as well as Russia and China, to what they have long considered a uniquely Western liberal interventionist agenda.

The second set of issues arises from Freedman's writings on strategy and the use of force. The specific concern here is the relevance of those writings to questions generated by the ambiguous and uneven record of employment of military force for humanitarian purposes in the post-Cold War era. A central and recurring theme to emerge from Freedman's work in this respect is an insistence on the importance of ensuring—whenever, and in whatever capacity, the use of military power is contemplated—that military actions are aligned to wider political purposes: or, to put it differently, never to forget that, in the final analysis, 'military actions must be evaluated by reference to their political effects'.[5] For military action to be truly effective, also when it is used to advance humanitarian objectives, it must be integrated with a coherent political strategy. The need to reassert the close connection between political purpose and military action is all the more important in and for an age when both normative pressures and technological developments, as Freedman's work makes clear, have had the effect of 'playing down the importance of the political dimension in shaping contemporary conflict'.[6]

Finally, there is the question of what Freedman's thoughts and writings on the New Interventionism tell us more generally about his approach to the study of international relations. The focus and consistency of his scholarly preoccupations—a life-long concern with problems of war, force and strategy in international affairs—would, for many, be enough to place him firmly within the realist paradigm of International Relations. But to leave it at that would be too crude and not terribly illuminating. In fact, Freedman's work in this area, while revealing of what he himself aptly describes as 'realism as an intellectual temper', also shows how misleading and unhelpful is the tendency to divide the field of international relations scholarship sharply into competing schools or paradigms. As will be argued more fully, it is possible to see in his varied writings on aspects of the New Interventionism a rejection of the analytical utility of the most established of dichotomies within the field of international relations, namely that between realism and idealism. In important ways, his work seems to suggest, this long-standing dichotomy is a false one.

The New Interventionism, 1991–2011: stocktaking and prospects

From 'human security' to the Responsibility to Protect. In Western academic and policy discourse of the 1990s, the rise of the New Interventionism was closely associated with changes in the normative context of international relations following the end of the Cold War. The general direction of those changes was towards a much greater emphasis on what the United Nations Development Programme, in its annual Development Report for 1994, first labelled 'human security'.[7] A broad and all-encompassing term, human security soon became a convenient shorthand capturing the shift—in scholarly preoccupations as well as in the foreign policy priorities of Western governments—away from a narrow or traditional focus on the security of states to a new focus on that of 'ordinary people'.[8] This more 'people-centred' approach—expressly concerned 'with human life and dignity'[9]—inevitably brought questions to the fore relating to internal governance and the domestic affairs of states, including the treatment of populations by their rulers. The growing salience given to human rights, the rule of law and democracy promotion as legitimate bases for involvement in the internal affairs of states in the 1990s all reflected this trend, so much so that, by the end of the decade, some observers were suggesting that a solidarist consensus was emerging among states.[10]

This was not an unreasonable reading of developments if—and it is a big 'if'—one's focus remained confined, like much of the writing on New Interventionism in the 1990s, to the discourse and policy priorities of Western liberal democracies. Throughout the 1990s both China and Russia, whose ruling elites have never embraced, let alone internalized, solidarist norms, were preoccupied with domestic political upheaval, while the dissenting voices of those that would soon come to be known as the emerging powers—India, Brazil and South

Africa—were more muted than they would become after NATO's involvement in Kosovo and, quite especially, after 9/11 and the American-led wars in Iraq and Afghanistan. In the meantime, buoyed by the emphatic and comprehensive collapse of communism in Eastern Europe, the liberal democratic model with its emphasis on free markets and political and civil liberties was triumphantly promoted as the key to both economic prosperity and political stability. In the West, as Freedman would later observe of the decade, the 'general impact of concerns about human security was to encourage attempts to rebalance political structures in other countries, in favour of the weak and the vulnerable, while encouraging, as an underlying theme, more open political systems, with improved governance, popular participation and respect for civil liberties'.[11]

The most visible expression of this change of priorities was the dramatic increase in the scale, scope and transformative ambition of field operations launched by the UN and regional bodies in the first post-Cold War decade. While the peacekeeping disasters of Somalia, Rwanda and Srebrenica were followed by a marked decline in the number of UN-mandated operations in the second half of the 1990s, the period of retrenchment proved temporary. In fact, both the genocide in Rwanda and the fall of the 'safe haven' of Srebrenica strengthened the hands of those who now stressed the conditional nature of sovereignty and its corollary, the rule of non-intervention. Capturing the mood, Kofi Annan, in an oft-quoted speech at Ditchley Park in June 1998, insisted that sovereignty must never again serve 'as a license for governments to trample on human rights and human dignity'.[12] The following year two developments in particular appeared to reinforce momentum in favour of a trend 'towards acceptance of the need to intervene and that this might require resolute and robust force'.[13] One was the first meeting, the first of what is now a regular occurrence, of the Security Council in a session specifically devoted to 'the protection of civilians in armed conflict'.[14] The second, seemingly still more significant, was NATO's decision in March 1999, taken without explicit authorization from the Security Council, to launch a bombing campaign against the Federal Republic of Yugoslavia. Justified on 'grounds of overwhelming humanitarian necessity' (that precise wording was proposed by the UK), the declared aim of NATO's operation was to halt Slobodan

Milošević's continuing and violent crackdown against the Albanian community in the Serbian province of Kosovo.[15]

NATO's 'humanitarian war',[16] the justification given for its initiation and the conduct of the campaign itself, could not but generate controversy and resistance within international society at large. In its aftermath attention was increasingly drawn, in scholarly analysis as well as among governments, to the dangers inherent in any Western-led military action ostensibly aimed at advancing humanitarian objectives.[17] Three closely connected concerns were now raised more openly, none of them new in the debates surrounding the theory and practice of humanitarian intervention: (1) abuse, or cloaking narrowly interest-based interventions in humanitarian principles; (2) selectivity, focusing on some cases while ignoring others; and (3) inconsistency, evoking humanitarian goals only when these suited would-be interveners. These concerns intensified dramatically after the events of 9/11 and the American-led wars in Afghanistan and Iraq, which profoundly changed both the terms and the geopolitical context of the debate about the bases for intervention in the internal affairs of states.

And yet, the humanitarian impulse did not cease with the events of 9/11. This is clear not only from the increasing number of missions launched by the UN on humanitarian grounds but also from the continuing and intense debate surrounding the rights and wrongs of humanitarian intervention, with the terms of the debate, if not its substance, reframed after Kosovo to a focus on 'intervention for human protection purposes' and later 'the responsibility to protect (R2P)'.[18] Set up in the wake of the controversy surrounding NATO's Kosovo intervention, the International Commission on Intervention and State Sovereignty (ICISS) first introduced the notion of a Responsibility to Protect in order to take the sting out of the more politically loaded term 'humanitarian intervention'.[19] In its original report, the ICISS argued that in cases 'where a population is suffering serious harm, as a result of internal war, insurgency, repression or state failure, and the state in question is unwilling or unable to halt or avert it, the principle of non-intervention yields to the international responsibility to protect'.[20] Modified and refined since (notably by tightening what seemed an alarmingly vague category of 'suffering serious harm'), the central idea underlying R2P—that individual states and, should they fail, the 'international community, through the UN', have a 'responsibility to protect populations from genocide, war crimes, ethnic cleansing, and crimes against humanity'[21]—was endorsed by member states at the meeting of heads of state and government marking the UN's 60th anniversary in 2005. For many, its inclusion in the final document agreed to by member states at the summit in New York—the so-called World Summit Outcome Document—represented the high point in the normative shift under way since the end of the Cold War.

The readiness to contemplate the use of force for humanitarian ends, even without Security Council authorization, the growing salience of civilian protection in peace support operations, and the commitment in principle to R2P reflected a change in normative context which Freedman clearly welcomed and indeed, through his policy advice, encouraged. Asked to submit 'some suggestions' for a speech that Prime Minister Tony Blair was preparing to deliver in April 1999, against the backdrop of mounting controversy surrounding NATO's military campaign in Yugoslavia, Freedman responded by noting that the principle of non-interference had long been considered 'basic to international order' and was 'not one that we would want to jettison too readily'.[22] Still, he added, it 'must be qualified in important respects', including 'acts of genocide', when 'oppression produces massive flows of refugees' that destabilize neighbours and when 'regimes based on minority rule' lose legitimacy.[23] As one could not intervene to rectify every wrong, the real challenge, he argued, was to decide whether to intervene and what tests to apply when making the decision.[24]

And yet, while Freedman welcomed the normative 'shift towards what is happening within states', his writings—always informed by a keen sense of history and an implicit recognition of the realities of power, hierarchy and interest in international politics—acknowledge the admixture of motives involved in decisions regarding intervention, and are clearly sensitive to the unforeseen and unpredictable consequences attendant upon any initiation of the use of force. 'The ideal type' for a war 'conducted in pursuit of a humanitarian agenda', he noted, 'is that it is altruistic in inspiration and execution'.[25] Implicit in this is an appreciation of a different reality, that decisions regarding intervention and the use of force, even though ostensibly for humanitarian purposes, inevitably reflect an uneasy coexistence of altruistic motives with interest-based and power-political considerations on the part of intervening powers and coalitions. Significantly, however, this does not mean, Freedman insists, that the pursuit of liberal values should simply be abandoned, nor does it mean that the inherent and undeniable risks of abuse, selectivity and inconsistency should always serve as an excuse for turning 'a blind eye to crude forms of repression and persecution for the sake of a quiet life'.[26] Freedman's writings make it clear that the tensions facing decision-makers as well as any morally engaged and concerned citizen in this area are real and inescapable, and simply cannot be wished away without a measure of intellectual dishonesty. There will always, he acknowledges more than once, be powerful reasons, both principled and prudential, for questioning 'wars as a means of achieving supposedly liberal goals'.[27] And, certainly, the American-led wars in Iraq and Afghanistan in particular (leaving aside the question of their deeper motives) cannot but induce extreme caution, if not downright cynicism, about any scheme to transform politically and culturally complex societies by means of external intervention and force of arms. However, against the realities of what occurred in Rwanda, Srebrenica and, now, South Sudan and the Central African Republic, the question remains whether 'the inherent illiberality of war may [not] at times have to be set against the even more illiberal consequences of inaction',[28] and the moral imperative of exploring the 'possibilities of mitigation'.[29]

Libya and after: whither the New Interventionism? If endorsement of R2P by the General Assembly in 2005 marked a symbolic high point in the normative shift underlying the New Interventionism, a number of developments have since combined to raise the question whether the humanitarian impulse, so prominent a factor in Western policy especially in the 1990s, has been decisively weakened, perhaps even reversed. One way to explore the question is by looking more closely at the fate of R2P and the controversies surrounding it before and after NATO's military operation in Libya, which culminated in the toppling of Muammar Gaddafi in 2011. Writing in 2010, Edward Luck, Special Adviser to the UN Secretary-General on R2P at the time, argued that 'resistance to operationalising the R2P remains, but appears to be a receding impulse'.[30] Whether or not that was an accurate reading of attitudes within the wider UN membership even then, there is no doubt that the course, conduct and outcome of NATO's operation in Libya would soon have the effect of reigniting controversy around R2P and, specifically, over the use of military force for humanitarian purposes.

In view of the now widespread perception that events in Libya unsettled and derailed an emerging consensus on R2P, there is a certain irony in the fact that the immediate reaction to the adoption of Security Council Resolution 1973 (at least among the most ardent proponents of R2P) was to view it as a successfully passed test case in the evolution of 'R2P as a powerful new galvanizing norm'.[31] 'Had the international community shirked [its] responsibility', Ramesh Thakur wrote at the time, 'Libya could have become R2P's graveyard'.[32] According to David Hannay, the significance of the resolution was partly that it had 'given lie' to the view that 'the responsibility to protect would remain just so many words on paper—an empty aspiration but not a reality'.[33] And, in May 2011, the Secretary-General himself confidently presented what was 'happening in Libya [as] … a watershed in the emerging doctrine of the responsibility to protect'.[34] Already by this time, however, Russia, China and prominent members of G77 serving on the Council (South Africa, Brazil and India) had publicly reached a very different conclusion. Their position was fairly captured by China in the General Assembly in July 2011: 'No party should engage in regime change or get involved in civil war in the name of protecting civilians'.[35] Inevitably, that perception—even though it rests on what is far from an ingenuous or disinterested reading of events—has adversely affected further discussions of R2P. More fatefully, it has severely weakened, if not paralyzed, the Security Council in its efforts to respond meaningfully to civil war and mass atrocity crimes in Syria (even though, it should be added, far too much has been made in some quarters of the supposed connection between NATO's action in Libya with the Council's inaction in Syria). To many, it has brought the very era of the New Interventionism to an end, signalling the return to a period in which considerations of power and interest again reign supreme in international relations.

How accurate is this reading of developments? While the debate about R2P since 2011 provides a barometer of sorts for wider trends and attitudes among states, the claims and counter-claims about the true status of the R2P norm have not proved terribly illuminating. At one end are those who maintain that the norm has already been endorsed by states and that consequently the only remaining challenge, temporarily delayed by the fallout from Libya, lies in its effective implementation. The other extreme is an equally stark position that sees R2P as dead and buried. Both claims are unwarranted and miss the larger point. Indeed, any conclusion about the lasting effects of the New Interventionism on international society must necessarily be more tentative than either of these extremes.

Clearly, the reference to R2P in the final document from the UN summit in 2005 does not indicate that a general right of humanitarian intervention has been widely endorsed by the member states. A careful reading of the relevant provisions of that document, as well as the accompanying commentary provided by states, reveals much greater caution than R2P advocates claim. Events since 2011 have only underlined that caution. Nonetheless, there is still an important sense in which the clock cannot be turned back, however much this may now be a matter of regret to some countries. While it is difficult to pin down that sense precisely, it may usefully be illustrated both by a historical reference and, more pertinently, by a closer look at the background and the decision-making leading up to the adoption of Resolution 1973 itself in 2011.

First, on history, it should be recalled that when, in early 1979, the Security Council debated Vietnam's invasion of Cambodia, Norway— on the Council at the time and already then a self-styled humanitarian superpower—was unequivocal in stressing that the domestic policies of Pol Pot's genocidal regime were entirely irrelevant to any assessment of the rights and wrongs of Vietnam's action. Indeed, Michael Akehurst concluded at the time that the Cambodia debates at the UN 'provide some evidence that there is now a consensus among states in favour of treating humanitarian intervention as illegal'.[36] That kind of argument simply could not be made today. Hence the sheer fact of R2P being a central and heated topic of debate within international society reinforces a presumption that has been growing in strength over the past two decades and has acted as a spur to the New Interventionism: the presumption that the manner in which governments and rulers behave towards their own population is not simply a matter of domestic concern. More than that, massive violations of human rights demand an international response. The growing acceptance of this view is real and not reversible.

This conclusion is supported, more interestingly, by a closer look at the context and the decisions leading up to the adoption of Resolution 1973 in March 2011. That context was one of a rapidly changing, confused and deteriorating humanitarian situation on the ground, played out against the backdrop of Gaddafi's stated intention of showing 'no mercy or compassion' to the citizens of Benghazi as he was, or so it seemed, preparing to overrun the city. [37] In view of the murderous and brutal history of Gaddafi's regime, there was every reason not to treat this as an idle threat. Against this, what drove France and the UK to press for the adoption of Resolution 1973 was not that it represented a defining test case for R2P, nor was it part of a deliberate strategy to effect regime change in Libya. It was simpler and more immediate than that. In the words of one senior official involved, to key decision-makers it was all about 'avoiding another Srebrenica in North Africa'. [38] The prospect of large-scale massacres in Benghazi simply could not be ignored, even by Russia and China, which chose to abstain rather than veto Resolution 1973. More significantly, the previous month—as violence was escalating and the humanitarian crisis deepening on the ground in Libya—both countries along with South Africa, Brazil and India chose to vote in favour of Resolution 1970, calling on the Libyan government 'to meet its responsibility to protect its population'. Indeed, in terms of the evolution of ideas about what is and what is not acceptable behaviour in international society, the unanimous adoption of Resolution 1970 is more revealing than the resolution that, in the end, authorized NATO action. Under Resolution 1970 the Council, inter alia, 'deplored the gross and systematic violations of human rights' by the regime, imposed an 'arms embargo' on the country, referred the 'situation in Libya to the International Criminal Court (ICC)', and committed itself to 'review the appropriateness of measures taken' in the light of Libya's compliance with the resolution. [39]

What all of this means is that the issue of the use of force and intervention in defence of human rights, especially when mass atrocity crimes are being committed or look certain to be committed, is likely to come back to the Security Council, even though, plainly, broader concerns 'about how R2P standards might be enforced, by whom, and under whose authority' will not go away.[40] In addition to those concerns, other developments since 2011—including, most notably, the further deterioration of East–West relations following Russia's annexation of Crimea in March 2014 and a rapidly diminishing appetite for Western involvement in zones of conflict following the sobering experience of Afghanistan—make it more difficult still to see the Security Council agreeing on military action in support of humanitarian purposes. And yet, in April 2014, the Council—despite massive logistical challenges, operational overstretch and tensions among its permanent members—unanimously voted in favour of establishing a new, ambitious and large-scale peacekeeping operation for the Central African Republic under Chapter VII of the Charter. It did so in response to 'multiple violations of international humanitarian law and widespread human rights violations and abuses', and it placed the protection of civilians at risk from mass atrocity crimes right at the centre of its mission.[41] Arguably more telling still, in terms of how far attitudes and normative assumptions have shifted, was the adoption, also in April 2014, of Resolution 2150 marking the 20th anniversary of the start of the Rwanda genocide.[42] Following an intense debate over the precise wording of the resolution, the Council unanimously called on states to 'recommit' themselves 'to prevent and fight against genocide, and other crimes under international law', and, more significantly, explicitly reaffirmed the relevant paragraphs of the 2005 World Summit Outcome Document 'on the responsibility to protect populations from genocide, war crimes, ethnic cleansing and crimes against humanity'.[43]

The creation of the UN Stabilization Mission in the Central African Republic, MINUSCA, and the passage of Resolution 2150 bring to mind an observation made by Freedman at the time when the full and catastrophic consequences of the ill-conceived US invasion of Iraq were played out on television screens around the world. 'For a variety of reasons', he suggested in 2006, 'I believe that, over the medium and long term, non-intervention will be a difficult position to sustain although in the short term it may be a tempting one to try'.[44] While many of the features that made the 1990s unique in terms of the growth of the New Interventionism have ceased to exert a decisive influence on international politics, it is safe to say that non-intervention as a response to humanitarian catastrophes, especially to mass atrocities, will remain a much 'more difficult position to sustain' than historically it has ever been.

Strategy and the use of force for humanitarian purposes

'Military power', Freedman wrote in *The Revolution in Strategic Affairs*, 'can only be truly judged against the political purposes it is intended to serve'.[45] The observation captures a central theme that runs through his writings on strategy and the use of force. As he lamented in a stock-taking exercise for *Daedalus* following the experiences of war in Afghanistan and Iraq: 'politics is often treated in military theory as an awkward exogenous factor, at best a necessary inconvenience and at worst a source of weakness and constraint—a disruptive influence interfering with the proper conduct of war'.[46] While these observations may well strike students of war studies reared on Clausewitz as truisms, the use of military force for humanitarian purposes since the end of Cold War shows that their full implications have all too often been ignored.

To appreciate more fully the importance of reasserting the link between political purpose and military action, it is helpful to recall the distinction—made by General Rupert Smith in 1994 before he assumed command of UN peacekeeping forces in Bosnia and Herzegovina—between what military force can do as distinct from what it can achieve.[47] NATO's air operation in Libya in 2011 was an extraordinary display of what military force can do: the first air campaign in history in which only precision-guided munitions were used, with devastating accuracy and unprecedented ability to discriminate among targets, far surpassing the performance of NATO's Kosovo operation just over a decade earlier. The real test, however, lies in what military force can achieve, meaning how military action can best be employed so that its effects support and reinforce, rather than become severed from and undermine, the attainment of overall political objectives. This does not mean, nor does the post-Cold War record suggest, that the military instrument cannot play an important role in mitigating and containing humanitarian emergencies. The point is rather to emphasize that the underlying sources and drivers behind the humanitarian emergencies to which the New Interventionism has been a response are also deeply political in nature.

Accordingly, the starting point for thinking through what role military power can play must be to focus not just on mitigation and containment, but on how military means and methods are aligned and continuously adjusted in the light of developments on the ground, alongside diplomatic, humanitarian and conflict-resolution efforts to advance a clearly defined political aim or end state. Where, for whatever reason, that aim is ill-defined or absent, the utility of force is likely to be limited, apart from the psychological satisfaction, itself usually short-lived, of having 'done something'. As Rupert Smith would later reflect, until the late summer of 1995 the basic reality he faced as commander of UNPROFOR in Bosnia was the absence of 'an agreed outcome, or aim' for the operation.[48] This did not prevent a large-scale humanitarian relief operation from being undertaken in Bosnia, where more than 700,000 metric tons of humanitarian aid was delivered by road during the war. Crucially, however, as the conflict dragged on the humanitarian action not only became a substitute for meaningful political action by outsiders; inevitably, the humanitarian operation itself became an ever more significant 'factor in the political considerations of the parties to the conflict and of the international community'.[49] This pattern is familiar from other post-Cold War intrastate conflicts in which an external military force has been deployed in support of humanitarian objectives and the nature of the conflict makes it impossible for outsiders to remain indefinitely above the political fray.

It is easy, of course, to state all of this in the abstract. And, no doubt, the benefit of hindsight too is helpful. The reality is that, faced with overwhelming, fast-moving and conscience-shocking humanitarian emergencies, governments—hemmed in by resource constraints and anxieties about the fickleness of public opinion at home—have frequently resorted to the military instrument as a means of demonstrating resolve, leaving until later, if it is addressed at all, the thornier but critical issue of investing in the necessary political process to accompany military action. Even so, acknowledging the admixture of motives that influence the decisions of governments to deploy military force does not diminish the importance of highlighting the close and critical connection between political purpose and military action. Indeed, as

Freedman's writings on strategy help illuminate, a combination of two developments in the era of the New Interventionism makes restating its importance all the more necessary.

In *The Revolution in Strategic Affairs* Freedman pointed to a combination of political, normative and technological developments in the West that were converging towards a view of the future of warfare, whose defining features he saw as threefold: firstly, growing professionalization of armed forces; next, mounting aversion to, even intolerance of, casualties; and, finally, a determination to avoid 'collateral damage', made possible by dramatic and rapid advances in information, communications and processing technologies.[50] The latter two features in particular combined to produce what elsewhere he described as a 'vision of victimless, virtual war … suitable for a post-heroic age, in which casualties on all sides, but especially our own, are kept to a minimum'.[51] It is certainly possible to debate how far the development of that vision has in fact gone. The suggestion of a developing 'Western way of warfare' was advanced in 1998; now those, most notably within the US military, who embraced the 'vision of a victimless, virtual war' must surely have been disabused of it by the experiences of war in Iraq and Afghanistan, both places where the attempt by Western powers to take advantage of unprecedented technological superiority to create a desired political end state met with dismal failure. Arguably, these wars also showed that the intolerance of casualties, received and especially inflicted, has not been as great as was assumed by those who wrote about post-heroic warfare in the 1990s. Even so, the 'Western way of warfare' as identified by Freedman still captures important underlying trends, which have exerted a powerful influence on how Western powers, above all the US, think about the use of force and the employment of the 'military instrument' in conflicts. In particular, it has reinforced persistence in the belief or, rather, the hope—a recurring one in Western thinking about war—that technological breakthroughs will eventually eliminate the forces of friction and help lift the fog of war.

This in turn has spurred the temptation of governments to look to military power in terms of what it can do rather than what it can achieve: if the risk that you will sustain casualties is minimal and you can avoid or minimize 'collateral damage', you may be less likely to dwell on the wider political purpose that force is meant to achieve. The temptation to think along these lines has been especially strong (though less so now, one would hope, after the sobering experience of Western involvement in Afghanistan) in relation to the challenges posed by deep-seated conflicts emanating from weak and fragile states. Freedman strongly cautions against the temptation. For while Western powers may enjoy unprecedented technological advantages, the post-Cold War period has shown that these are of limited utility and certainly do not confer a decisive or critical edge when intervening to meet the challenges in weak and fragile states—settings where the very purpose of conflict may be to create humanitarian emergencies and where, accordingly, the advantages of precision and the ability to discriminate in the application of force will generate, borrowing the jargon, an asymmetrical response. In other words, to counter Western technological advantages, opponents will seek to draw civil society into conflict.

In his work mentioned above, Freedman drew a distinction between 'wars of choice' and 'wars of necessity'.[52] Wars and military involvement justified primarily on humanitarian grounds fall into the former category, a central aspect of which is the absence of a compelling, core or easily identifiable national interest at stake. While Freedman would later concede that the distinction between wars of choice and wars of necessity was strictly misleading—in the sense that 'there is always a choice'—it still conveys significant differences in the perception of the stakes at issue and, therefore, in the degree to which decisions to act are viewed as discretionary or not.[53] If the perception of what is at stake in terms of core interests when intervening for humanitarian purposes is, ultimately, limited by comparison with interventions deemed necessary for the defence of 'vital' interests, the normative pressures to act may still, for good and powerful reasons, be strong. In the era of the New Interventionism, these normative pressures have strengthened the urge of governments to use the military as a means of 'demonstrating resolve', though it is then typically at the price of political resolve and without proper attention to the complexities of relating military means to political ends.[54] Indeed, when Freedman later questioned the validity of drawing too crude a distinction between 'choice' and 'necessity' in matters of intervention, it was, in part, because he felt (and experience has vindicated that feeling) that the dichotomy would encourage both proponents and opponents of military action 'to overstate their cases', with 'those asserting the discretionary nature of war ... minimising the dangerous consequences of inaction'.[55]

It is necessary to re-emphasize here that military involvement for humanitarian purposes over the past two decades—through the lending of organizational skills, logistical capacity and the provision of security—has undoubtedly produced some impressive and life-saving results. In the acute or short-term phase of an emergency, such involvement has, arguably, even played a role in the prevention of mass atrocity crimes. But over time and once they are engaged—and this is the key point—the deepening of conflict-generated humanitarian emergencies has tended to displace diplomatic and political investment in vital parallel political processes, which alone can address the underlying causes of an emergency. Furthermore, as humanitarian activities in the midst of an ongoing conflict feed into the political economy of that very conflict, contributing to its mutation and fragmentation, the search for a coherent political strategy becomes more, not less, complicated.

These lessons are nowhere better illustrated than in the case of the Democratic Republic of Congo (DRC), where the international community through the UN continues, after a decade and a half, to be confronted with one of the most catastrophic man-made humanitarian emergencies of modern times. The UN peacekeeping involvement in the DRC began in 1999 with the deployment of a small observer mission following the end, in theory, of the Second Congo War. In reality, fighting and violent preying on civilians never ended in the eastern part of the country. Against the background of continuing violence, the UN Mission in the DRC (MONUC) has not only expanded in size, eventually numbering well over 20,000 troops, but it has also been entrusted with an ever more ambitious, complex and robust mandate.[56] In particular, the centrality of MONUC's civilian protection responsibilities has steadily increased over time so that by 2008 the 'protection of civilians' had risen to the top of its operational priorities. To this day it remains a core objective for the force. At one level, this evolution of priorities is itself testimony to the change in normative climate underlying the New Interventionism. But it is also a response to repeated emergencies and atrocities, which an overstretched and under-resourced external force, lacking in clear political direction, has struggled to address. Indeed, in some places, MONUC has, perversely,

contributed to the state of continuing insecurity, violence and preda-
tion against civilians, as it has had to cooperate with the Congolese
government and its armed forces, whose own human rights record has
been and remains appalling. Elsewhere, efforts to provide more effective protection, including efforts relying on the more 'robust' use of
force by peacekeepers, have seen some local results. They have not,
however, been able to provide, as indeed they could not, a meaningful
political strategy that could drive MONUC's work forward. The lack
of such a political dimension has been the fundamental challenge facing
the UN in the DRC. A perfectly understandable preoccupation with
addressing the humanitarian crisis, through 'beefing up' and otherwise
improving the performance of MONUC, has over the long run—in
effect, if not with intent—diverted both focus and effort away from the
underlying political causes, local and regional, of the protection crises
and mass atrocity crimes in the eastern part of the country.

Realism as 'an unsentimental intellectual temper'

In view of his life-long scholarly preoccupations, it is tempting to place
Freedman firmly within the realist 'paradigm' of international relations
studies. To leave it at this, however, would be to simplify a more complex, nuanced and interesting position. Indeed, it is a position that
would likely start by endorsing the scepticism expressed by Philip
Windsor about the very 'utility of the idea of the paradigm', let alone
that of grand theories generally in the field of international relations.[57]
In a brief and trenchant survey of the field written as East–West relations were beginning to thaw, Windsor maintained, or was rather
expressing the hope, that 'most scholars are not casting around either
for paradigm shifts or paradigmatic unity; they are engaged in a discourse … [one] that takes place where other disciplines meet, and
clash on occasion'.[58] The idea of a discourse among scholars that rests
on diversity of both methodological approach and subject-area focus is
one that also fairly captures the ambition of war studies, a field of academic inquiry rather than a discipline as such, whose intellectual credibility Freedman has done so much to enhance.

To welcome discourse and diversity is not to say, however, that we
are not drawn towards established traditions of thinking about interna-

tional relations—traditions that reflect our research priorities as well as the set of values we bring to bear on our inquiries. In this context, Freedman draws a vital distinction between 'realism as an unsentimental intellectual temper' and realism as a 'theoretical construction'.[59] It is the former that informs and illuminates his approach to the study of international relations. What, one might ask, beyond the general features shared by the realist tradition as a whole (most obviously an appreciation of the continuing relevance of considerations of power and interest in international politics), are some of its distinguishing features? Viewed through the prism of Freedman's engagement with the issues of the New Interventionism—whether as a scholar, a policy adviser or simply a morally engaged citizen—realism as an 'intellectual temper' may, I suggest, be seen as encompassing three necessarily connected features.

The first of these is a distinctive view of the nature of progress in international relations, one that sees it as real and possible but, invariably, also as uncertain, fragmentary and susceptible to reversal. This is not progress in the sense that social scientists have borrowed the notion from the natural sciences, seeking to quantify and measure it in accordance with the rules and methods of the scientific experiment. Above all, it is an understanding of progress that recognizes how improvements in one area will often generate countervailing tendencies, have unintended consequences, add complexity, and even cause deteriorations and setbacks in another. This Janus-faced character of progress is evident in the sometimes ambiguous effects of what are otherwise undoubted normative gains, or signs of progress, made under the New Interventionism.

Thus, the endorsement by states of R2P is plainly a significant milestone in terms of embedding the norm that the rights and privileges that go with sovereign statehood do not automatically trump steps taken by international society—including in extreme cases the use of force—to prevent mass atrocity crimes. At the same time, the formal adoption of R2P in 2005 may, perversely, have complicated efforts for the UN actually to intervene and respond effectively in a humanitarian capacity, including action for the prevention of mass atrocity crimes. A hard-hitting internal appraisal of the UN response to the final phase of the civil war in Sri Lanka in 2009, during which as many as 40,000 civilians may have been killed, concluded that, while the 'concept of a

"Responsibility to Protect" was raised occasionally during the final stages of the conflict', this had been 'to no useful result'.[60] 'Differing perceptions among Member States and the Secretariat of the concept's meaning and use', it added, 'had become so contentious as to nullify its potential value'.[61] Indeed, making references to the Responsibility to Protect was seen as 'more likely to weaken rather than strengthen UN action'.[62] Similarly, the establishment of a permanent International Criminal Court (ICC) provides evidence of a growing and welcome intolerance of impunity by international society for particularly heinous crimes—but in several instances since the Rome Statute came into force in 2002 the workings of the ICC and the uses made of it by states have made the search for peace, as well as the conduct of humanitarian work in protracted conflicts, more complicated, not less.[63]

Yet another example of the ambiguous effects of seemingly progressive developments in the post-Cold War era is provided by the often perverse consequences of seeking to implant democracy by means of early elections and competitive party politics *alone* in conflict-torn, ethnically fragmented and economically weak states that lack robust democratic traditions and cultures. All too often, the introduction of electoral politics in such circumstances has had the effect of sharpening societal tensions and encouraging, even precipitating, violence rather than acting as an effective bulwark against it.

The second feature of the realist intellectual temper exemplified by Freedman's work flows from the first. It may be summed up as a rejection of the belief—embedded within an influential strand of liberal thinking—that, in essence, all good things go together. In his writings on the use of force for humanitarian purposes, Freedman draws attention to the coexistence of two distinct strands of thinking on intervention and the rights and duties of states within the same liberal tradition; strands whose implications for the conduct of foreign policy differ sharply. The paradox is best illustrated by the differing attitudes held towards the cardinal norm of non-intervention itself, which has been presented both as 'a vital principle of international order' and a 'charter for domestic repression'.[64] It is perfectly possible to embrace the regulative ideas of liberalism that cut across different strands of the liberal tradition—embracing its definition of the 'essence of a good society: individualism, civil and political liberties, the rule of law, the consent of the governed and opposition to arbitrary rule'[65]—while still recognizing, even rejecting, specific strands as deeply problematic.

The strand with which a realist temper would take issue is the one that grows out of a 'certain innate optimism' characteristic of liberal philosophy, which, in the words of Leszek Kołakowski, involves the tendency 'to believe that there is a good solution for every situation and not that circumstances will arise in which the available solutions are not only bad, but very bad'.[66] The history of using military power to advance humanitarian objectives would support scepticism of this kind of 'innate optimism'. And the same scepticism would also recognize the inherent challenges—by contrast with the hubris of the New Interventionism in its early days—of seeking to implant template models of democracy, good governance and free market solutions in societies which, though conflict-strewn and deeply fractured, possess a keen and proud sense of their own history and cultural worth. This kind of scepticism runs through Freedman's work and there is an inevitable tension between, on the one hand, the importance he attaches to championing core liberal values and asserting their universal validity and, on the other, his awareness of the dangers and difficulties of seeking to impose or implant those values by means of external intervention. To Freedman, not the least of reasons for championing and being explicit about liberal values has been brought into sharp relief by the sad record of serious abuses committed, and the questionable alliances entered into, by Western governments in the 'war on terror'. 'The advantage of stressing the importance of the liberal dimension', he insisted in 2005, 'is that it sets standards for Western governments, against which they [too] should be judged'.[67]

Finally, these considerations lead naturally to a basic acceptance of tragedy in international relations. The international system, consisting of nearly 200 legally equal states recognizing no overarching authority but otherwise of enormous diversity in terms of interests, historical experience, and cultural and political forms, is underpinned by, and rests on, a set of values that ultimately cannot be perfectly reconciled but do not for that reason cease to be important and cherished values. The point is perhaps best illustrated by the tension that exists within the UN Charter itself, a document aptly described as 'a remarkable amalgam of realism and idealism'.[68] On the one hand, it enshrines basic principles and derivative rules on which international order rest: the sovereign equality of states, the principle of non-intervention and a general prohibition against the use of force. On the other, it also speaks of 'promoting and encouraging respect for human rights', and it affirms the 'principle of equal rights and self-determination of peoples'. All of these affirm commitment to certain values. The history of humanitarian intervention and various attempts to work out the principle of self-determination in the era of the New Interventionism bring out clearly the tensions that exist between these partly competing values. And yet there are good reasons for not entirely discarding any one of them, even though the attempts by states (with the admixture of motives that governs their behaviour within the international system) to work out the resulting tensions can and do lead to tragic outcomes. Even so, as a feature of the realist intellectual temper, tragedy is not necessarily meant as a cause for despair. It signifies instead a recognition of the fact that tensions and conflicts in a multi-state system divided by interest and value are inescapable, and that, against this, the aim of international relations as a discourse, in the sense outlined above, should be, as Windsor put it, to 'harmonise positive analysis with normative aims, the principles of order with those of justice, and the interests of states with those of humanity'.[69]

So, what emerges from Freedman's engagement with and approach to the New Interventionism is an awareness of the fragmentary nature of progress, not its impossibility; the recognition that not all good things go together; and that tragedy, in the sense described above, cannot be avoided. As an expression of a realist intellectual temper, it is perhaps best captured by his own 'case for a realist revival' or 'approach', written at a time when the 'inheritors of the idealist tradition were [still] riding high'. The approach, he wrote, would

> assert the conditionality of the most progressive developments and the fragility of long-established institutions when under stress, keeping in mind how human relations can turn vicious in short order, while potentially creative political, economic, and social movements can suddenly take on a disruptive and vengeful aspect. The underlying purpose of a realist revival would not be to peddle despondency for its own sake but to challenge complacency, sustaining an awareness of the dark side of international affairs to encourage measures to protect and promote the light.[70]

Final thoughts on a false dichotomy

In his superb study of Leonard Woolf and twentieth century idealism, Peter Wilson notes how Woolf's scholarly output has often been dismissed, whether in his own time or by a later generation of International Relations scholars, as an unsophisticated and naive species of idealism or, worse still, 'utopianism'. And yet, although Woolf got things wrong and his purely academic work was of uneven quality, he nonetheless left an important and under-appreciated legacy. According to Wilson, this consisted in showing that 'not all ideals are impractical ideals':

> To have ideals in international politics does not mean that one is unrealistic in pursuit of them. This is the implication of the idealist–realist dichotomy: idealists, those with ideals, cannot by definition be realists. This dichotomy has done much to damage the evolution of IR thinking.[71]

Although Freedman does refer, sometimes in sceptical undertones, to the 'idealist tradition' in the field of international relations, there is also in his writings, especially as they pertain to the New Interventionism as covered in this chapter, a real sense in which he too rejects the simple idealist–realist dichotomy. Unlike Woolf, though, he rejects the dichotomy while coming to it, as it were, from the realist tradition: that is, to be a realist in international politics does not mean that one cannot have ideals. Working out the implications of that position, grappling with the dilemmas and complexities it raises in terms of moral and political choice, is another way of looking at his extraordinarily rich, sophisticated and, not least, deeply humane contribution to scholarship and public debate.

PART 3

HISTORY AND POLICY

9

ESSENCE OF INDECISION

COUP SCRIPTS, NGO DINH DIEM
AND THE KENNEDY ADMINISTRATION

Jeffrey H. Michaels

At around 1.30 p.m. in Saigon on 1 November 1963, a military coup was launched that led to the overthrow of South Vietnamese President Ngo Dinh Diem. The next day, Diem and his brother Ngo Dinh Nhu were assassinated. The responsibility for both the coup and the assassination of Diem has often been laid at the door of the Kennedy administration. This view presupposes both that the US had a clear policy to overthrow Diem and that US support was the most important factor in motivating the South Vietnamese generals to launch the coup. However, even a superficial examination of the willingness and capability of the South Vietnamese generals to 'remove' Diem demonstrates that the 'American factor' was only one of many they needed to consider and was almost certainly less important than their belief that they could actually succeed in launching a coup by physically defeating the military forces loyal to the President. Indeed, it was precisely this tactical appreciation of the 'balance of forces', as well as their awareness of problems with previous coup attempts, that led both Kennedy and most other senior US officials to adopt a cautious attitude towards supporting a coup only days before it occurred. While they were unwilling to support a coup out of fear that it might fail and leave US policy in Vietnam worse off, they also recognized that attempting to 'thwart' a coup would have its own consequences. Accordingly, prior to the November coup, the administration's policy could be characterized as one of unenthusiastic drift, in which US officials recognized they had little control over the actions of the South Vietnamese.

In arguing this, the present chapter builds on the foundation laid down by Lawrence Freedman in two of his key works. Most notably, his book *Kennedy's Wars* touches on the Kennedy administration's deliberations in the run-up to the coup.[1] More recently, Freedman's development of the concept of 'strategic scripts' in his book *Strategy: A History* provides a useful prism for understanding the ideas guiding US policy on this issue.[2] For the purposes of this chapter, the scripts considered include the analogies, metaphors and other cognitive schemata of senior officials that are found in US policy documents and transcripts and minutes of high-level meetings.

The chapter will begin by focusing on the evolution of perceptions of Diem in the Kennedy administration and how these perceptions affected US approaches to dealing with him. This will be followed by a discussion of the various ideas American officials put forward about how a coup might transpire and the role Washington would play in bringing it about. Related to this, the crucial National Security Council (NSC) meetings held in late August and late October 1963 will be examined to determine the extent to which officials believed a coup would actually occur. As part of this examination, particular attention will be given to assessments of the balance of pro- and anti-Diem military forces in the Saigon area and the importance of these assessments for US policy will be highlighted. The chapter will conclude by looking at what alternatives to supporting a coup were discussed, to show why there was a perceived need to adopt the policy line of 'not to thwart' a coup.

Perceptions of Diem

The US never had an easy relationship with Ngo Dinh Diem. In many respects he represented the ally the US had, rather than the ally the US would have preferred to have. Had it not been for the crucial support provided by the US in 1954–5, Diem would probably not have come to power, much less remained in power. Nevertheless, from Washington's perspective, Diem was far from an ideal leader. Not only did he run South Vietnam as an autocrat rather than a democrat, he was also a leader who was often reluctant to take American 'advice', especially when it came to instituting political reforms. Moreover, though a clever politician and ardent nationalist, Diem was first and foremost a devoted family man who refused to dissociate himself from the excesses of other members of his family, especially his brother Ngo Dinh Nhu. His insistence upon putting his family before his country would be one of the primary causes, if not the primary cause, of his downfall. In the late summer of 1963, as several key South Vietnamese generals were plotting a coup, they made it known to the Americans that their main aim was to 'get rid' of Nhu, and they would be willing to consider leaving Diem in place, albeit with less power.[3] However, it was gradually accepted that Diem and Nhu were 'Siamese twins' and that no amount of pressure could be brought to bear that would separate them.[4]

At the time the Kennedy administration came to power in January 1961, the US relationship with Diem that had been inherited from the Eisenhower administration was poor. During the course of the attempted coup in November 1960, US Ambassador Eugene Durbrow sought to negotiate a resolution by attempting to persuade Diem to compromise with the coup plotters. After pro-Diem forces put down the coup, Diem was quite angry with Durbrow for failing to offer his unqualified support.[4] As Brigadier General Edward G. Lansdale complained,

> The actions of the US Ambassador undoubtedly have deepened President Diem's suspicions of his motivations … At the most critical moment of the coup attempt, the US ambassador urged Diem to give in to rebel demands to avoid bloodshed.[5]

Another US official observed that the US had scarcely expressed unequivocal support for Diem, not least because the official US position given to the press after the coup attempt began was: 'The

American Ambassador remains accredited to President Diem so long as he remains president'. Yet the reasoning behind this statement was that officially it would have been problematic for the US to back Diem regardless of the circumstances, but if for 'purely internal and non-Communist reasons there is a change of Government, it would under most circumstances be wrong for us to interfere'.[6]

In reality, the key question that recurred time and again for US policymakers from 1954 onwards, and especially after the November 1960 coup attempt, was whether to support Diem or to refrain from providing support, in which case an alternative leadership would emerge. Given the risks associated with both options, the pros and cons were debated for years, but while these debates were ongoing, US policy remained in favour of supporting Diem, despite considerable disenchantment with his leadership.[7] The problem of dealing with Diem was one that divided policymakers, and to a significant degree this divergence of opinion is reflected in the way different American policymakers viewed Diem. In their private discussions, two main issues stood out.

The first issue was whether the war against the Vietcong could be won with Diem in charge and whether there was anyone else that could do a better job. On this issue there were sharp divisions of opinion. At the end of August 1963, Defense Secretary Robert S. McNamara stated that he saw no alternative to Diem, and therefore it was necessary to make a further effort to persuade him to reform his government.[8] Similarly, in early September, Chairman of the Joint Chiefs of Staff General Maxwell Taylor said that both he and other senior military leaders believed that the war could be won with Diem.[9] According to General Paul Harkins, head of the US Military Assistance Command, Vietnam, 'In my contacts here I have seen no one with the strength of character of Diem, at least in fighting communists. Clearly there are no Generals qualified to take over in my opinion'.[10] Another important voice arguing against a coup was former US Ambassador to South Vietnam Frederick Nolting. He characterized Diem as the only person that could hold the country together and praised his determination and leadership capabilities relative to the generals.[11]

However, there was also a significant body of opinion that argued against Diem retaining power. State Department officials such as Roger Hilsman, Averell Harriman, Paul Kattenburg and Michael Forrestal all believed the war would be lost if Diem remained in power.[12] Furthermore, just one week after taking charge of the US embassy in Saigon, Ambassador Henry Cabot Lodge wrote to Secretary of State Dean Rusk that 'there is no possibility in my view that the war can be won under a Diem administration'.[13]

But if Diem were removed, who would take his place? In the NSC meetings that occurred at the end of August, this question was raised on several occasions, although it was never answered to anyone's satisfaction. In one meeting, Kennedy requested that a 'who's who' be prepared listing the various personalities that might succeed Diem. Vice-President Nguyen Ngoc Tho was regarded as the most likely civilian candidate to take over, but he was considered a nonentity. Alternatively, a military junta would come to power, though it was unclear which of the generals would lead it. In their conception of what a post-Diem government might look like, several administration officials employed the analogy of the South Korean government after the May 1961 coup, in which the generals kept a civilian face to legitimize military rule.[14] Disregarding the uncertainty over the character and personalities of a successor regime, those within the administration advocating a coup placed their main emphasis on arguments against Diem rather than arguments for a successor.[15]

The second main issue debated by US policymakers was the tactics to be employed in dealing with Diem. Precisely because of the concerns expressed about the lack of good alternative leaders, Kennedy sought to find a means of pressuring Diem to reform. Nolting, whose tenure as ambassador was characterized by offering Diem 'carrots' rather than 'sticks',[16] urged Kennedy to instruct Lodge to have a 'cards down' talk with the South Vietnamese leader. For Nolting, only in the worst case should the US resort to economic and political pressure, but he was against any attempt to encourage a coup.[17] By contrast, Lodge viewed this idea with disdain. Unlike Nolting, Lodge preferred 'sticks' to 'carrots'. From Lodge's point of view, a meeting with Diem in which he would merely repeat US requests for reform was not only a waste of time, but would also make the US look weak.[18] With the failure of a coup to materialize in late August, the administration opted for a policy of placing economic pressure on Diem's government, largely for reasons of presenting a public image of American displeasure with the regime, and not because it was believed that this policy would have a chance of getting Diem to reform.

Coup scripts

Prior to the 1963 coup, the US government had considerable experience instigating, preventing and responding to military coups around the world. In cases such as Iran in 1953, the US took an active approach to promoting a coup against a regime it wished to depose. But neither the Iran analogy nor other analogies of covert promotion of coups were employed by US policymakers in relation to the Diem regime. Instead, the US role was viewed as being mainly of a peripheral nature, while it was still appreciated that the US had some role to play. As Lodge later wrote in his memoirs:

> The coup of November 1 was essentially a Vietnamese affair. Because of our lack of involvement in the intricacies of Vietnamese political life, we could not have started the coup if we had wanted to. Nor could we have stopped one once it had started. Our policy, under instructions from President Kennedy, was 'not to thwart' a coup. We adhered scrupulously to that policy … The common assumption that the American position was so strong in Saigon that all we had to do was to push the button to set a coup in motion was baseless. Actually, there was no button to push.[19]

Unfortunately, as the bulk of historical commentary on Vietnam is US-centric, in which the actions of the South Vietnamese are viewed as insignificant as a matter of course relative to those of the Americans, the US role in the coup has received more attention than it probably merits. To set the record straight, it is therefore crucial to examine the assumptions of US policymakers about what they believed Washington's role in a coup would amount to. As the prospect of promoting a coup had been discussed on numerous occasions prior to 1963, it is possible to trace the continuities in US thinking. Therefore, before proceeding to examine the August–October 1963 period, in which US leaders were at their most active in engaging with the idea of overthrowing Diem, it is worth highlighting several instances of earlier discussions in Kennedy's presidency.

Two documents from November 1961 are particularly noteworthy. In the first, US Ambassador to India John Kenneth Galbraith provided

Kennedy with his appreciation of the situation in Vietnam and the US relationship with Diem. His conclusion was that the US should 'drop Diem' and that 'dropping Diem will neither be difficult nor unduly dangerous'. Noting that 'rumors of coups are endemic', he went on to say that if the US made it 'quietly clear that we are withdrawing our support from him as an individual … [h]is day would then I believe be over'.[20] In the second document, an NSC staffer who was tasked with providing a paper considering alternatives to Diem similarly observed: 'The evidence suggests that all we will probably have to do to ensure that a coup takes place is to indicate clearly, but in an indirect fashion, that we will support a coup effort'. The reference to 'indirect fashion' was based on the premise that: 'No matter how unpopular Diem may be and no matter how popular his successors, our identification with the change would be a definite drawback in Vietnam and the world at large'.[21] Interestingly, in August 1962, another senior US official involved with Vietnam policy recommended that the US 'get rid of Diem, Mr. and Mrs. Nhu and the rest of the Ngo family'. Once again, it was noted that it: 'would be desirable to keep the US hand in the coup concealed to the maximum extent feasible. We would want to avoid any public connotation that the new government was our puppet'.[22] The assumption underlying all of these scripts was that quietly signalling the withdrawal of US support from the Diem regime would automatically trigger a series of actions by the South Vietnamese military resulting in Diem's downfall. When examining the internal discourse of US policymakers in late August 1963, one can clearly see this same assumption serving as a guide. As will be discussed in the next section, it was only after a coup failed to materialize that policymakers began to recognize that merely offering covert assurances of support was insufficient to unseat Diem, and that factors internal to the South Vietnamese military were more important.

It is noteworthy that in the crisis atmosphere of late August, with the NSC's executive committee meeting at least once daily as it had during the Cuban missile crisis, US officials discussed a broad range of ideas, including the possibility of a more direct role in supporting a coup.[23] For instance, in order to get South Vietnamese officers to abandon their support for Diem, it was believed essential that US military officers, whose views would carry greater weight with their counterparts than those of

CIA officials, should be directly involved in persuading them. Other ideas that were floated included cutting off economic aid, suspending all US operations in South Vietnam, conducting psychological operations, providing military equipment such as helicopters and communications facilities, and making a public announcement supporting the forces trying to overthrow Diem.[24] Although such ideas about direct US involvement were discussed in August, by late October these same officials had convinced themselves of the need to maintain a strictly hands-off approach, almost certainly because they had little confidence in the ability and willingness of the South Vietnamese generals to carry out a coup, and were therefore wary of risking a political and public relations catastrophe if the US were seen to be intimately involved.

One other assumption in the US scripts for a coup was that Diem and his family were to be exiled rather than killed. According to one State Department official, their deaths were a 'traumatic experience for the Administration because they had no anticipation that Diem and Nhu would be assassinated. It was thought that they would be exiled'.[25] At the time, Hilsman stated: 'We should be prepared, with the knowledge of the coup group, to furnish a plane to take the Ngo family to France or other European country which will receive it'.[26] It was believed to be paramount that Diem should be removed not only specifically from Vietnam, but also from South East Asia more generally. Hence there was a concern that if the plane carrying Diem stopped elsewhere in Asia to refuel, he would use the opportunity to disembark and claim asylum. Thus a key requirement for exiling Diem was to have a long-range aircraft on standby that could transport Diem directly to Europe.[27] There was also some discussion about initially flying Diem to the US Pacific island of Saipan, due to its relative isolation, and then on to another location.[28] Regardless of the US assumption about Diem's exile, he and his brother were executed, almost certainly on the orders of the coup leader, Major General Duong Van Minh.

The balance of forces

Apart from the pros and cons of removing the Diem regime in principle, there was also the practical matter of whether a coup plot was likely to succeed. Thus the relative balance of forces between the pro-coup and anti-coup elements probably became the most important factor considered by US officials. Although there was some limited discussion within the NSC in late August of the balance of forces, this issue became considerably more prominent by late October, especially since it was considered the main reason why no coup had occurred earlier. Interestingly, just days before the coup occurred, the general consensus of opinion was that a coup would be a very close run thing and that Diem probably still had the upper hand.

In contrast to the script of an inevitable coup once US intentions were made known, the reality on the ground highlighted that such a script was hardly inevitable at all. At the 27 August NSC meeting, McNamara circulated a list of coup generals and the forces they controlled, noting that those forces were 'few and scattered'. Afterwards, Kennedy concluded the meeting by casting doubt on whether the generals could actually bring about a coup.[29] At another NSC meeting the following day, Taylor stated that the Vietnamese forces loyal to Diem in the immediate vicinity of Saigon outnumbered by two to one the forces believed to be disloyal. By the end of the meeting, Kennedy again admitted that it did not appear the dissident generals were able to mount a coup, but suggested that options be considered for promoting defections. There was also the problem of security, as it was believed that the secret police were aware of the plotting by the generals and might arrest the plotters at any time. But as Hilsman observed, it was precisely because the generals were aware that the coup plot might have been penetrated by the secret police that they had no choice but to press forward with a coup.[30] Ironically, the inferior forces and the combined fear that the Americans might have exposed the plot to the secret police were cited as reasons why the generals called off the plot. Two weeks later, Director of Central Intelligence John McCone noted that the 'original abortive attempt to stimulate a coup was based on hope rather than reality with the SVN [South Vietnamese] generals'.[31]

By early October, US officials became aware that the generals were again plotting a coup, but, unlike in August, there was little sense of perpetual crisis to cause the NSC to meet every day to discuss it. With the experience of late August behind them, officials had all the more reason to be cautious and not get overexcited. Nevertheless, they were keen to obtain as much tactical intelligence about the coup plan as possible so that they could determine its chances of success. Such was the perceived importance of the relative balance of forces that this topic became the centre of discussion at the 29 October NSC meeting, which was dedicated entirely to discussing the prospect of a forthcoming coup.

The meeting opened with a briefing by CIA Far East Division chief William Colby, which provided an overview of the loyalties of the various units in the Saigon area.[32] In the course of the discussion that followed, Kennedy referred to coups that had occurred in South Korea, Pakistan and Iraq to try to ascertain how important the issue of the balance of forces was relative to other considerations.[33] Moreover, Kennedy wanted to know what lessons could be derived from the failed November 1960 coup, as well as what precautions Diem had taken since that time. Colby replied that the critical issue in 1960 was that Diem was able to retain the loyalty of units outside of Saigon and in the aftermath of the coup attempt he had increased his immediate defences, established early warning mechanisms, and improved his communication with outside units.[34] Later in the meeting, Kennedy again referred to the relatively even correlation of forces in the Saigon area and suggested that, if the balance favoured neither side, 'then of course it doesn't make any sense to have a coup'. Furthermore, Kennedy stated that unless there was some evidence that dissident units outnumbered loyal units, then the US should try to discourage a coup.[35]

The following day, General Paul Harkins cast further doubt on the ability of the generals to mount a coup with the forces they claimed to have on their side.[36] Harkins seems to have assumed that unless the generals could bring superior forces to bear, they would be unlikely to attempt a coup. Thus it was that only 40 minutes before the coup began on 1 November, Harkins sent a cable stating that 'MACV [Military Assistance Command, Vietnam] has no info … which could be interpreted as clear evidence of an impending coup'.[37] For Harkins as well as US officials more generally, the assumption about the possession of superior forces being a necessary condition for a coup was correct. That they were taken by surprise was principally due to a lack of accurate information about the composition of the coup forces; in addition, they were not provided with details of the coup plan. Unbeknownst to the Americans, the generals had made secret arrangements to ensure they would have superior forces in Saigon.[38] It must be remembered that the generals had little faith in the Americans and, out of fear that they might interfere or expose the coup plot, chose to avoid providing them with many details.

To thwart or not to thwart a coup?

American policy with respect to supporting a coup was somewhat akin to a high-stakes poker game, except that if a coup were successful the gains would be minimal, whereas if the coup were unsuccessful the losses would be disastrous. Both Taylor and McCone argued that a successful coup would bring with it a whole set of new problems, such as the political confusion caused by a wholesale shift in personnel. At best, they believed a coup might be good in the long term but would be bad in the short term.[39] On the other hand, an unsuccessful coup would have worse consequences. As Harriman observed, 'we have lost Vietnam if the coup fails'.[40] Similarly, Hilsman stated that if the coup was unsuccessful, the only choices left open for the US would be to get out of Vietnam or to overthrow the government and put in its own preferred government.[41] Robert Kennedy also complained: 'I would think we are just going down the road to disaster'.[42]

President Kennedy's policy—not to support a coup but not to thwart one either—had one crucial flaw. By taking a hands-off approach, the US had the advantage of 'plausible deniability' but the disadvantage of a lack of control. Thus, if the US was convinced that any coup would fail, it would be unable to stop it from occurring. Lodge's ability to stop a coup had first been called into question in late August. Having been requested by Secretary of State Dean Rusk to assess how long the US could delay conveying to the generals Washington's agreement to their proceeding with a coup, Lodge replied: 'We are launched on a course from which there is no respectable turning back: the overthrow of the Diem government. There is no turning back'.[43] Kennedy insisted, however, on reserving 'a contingent right to change course' if failure was likely. Lodge politely replied that he would do his utmost to follow Kennedy's instructions, but that to 'be successful, this operation must be essentially a Vietnamese affair with a momentum of its own. Should this happen you may not be able to control it, that is, the "go signal" may be given by the generals'.[44]

The prospect of stopping a coup was also discussed at the 29 October meeting when US officials believed the prospects for a successful coup were limited. National Security Advisor McGeorge Bundy cabled Lodge with instructions to dissuade the generals from going ahead with a coup plot if he thought it was going to fail. Lodge replied that he did not think 'we have the power to delay or discourage a coup' short of exposing the coup plot to Diem. He also argued that, even in the unlikely event that the US was able to discourage the generals from acting, the American relationship with the generals would be harmed and it would undermine the war effort. Worse still, Lodge believed that younger officers would probably attempt a coup anyway and this would lead to further chaos.[45]

Bundy was unwilling to accept Lodge's argument and responded that exposing the coup plot was unthinkable. Instead, he argued that Lodge should do his best to communicate American doubts to the generals and persuade them to delay a coup until the prospects were better.[46] It seems unlikely that, having identified himself so closely with supporting a coup, Lodge would have been enthusiastic about 'putting the brakes' on a coup. In fact, many of Kennedy's advisers felt, perhaps not unjustifiably, that Lodge had his own agenda, and that it was difficult enough to control him, much more to get him to stop the generals from launching a coup.

In fairness to Lodge, it should be pointed out that the notion of thwarting a coup not in US interests was one that bedevilled American diplomats throughout this period. For instance, only a month before the November coup in Vietnam, another coup had taken place in Honduras. Although the US ambassador had tried to dissuade the leader of the coup beforehand, it was to no avail, and the coup went ahead.[47] Numerous other cases of failed US efforts to dissuade military coups during the Kennedy administration, particularly in Latin America, could also be cited, which makes the notion of Lodge being able to succeed in thwarting a coup quite far-fetched.

Conclusion

The Kennedy administration was surprised by the coup's precise timing and its degree of quick success. There was also considerable shock at the assassinations of Diem and Nhu. Once the coup got under way and in the immediate aftermath, the first order of business was to consider when the US would provide official recognition for the new government. However, this seemingly mundane task was fraught with its own problems because the administration had publicly opposed military coups in Latin America and was afraid of looking hypocritical.[48] Fortunately, Diem's regime was so unpopular that, when the coup occurred, there was widespread jubilation. The US sought to exploit this by publicly stating that Diem's government was authoritarian, opposed by the people and incompetent, whereas the new government was less repressive and enjoyed popular support, and the military leaders had declared their intent to shift to civilian authority.[49] Bundy later said half-jokingly that in future when Latin American generals launched coups, they should be advised that obtaining US recognition would be easier if they ensured that there was a public demonstration of support accompanying it, as had occurred in Saigon.[50]

On a more serious note, in the years after the coup, and into the present day, US policymakers have continually employed the Diem analogy as a means of discouraging any discussion about overthrowing friendly governments whose leadership is viewed as problematic. As Freedman notes in *Kennedy's Wars*: 'In the end, Kennedy did not really choose to overthrow Diem, although his indecision had the same effect as an anti-Diem choice'.[51] As this chapter has highlighted, this indecision can be understood by the lack of a script in which the US stood to benefit, or even a script that clearly identified the least bad option. The decision-making process was further complicated by the numerous and overlapping issues under consideration. Strategic scripts for US policy towards Vietnam revolved around debates about whether to maintain relations with Diem or to seek a successor regime. Yet these debates could not be disentangled from tactical scripts detailing how a coup would transpire, assuming it transpired at all. The scripts reflected the broad spectrum of dilemmas facing the Kennedy administration in its Vietnam policy, but they also served to paralyze it by forcing policymakers to confront the complexities and contradictions of the policy. Yet even indecision can be construed as a decision in its own right, or at least a decision not to take a decision and to hope for the best. Lacking a positive way forward, these policymakers chose to 'pass the buck', and to adopt a policy of non-interference in the internal political struggles among its non-communist allies in South Vietnam. Therefore, although the coup would often be attributed to a deliberate US policy to overthrow Diem, it is perhaps more accurate to say that the coup was partially encouraged by Washington's unwillingness to stop it.

10

THE OPERATIONAL LEGACY
OF THE FALKLANDS WAR

Julian Thompson

The Falklands War of 1982 was, in the words attributed to a cynical parachute regiment officer, 'a come as you are party'. Professor Sir Lawrence Freedman expressed the same message in more scholarly language:

> Wars, as one of the post-conflict reviews noted, 'have a habit of occurring at a time and place other than those expected in formal policy assessments or scenarios.' They have to be fought with the forces and equipment in hand, not what was planned for the future. The Falklands was exactly the sort of war that Britain's forces had not planned to fight.[1]

Furthermore, the Falklands War included an amphibious operation conducted at a greater distance from main base to intermediate base and from intermediate base to objective than any comparable campaign in recent history, including the Central Pacific campaign of the Second World War.

As the first major British naval operation in decades, involving new generations of weapons systems and communications capabilities, the

Falklands War of 1982 might be expected to reveal operational and organisational innovations, or perhaps just improvisations, that would have significant knock-on consequences. This chapter discusses the war itself and the British military organisations and military systems that were involved. Then it assesses what, if any, footprints can be seen in the British military today.

Much of this chapter must perforce be based on open sources, conversations and personal observations. A complete examination of this subject would require access to the papers of the various departments involved, including minutes of meetings at various levels in government and position papers and briefings, but these will not be open to public scrutiny for many years.

Operation of the Falklands War

The Ministry of Defence (MoD) initially did not accept that the experience of the Falklands War changed anything as far as the general strategic and operational plans for the future conduct of defence were concerned.[2] The MoD view was mirrored and articulated on more than one occasion to this author by senior naval and army officers in words to the effect of 'nothing has changed, we will all proceed as before'. This somewhat jaundiced view proved to be incorrect. 'Jaundiced' because senior army officers regarded the Falklands War as an aberration, which distracted attention from the central front of NATO, in general, and the British Army of the Rhine, which had been the centrepiece of their careers since they were junior officers. Resentment on the part of the Royal Navy was confined to those who had not taken part in the Falklands War, headed by the then Vice-Chief of the Naval Staff, and the anti-naval aviation and anti-amphibious force factions, who wanted to dispense with these two capabilities in favour of an all anti-submarine navy. What nobody could deny was that the Royal Navy had demonstrated that the object of the 1981 Nott defence review (reducing the navy to an anti-submarine and nuclear deterrent force) had been overtaken by events. Furthermore, the perception of British military competence in the eyes of other nations had changed.[3] Sir Christopher Meyer wrote about his experience as political counsellor to the British ambassador in Moscow during the Falklands War:

My ambassador, Curtis Keeble, and I were regularly summoned to the Soviet Foreign Ministry. We would be handed a protest about the Royal Navy's expelling Soviet trawlers from the exclusion zone … Once, after delivering a particularly stern protest, Vladimir Suslov, the head of the ministry's Second European Department, muttered to us as we were leaving: 'When are you going to drive those bastards [the occupying Argentines] into the sea? For God's sake hurry up.' … Another Soviet diplomat remarked to me: 'We would no longer have considered you a serious country if you hadn't defeated the Argentines.'[4]

The management of the campaign at political level worked well. In particular, the well-tried Defence and Overseas Policy Committee (DOPC) met regularly, usually as a subcommittee of the DOPC and named the South Atlantic and Falkland Islands: Overseas and Defence South Atlantic 1982 (OD(SA)(82)), known simply as the 'War Cabinet'. Chaired by the Prime Minister, it comprised the secretaries of state for the Home, Defence, and Foreign and Commonwealth Affairs departments, the Chancellor of the Duchy of Lancaster (Cecil Parkinson, the Conservative Party chairman), the Attorney General, the chiefs of staff, the Permanent Under-Secretary (PUS) at the Foreign and Commonwealth Office (FCO), the Cabinet PUSs, and the Cabinet Secretariat. It did not include the Chancellor of the Exchequer because in the words of Prime Minister Thatcher, 'he always says "no"'.[5] The exclusion of the Chancellor of the Exchequer obviated any tiresome and counterproductive objections to expenditure, much less refusal to produce the necessary funding by the Exchequer that occurred in later conflicts. The members of Thatcher's War Cabinet came to meetings fully briefed by their respective departments, the proceedings were minuted, and the well-lubricated machinery of government worked as intended. This is in marked contrast to the manner in which Britain's wars in the twenty-first century have been run to date, a subject to which we will return.

At the highest military level, that of the chiefs of staff, the existing system worked competently. The Chiefs of Staff (COS) committee met regularly, and thus all three heads of services were kept fully in the picture. As we shall see, this was not the case during the Iraq and Afghanistan wars of the period 2001–14. Below MoD level, the command arrangements for the Falklands War did not run smoothly; summarized below, this subject is covered in more detail by Sir Lawrence

Freedman in his *Official History*.[6] The Falklands task force was commanded by the Commander-in-Chief Fleet (Admiral Sir John Fieldhouse) from his headquarters at Northwood, just north of London. The fleet headquarters' task in peacetime was the provision of ships, for both overseas and home waters deployments, and the administration of each fleet. It had no wartime role. That was the job of the fleet NATO staff, located in a different part of the bunker in Northwood. The NATO staff were debarred from involvement in the Falklands War. The fleet staff had no amphibious expertise. Suddenly, without warning, the headquarters found itself responsible for an amphibious operation followed by a land campaign, both undertakings of which it was entirely ignorant. Fortunately, Royal Marine Major General Jeremy Moore went to Admiral Fieldhouse and told him that his fleet staff needed help. Moore and some of his staff remained at Northwood until he left to command the land forces in the South Atlantic. At which point his place was taken by the General Officers Commanding (GOC) South East District, Sir Richard Trant and his staff. Trant and his staff knew no more about amphibious operations than the fleet staff.

From 12 April there were five task groups under Fieldhouse's direct command: the carrier battle group (Rear Admiral Woodward), the amphibious task group (Commodore Clapp), the landing force task group (Brigadier Thompson), the South Georgia task group (Captain Young), and the submarine task group (Vice Admiral Herbert). Eventually all but one of the task group commanders were about 8,000 miles away from Northwood; Herbert was located with Fieldhouse throughout. This organisation, shown in Fig. 1, superseded an earlier version, which is not included here in the interests of saving space.

On 12 May it was changed to the organisation shown in Fig 2. to reflect the arrival of Major General Moore in theatre with his divisional headquarters and another brigade, 5 Infantry brigade. The ships in the South Georgia group were dispersed to the carrier and amphibious groups following the recapture of South Georgia on 25 May 1982.

What was lacking in both organisations was an overall in-theatre commander between Fieldhouse and the forward task group commanders. Such a commander could have been located in either HMS *Antrim* or *Glamorgan*. Both of these ships were fitted with flag officer accommodation and communications. An overall in-theatre comman-

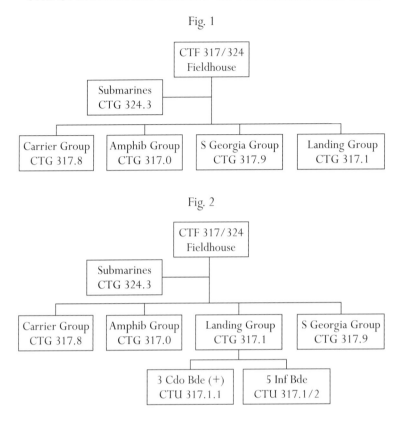

Fig. 1

Fig. 2

der could have moved between the carrier battle group and the amphibious and landing force groups, especially after the landings. He would have been able to assess the situation for himself, draw together the strands of the operation, keep Fieldhouse in the picture, and kept him off the backs of the task group commanders. Finally, his presence in-theatre would have resolved instantly any ambiguity over who was in charge of whom. Woodward as a two-star thought of himself as being in charge of Clapp and Thompson, as did Fieldhouse, despite the command diagrams making it perfectly clear that Woodward was one of three coequal commanders. For example, Fieldhouse expected Woodward to overrule decisions made by the other task group commanders and in effect act as the in-theatre overall commander, despite having enough on his plate already, and having neither the staff nor personal expertise to fulfil this role. Also lacking was clarity on the relationship between the commander of the amphibious group (Clapp) and the commander of the landing group (Thompson, until Moore arrived).[7] This relationship was proscribed in *Allied Tactical Publication Number 8* (ATP-8), a NATO document, which the UK had signed years before and was the Bible for amphibious operations.

The final organisation, brought into effect on 12 May, was flawed because Moore did not arrive in theatre until 30 May, nine days after the initial landings by 3 Commando Brigade. During the eight days following promulgation of the final command structure, Moore remained at Northwood (he left on 20 May). Consequently he was unable to fulfil the role of commander of the landing force (CLF), because this required that he be co-located with the commander of the amphibious force and be in a position to make on-the-spot decisions together with him before, during and after the landing. Having embarked on the liner *Queen Elizabeth II* at Ascension Island, the secure communications specially fitted in that ship immediately broke down on 21 May (the day of the landings). Not only was he still separated by considerable distance from the amphibious group commander, but he was unable to keep himself informed of the progress of the operation ashore because no one could communicate with him. Despite this, Fieldhouse persisted in sending him signals which he could not receive, ordering him to take certain steps in the prosecution of the land campaign. These signals were copied to Thompson as an information addressee, although he was de facto commander of the landing force. Either Fieldhouse was unaware of the situation or was oblivious to the potential chaos caused by the command structure.

The performance of the Sea Harrier (SHAR) as an air defence fighter came as a great surprise to many, including several senior officers in the Royal Navy. As well as outperforming all of the Argentine fighters and fighter-bombers, SHARs launched from the two carriers were able to generate a greater sortie rate than the opposition. As we shall see, this was a lesson that was forgotten. Another of the great success stories of the Falklands War was the use of British-flagged merchant ships to support all facets of the operation. Without the participation of the merchant navy the operation would have been impossible.

So, in sum, what was the potential operational legacy of the Falklands war?

- The value of a 'war cabinet' in time of war or conflict was shown.
- The importance of the Chiefs of Staff Committee was demonstrated.
- The need for a properly constituted and staffed UK-based headquarters to run an overseas operation was shown to be necessary.
- The requirement for an in-theatre overall commander in future operations was demonstrated.
- The value of the carrier equipped with SHAR was demonstrated.
- The value of an amphibious capability was proven.
- Sufficient escorts in the form of destroyers and frigates were needed.
- An adequate number of British-flagged merchant ships needed to be maintained.
- Last, but not least, the UK regained confidence in itself.

In the intervening thirty-odd years since the Falklands War, what remains of the operational legacy of that conflict? As access to the papers of the various departments involved is at present denied, much of what follows is based, as I have already noted, on open sources, conversations and personal observation. A recently published book has thrown some light on how the UK conducted operations under the Blair, Brown and Cameron governments.[8] For similar reasons, the book is based on personal interviews with key players, not on the relevant papers. One is therefore reliant on the veracity of those interviewed, which can only be confirmed when the relevant papers are released. Two other books, which are critical of the UK's conduct of war and operations in the first years of this century, also provide valuable insights into the subject.[9]

The organisations of war

The War Cabinet. As Sir Hew Strachan reminds us, Lloyd George created a workable War Cabinet in 1916, which produced a strategy that led to victory, but Winston Churchill did not follow his example in the Second World War. He preferred to deal directly with the chiefs of staff. By the time he became Prime Minister, Churchill, for all his faults, had acquired vast experience in the business of war from the lowest to the highest level for over forty years; he was therefore intellectually fitted to dispense with a war cabinet. His chiefs of staff, especially their chairman in the latter half of the war, Field Marshal Sir Alan Brooke, may have despaired at times, but they had the moral fibre, integrity and practice in command at high level that equipped them to deal with Churchill's wilder notions. But that begs the question: are the present-day chiefs in the same league as their Second World War counterparts?

Because Churchill did not establish a War Cabinet, there was no institutional legacy for one in Britain. But, as alluded to above, Margaret Thatcher revived the War Cabinet—OD(SA)(82)—for the Falklands War. Tony Blair created an 'ad hoc' War Cabinet in 2003, which, according to Strachan, met infrequently and to little practical effect. Blair preferred 'sofa government'.[10] This view is expressed more formally by Jonathan Bailey: 'The British constitution was undergoing rapid modification with the decline of cabinet government and the concentration of defence and foreign affairs in the office of the Prime Minister, a quasi 'White House'.[11] 'Sofa government' (Freedman's term, not Bailey's, and used here as convenient shorthand for the casual methods favoured by Blair), produced:

> a cultural gap between rigorous, closely argued and documented military staff planning and ad hoc subjective intuition. In the past such a gulf has been bridged by collaborative working. In this case, it was not. The deliberate absence of the military staff from strategic summit meetings, such as Mr Blair's meeting with President Bush in Crawford, Texas, in April 2002, was the most damaging example of this defect in British policy.[12]

A further disturbing trend of the Blair years was the ascendancy of the Chancellor of the Exchequer, who became 'the second dominant figure shaping defence and military capability ... more so than the defence secretary'.[13] The Chancellor of the Exchequer retained this dominance under David Cameron. Thatcher, Blair and Cameron knew nothing about war. Of these three, only Thatcher had the humility, insight and strategic intellect to form a War Cabinet and to then use it to good effect. She also heeded the advice tendered by the chiefs of staff, and the Chief of the Defence Staff (CDS) in particular. This was in marked contrast to Cameron whose response to being warned about the possible outcome of supporting the rebels in Libya by the CDS was to say: 'You do the fighting and I'll do the talking'.[14] The predictions of utter chaos in Libya, made by the CDS at the time, came to pass.

Not only has there been no proper War Cabinet since Thatcher, but, in addition, the DOPC itself (of which ODSA 82—the 'War Cabinet'—

was a subcommittee) seems to have fallen into disuse. The DOPC was attended by the chiefs of staff of all three services, in addition to ministers from the other relevant government departments. Before attending meetings of the DOPC, the chiefs met in committee to consider the agenda and the briefing papers and came to an agreed view, which was minuted by their secretariat. Furthermore, the secretary to the Chiefs of Staff Committee attended the DOPC, and took minutes alongside the members of the Cabinet Secretariat. The creation of a National Security Council by Cameron's coalition government was not an adequate substitute because 'strategy is inherently unstable and needs constant management and correction', so, in the further opinion of Strachan, 'the National Security Council's lack of a strategic staff or of a sufficiently resourced secretariat capable of hands-on management is a serious weakness'.[15] Furthermore, the CDS is no longer a permanent member, unlike the Secretary of State for International Development (DFID). Perhaps this is an indication of the priority the Cameron government accorded to defence.

The Chiefs of Staff Committee. Reforms over the years since the Second World War have made changes to the Chiefs of Staff Committee. Until 1982, the chairman, initially one of the service chiefs and, from 1964, the chief of the defence staff, was, as the name implies, *primus inter pares*, merely first among equals. Decisions were arrived at by the chiefs of staff as a body, either 'in committee' or 'out of committee'; the latter by the circulation of papers.[16] The Nott–Lewin reforms in 1982 elevated the CDS above the chiefs of staff, creating a staff for him, and making him 'the government's principal strategic adviser'.[17] Further tinkering by Michael Heseltine (Secretary of State for Defence, 1983–6) relegated the chiefs of staff, including the CDS, to budget managers, diluting the effectiveness of the service chiefs as strategic advisers to the government.[18] Field Marshal Sir Edwin Bramall, then CDS, considered that the effect of the Heseltine reforms 'was to emasculate the chiefs of staff as a strategic advisory body and to elevate financial management over professional military thought'. Bramall argued that 'without an effective chiefs of staff committee, the CDS is little more than the head of a bureaucratic structure subject to political manipulation'.[19] This is certainly the case today.

But the chiefs of staff still continued to meet, which ensured that at least the heads of the three services were kept informed, even if they had little power to act. Although the various reforms through the years had effectively relegated the service chiefs to providers of assets in the form of ships, aircraft, tanks and other equipment, along with the people to man them, at least they knew how these were to be deployed, when and where. Now it would seem that this has changed. Some of the chiefs interviewed by Christopher Elliott claim that they were kept in the dark about such matters as the decision to deploy British forces to Helmand Province in Afghanistan.[20] From this one could infer that either the Chiefs of Staff Committee does not meet or, if it does, not very often, and that nothing of note is discussed. Until the papers are opened to the public, we shall not know.

UK-based headquarters to run overseas operations. After the Falklands War, it was decided that in the event of future overseas operations, a nominated UK-based headquarters would be put in overall charge. The headquarters would be selected on the basis of the type of operation and the 'lead' service. This followed the precedent established in 1982 when C-in-C Fleet (Fieldhouse) ran the war in the South Atlantic, an overwhelmingly maritime operation. The other two potential headquarters were HQ South East District (army) and HQ Royal Air Force (RAF) Strike Command. When the British joined the US-led coalition against Saddam Hussein, following his invasion of Kuwait in August 1990, the initial UK contribution was overwhelmingly RAF; hence the HQ RAF Strike Command took the lead role.

In 1994–6, in response to the lessons of the Falklands War (Operation Corporate) and the 1991 expulsion of Saddam from Kuwait (Operation Desert Storm), a permanent joint headquarters (PJHQ) was set up at Northwood under a Chief of Joint Operations (CJO). It was given the staff and communications to run any future overseas operation. At last, it was thought, the UK's command and control organisation was well fitted to meet any unforeseen threat.

In Christopher Elliott's view, the PJHQ has not lived up to expectation.[21] Hew Strachan regards the PJHQ as 'the fifth wheel to the coach'.[22] Space does not allow a full discussion of the subject. But the essence of Elliott's argument is that experience in Iraq and Afghanistan has shown that, between the MoD, PJHQ and the British in-theatre overall commander (when there was one), there was a muddle and excessive interference with the decisions of commanders on the ground. He also makes the point that PJHQ is one hour's journey from the MoD—too far to be convenient, but close enough to make 'back-seat driving' easy.

Strachan is more critical of the MoD:

A few miles away [from PJHQ] the Ministry of Defence has remained not only a department of state but also a military headquarters. The latter itself is an awkward relationship, resulting in a convergence of financial needs with operational and military that is not necessarily to the advantage of either ... It can also result in 'group think' and the subordination of military imperatives to the needs of Whitehall. Civil servants see their primary function as serving their ministers and saving them from embarrassment, not winning the war.[23]

Elliott recommends setting up a smaller PJHQ-type cell in the MoD in order to rectify these drawbacks. I am not entirely convinced; it may be that the fault lies with the terms of reference of the overall in-theatre commander, combined with the tendency of ministers to wield 'long screwdrivers' from their offices in Whitehall all the way to the headquarters in-theatre. Nevertheless, Elliott makes a good case, and it is a subject worthy of more study. Such a study needs to decide where responsibility lies with each headquarters: MoD and PJHQ. Strategic decisions, as part of national policy—where this exists—should be the responsibility of the MoD. Operational-level decisions should be PJHQ business or that of whatever organisation is finally devised after study.

Overall in-theatre commander. In the Afghanistan and both Iraq wars, the UK established a UK overall in-theatre commander responsible for the British effort in that campaign. Their terms of reference and lines of command changed from time to time to take account of the situation in-theatre, and this chapter is not intended to give a detailed account of how this evolved in over a decade of campaigning.

In the run-up to Operation Desert Storm, the British army contingent grew to over a division, so it was decided to position an army officer as UK overall commander in-theatre. Lieutenant General Sir Peter de la Billière, GOC South East District, was sent out. Although de la Billière was designated Commander British Forces Middle East (BFME) with operational control over all British forces in-theatre, he was in effect a liaison officer with General Schwarzkopf, the US and coalition commander, and charged with overseeing the UK contingent's interests, rather than a true overall UK commander—he did not have any command and control function in the actual battle. He reported to HQ RAF Strike Command at High Wycombe. All of the UK component commanders were under the operational command of the relevant US commander. For example, the British 1 Armoured Division was under the command of US VII Corps with a 'dotted line' to HQ BFME. Although this was an improvement on the command structure in the Falklands War in that the UK component commanders in the Middle East were spared dealing with a headquarters thousands of miles away on most matters, there was still a degree of 'back-seat driving', for example by the MoD and other UK-based headquarters, directly with component commanders—land, sea and air.

Furthermore, the size and nature of Desert Storm (the first Gulf War) make direct comparisons with the Falklands War almost impossible. Suffice it to say that because both campaigns were conducted with allies, and the British contribution was small compared to that of the lead nation, the US, the job of the overall in-theatre commander was more complex than it would have been for such a commander in the Falklands War, had there been one. However, none of that alters the fact that there will almost always be a need for an overall in-theatre national commander in any future operation.

Military systems in the war

The value of carriers and Sea Harriers. The Sea Harrier (SHAR) was dispensed with in 2007, unwisely in my opinion. However, the Royal Navy continued to embark the Harrier GR9A (upgraded GR9) on their aircraft carriers. The *2010 Strategic Defence and Security Review* (SDSR), as originally drafted, included keeping the latter Harrier and dispensing with the ageing RAF Tornado fleet. Over one weekend the CDS persuaded Prime Minister Cameron to reverse this decision and eliminated the Harriers entirely (committing the government to a small number of Joint Strike Force jets for the new class of carrier that the government thought would not go into service fully).[24] This was achieved without consulting the navy department to which this chicanery on the part of the CDS came as a complete surprise.

When Cameron decided to back the rebels in Libya and topple Colonel Gaddafi, one of the first questions he asked was: 'Where is the carrier?' The British air operations carried out by Tornados, initially from bases in the UK and later from Italy, cost nearly nine times as much as operating Harriers from a carrier, or considerably more if infrastructure costs are added.[25] In summary the British part in the operation would have been greatly improved, and cheaper, using a carrier–Harrier combination, together with Apache helicopters and TLAM-equipped nuclear submarines (the latter two methods were employed to good effect). All land-based air operations could have been dispensed with. Contrary to the misinformation fed to Secretary of State for Defence Liam Fox, there was an effective naval alternative to the air-launched weapons carried by the Tornados. But thanks to 'sofa government', the disastrous decision was made to dispense with the carrier-Harrier combination.

The value of an amphibious capability. Had the UK not possessed an amphibious capability, the Falklands would now be part of Argentina. A viable amphibious capability requires not only the necessary ships and ship-shore movement assets (helicopters and landing craft), but people trained in their use. This includes commanders and staffs able to plan and execute one of the most complicated operations of war—an amphibious assault. An amphibious operation should not be confused with a sea-transported one, where troops and equipment are landed into a friendly country which provides plentiful host nation support in the form of docks, slipways, mechanical handling equipment, fuel, airfields and road transport—as occurred in the case of the operations to expel Saddam Hussein from Kuwait. Without the support of carrier- or land-based aircraft, an amphibious operation against an opponent with a strike capability is so hazardous as to be unlikely to succeed.

Had the UK not won the Falklands War, or even not engaged with Argentina at all, what existed of the amphibious capability in 1982 would have been gone long before the 2000s decisions—including the Royal Marines. Instead, in the years following the Falklands War, the two amphibious ships, *Fearless* and *Intrepid*, were replaced by bigger and better equivalents: *Albion* and *Bulwark*. A new helicopter carrier (LPH), the *Ocean*, was launched. New and improved landing craft were built, including hovercraft (landing craft air cushion, LCAC). New amphibious support ships were also brought into service to replace the old landing ships logistic (LSL).

In subsequent years, however, the capability has steadily been eroded. The Royal Marines remain, as vibrant and effective as before, and if anything more so. But cost-saving measures have led to some of the amphibious shipping being 'mothballed' and to talk of dispensing with some vessels. So although the capability is retained, its potential is reduced; and it will remain so unless the decisions outlined above are rescinded.

Escorts. Twenty-three British frigates and destroyers took part in the Falklands War. This was less than half the total number of such vessels in the Royal Navy at that time. Now the frigates and destroyers in the navy total a mere nineteen. Those responsible for this parlous state of affairs argue that ships today are more capable than their predecessors, so one can do more with fewer. That may be true, but the discussion evades the big question: how many fewer? It is a 'how long is a piece of string' question. Very few, if any, maritime experts are convinced that this piece of string is long enough. It is perfectly feasible to envisage a situation in which there are not sufficient ships to cover the tasks. If a ship is in the wrong place, it makes no difference how capable it is.

British-flagged merchant ships. Fifty British-flagged merchant ships were taken up from trade (STUFT) for the Falklands War. Provided the crews were British subjects, all that was required was an Order in Council signed by the Queen to requisition them and their crews to be subject to the Naval Discipline Act. Crew members who were not British subjects were replaced by people who were. In time of war, STUFT can be armed, ordered to sail in convoy, and carry out manoeuvres such as replenishment at sea. If merchant vessels in support of an operation are to be taken into waters where there is an enemy threat, they must be STUFT. Ships that are merely hired for the purpose, and from a variety of 'flags', cannot be ordered into a hazardous situation; if they are so ordered, they will probably refuse. So, for example, because the shipping involved in the sealift in the build-up to Operation

Desert Storm in Saudi Arabia was not taken into potentially dangerous waters, a merchant ship under any national flag could be hired for the purpose. In contrast, in the Falklands War merchant ships were taken into hazardous situations. They spent weeks at sea, hence the need to refuel thousands of miles from the nearest port, using replenishment-at-sea techniques, which are not among the normal skills of merchant seamen. They needed to defend themselves. Too few were fitted with the means to do so (there was neither the time nor the equipment available), though some were.

What is not clear at the present time is the number of suitable British-flagged ships available for taking up from trade for wartime use. The number of ocean-going ships worldwide has grown threefold in the last fifty years.[26] But the number of ships under 'flags of convenience' has grown at an even greater rate. A recent survey revealed that the British merchant navy consisted of 285 ships, with another 446 registered in other countries. But not all of the 285 would be suitable. Only a detailed study will reveal whether there are sufficient suitable British-flagged ships still in service. The study needs to include questions such as: Are there sufficient naval and commercial dockyards to carry out the necessary modifications to STUFT before they can be used to support operations? Is there enough naval manpower to provide the necessary naval parties needed on board to provide communications and other services? How many of these ships are crewed by British subjects?

Conclusion: UK confidence in itself

The First Sea Lord and Chief of the Naval Staff at the time of the Falklands War wrote later, speaking of the early 1980s: 'At that time the UK's stock in terms of world opinion was not at its highest: as a nation we were increasingly regarded as long on advice but short on muscle to back it'.[27] After the Falklands War, the picture changed dramatically. For example when Saddam invaded Kuwait in August 1990, the Prime Minister, Margaret Thatcher, is credited with saying to the President of the United States, George H.W. Bush: 'Remember, George, it's no time to go wobbly'.[28] Without the experience of the Falklands war, it is unlikely that the UK would have been so enthusiastic about supporting the US in Operation Desert Storm.

Now, after two disastrous wars—Iraq and Afghanistan—the mood is very different. In my opinion, the invasion of Iraq and the toppling of Saddam Hussein was a huge strategic error. The removal of Saddam Hussein and the subsequent chaos have destabilized the whole region. The US-led coalition should never have invaded Iraq in the first place. We will be living with this for the rest of this century.

The decision to move into Afghanistan to remove al-Qa'ida and the Taliban was correct. After that it all unravelled. Several British senior officers with considerable experience in Afghanistan have told this author that 'we got it wrong'. A better strategy, which some of these officers have come around to believe in, would have been to destroy the Taliban and get out, but, if they became a threat to security outside their country, to be prepared to go in again and destroy them a second time, and so on. But on no account should coalition forces maintain a permanent presence in the country or attempt to 'nation–build'.

So thirty-odd years on, what remains of the operational legacy of the Falklands War? The answer is very little. The practice of forming a war cabinet to run wars has been abandoned. The advice tendered by the CDS is frequently ignored. On one of the few occasions when it was taken, it was deeply flawed: the scrapping of the carrier-equipped Harrier. This did nothing to increase the Prime Minister's faith in the CDS when he discovered, too late, that he had been given what might crudely be called a 'bum steer'. The chiefs of staff are largely powerless and ignored. The Ministry of Defence is probably unfit for purpose. The Chancellor of the Exchequer has too powerful a voice in defence and foreign policy, a trend started by Blair. As a result, economic factors dictate what defence the UK requires, whereas it is the 'enemy' or the threat that should influence how the country is defended. First, it is necessary to establish the UK's foreign policy and identify the threats both at home and abroad. Then, and only then, should economics be introduced into the assessment of what defence resources are required. Despite ministerial protestations to the contrary, the 2010 strategic and defence and security review, despite its high-sounding name, was no such thing. It was cost-based and not strategy-based.

The PJHQ formed to run overseas operations has been shown to be less effective than hoped. The UK has to operate without a carrier for several years, and perhaps without the aircraft to go with it for even longer. There are insufficient escorts in the Royal Navy. It is possible that there are sufficient suitable British-flagged merchant ships, but only a concerted study will establish whether this is so.

The British have lost confidence in themselves and are led by ministers who know little about defence and care even less. They lack the ability to think strategically—a state of affairs that would continue whichever party is in power. There are, however, two brighter spots among the gloom. The principle of an overall HQ in theatre has been maintained although the results have been patchy, largely due to the command structures in allied operations in the country concerned. But at least the attempt was made to get it right. The other bright spot is the amphibious capability, which remains, though reduced. Taken all round, we are left with a sorry tale.

11

THE IRAQ SYNDROME REVISITED

AMERICA'S USE OF FORCE DEBATE UNDER OBAMA

David Hastings Dunn

In an analysis of the quagmire that the United States found itself in at the height of the Iraq insurgency in 2005, Lawrence Freedman contemplated what the long-term consequences of this episode would be for American foreign policy.[1] Comparing the decisions taken by Secretary of Defense Donald Rumsfeld in Iraq with Robert McNamara's role in Vietnam, Freedman speculated that Rumsfeld's legacy might well be a renewed version of the 'Vietnam syndrome', the persistent American reluctance to get involved in overseas wars. For Freedman, however, Rumsfeld's legacy was likely 'to leave behind an even more burdensome Iraq syndrome—the renewed, nagging and sometimes paralyzing belief that any large-scale US military intervention abroad is doomed to practical failure and moral iniquity'. It is the purpose of this chapter to examine the extent to which these considerations shaped America's attitude towards the use of military force in the Obama administration and the enduring legacy of this debate.

The importance of the Vietnam syndrome to the American use of force debate has been much analyzed. A great deal has been written on America's aversion to the acceptance of military casualties in the aftermath of the loss of 58,220 servicemen in what was seen to be an ultimately unsuccessful intervention.[2] Importantly, the Vietnam syndrome brought into question the utility of the large-scale use of force in achieving American foreign policy aims, and the moral righteousness of using American soldiers to promote or defend US values and interests on a global scale. It also raised questions about the political use of the military, the nature of the national interest and the legitimacy of military instruments in war, such as special operations. The legacy of that experience served as a strong inhibition against the use of force in the immediate post-conflict period, but it has gone on to influence all subsequent debates in the US body politic on the use of force. Even though the election of Ronald Reagan in 1980 can be partially understood as a counter-reaction to the response to the war in Vietnam, his administration's attempts to rehabilitate the use of force were limited in scale, scope and duration.[3] Indeed, the articulation of the Weinberger Doctrine in 1984 was an attempt by the Pentagon to codify the effects of the Vietnam syndrome in a set of guidelines as to when and how force should be used by the US, in the wake of the Beirut bombings.[4] Concerned that the State Department, under George Shultz, wanted to task the military to go after terrorists, the Pentagon came up with six tests to justify the US use of force: it must be shown that a vital American interest was concerned; that troops should be committed wholeheartedly and to win; that they had clearly defined objectives; that their use was monitored and adjusted; that there was 'reasonable assurance' of Congressional and public support; and that the use of force was a last resort.[5] The Pentagon even configured the military to fight large-scale conventional operations, in part, as a means of limiting its use for lesser operations.[6]

Not until the end of the Cold War and the expulsion of Iraqi forces from Kuwait in 1991 did a US President feel confident enough, as George H.W. Bush did, to declare; 'By God, we've kicked the Vietnam syndrome once and for all'.[7] In this self-appraisal, however, Bush failed to appreciate how much his own decision-making had been influenced by the Vietnam syndrome and the subsequent reactions to it. In seeking

UN and Congressional authorization for the intervention to remove Iraq forcibly from Kuwait, he was mindful of the need to legitimize his actions at home and abroad. In limiting the scope of the war to the removal of Iraq's forces from Kuwait and limiting the conflict to a 'hundred hours' war', Bush avoided testing the limits of what military force could achieve, or what international and domestic opinion would tolerate. And, crucially, Bush used 'overwhelming force' to achieve his objective quickly and decisively, and then withdrew forces in order to avoid the possibility of fighting a counterinsurgency war. So, while the largest American use of force, since the 1970s, may have looked as if it had exorcized the ghost of Vietnam, the reality was quite different. The war was fought according to its strictures. Yet, while the US was learning the wrong lessons about its new-found capabilities, others were drawing their own conclusions from the conflict. As Freedman notes, 'The very success of Operation Desert Storm … made it less likely that future enemies would fight in a way that conformed to American preferences: accepting a conventional battlefield, where they would be comprehensively destroyed by superpower firepower'.[8] The rapid exit of US forces from Somalia, following the death of 18 US Rangers in Mogadishu, in 1993, proved the effectiveness of 'asymmetric warfare' and the lingering influence of the Vietnam syndrome. America's subsequent unwillingness to incur casualties in Haiti, Bosnia and Rwanda was further testimony to the legacy of this experience. While the attacks on the US in September 2001 undoubtedly raised the bar considerably in support of the use of military force to defend America and to vanquish its foreign enemies, the assumption that this was a licence to act at will has subsequently been proved false by American policy since Iraq, as this chapter will demonstrate.[9]

George W. Bush and the creation of the Iraq syndrome

In the responses to the September 11 attacks, with the Pentagon taking the role of lead agency, George W. Bush and his advisers were keen to use force in a transformative way. While his predecessors had merely contained Iraq and reacted to acts of violence, Bush was confident that he could remake Afghanistan and Iraq and, through them, transform the entire Middle East.[10] While President Wilson had wanted to 'make the world safe for democracy' in 1919, George W. Bush went one further, wanting to make the world democratic in order to be safe.[11] For him, the world's most powerful military could destroy a despot and his army and, in so doing, allow freedom to blossom. It was a most ambitious foreign policy agenda and one that was backed by the most permissive domestic mandate of modern times, witnessed by the passage of the Authorization for Use of Military Force Act, 2001.[12] Yet, in its execution, it failed at nearly every step, turning the swift decapitation of the regime into a bloody insurgency by deploying too few troops, failing to plan the post-invasion period, disbanding the Iraqi army and seemingly flouting the rules of war through mass detentions and torture.[13] In its planning and execution, it deliberately sought to eschew all the lessons and legacies of Vietnam. Secretary Rumsfeld established his office as lead agency, reversing the military's dominance in operational planning and insisting on a small footprint force rather than 'overwhelming force'.[14] Buoyed by optimism from the first Gulf War, it ignored the criteria that Weinberger had warned were necessary. But, by acting as if it were both invincible and immune to any limitations on its freedom of action, the Bush administration tested the wisdom of its preventive invasion model to destruction. In doing so, it not only revived the Vietnam syndrome that it had sought to vanquish, but it added to the syndrome's effects.

As Freedman argued, the resulting Iraq syndrome posed 'an even more serious challenge to US foreign policy than the Vietnam syndrome did', because it called into question 'not only the wisdom of intervention but the integrity of US intelligence and judgement about what poses a direct threat to US national security'. Like Vietnam, this war led to a questioning of the White House's judgement, but this time that questioning extended to all of government, if not all politics. While in many ways both conflicts were wars of choice, the fact that Vietnam was responsive in the context of containment while the Iraq war was presented as pre-emptive left additional problems in its wake. For the general public, the war was justified on the basis of the threat of weapons of mass destruction, and the fact that none were found in Iraq was consequently seen by many to delegitimize the war. For them, America fought what Barack Obama called a 'dumb war' based on a bad judgement of faulty intelligence. Not only, therefore, did Iraq puncture the myth of the transformative power of the US military, it also questioned the competence of America's leaders to judge the veracity of future threats. This ensured that all subsequent calls to arms based on intelligence data would be treated with extreme scepticism. Attempts by Israel and its Congressional allies to get the Obama adminisration to respond to the 'imminent' threat of an Iranian nuclear weapon in the following years were discounted in this context.

The Iraq syndrome therefore went much deeper than the Vietnam syndrome in that it concerned not just the issues that gave rise to debates about the political control of the military—how the military could ensure that it was not misused, and how it could ensure that the interventions it undertook were optimized for success. Instead, it brought into question the very idea of whether it was possible for political leaders to know whether any intervention would succeed, and whether the military had the capability to make it succeed if intervention was ever deemed necessary. In short, the difference is between considering how to intervene effectively and asking whether it is ever effective to intervene at all.

Obama and the use of force

The election of Barack Obama in 2008 was perhaps the first tangible manifestation of the Iraq syndrome. Obama was elected President because he was the antithesis of President George W. Bush. Internationally, he was immediately given the Nobel Peace Prize as a symbolic representation of that sentiment.[15] He won the Democratic Party nomination, in large part, because, unlike Hillary Clinton, Obama had opposed the invasion of Iraq in 2003.[16] He won the presidency on a platform of ending America's ground wars in Iraq and Afghanistan. Talking about his opposition to the Iraq War in January 2007, Obama exclaimed: 'I don't want to just end the war, but I want to end the mind-set that got us into war in the first place'.[17] A month later he expanded on this with regard to Iraq by stating: 'It's time to admit that no amount of American lives can resolve the political disagreements that lie at the heart of someone else's civil war'.[18]

As President, downplaying the resort to the use or threat of use of military force has been a constant theme. This was articulated most fully in his May 2010 National Security Strategy document which stated: 'We will draw on diplomacy, development, and international norms and institutions to help resolve disagreements, prevent conflict, and maintain peace, mitigating where possible the need for the use of force'.[19] In order to achieve these goals Obama sought an inclusive diplomatic approach which tried to utilize what power America had in the international system towards the creation of a multilateral approach to what it viewed as an increasingly multi-polar world. It was an approach not dissimilar to that adopted by President Jimmy Carter in the wake of the Vietnam War in the late 1970s. Indeed, Henry Kissinger described Obama's approach as a return to:

> some sort of concert diplomacy … in which groupings of great powers work together to enforce international norms. It is a kind of world order either without a dominating power or in which the potentially dominating power leads through self-restraint.[20]

An important aspect of that self-restraint was the need to prioritize cooperation in its relations with other great powers. It was for that reason that Obama sought to 'reset' relations with Russia, rekindled the START (Strategic Arms Reduction Talks) and concluded a treaty in 2010, and similarly sought to play down differences with China on human rights and other issues.[21] It was also in this vein that Obama reached out to Iran to seek a negotiated deal on the issue of Tehran's nuclear programme. Whereas George W. Bush had stated, 'The Iranians should not have a nuclear weapon, the capacity to have a nuclear weapon, or the knowledge as to how to make a nuclear weapon', for Obama this changed to the much less exacting statement that '[w]e will not allow Iran to get a nuclear weapon'.[22] By demanding less, Obama was at once drawing back the red line on the implicit threat of force and making a potential negotiated settlement more realizable. He was also signalling more generally the new attitude to force in the Iraq syndrome era. It was an attitude that also reflected the new reality that the US was in a much weaker position to make great demands of its interlocutors.[23]

Despite Obama's commitment to downplay the use of force and to end America's military involvement in Iraq and Afghanistan as quickly as possible, 2011 saw the US undertake a third military intervention in a Muslim country in the Middle East. Overruling the advice of his Secretary of Defense, Robert Gates, Obama endorsed the calls of the

League of Arab States for a humanitarian response to the murderous crackdown of the Gaddafi regime on the Libyan people.[24] Crucially, Obama only embarked upon this mission after securing a United Nations Security Council Resolution (1973), the endorsement of the League of Arab States and the active support of the NATO allies. Even more tellingly of the new mood in Washington, the US, in an unprecedented move, allowed its European allies to fly the majority of the combat missions and a Canadian general to assume overall command of the operation. According to one administration official, this new approach was characterized as 'leading from behind'.[25] For the administration, this was an attempt to demonstrate a less domineering, more pragmatic and cautious approach to a world in which Washington recognized both its limited capacity to shape events and the critical way its foreign policy was often perceived abroad. It was clearly shaped by the fatigue of having fought two long wars and the desire to ensure that the effort to rebuild America's image in the world was not damaged by being seen to lead a military campaign. Where its allies were able to lead and be seen to fulfil the combat role, they were encouraged to do so, while the US played the facilitator for the operation. This fitted the concert idea, playing down the role of the US as alliance leader, seeking to be more the invisible power than the indispensable power.

The impact of the Iraq syndrome here is interesting to note. While determined to avoid another military engagement on the ground, Obama was still willing to make foreign policy demands—that Gaddafi must go—backed by the threat and eventual use of surgical air strikes. Yet, despite the success of the decapitation of the regime, the desire to avoid another foreign policy commitment meant that neither the US nor its NATO allies followed through on the military action in Libya with meaningful efforts to support and stabilize the post-conflict situation. The result of this neglect left Libya as a haven for instability, lawlessness and Islamic insurgency.[26] Having actively removed Gaddafi, the Obama administration has been widely criticized for its failure to offer leadership and support in order to bring stability to Libya and, indeed, the region as a whole during its period of turmoil and transition. Ironically, and most controversially of all for the Obama administration, its actions in Libya also encouraged protesters elsewhere to believe that similar popular uprisings could also rely on active US support against their own dictators. In the case of Syria, as elsewhere, these expectations were to prove unjustified.

Encouraged by the international support for the uprising in Libya, in the spring of 2011, Syrian protesters demanded a public voice in the governing of their country. Their brutal suppression led to a long and bloody civil war, in which more than 160,000 people had been killed at the time of writing and millions displaced. Having demanded that the regime of Bashar al-Assad stand down in favour of free and fair elections, Washington failed to deliver the means to achieve this goal. Conscious of the myriad forces fighting Assad, many of whom had Islamist agendas, the Obama administration has procrastinated over whom to aid among the insurgents and how to aid them. More fundamentally, his strategy of American international restraint as a way of building influence and an international consensus among the great powers proved ineffective for facilitating an end to the Syrian crisis. Both China and Russia blocked all attempts through the UN to intervene, while Iran and Russia actively armed and aided Assad's regime against the rebels. Reports of divisions within the Obama administration, between the State Department, eager to actively arm the rebels, and a more cautious Pentagon, fearful of the blowback that could result from aiding inchoate groups, added further to the sense of division and the perception of indecisiveness and irresolution on the part of the White House.[27] Its own lack of clarity on when and where the US should intervene abroad was most dramatically demonstrated by its ad hoc responses to the unfolding conflict. The incident is worth closer examination as an example of the conflicting impulses within the Obama White House on the use of force in the post-Iraq War period and the prevailing mood in Washington against intervention.

The Syrian red line

What started in Syria as a call for popular representation has become a complex conflict with many actors and agendas that reflect competing religious, ethnic and political cleavages. Russian support for the regime has blocked any attempt at outside mediation; and support from Hezbollah and Iran, on the one hand, and Turkey, Qatar and Saudi Arabia, on the other, has ensured that the conflict has become ever more violent and intractable. While at one stage the rebel forces seemed to be making progress against the Assad regime, bringing the fighting to the outskirts of Damascus, the use of rockets and aerial bombing against rebel-held areas blunted this advance and entrenched the stalemate. This renewed offensive by the Assad regime followed the limited use of chemical weapons against rebel areas in early 2013. This transgression of the norm of non-use of chemical weapons, accompanied by fear that these munitions could fall into terrorist hands, violated previous warnings from the White House against their use. Indeed, at a press conference in August 2012, Obama, speaking extemporaneously, escalated the potential American stake in the conflict by stating: 'We have been very clear to the Assad regime, but also to other players on the ground, that a red line for us is [if] we start seeing a whole bunch of chemical weapons moving around or being utilized'. He continued: 'That would change my calculus'.[28] In crossing his own previous line of non-intervention, Obama put America's credibility at risk in the conflict. Once chemical weapons were used on a small scale, in 2013, the Obama administration tried to dismiss these as minor transgressions that did not themselves warrant a response. But, almost a year to the day after his 'red line' speech, an attack on 21 August 2013 in Damascus left a reported 1,429 people dead. As the President had threatened to respond to such an attack, all eyes fell on the White House.

Having avoided intervention in Syria for the very good reason that there were no good or easy options to intervene militarily, the US now felt obliged to act. What followed was an attempt to elicit support for military action of a 'limited' and 'calibrated' form. In an echo of the Kennedy administration's policy in Vietnam, Obama sought a calibrated, flexible response, designed to be robust enough to punish the Assad regime and thereby to deter further use of chemical weapons and reinforce the norm of non-use, but also sufficiently limited to avoid embroiling the US in a messy sectarian war, where the stakes and motivations of other players were a great deal larger than those of the US. This was a difficult case to argue and one that the Obama administration articulated in a way that demonstrated all the moral-political complexities and contradictions involved. Secretary of State John Kerry, for example, talked about air strikes as being 'limited', 'targeted' and 'unbelievably small', while Obama spelled out that they were not intended to target the leadership, that the US should not 'remove another dictator with force', that there would not be an extended air campaign like that over Libya, and that there would be no 'American boots on the ground'. And yet at the same time the administration justified its intention to intervene by describing the deaths of innocents 'foaming at the mouth, gasping for air', explaining that chemical weapon use was a 'crime against humanity' deserving to be punished by a mission to 'deter and degrade' Syrian forces, and that 'the United States military doesn't do pinpricks'.[29] The implication of the rhetoric was that the US would end this suffering, but the caveats and limitations also demonstrated that the US did not have the will to use the means to achieve that end.

In navigating this difficult position, Obama started out by explaining that he had 'resisted calls for military action, because we cannot resolve someone else's civil war through force, particularly after a decade of war in Iraq and Afghanistan', but, then, he went on immediately to argue that 'the situation changed, though, on August 21st, when Assad's government gassed to death over a thousand people'. What Obama failed to do, however, was to persuade people of the logic of the relationship between these two impulses. Attacking Assad in a limited way might deter him from further chemical use, but could not guarantee preventing it. And even if it did deter further chemical attacks, it would not stop the vast majority of the killings through rocket, bomb and shell-fire. It would also be an intervention in a civil war in such a limited way that it would show both the inability of the American military to end it decisively and the lack of American political will even to try. Nor would it have advanced the cause of a negotiated end to the conflict. It would likely have antagonized the other outside powers, Russia and Iran, which had a greater capacity than America to determine how and when the conflict would end. It would also have been an attack without international backing, or legal authority, and in the face of opposition from regional actors, such as Russia, Hezbollah and Iran, who might escalate their involvement in the crisis as a result of any such attack. It was not even evident that the US had a clear idea of the sort of solution that it would like to see in Syria, other than the departure of President Assad himself and his butchering henchmen. Indeed, the opposition to Assad was now so fractured, fratricidal and riddled with Jihadist fighters that it is not impossible to imagine many potential outcomes worse than the current situation.

The contradictions in the logic of the threat to use force resulted, in part, from the refusal of the British Parliament to back the US in its military threat. In the face of this, and having been criticized for not consulting Congress over the Libyan campaign, Obama surprised many by announcing a delay in the threatened strike in order to seek Congressional approval and, implicitly, responsibility for such an attack. As former Secretary of Defence Leon Panetta observed, this move was 'an almost certain way to scotch any action'. He judged that, by mid-2013, 'a majority of Congress could not agree on what day of the week it was, much less a resolution authorizing the use of force in the Middle East'.[30] Having effectively asked Congress to curtail his ability to threaten force, the Obama administration was left looking defeated on this issue. Panetta was not untypical in seeing this as a 'blow to American credibility'. He stressed that when 'the commander in chief draws a red line, it is critical that he act if it is crossed'.[31] Events interceded at this point, however, through the happenstance of an off-the-cuff remark by Secretary Kerry at a news conference, to the effect that military strikes could be averted if the Syrian government would agree to give up its chemical weapons under international control. The Russians seized on this announcement, explained that this was their idea, and offered to work with the Americans on its fulfilment. A plan that had initially been rejected by Washington because it meant working with, and therefore legitimizing, the Assad government, and that advanced the role and standing of Russia in the region, was now up and running. As it was impossible to stop the initiative that the Russians had taken, the plan also began to look like a face-saving way of addressing the issue of chemical weapons while allowing the US to back away from its plan for limited military strikes.

The artless symmetry of foreign policy by press conference misstatements, first Obama's and then Kerry's, led to much speculation as to what the episode meant for American foreign policy in the aftermath of the Iraq and Afghanistan wars. For some commentators, the end result is a vindication of Obama's agonized approach to the conflict and the use of chemical weapons. His instinct was not to get involved, and yet when he was provoked into threatening punitive air strikes, this proved enough to coerce the Syrian regime to accede to the Russian plan to internationalize the destruction of Assad's chemical weapons. For some observers President Assad's decision to join the Chemical Weapons Convention and to provide the Hague-based Organization for the Prohibition of Chemical Weapons (OPCW) with an inventory of its chemical capabilities as part of a plan for their phased destruction was a better result than could have been hoped, or planned, for a few weeks earlier.[32] The move was also popular in the US, where both public and Congressional opinion were not persuaded by the case for military action, and where support for the 'US–Russian' plan to dismantle Syria's chemical weapons capability within a year had 79 per cent approval.[33]

While Obama's Syria policy now looked better than it deserved to be at the height of the crisis in September 2013, it was hardly a model for how to make foreign policy. Nor was the problem over, by any means, whether that was defined as the issue of chemical weapons, the Syrian crisis in general, the turmoil of the Middle East more broadly, or the ability of the Obama administration to navigate an incredibly complex situation where there were no obvious or easy answers. In the absence of the American threat, Assad's compliance with the chemical disarmament process was slow and incomplete.[34] Worse still, there were further reports of chemical weapon use in Syria which the administration chose largely to ignore in the absence of a clear idea of how to respond to such evidence.[35]

To his critics, Obama's missteps over Syria demonstrate the clear lack of an active strategy. Other than moral condemnations and calls for a negotiated settlement, the US has offered little leadership over Syria and had an inconsistent attitude to when and why force should be used. In this context, the red line decision, such as it was, seemed to be an empty gesture, at odds with the approach. To many observers, America missed several opportunities to intervene more effectively through the use of air power, special forces, and arming the moderate rebels in order to strengthen their position against both Assad and the growing threat of Islamic State.[36] If the US strategy was not to get involved militarily, then why threaten intervention over one small aspect of the Syrian civil war? For Joe Klein of *Time*, Obama 'willingly jumped into a bear trap of his own creation' and 'in the process, he has damaged his presidency and weakened the nation's standing in the world'.[37] For his critics, this episode resulted from the tension between the impulse not to intervene and the desire still to call the shots. Obama, one of the most eloquent presidents of modern times, caught up in his own rhetoric, made demands of Assad on the assumption that the mere threat of action would prevail upon him. Yet, when the bluff was called, Obama recognized that the consequences of the use of force were so incalculable that restraint was called for. If the threat of military action was an attempt to give credibility to the 'red line' statement, however, then not striking Syria undermined that threat. Having presented the threat as being of modest and specific means and ends, and even then being unwilling, and in the end practically unable, to carry them out, both the administration and the US lost credibility as a result. But, interestingly, the Obama administration by its own actions and inactions clearly made the calculation, based on both the complexity of the situation and the lessons learned from the post-9/11 wars, that such a reputational hit was better than the alternative of US involvement in another 'dumb' war.[38]

While it can be contended that Obama's red line diplomacy advanced the internationalization of the Syrian civil war and arguably reduced, if not removed, the threat of further use of chemical weapons, it did so at the expense of America's standing in the region. In this sense, the Syrian crisis fits the wider pattern of US diplomacy in the post-Iraq period. In face of the political turmoil in the wider Middle East, with revolutionary forces bent on the removal of unrepresentative regimes and the reduction in regional influence of external actors such as the US, the Obama administration presented a faltering and inconsistent response. His administrations judged that Assad would fall quickly and that the Arab Spring was best left to run its own course. On both counts those judgements turned out to be wrong. As a result, his critics felt vindicated in asking why the US and its NATO allies acted to prevent the Libyan army from committing atrocities against the civilian population in Benghazi, but failed to intervene in similar circumstances in Syria.

The unarticulated answers to these questions concerned, in part, the limits of US power in the region and, in part, the legacy of the Iraq syndrome. Obama rightly calculated that US military power could facilitate the allied decapitation of the Gaddafi regime without either engaging US ground forces or risking America's reputation in the region. But the action would offer no more than that, for fear of entanglement.[39] With regard to Syria, the calculation consistently looked both more complex and more difficult. While previous administrations would have more actively sought to train and arm friendly forces in an effort to shape the future direction of post-conflict Syria, to raise the costs to its enemies and to stand by and reassure its regional allies, the Obama administration resisted such calls, limiting its early efforts to non-lethal aid.[40] To have armed the rebels would at least have matched his actual policy to his rhetorical demands, but because the crisis was so complex and the potential unintended consequences so unpredictable, it was easier and wiser, in this view, to stay out of it. An alternative suggested by some conservative critics was that Obama should desist from calling for regime change and 'swallow the bitter pill of tolerating Assad', in the pragmatic realization that the US was powerless to engineer an ideal solution and that many alternatives might actually be worse.[41] For these critics, at least, such a policy would have the benefits of consistency and predictability, rather than one moving from 'bluster to retreat' in a way that damaged US credibility.[42] For Obama, however, the legacy of Iraq appears to require action of the kind enjoined by the Hippocratic oath—'First, do no harm'—with the result that the US was reluctant to take a decisive position of even limited active intervention on either side in this conflict.

The Obama Doctrine

Having been widely criticized over the Syrian red line episode, the Obama administration was keen to articulate the coherence of its policy on the use of force. Interestingly, its experiences, coupled with the President's initial approaches, seem to have resulted in the White House becoming progressively more ambivalent about the use of military power as his tenure progressed. It would appear from this evidence that the influence of the Iraq syndrome—the renewed, nagging and sometimes paralyzing belief that any large-scale US military intervention abroad must be doomed to practical failure and moral iniquity—has been reinforced by his own experience in office, such as the limited 'surge' in Afghanistan and the chaos rampant in Libya. As Landler observes:

He has learned that even 100,000 American troops were not enough to save Afghanistan from the predations of the Taliban. He has learned that while NATO airstrikes could avert a slaughter of civilians in Benghazi, intervention could not save Libya from becoming a violent, chaotic failing state.

He has also learned the lesson from the Syrian 'red line' episode that it is imprudent to make commitments, in a press conference or elsewhere, that you do not have the ability or will to follow through. Over the chemical weapons issue, Obama was engaging in an ad hoc policy but, when his bluff was called, the dominant influence that determined his response was that of the Iraq syndrome.

The major articulation of the administration's doctrine on the use of force was presented in May 2014 at West Point, a venue chosen to mark the distinction between Obama's approach and that of his predecessor, as it had been the venue where in June 2002 Bush laid out the case for preventive war. In this address, Obama played to his familiar themes of ending a decade of war, withdrawing all combat forces from Afghanistan by 2016, and having ended the war in Iraq.[43] He also reinforced several of the themes on the use of force debate of the post-Vietnam period, themes which the Iraq syndrome had resurrected. For a speech to a military audience, in part aimed to reassure allies, the tone was remarkably antithetical to the use of force. Speaking of casualties on his watch, the Commander-in-Chief spoke of how he was 'haunted by those deaths' and 'haunted by those wounds'. He quoted General Eisenhower, speaking at West Point in 1947, stating: 'War is mankind's most tragic and stupid folly; to seek or advise its deliberate provocation is a black crime against all men'. And he argued that, since the Second World War, 'some of our most costly mistakes came not from our restraint, but from our willingness to rush into military adventures without thinking through the consequences, without building international support and legitimacy for our action, without levelling with the American people about the sacrifices required'. He continued: 'Tough talk often draws headlines, but war rarely conforms to slogans'. In making the case for a more limited use of force, Obama also sought to caricature the arguments of his critics. As a *Washington Post* editorial put it: 'Mr. Obama marshalled a virtual corps of straw men, dismissing those who "say that every problem has a military solution", who "think military intervention is the only way for America to avoid looking weak", who favour putting "American troops into the middle of [Syria's] increasingly sectarian civil war", who propose "invading every country that harbours terrorist networks" and who think that "working through international institutions ... or respecting international law is a sign of weakness"'.[44] To this list might also have been added another straw man, arguing that 'U.S. military action cannot be the only—or even primary—component of our leadership in every instance'. He echoed the words of the former chairman of the Joint Chiefs of Staff: 'Just because we have the best hammer does not mean that every problem is a nail'. In presenting his opposition only to extreme examples, which no critic was actually proposing, Obama used a rhetorical device to ensure maximum agreement among his audience. But he also went further in limiting the occasions when the US should engage militarily. Beyond the defence of 'core interests', Obama explained:

> when issues of global concern do not pose a direct threat to the United States ... when crises arise that stir our conscience or push the world in a more dangerous direction but do not directly threaten us, then the threshold for military action must be higher. In such circumstances, we should not go it alone. Instead, we must mobilize allies and partners to take collective action. We have to broaden our tools to include diplomacy and development, sanctions and isolation, appeals to international law, and, if just, necessary and effective, multilateral military action ... because collective action in these circumstances is more likely to succeed, more likely to be sustained, less likely to lead to costly mistakes.[45]

It is here that the tone and content of the speech come together. In setting out the limited circumstances of when the use of force would be justified, Obama was echoing Caspar Weinberger's Doctrine of 1984, which sought to institutionalize the lessons of Vietnam. In raising the threshold for the use of force, however, the Obama administration could be accused of inviting its enemies to speculate about which actions directly threatened US national interests which did not, just as North Korea did in 1950 and Iraq in 1991. Similarly, Obama's formulation would have prevented previous unilateral uses of US military force, such as the operations against Libya in 1986, Panama in 1989, Somalia in 1992–3 and Haiti in 2004, actions which were post-Vietnam attempts to re-establish the credibility of the US use of force. Given the recent history of multinational operations, from Kosovo to Afghanistan, with their multiple rules of engagement and arguments over target sets, this could also amount to a real limitation on the threat or use of force by Washington.

The assertion that 'for the foreseeable future, the most direct threat to America, at home and abroad, remains terrorism' can also be interpreted as resulting from the Iraq syndrome. Despite having pledged to end the 'global war on terrorism' and to downplay the significance of terrorism since the Bush era, the administration's focus on such operations allowed it to conceptualize the use of force and foreign interventions as being restricted to limited strike operations and to support and training for affected states. This theme also fitted with the Obama administration's increased use of drone strikes and other targeted killings: operations that allowed the containment of foreign enemies rather than dealing with the political and situational issues from which they arose. It is a focus that also allowed it largely to ignore, as this speech did, the need to deter Russia and China militarily. Instead, the Obama administration's strategy was to stress the multilateral and international institutional levels of diplomatic influence, as it did over Ukraine, where the President argued:

> Because of American leadership, the world immediately condemned Russian actions, Europe and the G-7 joined with us to impose sanctions, NATO reinforced our commitment to Eastern European allies, the IMF is helping to stabilize Ukraine's economy, OSCE monitors brought the eyes of the world to unstable parts of Ukraine … [and] this mobilization of world opinion and international institutions served as a counterweight to Russian propaganda and Russian troops on the border and armed militias in ski masks.[46]

Yet this argument failed to acknowledge that such an approach had no tools to reverse the annexation of Crimea, or stop the further destabilization of areas of Ukraine with Russian minority populations, where Moscow placed a higher priority on these goals than on its global reputation. Such an approach might be successful if it included all the great powers, acting in concert to check the actions of rogue states, an approach the US followed in forging the coalition in 1991 over Iraq's invasion of Kuwait. Where the irresponsible behaviour of the great powers was part of the problem, it was a much less persuasive strategy.

Indeed, the very articulation of a policy where multilateral diplomatic instruments were the preferred tools of his statecraft was seen by some critics as likely not only to embolden the actions of Russia in its 'near abroad', but, also to increase the likelihood that China would escalate its disputes with its Asian neighbours. Indeed, a Chinese general even used the example of the US response to the Ukraine crisis to suggest to America's Asian allies that Washington would be an unreliable partner in any future conflict because it suffered from 'ED', by which he meant 'extended deployment' but also 'the male type of ED problem—erectile dysfunction'.[47] It is clear from this that at least General Zhu Chenghu believed there was something akin to the Iraq syndrome afflicting the Obama administration's foreign policy and that this, in turn, affected the virility of the American security guarantee to its allies. The Chinese, rhetorically, but perhaps also in practice, were happy to exploit this perception in relations with their regional neighbours.

Conclusions

The election and subsequent re-election of Barack Obama were symbolic of a nation exhausted and disillusioned by more than a decade of expensive, bloody and inconclusive war in which over a trillion dollars and over 7,000 American service personnel's lives were expended. Obama promised to end those wars and the mentality that committed America to those military engagements. He recognized the damage done to America's reputation globally by the Iraq War in particular, to the credibility of American military power in general, and to the notions of unipolarity built upon it, as encapsulated by the Bush administration's strategy of pre-emption. While, in many ways, Obama epitomized the American public and political mood at the end of the Bush administration, he also offered leadership in articulating that sentiment. For this reason, it is difficult to decide how much of the approach adopted by Obama was due to the Iraq syndrome (in Freedman's words, 'the renewed, nagging and sometimes paralyzing belief that any large-scale US military intervention abroad is doomed to practical failure and moral iniquity') and how much came from the personality of the President himself. Distinguishing what was cause from what was effect is difficult in this instance since 'President Obama' was the product of his opposition to war. Yet it is important to note that the effect of the Iraq syndrome predated Obama. In 2008, towards the end of the Bush administration, the Russian invasion of Georgia, involving real tanks and hundreds of deaths, provoked no noticeable response from a president who, only a few years earlier, had argued for Georgia's admission to NATO. In its post-Iraq torpor, the Bush administration had nothing meaningful to say to this provocative Russian act.

America's appetite for risk in the form of the use of force was blunted by its traumatic experience in Iraq. This also had an impact on public support for foreign policy engagement more generally. A poll conducted by the Pew Research organization found that, for the first time since 1964, a majority (52 per cent) agreed that the US should 'mind its own business internationally and let other countries get along the best they can on their own'; while 38 per cent disagreed. Similarly, 80 per cent agree with the statement: 'We should not think so much in international terms but concentrate more on our own national prob-lems and building up our strength and prosperity here at home'.[48] The success of the Tea Party and the election of Donald Trump as President are also evidence of this current of thinking. From this, it is possible to deduce that Obama's approach to foreign policy was predicated on an understanding of the Iraq syndrome without the need to articulate it, as such. He embraced the idea that military force could not solve other people's civil wars, that interventions could do more harm than good—both in places where force was applied and in the eyes of inter-national opinion—and that popular support for further entanglements was severely limited.

Obama ended US combat operations in Iraq in December 2011 and avoided looking weak while doing so by 'surging' additional troops into Afghanistan. But, as Bob Woodward reported in 2010, his focus was always 'about how we're going to hand it off and get out of Afghanistan … I'm not doing long-term nation-building'.[49] His announcement in 2014 that all combat forces would leave Afghanistan was an attempt to make good on that promise before he left office. There was consider-able popular support for this approach in the US and Obama has made a virtue of America's diminished standing internationally by stressing the differences between his approach and that of his predecessor. Obama's willingness to apologize for the excesses of the Bush administration and to offer a less militarized and dogmatic foreign policy proved popular at home and abroad—and appeared to reap benefits with Iran, as a historic nuclear agreement was reached in early 2016. In Europe in particular, popular and political opinion broadly supported this apparent willingness to move beyond Bush's view of the world and to end combat operations of which other NATO states were becoming weary.

Yet his approach was not universally popular or effective. An American president must satisfy a multiplicity of different audiences, and what works for the US and Western Europe could cause concern elsewhere. His willingness to leave Iraq and Afghanistan without having ensured their future stability, prosperity or even viability as functioning states was seen by many as troubling. In the Middle East, key American allies, such as Israel and Saudi Arabia, saw what they perceived as the abandonment of Iraq and Afghanistan as problematic for the region. The loss of Fallujah and Mosul in Iraq to the Islamic State of Iraq and Syria (ISIS), and the potential return of the Taliban in Afghanistan, were seen by many as creating potential havens for extremists, which were a danger to the region and wider world. Obama's willingness essentially to admit defeat in the face of these challenges, and to withdraw without leaving behind the prospect of sustainable governmental authority able to provide security and prevent insurgency, was regarded as the abandonment of previous commitments to the region. Such actions are perceived by some to undermine confidence in America's guarantee to its treaty allies more widely. If America was unwilling to fight for what it previously categorized as its 'vital interests', such as a non-threatening and stable Iraq, would it be willing to fight for its allies in Eastern Europe, the Middle East or Asia?

In this context, Obama's announcement that the US would only be prepared to fight unilaterally for core interests, which included commitments to treaty allies, caused further concern for the signals it sent. Defining core interests more narrowly could invite other states to pick away at interests that were not so defined, as Freedman observed: 'It is notable that Russia and China have taken more risks with Ukraine and Vietnam, neither allies of the United States, than with, say, Estonia or Japan'.[50] Obama's pledge to stand by such treaty allies did not help those outside the fold or reassure those who were facing external provocations. Making statements about the folly of war, about the need to avoid 'doing stupid stuff', while popular at home, was not without its consequences abroad.[51]

The US, as the dominant power since the Second World War, has prevented major war in the international system by guaranteeing its allies' security. In order for this to be credible, Washington had to be 'ready to threaten major war on behalf of its allies'.[52] Despite efforts to reassure allies in Asia of America's commitments and despite force deployments to Eastern Europe in the wake of the Ukrainian crisis, the Obama administration acted and spoke in a way that indicated the influence of the Iraq syndrome in its foreign policy disposition. But, as Michael Gerson observed, Obama's 'doctrine of risk aversion can only be justified by minimizing the seriousness of global challenges and miniaturizing the role of presidential leadership', which is what was displayed in relation to the challenges presented by the emergence of chaotic Jihadist havens in the Middle East, by the Russian actions in Crimea and by China's provocations in the East China Sea.[53] While understandable in relation to the influence of the Iraq syndrome, Obama's opposition to the use of force, by characterizing it as 'dumb war', was unhelpful. As the Russians masterfully displayed in their 'influence operations' in Ukraine, the tools available to influence events were multifaceted.[54] Obama himself, however, despite his willingness to use drones in Afghanistan, Pakistan and Yemen and to kill Bin Laden in Pakistan, seemed committed to embracing and embodying the implications of the limitations of American power and, with them, a risk aversion regarding the use of force that stemmed from what Lawrence Freedman identified in 2005 as the Iraq syndrome.

12

BRITAIN'S JOURNEY TO A NATIONAL SECURITY APPROACH AND THE EVOLUTION OF A DEFENCE ACADEMY

John Gearson

Over twenty or so years, from the early 1990s, a project developed to deliver a national security approach in Britain. Partly as a response to a changing threat environment, governments dropped rigid notions of internal and external security, in favour of an extended and broader concept of national security. The goal of a national security approach advanced significantly in that time, but it remained very much a work in progress, as demonstrated not only by some key events, but also by the release of the November 2015 UK National Security Strategy and, concurrently, and indeed embedded within it, the Strategic Defence and Security Review of 2015. A number of important innovations were initiated over two decades: the development of the UK's counter-terrorism strategy known as CONTEST, the publication of the country's first National Security Strategy in 2008, and the establishment of a National Security Council in 2010 were three prominent examples.

Alongside such developments, there was increasing recognition that the UK government could organize its central policy machinery for protecting national security more effectively.

It is a journey that began during the Cold War, passed through the end of history (and its return), stumbled through the rise of the non-state terrorist organizations as these challenges to be considered in strategic terms, even if not as opponents capable of strategic effect, emerging into the confusing public glare of citizen-based security, accountability, interdepartmental working, the chill winds of austerity, and the resultant remaking of what Peter Hennessy has termed the 'secret state', but which perhaps should now be called the 'secretive but unsecret state'.[1] This journey both intertwined with and paralleled the development of several careers, including my own and, at the fore-front, Freedman's.

The national security project, in various ways, focused the minds of the security policy-engaged academic community—especially the ever-growing part of it at King's College London, led and, in many ways, inspired by Lawrence Freedman—just as it did parts of the British policymaking establishment itself. It did so, even if, at times, it appeared that neither the academy nor the UK's nascent national security structures had a clear idea of where this project was leading. But the endeavour significantly narrowed the academic–policymaker gap thanks in no small part to the example offered by Freedman to a generation of scholars and a number of policymakers and their advisers. To this should be added the generation of students who were introduced to broadening horizons and benefited from the academic-policy alliance, including, increasingly, those in military education, where the involvement of the academy, again under Freedman's leadership, grew from nothing to become a flourishing phenomenon—an important leitmotif in the evolution of the national security approach. The present chapter will chart the evolution of this approach, starting in the 1980s during the Cold War, and following it through various key points in its history.

Berlin, bombs and the beginnings of the national security approach

In the mid-1980s, I almost came to King's to do a master's in war studies. The Department of War Studies was not quite a one-man band (there were four and one half-time academics), much smaller than the giant it would become. Having got past the fearsome gatekeeper, Wendy Everett, somehow Freedman was convinced that I should join the MA programme at one week's notice. After withdrawing from the programme to take up a job offer, I returned to begin an MA degree in 1988. A proposal for PhD research during that year led to my appointment as a King's College Scholar and to doctoral research under Freedman into nuclear contingency planning during the Berlin Wall crisis of 1958–61. Under the thirty-year rule for release of government papers, this study was set to be the first assessment of the relevant material and the originality of the thesis was guaranteed—or, so it seemed. The Cold War had not quite ended when the vetting process was undertaken and, after several months at Kew Gardens, in what was then the Public Record Office, it became clear that all of the nuclear contingency planning documents had been held back: so, no original military planning assessment files, no original thesis and, on that basis, no doctorate.

The initial research approach to the Berlin Wall crisis had judged the crisis in many ways as national security policy was conceived in the years of the Cold War, as one in which the politics had been removed or at least were frozen by the realities of the mega-security challenge of facing down the Soviet Union for which defence planning took primacy. And yet, Berlin was that irritating and intractable problem that appeared to defy military and diplomatic logic. How could one defend an enclave without recourse to nuclear deterrent threats, while seeking to de-escalate tensions and normalize relations between NATO and the Warsaw Pact. The eventual thesis, *The Limits of Interests and Force*, reflected what would now be understood as an emerging national security approach by King's academics and British policymakers, considering the crisis in all its aspects and not through a narrow defence-planning prism alone. The limits of interests and force have occupied many security policy academics ever since, as the Cold War ended (and the nuclear planning documents were then actually released, but too late for that thesis) and Britain moved into the 'end of history' period and a time of apparent choice in national security planning.

The nature of security came to be discussed in different ways in this period, of course. No longer solely thought of in terms of the state, the concept embraced individuals and groups and was thought about in ways transcending national perspectives. Furthermore, the deliverers of security were not just seen as states, but now embraced the private sector, non-governmental organizations, and nature itself for some.

However, not all British security planning was subject to choice. The campaign by the Irish Republican Army (IRA) against the British presence in Northern Ireland had continued throughout these years of upheaval in interstate and interbloc relations. Bombings in the province and even on the mainland had become a normal fact of life—lest we forget, the campaign, such as the Balcombe Street gang's targeting of restaurants and pubs in the 1970s, presaged some of today's so-called novel terrorist tactics of Mumbai or Paris-style attacks. The IRA's targeting of the City of London (a previous target as well, including the attempted bombing of the Stock Exchange) in the early 1990s, using two of the largest explosive devices seen in the capital since the Second World War, was an important stage in the realization of the need for a national security approach.

The Baltic Exchange bombing of 1992 and, even more so, the Bishopsgate bombing of 1993 shocked the City's elders; and Lawrence Freedman was asked to undertake a threat assessment for the City as it pondered how to respond and to avoid a riptide of foreign financial institutions leaving the City to alternative centres such as Paris and Frankfurt. As his research assistant, I spent months talking to institutions across the Square Mile and wider Greater London about the nature of the threat and their expectations of security provided by the state. What became very apparent was that total security was not expected or desired, but a much greater level of national and local resilience was: poor disaster recovery would not be tolerated. The initial estimated costs of the bombings ran into the billions, which, although later downgraded, did focus minds. Even so, the private sector repeatedly complained about the lack of transparency by the security services and the extent to which they were treated as supplicants of the state purveyors of security. In fact, it became apparent that resilience (then a novel term) was not achievable without the co-opting of the public themselves and the private sector more widely, which increasingly owned and operated the structures of what came to be termed critical national infrastructure. The City adopted unprecedented security measures in the aftermath, including the closing of entry and exit points, the monitoring of all vehicles entering the City, and the deployment of police officers on the streets in unprecedented numbers. Disaster recovery schemes were encouraged and CCTV coverage from private sources was integrated with traditional security systems.

The City demonstrated itself to be better defended and also better able to deal with the consequences of any future attack. And the appearance worked: when the IRA returned to target the financial services sector (a uniquely attractive target in terms of office value), they attacked Docklands, which was outside the City's security cordon. This was an example both of deterrence by denial and of a sector more resilient to any external shock. However, this was not a result of central government machinery delivering a national security approach. The response was integrated and cross-sector in its outlook because it was not delivered by the central government, but by a city corporation with unique powers and, crucially, its own police force, which decided to prioritize defence against truck bombings and the delivery of effective disaster recovery measures. The Security Service (MI5) coordinated an intensive counterterrorism (CT) operation in the months following Bishopsgate and discovered 'materials for six car bombs which PIRA [Provisional IRA] had intended to use to continue its attacks on the Square Mile'.[2]

In the City's approach one can perhaps see the genesis of what eventually became the Civil Contingencies Secretariat (CCS), built on the desire to adopt a national security approach, although the policy driver of its establishment was the fuel protests of 2000, when the distribution of petrol and diesel across Britain was disrupted by blockades at oil refineries and distribution depots by farmers and hauliers, with the cabinet apparently amazed to find that they could apparently lose control so easily—demonstrating the limits of interests and force again.[3]

The changing nature of security

Politicians and officials everywhere recognize that the first duty of government is security—a principle familiar in the political philosophy of Thomas Hobbes and John Locke.[4] This impetus can be seen through all of the iterations of the UK National Security Strategy: 'We are agreed that the first duty of government is to safeguard our national security … and we will fulfil that duty'.[5] Rooted in eighteenth-century common law and doctrines of allegiance and protection between sovereign and people, the concept came to define understandings of the role of government, for writers such as John Locke and Adam Smith, including ultimately the protection of the state against invasion. In this way the protection of the state became the goal of security. Such concepts of national security had come to be challenged over many decades and especially following the end of the Cold War. Constructivist security theorists and the Copenhagen school, emblematized by Barry Buzan, argued for a shift away from state and military threats as drivers of policy and called for a focus instead on individuals and communities, a call latterly promoted by so-called critical theorists. As one critic has noted:

> The traditional notion of security as state security has been contested. The critical security studies and human security literatures have done much to dispel the notion that "security" is an objective, rational, apolitical and unproblematic concept.[6]

National security, therefore, was apparently what policymakers wanted it to be: in effect, a political rather than an objective assessment.

The 2009 update to the first UK National Security Strategy of 2008 reflected some of this thinking: 'Providing security for the nation, safeguarding our citizens and our way of life, remains the most important responsibility of government'.[7] In his introduction, Gordon Brown stated:

> In the past, Governments thought about national security as being about protecting the state and its interests. This remains important, but the nature of the risks we face in today's world means our approach to national security must be focused just as much on protecting individual citizens and businesses.[8]

Then again, if definitions of security are sought, one quickly is taken to concepts of 'the condition of being secure' or 'feelings' and even 'a freedom from doubt' as sources of security. In the Cold War this would in all likelihood have been seen as the freedom from armed conflict. In the new post-Cold War world it could mean something very different, as national security became dependent on the feelings of security felt by actors other than the state, including the state's own citizens and even some of its violent opponents—away and at home. The leader of the 7/7 suicide terrorists, Mohammad Sidique Khan, in a video message found after their murderous attacks on the London transport network, stated: 'Until we feel security you will be our targets … We are at war and I am a soldier. Now you too will taste the reality of this situation'.[9]

In these post-Cold War years, the growing incidence of terrorism and the rise of non-state actors, as well as what became fashionable to term 'wicked problems', pressed up against economic constraints and widening concepts of a Responsibility to Protect (R2P) and later notions of duty of care across all levels. If national security had broadened so much, how to bound it? As one observer wrote: 'The obvious shortcoming of the new ideas or principles of security of the 1990s … is their inclusiveness: the dizzying complexity of a political geometry … in which individuals, groups, states, and international organizations have responsibilities for international organizations, states, groups, and individuals'.[10]

What slowly dawned on many working in the national security space was the realization that no department or agency could do it on its own. Rather, together each could contribute to what had become a process, not a competition. Is mass migration a national security issue or only a concern of national security if Jihadists are disguising themselves as migrants to access target countries? Non-military issues such as cyber security, counterterrorism, organized crime and border controls have been included in the British National Security Strategy documents now, but, as the concept broadens, how can governments maintain strategic focus, and therefore how can they prioritize in the absence of a clear understanding of what national security is and what it is not? A Joint King's Policy Institute–Institute of Government report in 2015 offered the following definition: 'Broadly construed, national security encompasses defence, intelligence, foreign affairs (including trade and development assistance), internal security and civil contingencies'.[11]

Such a broad definition leads to a wide range of hard-to-quantify costs. Defence spending, the largest component, has of course been on a downward trajectory for many years, as shown in Figure 1, from the Defence Select Committee.[12] However, this was not the whole story. An IPPR *Report into National Security* in 2009 suggested that national security spending had spread out well beyond defence and accounted for three per cent of GDP.

Taking the total annual budgets for 2007/8 of the Ministry of Defence (MoD) and the Foreign and Commonwealth Office (FCO), relevant streams of the Home Office budget and ten per cent of the budget of the Department for International Development (DFID), the figure for 2007/8 comes to approximately £43 billion, or three per cent of GDP.[13]

In fact, despite cuts in defence spending, overall national security spending actually increased in the 2010 Strategic Defence and Security Review (SDSR), in which the government said it would increase funding to the Conflict Pool up to £300m. The National Cyber Security Programme was given £650m of new investment over four years, and a new multi-agency National Maritime Information Centre was planned at a cost of £450,000. Funding for counterterrorism and intelligence had exceeded £3.5bn by this stage and spending on flood management was expected to top £800,000 by 2010/11. Writing for the Royal United Services Institute in 2015, before the 2015 SDSR, Malcolm Chalmers estimated a core national security outlay of about £56bn, plus a planned Joint Security Fund of £1.5bn by the end of the Parliament, giving a total of £57.5bn, excluding the national security elements of the National Crime Agency (£427m), FCO (£660m) and the borders and immigration service (£445m):[14] almost £60bn—nearer four per cent of GDP than three—a very significant piece of government spending. As American political scientist Arnold Wolfers noted in the 1950s:

> Efforts for security are bound to be experienced as a burden; security after all is nothing but the absence of the evil of insecurity, a negative value so

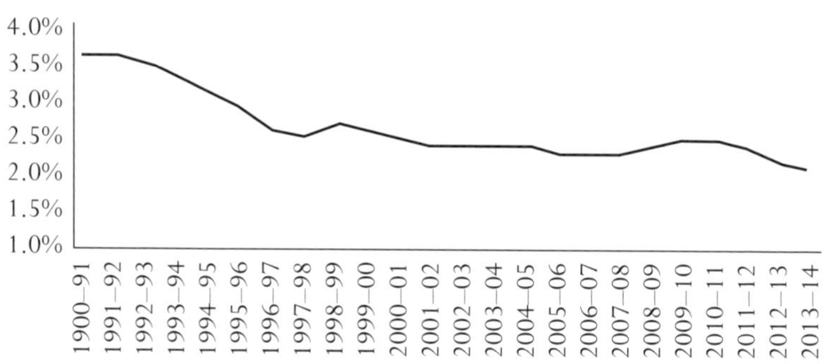

Figure 1: Defence spending trend. Source: House of Commons Defence Select Committee

to speak … Nations will be inclined to minimize these efforts … Together with the extent of the external threats, numerous domestic factors such as national character, tradition, preferences and prejudices will influence the level of security which a nation chooses to target.[15]

There is more to security than conventional defence.

Dealing with security strategically: towards the defence academy

National security is an expensive policy area, focused on dealing with a concept—security—that is highly subjective, with individual, national and international levels, and fundamentally about perception. That perception increasingly became one of insecurity rather than security on the part of the public, despite the sources of insecurity at the top level (nuclear war) being much less severe after the end of the Cold War. Government's perceived and actual ability to control events diminished and, with the rise of non-state actors, state dominance of security dissipated. As such, there could be little surprise that policymakers sought to define what those feelings were on behalf of their citizens. While usually couched in terms of threats, the more interesting questions perhaps were how to manage the risks to the security affecting their citizens and how to balance the costs that this entailed with the level of risk that they had to accept. For that, policymakers needed to be able to think strategically.

Strategy was perhaps easier when national security was conceived of in institutional terms during the Cold War and within the 'secret state' that grew up to defend against the Soviet threat (although this did not seem so easy at the time to many students of strategy). At the end of the 1990s Freedman noted the following in an influential article:

The link between the military and political spheres is the realm of strategy. If there is a revolution, it is one in strategic affairs, and the result of significant changes in both the objectives in pursuit of which governments might want to use armed forces, and in the means that they might employ. Its most striking feature is its lack of fixed form. The new circumstances and capabilities do not proscribe one strategy, but extend the range of strategies that might be followed.[16]

The problem was that many of our structures for national security appeared ill suited to respond to such challenges.

The UK's armed forces, while generally conceived of as status quo actors and conservative (with a small 'c'), had actually begun to grasp some of these difficult challenges in the defence reviews which followed the end of the Cold War. By the middle of the 1990s, the concept of jointery (or 'thinking purple'), whereby the three services were encouraged to work together, was well established in the MoD and found institutional and academic expression in the bold decision to do away with the three individual service staff colleges of the Army, the Royal Navy and Royal Air Force, creating a new Joint Services Command and Staff College (JSCSC) in 1997, after protracted negotiations led by Freedman, supported by independent academics from King's College working in partnership with military directing staff.

The subject area of terrorism and asymmetric threats grew in importance at the JSCSC in the later years of the 1990s. This focused attention on the security, rather than defence policy, aspects of international affairs, with good reason. This, after all, was the period after the first World Trade Center attack; after the use of sarin gas by the Aum Shinryko sect on the Tokyo underground, the first non-state group to develop, weaponize and deploy a biochemical agent without state support; and after the Khobar Towers attack on US forces based in Saudi Arabia. US scholars were developing thinking around the idea of a New Age of Terrorism (several years before 9/11) which, though much of their analysis was contested, did take the growth of networked international terrorism seriously. This was not mirrored in the UK, where international terrorism was only slowly assuming greater importance in the defence academy's work, and this relative lack of interest in the subject area was mirrored in UK intelligence and security structures. While it later emerged that the first al-Qa'ida-inspired plot against the UK was disrupted by MI5 in 2000, the reality was that Britain saw little threat to the UK from such manifestations of terror in this period. As the head of CT policing noted in 2007: 'During the 1990s many people believed that the extremists and dissidents from overseas regimes who were active in the UK were, if anything, pursuing agendas against foreign governments, and posed little or no threat to the UK'.[17]

Osama Bin Laden was seen primarily as a potential financier of terrorism; really only after the US embassy bombings in East Africa in

1998 and the US response with cruise missile strikes against al-Qa'ida targets in Afghanistan and Sudan, did UK intelligence assessments start to see state-sponsored terrorism as being supplanted by transnational Islamist terrorism.[18] The Security Service had, though, started to study the problem of radicalization as early as 1995. But the threat was not seen as likely to lead to attacks inside the UK.[19] According to Peter Hennessy, in the 1980s and 1990s, MI5 deployed 'about half a dozen officers' on international counterterrorism.[20] Under-resourced agencies do not tend to go looking for future threats, but rather concentrate on those of the moment, while critics of intelligence failures rarely are shown to have been supporters of increased budgets for security structures before significant events.

While the end of the Cold War and the rise of transnational terrorism may not have been predicted by the UK's national security structures, as noted above a national security approach was nevertheless emerging in various ways as it slowly dawned on many in the national security space: no single service, department or agency could do it on its own, but together each could contribute to what had become a process, not a competition. A national security approach was emerging in other ways in this period.

Towards a new approach to national security: the Strategic Defence Review

The Strategic Defence Review (SDR) of 1998 was perhaps the first attempt to do just that. The decision to have a defence review had been a manifesto commitment of the Labour Party in 1996 and with New Labour's sweeping victory in 1997 the review was undertaken with a small team assembled by the new Defence Secretary, George Robertson. The term 'strategic' was inserted to protect against Treasury protests by suggesting an overriding priority for the review. The label stuck, as did some of the crosscutting initiatives that emerged from the exercise.

The aim was to 'conduct a foreign policy-led strategic defence review to reassess Britain's security interests and defence needs'; the resultant document was generally well received. It is now known that the foreign policy baseline upon which the review allegedly stood was not published due to disagreements between the MoD and the FCO, and unwillingness on the part of Foreign Secretary, Robin Cook, to sign off on the document. A national security approach was not quite achieved. But, in its aspirations, the SDR was outward-looking and wide-ranging, emphasizing the role of defence diplomacy, the challenge of 'new risks' and vulnerabilities stemming from organized crime, terrorism and environmental degradation.[21]

The SDR called for 'an integrated external policy ... using all the instruments at our disposal, including diplomatic, developmental and military', moving the UK from 'stability based on fear to stability based on the active management of these risks, seeking to prevent conflicts rather than suppress them'.[22] In other words, the UK would go to crises before they came to us. This was rooted in an internationalist agenda of being 'a force for good' in the world and 'giving a lead' (breezing over the question whether the world wanted to be led by Britain, of course).

Robertson continued the process of jointery initiated by his Conservative predecessors in the MoD. He created a Joint Rapid Reaction Force, a joint force of Harrier jump jets, a joint helicopter command, and an expanded role for the Chief of Joint Operations. This last development was another step towards the Joint Forces Command that would exist without question two decades later.

It was not all positive for national security, though. The review also saw the transfer of almost £1bn from the defence budget to that of the new DFID), in what some saw as an historic shift in security spending. One unintended consequence of the separation of DFID from the Foreign Office was even more significant, according to Daniel Korski: 'Whatever its benefits for aid policy, creating DFID had the result of ring-fencing aid and complicating cooperation with the MoD, especially in post conflict stabilisation missions'.[23]

The SDR came out in 1998 and was intended to look forward seventeen years to 2015. In the event it lasted but three years. Nevertheless, the review could be seen as the genesis of an approach to thinking about defence and security still evident in the 2015 Strategic Defence and Security Review.

The emergence of resilience and oversight

Steps towards a national security approach continued with moves towards thinking about the concept of national resilience, a key aspect of the national security approach, most demonstrably through the creation of the Civil Contingencies Secretariat (CCS) in 2001, which grew out of work on successive events: the Y2K bug scare (the resilience part of which fed back to CT resilience work after the Bishopsgate bombing for many companies), the fuel protests of 2000, and the foot and mouth epidemic of 2001 in which the Army had to be called upon to support the Ministry of Agriculture, Fisheries and Food—events which 'brutally exposed' a lack of national preparedness.[24]

These events appeared to demonstrate that the UK's emergency management policies and structures were not up to the task. The fuel crisis in particular influenced ministers. As David Omand observed: 'That crisis was the first time a UK government had recognised the extent to which a modern economy was dependent upon complex supply chains and how just-in-time value engineering had reduced the buffering that stocks of goods and works in progress would have provided in a previous era'.[25] Omand further advised the Home Secretary to run the crisis as if it were a major terrorist incident using procedures for CT information management and decision-taking. While doing so was straightforward in principle, it proved time-consuming in practice and revealed gaps in communications between local and central government, and the need for central direction in an emergency.[26]

The CCS began to work on resilience ten weeks before the attacks of 9/11. International terrorism became the key topic of interest and the MoD reached out to all of the academics it could to gain insights into the nature of the threat it now faced. Many people in MoD were apparently receptive to a 'whole government' approach, but there was resistance among some senior officers to the idea that countering terrorism might be a core task for the armed services or that the military had an important role to play at home as well as away—indeed, the idea that al-Qa'ida represented a strategic challenge was also questioned.[27]

Oversight

Parliamentary oversight of government policy was given a shot in the arm with the establishment of the select committee system in 1980, under which several committees made up of members of Parliament from various parties scrutinize the main departments of state. The focus was on departments rather than government policy or strategy in general. The events of 9/11 helped change some of those attitudes, with the House of Commons Defence Committee (HCDC), in particular, showing itself open to a broad interpretation of defence matters and beginning to conduct crosscutting inquiries alongside the traditional reports into military operations, major procurement projects and departmental reports.

At the start of 2002, the HCDC began an inquiry into defence and security in the UK, which, unusually for the time, saw the committee take evidence from ministers and officials from across Whitehall, well beyond the defence brief. Parliamentary turf wars were put aside, given the climate of the time, and the other relevant departmental select committees agreed to let the HCDC carry out its inquiry. However, this did not appear to represent a precedent concerning crosscutting scrutiny, with only the Intelligence and Security Committee—a statutory committee of parliamentarians appointed by and reporting to the Prime Minister (only changed in 2011) and not a select committee—attempting broader scrutiny. It was clear to some that a national security approach was the future and little in the following dozen years shook that belief, although institutional progress was slow. The establishment of a Joint Committee on National Security—made up of members from both Houses of Parliament to scrutinize 'the structures for Government decision-making on National Security, particularly the role of the National Security Council and the National Security Adviser'—was supposed to move things forward. But its remit limited the scope of its work. Scrutiny of the national security approach was yet to emerge, remaining split among a range of select committees and joint committees of Parliament, which held back coherence.[28]

SDR new chapter and the comprehensive approach[29]

The SDR lasted three years, before the MoD felt compelled to conduct a mini-review of policy in the light of the attacks on the US, launching a public consultation exercise into what it called 'a new chapter' to the SDR, testing whether the challenge of the new CT mission required fundamental changes. It was well timed. The SDR had set out the geographical limits within which the MoD could expect to operate at scale and these did not, unsurprisingly perhaps, include Central Asia and the Hindu Kush. The UK had, since then, deployed significant numbers of special forces and Royal Marines under Operation Veritas into Afghanistan, which culminated in the deployment of the 45 Commando unit as part of Operation Anaconda, designed to mop up remaining elements of the Taliban and al-Qa'ida. However, the 'new chapter' was far more significant in attempting to address the balance between home and away missions in confronting the challenge of terrorism and the military's role within it. The review considered a number of innovative solutions to the problem of how to respond to what had been termed low-probability, mass-consequence events. In the context of multiple attacks across the UK, could the civil authorities cope?

By 2002, the MoD was considering radical ideas for supporting home defence security—one proposal was for the reserve forces to be given responsibility for home defence in a recalibrated posture. But this was too much for the silo mentality of departmental responsibilities. The MoD appeared to blink in the face of Home Office and broader Whitehall obduracy. Instead, the MoD rolled out an enlarged network of military–civil liaison officers and launched the Civil Contingency Reaction Forces (CCRF) of 500 reservists in each of the 14 brigade districts of the UK, to stand ready for deployment in the event of an emergency. This impressive-sounding force of 7,000 trained troops ready to spring into action was not to prove enduring. In essence, the CCRF concept was flawed from the start due to existing demands on reserve forces; the difficulty of identifying obvious tasks for the units; and, most worryingly, its proven inability to be rapidly and easily deployed—which had been the whole point of the project. The CCRF was quietly dropped after a few years following scathing criticism from all sides, including the HCDC.[30]

Nonetheless, the principle that the armed forces should prepare to support the civil authorities at scale and more formally than under existing Military Aid to the Civil Authorities (MACA) arrangements appeared to have been accepted, although little more was done by the MoD to give effect to this. UK security policymakers, and indeed the armed forces themselves, were hesitant for the military to play anything other than a limited supporting role in UK domestic emergency preparedness, generally. The HCDC continued to review defence and security in the UK, holding further evidence sessions in 2003, and reported on the draft Civil Contingencies Bill in the summer of 2003,[31] having considered the role of emergency services, the police, and the CCS. The CCS concept was proving enduring and successful as a mechanism of cross-government coordination, now additionally spurred by the challenges posed by international and home-grown terrorism. But it struggled to engage with the providers of private sector capabilities, in contrast to its achievements in conceptual work in community engagement and resilience.

Military–civilian operational coordination was discussed conceptually at the time through the concept of 'effects-based operations', a US doctrinal concept that was adopted in UK defence literature, including the *New Chapter*. It influenced the emergence of a more enduring concept in British security thinking: the 'comprehensive approach'. This was another attempt at cross-government working, developed in an era of efforts towards what the Tony Blair administration termed 'joined-up government'. According to one commentator, the concept embraced much of what one might expect of a national security approach: 'The "comprehensive approach" means blending civilian and military tools and enforcing cooperation between government departments, not only for operations but more broadly to deal with many of the 21st century security challenges, including terrorism, genocide and proliferation of weapons and dangerous materials'.[32] MoD documentation from the period repeatedly referred to the concept, but its true institutional effect was opaque. The creation of the tri-department Post–Conflict Reconstruction Unit in 2004 (MoD, FCO and DFID) gave visible effect to the concept, but in the event was a poor example of cross-departmental coordination. It was beset by under-resourcing and unclear lines of authority. Its later manifestation as the Stabilization Unit (2007), though a bit more successful, still did not deliver what was promised; the same could be said for the Provincial Reconstruction Teams made up of civilian and military staffs that were set up in Afghanistan and Iraq.

> The Stabilization Unit, rather than offering strategic leadership, principally proved to be a forum for the various departments to meet as a committee and argue their own positions, rather than combining forces under an independent lead. As a result, the Stabilization Unit's leadership was less than the sum of its parts. In practice, most of the time, when the Unit

worked in something of the way intended, this was inevitably because one department, most commonly the MOD, or DFID, pushed an agenda, taking the lead.[33]

Concurrently, Gordon Brown's introduction of public service agreements was designed, in part, to encourage interdepartmental cooperation and the Global Pools initiative sought to get departments to agree on resource allocation.

But institutional reluctance to get behind the concept stymied its future. As a result, policy in Iraq and Afghanistan too often ended up being amalgamations of separate departmental plans. In the absence of a national security policy community, the failures of previous missions were too often lost:

> Governments have a sterling record of identifying lessons from post–conflict operations but not learning from them or institutionalizing change. Too often, "lessons learned" exercises identify that lessons from previous operations have not been acted upon.[34]

As Theo Farrell noted, the FCO and DFID were 'suspicious of military doctrine in general and not inclined to discard their own operational planning methods in favour of a new shared method'.[35]

What did happen in this period was the start of routine working between intelligence, military and civilian officials on an unprecedented scale (although sadly not matched by equivalent institutional development). A generation of junior and middle-ranking officials and officers gained experience of close interaction with colleagues from other agencies and departments.

Politically, the concept, in its wider form, was embraced with increasing calls for a review of UK security policymaking, with David Omand, recently retired from the role of the Prime Minister's Intelligence and Security Coordinator, as a leading voice in pressing for reform of national security structures. The Conservative Party, in opposition, appointed a national security adviser (NSA), Dame Pauline Neville-Jones, who in 2006, along with Lord Tom King, reviewed security policy and recommended the establishment of a National Security Council (NSC), following the longstanding US example of a cross-issue body serving the executive.[36] The Brown administration felt it had to respond and issued the UK's first National Security Strategy (NSS) in

2008 and created an embryonic version of the NSC, in the form of the NSID, a Committee on National Security, International Relations and Development—a broad remit for a single cabinet subcommittee.

Contest

Perhaps of greater significance on the road to a national security approach was the secret adoption of a cross-government CT strategy in 2003: CONTEST. A central idea within CONTEST was that it would dispense with the traditional home–away distinction associated with different forms of terrorism (and the variety of policy responses to it) and thus seek to introduce a genuinely 'joined-up' and 'fully integrated' approach across government in order to tackle the problem comprehensively. In 2006, the first of three published editions made this abundantly clear: 'The threat has grown and it has changed in character. It has both domestic and international dimensions'.

In order to achieve the level of interdepartmental coordination that would be needed to address the complex challenge, the basic organising structure of the strategy used the so-called 4Ps—four main organizing themes, or functional areas, as summarized in the latest edition of the strategy:

- Pursue: to stop terrorist attacks;
- Prevent: to stop people becoming terrorists or supporting terrorism;
- Protect: to strengthen our protection against a terrorist attack; and,
- Prepare: to mitigate the impact of a terrorist attack.

The longevity of the '4P' structure is important for any assessment of CONTEST, not least because it remained the guiding format for over fifteen years. Similarly, it is also valuable to note, for context, CONTEST's central stated aim: 'to reduce the risk to the United Kingdom and its interests overseas from international terrorism, so that people can go about their lives freely and with confidence'.[37] Often referred to as the preservation of normality (whatever such an expression means), the longevity of this strategic objective of CONTEST is important to bear in mind within the context of the evolution of contemporary terrorist threats facing the UK and its citizens.

The development of CONTEST was not always perceived to be as effective as it could have been. Indeed, questions were initially raised over the Cabinet Office's competence and capacity to take on leadership for its delivery. It was in this context, in 2007, against the backdrop of Home Secretary John Reid's controversial assessment that the Home Office was not 'fit for purpose', that the government moved CT policy from the Cabinet Office to the Home Office, establishing the Office for Security and Counter-Terrorism (OSCT) as an executive directorate there. The OSCT drew on the expertise of officials and outsiders drawn from a wide variety of departments and agencies—most notably second-ees from the MoD, the police, the intelligence agencies, and a handful of other organizations—proving over time to be a consistent advocate of the need for a 'multi-agency' approach to addressing terrorism. Since the creation of CONTEST, this strong emphasis on 'cross-departmental' cooperation has also been a consistent feature of other strategic UK security policy documentation (however effectively implemented), and the government's adherence to seeking more effective coordination was later reflected in the first National Security Strategy document in 2008 and its subsequent iterations.

Ultimately, despite the high-level rhetoric around the crucial need for effective coordination, the CONTEST strategy proved to be more siloed and reflective of the longstanding lead department model for addressing issues cutting across Whitehall—in practice, the Home Office first formulated the policy largely unhindered and then engaged other departments, only as required, to highly variable degrees.

Somewhat surprisingly, for such an apparently 'successful' policy approach to a crosscutting challenge, CONTEST did not actually seek to counter the problem of terrorism using all elements of state power. It remained, and arguably always was, to all intents and purposes, a non-military counterterrorism strategy. In other words, it was a strategy that focused primarily on preventing terrorist attacks within the UK, delivered mainly through civilian institutions, under the leadership of the Home Office (at least for most of its life cycle); and, even domestically, often not all of the possible partners were embraced. CONTEST, in this sense, was not truly strategic because it had not included proper consideration of the military's contribution to CT within a broader, overarching and long-term national vision of how to address the problem—what one might call a grand strategy for CT. Nor had it engaged in as wide-ranging a policy conversation as 'strategic' would imply, including partners and agencies beyond the core CT actors and one or two other ministries. Only the creation in 2003 of the Joint Terrorism Analysis Centre (JTAC), hosted by MI5, appears a true exception to the siloed domestic approach in the design of new structures for CT after 9/11, pooling all terrorism-related intelligence in one central location and under the direction of one central authority.

Despite these new structures, questions persisted about whether the arrangements have actually remained ad hoc, traditional and even out-dated, while the threat itself evolved considerably. Had the OSCT been placed in the Cabinet Office, for example, there might have been a greater emphasis on the comprehensiveness of the approach, with policy responsibility in the Home Office. Considering the tensions that clearly existed across Whitehall departments, it was perhaps hardly surprising that the level of cooperation that emerged between the civilian and military authorities on CONTEST was not optimal.

Arguably, the pragmatic approach established by CONTEST at least ensured a level of cross-departmental cooperation not seen in other areas of national security policy, notwithstanding repeated clashes over responsibilities regarding the 'Prevent' strand, concerning counter-extremism which had no obvious lead department to take things forward. Strengthening the country's intelligence machinery to counter domestic and international terrorism after 9/11 was another important way in which the UK sought to implement its strategic approach to countering terrorism and an area that attracted considerable additional resources, if not similar additional oversight, given the new scale.

The deeper question for CONTEST, therefore, was whether the UK government should develop, as part of its 'comprehensive approach', a more capable and potentially sharper political-military strategy of its own, in delivering the overseas elements of countering transnational terrorism. The Home Office clearly lacked the capacity of the MoD—in terms of personnel numbers, the maturity of its training infrastructure and its level of financial resources—to develop a full-spectrum approach to CT.

The situation was doubly problematic in the sense that the UK government never actually crafted a coherent strategy for guiding the

British military's contribution to CT in the CONTEST document. The strategy's domestic focus may happily have 'worked' in the sense of limiting the number of fatalities on UK soil, but members of the armed forces and the MoD, looking to CONTEST for clarity, might justifiably have felt disappointed. This oversight, deliberate or accidental, risked appearing dangerously complacent, in the sense that the apparently growing ability of terrorist entities to operate globally looked set to threaten UK national security more directly for many years to come. In this context, it was also noticeable that, in line with the diversity and scale of the threat that the OSCT confronted, considerable daily demands were placed on it to fight fires when constantly faced with short-term, urgent priorities.

For hard–pressed security officials (civil and military) and their political masters, the priority was (and would remain) stopping attacks. Given the stated central aim cited above—reducing the risks from international terrorism, 'so that people can go about their lives freely and with confidence'—any belief that CONTEST had succeeded was a narrow reading of the aim. The risk of terrorist attack could hardly be said to have diminished and public concerns about terrorism remained high, feeding into the sense of insecurity that the national security state appeared to engender as an unfortunate by-product.

Olympic security, the NSC and SDSR 2010

Another model of innovation in the crosscutting provision of security policy in this period was that of Olympic security for the 2012 Games, which proved to be the largest peacetime security operation on mainland Britain since the end of the Second World War. As Robert Raine, the director of Olympic security, explained: 'The platform was huge: thirty sporting and seventy other venues with ten million spectators; in nine cities besides London; 14,000 athletes and 40,000 media people'.[38] Over 50,000 people were involved in safety and security from government, police, military, the organizing committee and private security. The result was that no major incident—no terrorist attack, no cyber attack—occurred to disrupt the Games (there was daily evidence of probing); and there were only three serious protest attempts: one by massed cyclists and two by taxi drivers.

However, it did involve the late but highly effective deployment of a huge contingent from the armed forces, when the contract with the private sector firm G4S 'fell short', reflecting contractual weaknesses and corporate failure. The result was very effective use of the military contingent (despite some concerns over 'militarization') with a peak deployment of 18,200, including an additional 3,500 deployed at short notice and a 1,000 contingency reserve. As Lord Coe, chairman of the London Organising Committee for the Olympic Games, said, the security shambles was saved by the professionalism and humour of the military.[39] Home Secretary Theresa May, responsible for counterterrorism, was allegedly unhappy with the large numbers deployed, perhaps reflecting the now traditional Home Office view of military support for home missions, telling General Nick Parker: 'You are the general who deployed far too many troops'.[40] Of the many lessons learned on governance and machinery of government, Raine emphasized:

> It was right to set out the strategic framework and get it widely agreed: a published strategy and a common concept of operations. They provided the glue that this massive, multi-agency operation needed. They ensured there were a common purpose and a common vocabulary. And publishing these documents widely made sure that they were enforceable.[41]

We should not understate the deliberate integration of the planning for the security of the 2012 Olympic Games with the UK's broader national security and CT strategies during the latter stages of its implementation, and its ongoing connection to the UK's wider economic and national security objectives.

The decision to transfer overall policy responsibility for Olympics security from the Crime and Policing Group within the Home Office to the OSCT in December 2008 was a pivotal moment. The unsettled character of the governance arrangements that were in place before then was one of Whitehall's worst-kept secrets, with claims that senior police officers at the Metropolitan Police Service were exerting too much influence on the strategic direction of the security for the Games. By moving overall policy responsibility to the OSCT, the government was able to exert stronger control and oversight over the Olympic security strategy, directly connecting its delivery to its broader implementation of CONTEST and national security—the public version of the Olympics strategy published in March 2011 explicitly stated that this 'strategy supports the National Security Strategy'.

The positive benefits that the UK gained from its Olympics security experience—in terms of security policy integration—continued, as the 2015 Strategic Defence and Security Review stated explicitly: 'We have established a global reputation for hosting major international events safely and securely …creating opportunities for UK companies'.[42] The head of Olympics security emphasized how openness about the strategy and its publication was of great importance, ensuring 'common purpose and a common vocabulary'.[43] It was, he said, 'transformational' for domestic agencies and 'enabled a reengagement between the British public and their security forces, particularly the military and the police'.[44]

The 'success' of London 2012 security was used to seek to assist other Olympics organizers and to export UK capability and expertise (i.e. the economic dimension). A UK Trade and Investment (UKTI) Security Export Strategy document included a 'Major Event Security' section: 'Our hosting of the London 2012 Olympic and Paralympic Games presents us with a significant opportunity to harness and promote our experience to the benefit of UK security companies'.[45] For example, the UKTI Defence and Security Organisation (DSO) trade mission to Japan in November 2015 issued a UKTI press release saying: 'UK companies are also keen to develop partnerships with Japanese industry in the Security sector and to help with safety and security of the Tokyo's 2020 Olympic and Paralympic Games'. This was said to have had a 'transformational' effect on many relationships and would help with future work.[46]

NSC and SDSR 2010

The establishment on the first day of the coalition government, in 2010, of a National Security Council (NSC), therefore, should perhaps have presaged the blooming of a thousand flowers for national security thinkers. But Whitehall got its own back in the SDSR process that followed. Rather than a strategic approach, the NSC appeared to herald a return to Foreign Office control of advice to the Prime Minister and little institutional reform towards a genuinely national security approach. Instead of a strategic approach in shaping the SDSR, the

Cabinet Office assumed a coordinating role and the exercise had the appearance of stitching together various departmental agendas and hurried political decisions. The teams of officials brought together to support the process were swiftly disbanded and the opportunity was lost for the delivery of a coherent approach to the regular SDSR process established by the incoming government.

The future: delivering the national security approach

In February 2015, Sir John Sawers, the former Chief of MI6, spoke at King's College London, declaring that the way we think about security needs to change,[47] and the way security is delivered also needs to change. Three things are required in particular: the development of a cadre of national security officials and experts from across Whitehall (supported by regular and institutionalized outside advice) to maintain the strategy; the use of the private sector more actively and coherently in the national security process; and enhancement of means of oversight and, through it, public confidence in the process.

In the aftermath of the attacks on the United States in September 2001, many wanted to talk of failure—of intelligence and of security. *The 9/11 Commission Report* of 2004 tried to look forward:

> As presently configured, the national security institutions of the U.S. Government are still the institutions constructed to win the Cold War. The United States confronts a very different world today. Instead of facing a few very dangerous adversaries, the United States confronts a number of less visible challenges that surpass the boundaries of traditional nation states and call for quick, imaginative and agile responses … Ways of doing business rooted in a different era are just not good enough. Americans should not settle for incremental, ad hoc adjustments to a system designed generations ago for a world that no longer exists.[48]

The achievement of a national security approach in Britain will not happen without coordinated action and, if left as a top-down exercise, can only achieve so much. What was required was a genuine partnership between government, citizenry and other actors outside government, facilitated by true collaboration across departments. This was proving to be one of the greatest challenges:

> Interdepartmental working has not been an integral part of how Whitehall operates. The reasons are simple: political, financial and bureaucratic loyal-

ties stream vertically upwards rather than across departments, thus inhibiting integrated collaboration. Changing this remains one of Britain's main national security challenges.[49]

National security cannot simply be something that is dispensed from the top down anymore. If the changing nature of security had demonstrated anything over the past twenty-five years, it was that security was not just about elites and decision-makers—it was about citizens and the resilience of communities facing the challenges and risks. The public need to be brought into the process in a meaningful way because, if the terrorist attacks in Paris in 2015 showed anything, it is that creating a resilient public can be a powerful element of national power; but the creation of long-term public support requires openness. As James Gow and I noted in an article following the 2010 SDSR:

> It is fair to ask whether the sorts of roles assumed to be in Britain's interests are actually within its capabilities as a strategic player in international affairs, or within the bounds of long-term public support. Without such clarity, it is questionable whether public opinion can be carried along to accept that Britain should shoulder disproportionately more than others who fundamentally share similar security challenges and essentially occupy the same security space in many ways.[50]

The publication of a National Security Strategy (NSS) and the eventual establishment of the National Security Council (NSC) were generally positive steps. The chairmanship of the NSC by the Prime Minister clearly gave a fillip to the process, and the regular attendance of ministers from a variety of departments, attuned to a 'battle rhythm' of circulations of papers and background material for the often weekly meetings, meant that the NSC did appear to be more than simply a rebadging of Gordon Brown's National Security and International Relations and Development (NSID) committee and other previous cabinet subcommittees that had long considered matters of foreign affairs and defence. Similarly, the coordination of the NSS, in tandem with a regular five-year cycle of defence and security reviews introduced by the coalition government of 2010, was, on the face of it, a good thing.

Defence reviews were for many years something to be avoided by officials and ministers scared by the Nott Review of 1981, which was remembered for cutting the Royal Navy just before the Falklands War. As Freedman noted:

> As a result of this experience it became an article of faith that defence policy was best managed through the annual long-term costings process, allowing for regular reappraisals, rather than all the big decisions being saved up for a special occasion … A wariness crept in when it came to statements about 'new directions' in policy lest once again the direction stated turned out to be the opposite to the one travelled.[51]

Having a five-yearly SDSR and NSS cycle, guided by an ongoing National Security Risk Assessment Process, which could be updated more often (as the 2010 one was in 2012), could avoid the danger of not being responsive outside the regular review cycle. The intention of the 2015 SDSR to create a new NSC subcommittee, chaired by the Cabinet Office minister (making Oliver Letwin the first incumbent), to oversee implementation was, in principle, a very good thing. Although it stopped short of the creation of a minister for national security as such (too Cold War Warsaw Pact-like a title, perhaps), it gave political leadership and authority to the National Security Adviser and his secretariat, in the absence of prime ministers, who never have the time for medium to long-term policy assessment. Furthermore, since any NSC chaired at the highest level would always reflect what the prime minister of the day wanted most, its benefits needed to be acquired in this other way.

> Of course in the NSC we discuss strategy, but I want us to determine policy, I want us to agree action, and I want us to check that we have done what we said we were going to do … I find that the problem all too often is that people love sitting around talking about strategy. Getting people to do things and act and complete on the strategy is often the challenge.[52]

This traditional British suspicion of strategy (amateurs do strategy; professionals do logistics, as the military say) missed the opportunity of a strategic approach, which was to understand situations, and see the dangers and opportunities that they present. It also allowed a perspective beyond the immediate policy agenda.

British security policymakers might simply be uncomfortable with the notion of applying a strategic approach to the country's top contemporary security challenges. As Minister for Policy in the Conservative–

Liberal Democratic Coalition government of 2010–15, Oliver Letwin himself revealed this tendency when he explained in Parliament: 'We are not devotees of what I believe is called "grand strategy"'.[53] Perhaps this was reflective of wariness about MoD domination creeping through national security policymaking, when doctrinal terms, such as 'grand strategy', were used, but perhaps it was actually the usual preference simply to muddle along and not do anything too revolutionary that prevailed. This is a wasted opportunity because, as Freedman made clear, strategy was not about setting down in stone what the country's objectives were in all circumstances.[54]

Rather, as Richard Betts explains: 'Strategies are chains of relationships among means and ends that span several levels of analysis, from the maneuvers [of] units in specific engagements through larger campaigns, whole wars, grand strategies, and foreign policies'.[55] For Hew Strachan, strategy is conceptualized similarly as a 'declaration of intent, and an indication of the possible means required to fulfill that intent [—in short, the] matter of combining means, ways and ends [—and is] as much reactive as prudential; as much an exercise in flexibility and adaptability in the short term as a narrative'.[56] While not a panacea by any means, adopting a strategic approach to national security policymaking can only be a good thing if the establishment could just 'get over' their problem with the term. As Brands and Porter put it: 'Grand strategy is undeniably difficult to get right, but it beats the alternative, grand strategic nihilism, hands-down'.[57] The British establishment too often appeared to tend towards the nihilist's perspective.

Similarly, the appointment of a National Security Adviser (NSA), supported by a secretariat, based in the Cabinet Office, gave a clear focus for official support to the process of national security making, in theory. While the holders of the post after 2010 have all been men (and they were all men of exceptional talent and experience), they also all came from the FCO, and the signs were that Whitehall had given the role to that department. This was problematic, not only because national security was about more than foreign affairs, but also because the role of foreign policy adviser had moved out of No. 10 Downing Street and into the neighbouring Cabinet Office, where the NSA sat, alongside his secretariat. Access and proximity are the only thing at these levels of government.

The role of foreign policy adviser was reinstated by Margaret Thatcher in 1982, having been unfilled since Sir Horace Wilson, Chamberlain's foreign policy adviser, according to Anthony Parsons, her first adviser, who recalled: 'In her mind she wanted to replicate the American system, have a kind of competitor to the Foreign Office advice. I made it plain to her that I wouldn't accept the job on those terms, that I would only accept it on the terms of co-operating with the Foreign Office, not competing; and I insisted on this'.[58] The creation of the NSA role did not appear to have substantially changed the system of lead departments in the delivery of national security policy, nor fundamentally to have changed the silos approach that beset this area of public policy for decades. Even the SDSR process appeared, at times, to have been simply coordinated by the Cabinet Office, not led by a central team. In the 2010 SDSR, for example, the MoD did its own policy studies, without recourse to other departments, and the NSS team failed to prioritize tasks or set geographic priorities.[59]

What is needed for an effective national security approach is a profound change in ways of thinking among not only the decision-makers but also their officials and advisers. The teams dispersed following the publication of the 2015 NSS and SDSR (as they were following 2010) should in the future be retained as a permanent posting to keep a watching brief on the national security process, strengthening the capabilities of the NSS secretariat, to avoid the wasteful effort of reassembling all these teams once again in three years' time. In this way departmentalism could be minimized, as agencies and ministries would have a stake in the process between reviews.

In the context of continuing austerity and shrinking departmental budgets in many areas, this may seem an unrealistic proposal. But it was precisely because individual budgets were under continuing pressure that the need to bring all elements of national power together in a strategically coherent and structured manner was so important. The centre could never deliver the effect, which would, in all likelihood, be left to departments and agencies, but those individual elements could not be left to define what their individual roles should be in isolation. A central national security machinery freed from siloed departmental working practices should be left to initiate fresh and imaginative policies, because ensuring effective coordination of the levers of state power was a central task. As an American commentator noted: 'The largest challenge of the twenty-first century will not be terrorism or natural disasters; it will be the creative management of national security capabilities housed within departments and agencies to respond to crises effectively and collaboratively'.[60]

With the lessons of the faltering steps in the fifteen years after the 1998 SDR, nothing less than a national security version of jointery (embraced by the armed forces for several decades) could achieve this outcome. It probably means structuring careers and promotion within individual departments around national security outcomes for a cadre of national security practitioners—in the armed services it had become almost unheard of for the most senior appointments to go to candidates who had not held a significant 'joint' post in their careers.

The post of NSA should be opened to candidates from various departments of state, as the role of chairman of the Joint Intelligence Committee was and the head of the Joint Terrorism Analysis Centre and, in all likelihood, the OSCT would be. The deputy NSA teams should be modestly enlarged to include a permanent military representative and ideally a financially focused deputy NSA from the Treasury or Bank of England. Fixed-term secondees from the private sector and academia should be actively sought, allowing for fresh thinking and experience, and a national security studies programme of training and education should be adopted by the new (but virtual) National Security Academy. Overseeing this process should be a professional head of national security, along the lines of the professional head of intelligence.

An oversight committee of parliamentarians (ideally a select committee) should provide high profile and crosscutting oversight of the national security approach, taking evidence from officials and ministers of all relevant departments. The annual update to Parliament of progress announced in the 2015 NSS–SDSR would be a useful focus for starting this committee's work. Whether this should take the form of an expanded and better-resourced Intelligence and Security Committee, given the workload that the existing committee has, is unclear, but the needs of security and the sensitivity of some material may mean that a traditional select committee is not appropriate. The Joint Committee on National Security was not configured to deliver crosscutting oversight either. Whatever the solution decided upon, the principle should be that as much openness as can be allowed is an end in itself. The public should not be treated as the mere suppliants of national security from a secretive and distant apparatus of national security, but as part of national security and resilience. In bringing all elements of national power to bear on the risks and challenges of the modern world, it would be a huge mistake not to see the public as a source of strength rather than weakness. Through trust will come confidence. Similarly, Omand focused his definition of security on trust and management: 'National security today should be defined as a state of trust on the part of the citizen that the risks to everyday life, whether from man-made threats or international hazards, are being adequately managed to the extent that there is confidence that normal life can continue'.[61]

As the public are key players in this, the challenge was that there was too often a perception of insecurity, despite 'objective' evidence to the contrary, rooted in part in how national security was communicated in British political discourse. Government needed to communicate clearly what it could and could not do, and why. The MoD could usefully start defining itself by reference to supporting the citizenry of the UK, not the state as an abstraction. And the perception of insecurity needed to be challenged. The public needed to be treated as adults, not as child-like suppliants of the national security state. As Wolfers put it during the Cold War: 'Because the pendulum of public opinion swings so easily from extreme complacency to extreme apprehension, from utopian reliance on "good will" to disillusioned faith in naked force only, it is particularly important to be wary of any simple panacea, even of one that parades in the realist garb of a policy guided solely by the national security interest'.[62] The security challenge had shifted to one of understanding and acting upon security challenges as they arose and communicating policy effectively. Such policymakers needed, in the words of one US author, to be 'strategic artisans', with the intellectual breadth and competences to operate across domestic and international areas of policy.[63] This summed up the needed qualifications very well: people who understood the limits of interests and force.

This is not to advocate a national security solution, or any such thing, as a panacea, but rather the adoption of a national security approach to underpin the development of national security policies. The policy-focused work of the war studies group at King's College

London, educated and inspired by Lawrence Freedman over three decades, contributed to some of the innovations and new thinking. Now this will continue, as King's launched a national security studies programme in 2016, with the aim of supporting the creation of a cadre of strategic artisans by seeking to educate and inspire emerging generations of national security practitioners and future generations, from King's own student body and across Whitehall. The post-SDSR period saw substantial progress towards the adoption of such a national security approach in Britain, with many welcome innovations by successive governments. But, perhaps, they were not as many as were promised. As such, the adoption of a new approach to thinking about and delivering security remained a work in progress.

PART 4

THEORY

13

TRUST AND INTERNATIONAL RELATIONS

Richard Ned Lebow

Lawrence Freedman begins his *Strategy: A History* with a discussion of chimpanzees, noting how research shows them to be political and strategic, using cooperation and coalition-building, deception, rewards and occasional instrumental violence in managing and limiting their conflicts. It was evident that competition had to be limited because there would be moments where the same chimpanzees would need to join forces for the greater good of the group. The chimps had to kiss and make up after fights and, as Freedman observes, by 'showing their vulnerability they invited trust'.[1] Trust, or its absence, is a key feature of political and social relations.

Trust is a central concept in domestic politics and international relations literatures. In the latter it almost invariably applies to judgements about other actors: will they prove faithful allies, will they adhere to their treaty and other commitments, do they have benign intentions? These questions are critical, but surprisingly little work has been done on how policymakers reach these decisions and how they ought to. I further contend that trust has a wider application to international rela-

243

tions. It describes the belief policymakers have in their own judgement, the efficacy of their initiatives, and their ability to control or influence others to bring these initiatives to fruition. These beliefs are often misplaced and there is a large literature on this subject, much of it drawing on the work of cognitive and motivational psychology.

These two understandings of trust are obviously related, as trust in one's abilities and judgements influences not only the judgements people make about others but also the intensity and certainty with which they hold to them. Thucydides explores this relationship at some length and attributes the catastrophic decisions made by Athens in the Peloponnesian War to *hubris* (pride before a fall) and *elpis* (hope). The former prompts overconfidence and the latter is an expression of it. Leaders exaggerate their ability to understand and to control others, and to predict the consequences of their own and others' actions, and become correspondingly insensitive to looming catastrophes. Some historians and biographers have picked up on this theme in their treatment of such figures as Napoleon, Franklin Roosevelt, Jawaharlal Nehru and Lyndon Johnson. International relations theorists on the whole remain mute on the subject.

Where does trust come from? Deterrence and strategic choice models tell us it comes from assessments of the prior performance of those we are evaluating. Psychological and political research indicates that we feel more positive about people who resemble us, who have even features and are tall and not overweight. We are more likely to trust such people and vote for them. Thucydides and research in motivational psychology suggest that the wish is father of the deed; to the extent that we need to trust in someone, some elite, some organization or state, we are likely to do so regardless of the evidence. Sophocles in *Philoctetes* and Plato in *Protagoras* and the *Republic* offer a more fundamental explanation that has to do with friendship. The first and last explanations invoke learning as their mechanism, although in different ways. For deterrence and strategic choice, it is past performance in the same domain that counts. For Sophocles and Plato, friendship builds a generalized form of trust that extends to all areas of activity: violations of trust in any domain, in turn, undermine it in all others. These two explanations differ in a more fundamental way: many strategic choice models assume a pre-existing desire, or at least propensity, to cooperate and address features of context that make it difficult or impossible.

The goal of this chapter is to expand our understanding of trust and its application to international relations. I examine its application to domestic politics, first, and then its application to international relations. I critique two highly regarded works, Robert Putnam's account of social capital and Robert Axelrod's research on tit-for-tat. Putnam describes the benefits of trust but tells us nothing about where it comes from. He defines his actors as autonomous agents, a framework widespread in social science, but one that makes it difficult to account for the trust so essential to sustain political order, let alone cooperation among agents. Axelrod starts from the same premise and runs into the same problem. His strategy of tit-for-tat assumes a predisposition to trust and cooperate with others but tells us nothing about how it arises. In its absence, it is impossible to build trust and cooperation through tit-for-tat. Repeated iterations of the game only heighten mistrust and non-cooperation in the form of defection.

We need to go beyond approaches limited to strategic interaction and its context. I accordingly turn to Sophocles and Plato for accounts of why and how trust develops. They encourage us to think about the ways in which society and trust are co-constitutive and how each makes the other possible. We cannot understand trust by extracting actors from the societies in which they operate. Rather, we must embed them in their social context as it shapes their behaviour and expectations. Deterrence theory and realist models of international relations assume that trust is in short supply, the anomaly rather than the norm. The ancient Greek understanding of trust sees it as variable; the more robust the society is the more widespread trust will be.

Trust

Trust is a concept familiar to students of American and comparative politics. The conventional wisdom in these fields holds that it is important, even essential, for stable regimes, especially democratic ones. In their 1963 book *Civic Culture*, which involved a five-country comparative study, Gabriel Almond and Sidney Verba emphasize the importance of 'subjective competence' or the trust citizens have in their government's responsiveness to their needs. Trust is equally central to the writings of James Coleman and Robert Putnam, where it is the principal source of social capital. Coleman deployed the concept of social capital to describe the social norms and expectations which underwrite economic activity but which cannot be accounted for in economic terms. This concept explained the capacities of successful economic groups to extend their transactions across time and space and reduce transaction costs through 'soft' regulations of norms and mutual expectations instead of 'hard' rules of law or the logic of reciprocity. Coleman describes social capital as a form of generalized trust.[2]

Putnam argues that social networks generate social capital and comprise the people we know. They generate an inclination to do things for others in the same network. Neighbours are generally willing to keep an eye on one another's homes. Hasidic Jews trade diamonds among themselves without having to test each gem for its purity. Attorneys reach oral agreements secure in the knowledge that they will be honoured in situations where subsequent defection would seem advantageous to one side. Social capital describes a variety of benefits that derive from the information, trust, reciprocity and cooperation generated by social networks. Putnam maintains that it creates value not only for the people who are part of these networks, but often for bystanders or people connected to other networks.

Putnam's thesis has drawn equal degrees of praise and criticism. Some react negatively to the social and political conservatism inherent in his thesis. He seems to envisage the America of the 1950s—the era of 'Father knows best', racial and ethnic intolerance, the sexual double standard and women forced out of the post-war labour market—as an ideal to which we should want to return. Putnam has also been accused of playing into the hands of elitists who want to substitute self-policing for regulation and voluntarism for the welfare state.[3] Other critics maintain that trust in institutions and elites is very different from trust in neighbours, and that a decline of trust in governments and elites is not necessarily a bad thing; it might even benefit the country.[4]

I raise a different objection to Putnam, one based on his underlying assumptions about human beings and what moves them to cooperate. Working in the dominant social science paradigm, Putnam, like Coleman, frames cooperation as a narrow collective action problem: everyone would gain from cooperation, but no one is willing to take the first steps because of its possibly prohibitive cost. Not surprisingly, he invokes the same mechanisms as microeconomists to explain how this impediment to cooperation can be overcome: transparency and the shadow of the future. Economic and political transactions 'in dense networks of social interactions' reduce the incentives people have for defection and free riding (reaping the benefits of cooperation without assuming any of the costs) by increasing the flow of information and reducing transaction costs. People are assumed to be autonomous, egoistic actors, who evaluate the costs and benefits of cooperation rationally in terms of their individual interests.

Just where do these interests come from? Constructivists assume that interests derive from identities, which are in turn shaped by the societies in which we live and the relationships we form. Relationships encourage us to frame our interests primarily in collective terms, as members of partnerships, families, locales, businesses, ethnic groups, classes, religions and nations. We are inclined to cooperate with other members of these communities because we see our interests served by the attainment of collective goals. Such an orientation not only provides a deeper explanation for case-by-case cooperation, but it also explains why such cooperation often occurs in situations where it does not appear to be in the immediate interest of some of the actors involved. Social capital—as conceptualized by Putnam—describes at best a secondary process that can only function when there is a prior underlying inclination to cooperate on the basis of a common identity.

Putnam claims that his concept of reciprocity derives from Emile Durkheim and Marcel Mauss, and his understanding of civic participation and democracy from Tocqueville. Mauss, Durkheim and Tocqueville are representatives of a French intellectual tradition that extends back through the Encyclopedists, Rousseau and Montesquieu to the Greeks. While these thinkers disagree among themselves on many issues, they share an understanding of self-interest and cooperation that roots both in identity. They also distinguish between narrow and enlightened self-interest and explain the latter with reference to emotion as well as reason. For the ancient Greeks, as understood by Durkheim and Mauss, participation in a network of ritual exchange and mutual obligation built community by creating affective ties among individuals and providing important shared experiences that stretched their identities into what Durkheim called *la conscience collective*. Collective identities made cooperation possible. Durkheim was adamant that contracts—which included the kinds of associations emphasized by Putnam—could not create or sustain social order. This only happened in societies where such order already existed.[5]

In his desire to offer a parsimonious, scientific explanation for cooperation, Putnam has denuded Mauss, Durkheim and Tocqueville of their conceptual richness and profundity. Tocqueville observed that Americans were losing their social ties and theorized that democracy would become difficult to sustain in a world of fully autonomous individuals. Putnam, following modern economists, assumes that such individuals are to be welcomed and have become the norm, or are an appropriate assumption on which to base theories. A world of autonomous, egoistic individuals—even the fiction of such a world—assumes that cooperation and civic commitment are only valued when they serve selfish ends. This assumption rules out affection and sympathy as motives, and excludes the possibility of any kind of learning beyond the purely instrumental kind. By doing so, it makes sustained trust and cooperation something of an oxymoron. It is the very world that frightened Tocqueville because he thought it likely to promote a modern form of despotism. He is firm in his belief that successful democracy requires a commitment to community and transcendence by the political class of its parochial economic interests in favour of those of the community as a whole.

To understand the nature of self-interest, the ways in which conceptions of it change, and which formulations strengthen instead of undermining community, trust and civic participation, we need to free ourselves from the limited conceptual categories of microeconomics in favour of the richer, if less parsimonious, frameworks of the great philosophers and sociologists.

Tit-for-tat (TFT)

In 1981, Robert Axelrod and W.D. Hamilton used a computer tournament to detect strategies that would encourage cooperation among individuals engaged in an iterative game of prisoner's dilemma.[6] In a first round, fourteen more or less sophisticated strategies and one totally random strategy competed for the highest average scores in a tournament of 200 moves. A very simple strategy emerged as the victor: cooperate on the first move and then copy your opponent's last move for all subsequent moves. TFT won again in a second competition involving 62 contestants, in which all competitors knew the results of the first round. TFT has three characteristics that account for its impressive performance: it is nice (cooperates on the first move), retaliatory (punishes defection in the prior move with defection) and forgiving (immediately returns to cooperation after one cooperative move by an adversary). Like other rationalist explanations for cooperation, TFT starts from the premise that actors are autonomous and egoistic. Its wrinkle, which gained it so much attention, is its seeming proof that cooperation can emerge over time at the system level from entirely self-interested behaviour at the agent level. It is a high-tech version of Hegel's 'cunning of reason'.

In the computer tournaments won by TFT, 'tits' (punishment) and 'tats' (defections) were defined unambiguously, as were their consequences (assigned numerical values), and both were evaluated independently by the computer that kept score. None of these conditions can be replicated in the real world, where 'tits' are readily interpreted as 'tats', cooperation as defection, and either can be dismissed as noise.[7] The pattern of interaction between two actors, each of whom believes they are punishing the other for prior defection, is likely to diverge radically from a starting point jointly perceived as mutual cooperation, or defection and punishment. The Cuban missile crisis was the result of such an escalating spiral of mutually reinforcing defections, with each superpower convinced that its 'tat' was a 'tit' made in response to its adversary's 'tat'.[8]

In subsequent tournaments, Axelrod allowed for faulty attribution. He introduced a degree of randomization in outcomes, so that when players chose to cooperate or defect, it would occasionally appear to their opponents that they had done the opposite. Players would be informed afterwards if their choice had not been implemented correctly, but they would never be told if opponents' choices were intended or not. Nor did they know for how many moves the game would last. Axelrod explored two ways of coping with these uncertainties: making the response to defection somewhat less than the provocation (generosity); and encouraging the player who had defected by accident to recognize that the opponent's defection in response did not necessarily call for another defection in return. Both strategies coped well with the noise introduced by randomization, but too much forgiveness invited exploitation.[9]

In the original and subsequent tournaments, the outcomes of cooperation and defection were unambiguous, the payoffs of all possible combinations of cooperation and defection were known in advance, and all contests consisted of reciprocal moves. In the real world, none of these conditions hold. Outcomes and their payoffs can only be estimated imperfectly, as policies not infrequently bring about outcomes the reverse of those intended. Actors in the same political unit or faction, not to mention in different ones, frequently make radically divergent estimates of likely policy outcomes. Perception is everything, and it may also determine whether the other side perceives your behaviour as cooperation or defection—or anything in-between, as these binaries do not capture the more complex categories actors use to assess the motives and behaviour of others. The real world is characterized by opacity in actor motives as well as outcomes; the latter are often the result of complex interactions among multiple actors.

TFT may be the most extreme example of a theory of cooperation based entirely on external stimuli. As we have seen, it requires actors to replicate the previous move of their adversaries. If they cooperate, you cooperate, and if they defect, you defect. The strategy tells us nothing about the original choice of any actor, and it is easy to see that the nature of the world that emerges in any game is critically dependent on the opening moves of the players. They presumably reflect a prior disposition towards cooperation or defection. In this connection, it is interesting to observe that when Axelrod ran TFT with real American and Soviet defence analysts as players, they subsequently explained their initial and subsequent choices—mostly defection—in terms of their prior expectations about each other's motives.[10]

When we leave the abstract, transparent domain of games for the world of international relations, it is difficult to find an interstate rivalry that moved from acute conflict to cooperation by means of TFT. The Cold War ended because Mikhail Gorbachev refused to play TFT. He made a series of conciliatory moves, undeterred by Reagan's repeated unwillingness to reciprocate. Repeated efforts at conciliation in the face of no response or defection convinced many Europeans and Americans of Gorbachev's sincerity, and generated allied and domestic pressure on the Reagan administration to extend the olive branch. Ironically, the first major move the administration made towards cooperation—the 'zero option' arms control proposal—was never intended to be taken seriously by the Soviets. Its purpose was to put the onus of the expected failure of arms control on Moscow and make the administration look better in the eyes of its critics. Gorbachev's positive response compelled the administration to follow through on its own offer and led to an important arms control agreement.[11]

At best, TFT describes tactics that may facilitate cooperation in the long run when the outcomes of individual encounters are not critical. If you get beaten or conquered after one or two moves of cooperation by agents who defect, TFT is not a winning strategy. Moreover, it tells us nothing about why leaders seek cooperation. To understand why Gorbachev, Sadat and other leaders were moved to extend the olive branch, and willing to assume great risks in the process, we need to examine their internal as well as external incentives—that is, their domestic goals and political needs—and the ways in which both kinds of incentives were refracted through important processes of learning.[12]

A world of autonomous, egoistic individuals—even the fiction of such a world—when used as a starting point of analysis, fosters the belief that cooperation and commitments should serve purely selfish ends. If we work from such an assumption, which rules out social and emotional attachments and commitments and the communities they sustain, it is easy to see why social scientists working in the rational choice tradition must resort to the most extreme forms of intellectual conjuring to explain how any collaboration beyond the most short-lived and instrumental kind ever occurs. Having coaxed the rabbit of individualism out of its analytical hat, social scientists are now unsuccessfully casting about for tricks to put it back inside.

There are two further points to consider. In Axelrod's tournament, TFT only emerged as victor in the course of many rounds of the cooperation–defection game against all other programs. TFT had the luxury of being able to lose many games in the process. This is another way the tournament differs from the real world. Loss for a state could be final or, if not, sufficiently debilitating to seriously impede its security or standing. Failing that, it might still be perceived as likely to have that effect by relevant actors. Historically, such perceptions have been a strong motive for caution when it comes to concessions and self-restraint or overreactions to what are perceived as challenges from adversaries. Fear of loss and high levels of conflict produce emotional arousal, which is another significant way in which the real world differs from a computer game.

TFT is a thought-provoking concept that has inspired interesting work in evolutionary biology. However, it tells us nothing about politics, and it is not a practical strategy for reducing or overcoming international conflicts. Its appeal was nevertheless understandable. Axelrod published his findings at a time when the Cold War had heated up again and many people were searching for a route to peace. TFT was read by some—most of them outside the academic world—as 'scientific' support for their belief that cooperation was more effective than confrontation.

Trust and IR theory

Social scientists generally define trust with respect to particular behaviour. According to Henry Farrell and Jack Knight, trust is 'a set of expectations held by one party that another party or parties will behave in an appropriate manner with regard to a specific issue'.[13] Mark Suchman argues that trust is built by compliance with rules and established expectations of behaviour.[14]

In family life, domestic politics and international relations, indeed in all domains in which human beings interact, predictability of behaviour is essential. We trust that, depending on the country, everyone will drive on the right—or the left—side of the road. In the absence of this assurance, driving would be hazardous, insurance rates would be exorbitant, and many fewer of us would venture on the highway. This example is interesting in a second respect. We take it for granted that everyone will follow the rule because it is so evidently in one's self-interest. The principal violators are drunken drivers—people no longer restrained by reason—and, for a while, illegal immigrants in southern California who would race up the highway in the face of oncoming traffic to escape the Border Patrol.

Behaviour that is patently self-serving and socially mandated is for the most part unproblematic. People act in accordance with stipulated norms of this kind so regularly that their performance becomes habitual. This in turn makes their actions more predictable, heightens trust among others that the norm will be followed, and contributes to the stability and efficiency of the social order. Trust becomes problematic in situations where (1) there are no norms, or they are too weak to inspire confidence in their performance; (2) for whatever reason, actors have not been successfully socialized into behaving consistently with existing norms; and (3) violations of these norms promise great rewards.

Realists describe the international system as anarchical with few, if any, embedded norms. They further assume that 'crime pays'. Extortion, invasion and cheating in arms control or trade agreements bring significant advantages. During the Cold War, opposition to arms control agreements with the Soviet Union was driven by the belief that Moscow would cheat and secretly augment its arsenal and somehow derive a significant strategic advantage from doing so. Ronald Reagan's signature phrase—'Trust but verify'—became a catchword for American conservatives. This oxymoron reflects the belief that agreements can be valuable but are rarely self-enforcing and accordingly require careful monitoring by those affected.

Why would leaders negotiate and sign agreements that they have no intention of following? We can imagine several conditions in which this might occur. Leaders might do so under duress and hope to wriggle out and ignore their commitments in better circumstances. The Weimar Republic had little choice but to sign the Versailles Peace Treaty and violated key provisions regarding the size of its army and its weaponry as soon as it could get away with it. Circumstances can change, making agreements freely negotiated no longer appear to be good deals. Keen to end the fighting in Indochina, the United States signed an accord in Geneva in 1954 in which North and South Vietnam were established pending unification in 1956 following an election; then Washington and its South Vietnam ally refused to hold the election when the time came because they recognized the communists were likely to win. Agreements can provide camouflage, making it easier to violate a commitment successfully. Nikita Khrushchev promised John F. Kennedy that he would not send missiles to Cuba for this reason.

Given their assumption of anarchy, realists reason that security must be the first concern of states and that none can trust others to support them when it endangers their security. The liberal model presupposes a desire to cooperate because it is the most rational strategy for actors motivated by security or wealth. Liberals believe that institutions have the potential to overcome anarchy and in practice do so to a considerable degree. Institutions are created, expand and become influential when states and other actors in the international system consider them useful; those who join and support these institutions have varying incentives to follow their norms and procedures, and, to the degree that they do, compliance is largely self-enforcing.

Two kinds of trust issues arise for liberals. The first concerns defection and free riding. Defection is the principal concern of realists, but liberals consider it less likely because of the positive incentives that institutions provide for compliance. Defection undermines trust, making it less likely that actors who behave in that way will be invited to participate in other institutions, which further raises the cost to them of defection. The second concern of liberals is the problem of the commons. The possible costs and risks to actors who take the first steps towards cooperation are a significant barrier to doing so. Here, too, liberals think that institutions reduce these costs, as does the existence of a hegemon with the power and authority to coordinate collaborative behaviour and punish defectors.

Constructivists offer understandings sharply at odds with those of realists and liberals. They direct our attention to the underlying causes of cooperation, not to individual instances of it. According to Christian Reus-Smit, 'all political power is deeply embedded in webs of social exchange and mutual constitution—the sort that escapes from the short-term vagaries of coercion and bribery to assume a structural, taken-for-granted form—ultimately rests on legitimacy'.[15] Martha Finnemore and Stephen Toope spell out the implications of this approach for cooperation and defection from binding commitments.[16] They argue that law, domestic and international, is a broad social phenomenon that is deeply embedded in the practices, beliefs and traditions of societies. To understand the incidence of compliance and defection, one must determine the congruence of law, custom or rule with social practices. When there is a good fit and actors see the institutions with which they are associated as legitimate, they are likely to act in accord with the law, custom or rule even when it is perceived to be contrary to their interests.

I contend that cooperation, defection and trust depend on the value structure of society. I argue that individuals and their societies are motivated by security, well-being and self-esteem.[17] The last finds expression in the quest for honour and standing. By excelling in activities valued by our peer group or society and winning the approbation of others, we in turn feel good about ourselves. Each of these motives generates a different approach to cooperation and conflict, a different calculus of risk-taking, and a different kind of hierarchy. They are also associated with different principles of justice. Security, self-esteem and wealth are universal motives, but the relative importance is culturally and historically specific. We must map their distribution to explain and predict the extent to which trust among actors is likely to develop, as well as the specific ways in which it develops.

In societies where material well-being is the dominant motive, cooperation is issue-specific and motivated by narrow calculations of self-interest. Trust is not diffuse but is limited to situations where actors judge that others have the same incentives they have to cooperate or play by the rules. This is why liberals turn to institutions in the hope of creating incentives to put trust and cooperation on more than a case-by-case basis. This strategy was evident among the early US Federalists who expected the Congress to create a strong sense of comity among its members. As alliances would shift in response to changing issues, yesterday's adversaries could be tomorrow's allies and vice versa. Thoughtful representatives and senators accordingly had strong incentives to maintain a degree of personal trust and seek compromise outcomes even when they had the votes to impose their preferences.[18]

In societies where honour and standing are the dominant motive, cooperation is based in the first instance on ties of kinship and reciprocity. These ties tend to be enduring and override the perceived security and economic risks of providing support. Honour-based societies give rise to clientage hierarchies, where those at the apex receive honour from those beneath them in return for providing practical support. When the system works, it provides symbolic rewards for the powerful, while constraining their behaviour and thus protecting the interests and independence of the weak. In international hierarchies of this kind, support takes the form of providing security and commercial advantages. Classical Greece, eighteenth-century Europe and East Asia in the era of imperial China offer historical examples. In these systems, defection is less common and trust is greater, but limited to actors within the system. For this reason, war was relatively rare in East Asia during the centuries of Chinese dominance.[19]

When reason loses control over either appetite or *thumos*, actors begin to worry about their ability to satisfy their goals, and perhaps about their security as well. In this circumstance security becomes the overriding motive and fear the dominant emotion. Cooperation will extend only to other actors who have similar fears because they face the same threats. Trust among actors will be low, even when their level of cooperation is high. Consider the relationship among the Big Three during the Second World War. The US provided Lend Lease aid to Britain and the Soviet Union, and the leaders of the three countries met periodically to hammer out military strategy and post-war occupation policies. But their relationship was marked by distrust—between Britain and the US, not just between the Anglo-American powers and the Soviet Union—and led to an East–West Cold War within three years of the defeat of the Axis powers.

The downside of trust

Justice and legitimacy are closely connected to trust. Trust is the expectation that others will honour their promises. Political orders, like their economic counterparts, rely on a fair degree of trust, as many critical relationships find expression in sequential rather than simultaneous behaviour.[20] Trust rests on both the principles of fairness and equality. It involves reciprocity, an expression of fairness, and equal treatment of agents, regardless of other inequalities between them.

Elites everywhere propagate discourses intended to justify their power and wealth and often succeed in generating trust and respect for themselves. The more the *demos* trusts the elite, the more the elite can exploit it, which can lead to more unjust political, economic and social orders. The less faith the *demos* has in elites, the more it is likely to hold them accountable to relevant principles of justice. Too much trust undermines justice and order, while too much distrust can be disruptive of it. In practice, we must balance the needs of order and those of justice, and this requires a healthy degree of distrust, but not so much as to encourage total alienation.

Building on this understanding, James Madison wrote in the *Federalist Paper*:

> If men were angels, no government would be necessary. If angels were to govern men, neither external nor internal controls on government would be necessary. In framing a government which is to be administered by men over men, the great difficulty lies in this: you must first enable the government to control the governed; and in the next place oblige it to control itself. A dependence on the people is, no doubt, the primary control on the government; but experience has taught mankind the necessity of auxiliary precautions.[21]

The same holds true for regional and international orders. Governance invariably requires some hierarchy and, with it, privileges for elites. Power invites abuse and too much faith in these elites encourages the exercise of crude self-interest and the exploitation of others. For the most recent historical example, one need look no further than the way the US has exploited its dominance since the end of the Cold War and the collapse of the Soviet Union.[22]

The authors of the *Federalist Papers* nevertheless felt the need to put their trust in some group if the American political system was to function effectively. They portrayed the educated, affluent elite—or at least some of them—as people capable of subordinating their personal interests to those of the common weal. For this reason, they wrote indirect election of senators into the constitution in the expectation that state legislatures would elect the most distinguished among them to the upper house. They also gave the upper house more powers regarding foreign policy and the appointment of judges and a veto power over legislation initiated in the House of Representatives.

Their opponents, the Democratic Republicans, put their trust in small famers, whom they regarded as simple men of virtue. A century later, communists would describe the proletariat as the only trustworthy class. Democratic Republican politicians were for the most part elitists, and few of the small farmers that they idealized ever got to exercise power. The communists, especially in the Soviet Union and Eastern Europe, took this hypocrisy to new levels.

The same mix of cynicism and naivety pervades the contemporary practice and theory of international relations. From the time of John Bright and Richard Cobden, liberals maintained that democracies were peaceful and trustworthy by nature. Woodrow Wilson made similar claims, and today this ideology finds reflection in the Democratic Peace programme and the appeal by Ivo Daalder and James Lindsay for a concert of democracies to run the world.[23] During the Cold War, the Soviet bloc maintained with equal fervour that only 'fraternal' communist governments could be trusted. The People's Republic of China, India and other non-aligned states put their trust in developing and, for the most part, ex-colonial countries. Realists, by contrast, respect the powerful and claim, in contrast to rival perspectives, that they see the world as it is and not through rose-tinted glasses. American realists and liberals alike are committed to preserving what they believe to be their country's pre-eminent position in the global system, conceiving of the US as 'exceptional and indispensable' to the system's stability.[24] They ignore all the ways in which the US fails to live up to the responsibilities of hegemony and attempts to exploit its economic and military power to advance parochial ends, often to the detriment of the stability of the economic and political order.[25]

My examination of trust suggests several conclusions. The first concerns the close connection between trust and cooperation: the latter is certainly possible without the former, but it is greatly facilitated by it, and sustained cooperation, whether bilateral or institutional, requires a high level of trust. The second is about the source of trust: as Plato recognized, it comes from friendship and the demonstrable willingness to do things for friends that have nothing to do with one's own goals. Treating friends, elites and countries as ends in themselves, not means to our ends—as Kant would put it—builds trust. It facilitates cooperation, which in turn builds common identities and more trust. Finally, there is the question of international relations theory. My short review indicates that it is hardly objective in the sense of being separate from the subject it purports to study. Rather, international relations theory is part and parcel of intellectual and political projects, and theorizes trust in ways consistent with and supportive of them. We should not trust these paradigms and theories nested within them but become more cynical regarding them and their claims.

14

THE ESSENCE OF STRATEGY

CONSTRUCTIVIST REALISM AND NECESSITY

James Gow

In his *Confessions of a Premature Constructivist*, Freedman alludes to the constructivist aspect that has always informed his work and to the more pointed version, realist constructivism, attributed to him by Peter Katzenstein.[1] Freedman, somewhat whimsically, points out that he could have, indeed, characterized a whole school of thought—had he only realized this at the time, rather than just getting on with that which just made sense (or which he, at other times, described as the 'perfectly b—obvious'). Although Freedman says that he did not know what Katzenstein meant, this de facto provides an embryonic precursor for the concept, which implicitly and unreflexively might be said to have underpinned his work over the years. *Strategy: a History* is implicitly replete with it, while at times both the sociological theory of the constructivist approach and the rational-actor ethos of traditional realist thinking are discussed explicitly. Moreover, because strategy itself is replete with a blend of construction and reality—strategy is a product of largely unrecognized constructivist realism—Freedman's whole oeuvre is filled with those same qualities. This blend has also informed his practice and that of those who have studied and worked both with and for him over the decades, whether this is because they came to study and research in the area of Freedman's work because they shared implicitly the approach, or because they learned while working with and around him. It has been largely a dominant, though unstated, approach to problems of strategy and policy, regarding both matters of historical evolution and the real world events of any given moment. However, despite its ever-expanding application, the realist constructivist term was not used beyond the initial reference by Katzenstein or developed as a concept. [2]

Why is Freedman realist constructivist or constructivist realist? What does it mean to be a realist constructivist or constructivist realist? These are the questions addressed in the present chapter, seeking to explore the nature of a way of working, whether methodology or disposition, that has never been recognized as such, but that is at the core of good strategy, and has, nonetheless, produced some of the most important and influential strategic, policy and historical analysis of the late-twentieth and early twenty-first centuries in the body of work generated by Freedman. In making this case for a distinctive approach, I stress among other points the value it holds in overcoming the somewhat ideological weakness to be found in the application of the two terms that combine to label it—realism and constructivism. Whether these are seen as dispositions, theories or methodologies, their conjunction in a form of analysis that blends intersubjective social process with acceptance of power and reality presents a distinctive and beneficial approach. That approach is evident in strategy, as Freedman has shown implicitly.

This, indeed, is why there is some worth in taking the relatively unusual step (both personally and in terms of Freedman scholarship) of exploring explicitly the theoretical waters that have nurtured great work. Of course, this could be seen as some form of wallowing in international relations theory, or an exercise for its own sake, given that Freedman is not generally thought of as a political philosopher. Yet, neither political philosophy nor its subordinate field of international relations theory has been a personal focus, either—so the initiative in treating his work in this way is certainly not merely to touch on his work while indulging personal current interests. It is a serious attempt to uncover the mechanism at work across Freedman's diverse work. It is an intellectual exercise that involves touching on the work of theoreticians developing their work intrinsically—of scholarly necessity. It is also one that, in many ways, would leave the rose of his collected work smelling as sweetly, if it were not tried. Yet, it merits the trying not because the rose of his practice will be given other names, but because the elements of colour and scent that define it might be identified and understood.

While most scholars have regarded constructivism and realism as contrasting and incompatible approaches, there have been a few attempts to bring the two together, although they have concentrated in the main on trying to work out how and why the two concepts can be joined together. These are discussed in the middle section of the present analysis, following a first section that traces the emergence of constructivism as a challenge to the dominance of realism in the study of international politics. That section is followed by a discussion of how constructivist realism operates in practice by strategists, examining elements of that which contributes to such practice in Freedman's *Strategy*, and arguing distinctively that necessity lies at the heart of what might be dubbed a constructivist realist analysis. Where Freedman himself might say that the essence of his approach is the combination of understanding the social processes and a recognition that power counts, the way in which power counts is when it affects necessity, where it is one highly important factor, but never the only one—even if the term 'soft power' is used to embrace a range of the elements not traditionally regarded as 'power'. What counts is the sense of empirical realities as they meet concepts and ideas of action in processes of adaptive social interaction. That is the essence of strategy or practical, 'real world' politics and policymaking.

The apparent oxymoron

Constructivist realism, or realist constructivism, is an oxymoron. That is, it is an apparent contradiction that actually makes sense—in this case, a great deal of sense. It is not a paradox or a contradiction in terms.

Indeed, it is only an oxymoron to the extent that unreflexive understanding of 'constructivism' pitches it in opposition to realism, as a political theory, whether that opposition is a matter of direct challenge or of attempts to bridge seemingly irreconcilable approaches, as discussed in the following section. The relatively late arrival of 'constructivism' to the theoretical and epistemological worlds of international relations scholarship initially saw it developed as a challenger to realism, a position that remains in many quarters, as we shall see. Subsequent development has seen some attempts to bridge the gap between constructivism and realism; however, these attempts, and the gap which they seek to span, are themselves premised on an assumed opposition.

Most international relations theorists espousing constructivism have positioned themselves staunchly in opposition to realism. The latter has been the dominant ideology in the field. Narrow or broad, nature-based or structurally based, realism explains the world, and international politics in particular, in terms of material self-interest and benefit, exercised by rational actors, focused on the maximization of power, which is seen as necessary for achieving material interest and benefit, including, above all else, security—that is, the security of the state, in a world defined by states in an insecure, anarchical set of relationships with one another.[3] Realism has conventionally stood in opposition to various forms of idealism or liberalism.[4] Idealists, in all their variety, have lobbed critical shells at realism, as have socialists, Marxists and those proclaiming so-called critical perspectives.[5] US scholars, simply because of the scale of the US academic market and the quality of its institutions, have dominated the academic study of international politics. To some extent, a consequence of this has been that the status of realism has been confirmed as the most influential approach. Each challenge has confirmed the failure of any competitor to supplant it, simply by pitching criticism and analysis against it. In practice, the failure of realism's opponents to supplant it has underscored its salience, as does the alternative approach, which embraces elements of both realism and idealism, recognizing the inevitability of brute power but also the possibility of rules tempering it in the 'international society' Hedley Bull identified.[6]

Alexander Wendt introduced the concept of constructivism into the mainstream international politics literature as a decidedly liberal approach to international affairs.[7] He sought consciously to situate it in the idealist tradition as a counter to realism.[8] He was not concerned with the mechanisms of international politics, or with analyzing the ways in which particular interpretations developed. His mission was to identify how constructivism could be used to assail the ramparts of realism and uncement its rock-hard walls. Wendt sought to follow those challenging mechanically rational, or power-based, interpretations in other fields, by using constructivism to show that international politics was social, cultural and contingent and, in doing so, to confirm that realism was neither scientific, nor material, nor necessary.

The point of constructivism, for Wendt and even more so for some other authors,[9] was ideological. This position also rested on somewhat faulty logic. Because reality is constructed, it was assumed that it could also simply be reconstructed in some different way that suited the preferences of those advocating the approach, whatever those preferences were. This, indeed, is one of the hopes of Wendt, who did most to raise the profile of constructivism.[10] In his landmark article 'Anarchy is what States Make it: The Social Construction of Power Politics', the main message is situated in the title. The very intention in adopting social constructivism is to create the possibility of change. Anarchy—the absence of any overriding authority—may define international society, he accepts. But this does not mean, as realists suppose, that states are bound to self-interest and self-protection, best achieved by the maximization of power. Those same states hold their collective destiny in their own hands. This means that they can replace competitive security dilemmas with other realities, if they so choose. They can construct new realities through their interaction.

Despite its challenge to realism, Wendt's approach is regarded as weak and too respectful of realism by some other proponents of constructivism, in seeking to engage realists in discussion. These scholars adopt more consciously and openly reflectivist positions,[11] meaning that (similar to critical and postmodern theorists) they refuse even to argue on the same ground as the realists (or, indeed, their liberal counterparts whose thought is also founded on some sense of Enlightenment rationalism). In this purely normative worldview, there is no independent reality that can be tested and verified, in contrast to the reasoning of scientific positivism, and 'facts' (with some concessions perhaps for the physical world) are merely social agreements, not the product of empirical testing. Even though the point about 'facts' might well be taken—they are socially agreed phenomena, though they may also have empirical, observable or testable bases in the world around them and in events—this approach is somewhat misguided. Constructivism's real analytical strength is the capacity to identify social processes. This should apply equally to realism, idealism and any other normative, or ideological, school of thought or practice. The analytical strength of a constructivist approach should be in understanding processes and dominant interpretations. However, Wendt's original purpose was to show that international politics and the realist interpretation of it were not inevitabilities, but inventions produced by social process—a position only amplified by those who go much further than he did in their reflectivist-constructivist challenge to realism and their sense that the world is imagined, and, so, can be reimagined and recreated in what they view as a better way. The fallacy in this is not to recognize that a constructed reality is still a reality. As George Schöpflin challenged those, such as Benedict Anderson, who applied constructivism to nationalism, the only reasonable response to this might be: 'So what? That does not make it any less real'.[12]

The outcomes of social construction are still 'real'. Any social product has 'real' underpinnings. Although realism is constructed, this does not mean that it is either arbitrary or necessarily wrong. While scepticism is an important test of the worth of any interpretation, it is probably not unreasonable to infer that realism, although socially constructed through intersubjective processes, has considerable purchase precisely because it builds on something 'real'. This is the need for viability and security—and, of course, the relevance of power in meeting those needs. Moreover, because it is felt or perceived with real feelings and perceptions by real human beings, the products of social interaction are indeed very, very real. This is why Freedman's approach works and why strategy, when practised well, is successful—it perforce deals with empirical realities, including those that are constructed, constituted and cathectic.

Bridging the gap

While the majority of those adopting constructivism, in one form or another, have done so in direct opposition to realism, there have been two different initiatives that could be seen as attempts to 'bridge the gap' between the two. The first of these, the Copenhagen school, can also be seen as a challenger to realism—I shall discuss this below. The second is the conscious attempt by some scholars to combine the two conceptually, theoretically or spiritually. The remainder of this section discusses these two initiatives.

The approach of the 'Copenhagen' constructivists, Barry Buzan, Ole Weaver and Jaap de Wilde, could be seen as opposing realism. They certainly aimed to improve on realism, in an attempt to broaden the scope of security studies. But, as we shall discuss, their work should be seen more as a constructivist approach that engages with realism, rather than opposing it. It seeks to make connections and bridge the gap between the two. In doing so, it goes a considerable way towards something that might be constructivist realism, but in the end does not reach that point.

The purpose and primary focus of the Copenhagen school was to broaden the agenda of security studies and practice. While seeking to do so, this school also wanted to ensure that there were useful boundaries. Its approach forms an alloy that is consciously constructivist and, at the same time, explicitly realist. The Copenhagen school is constructivist to the extent that it regards 'securitization' as 'an essentially intersubjective process'. This means that only in the most extreme and imminent cases can threats be identified clearly and objectively.[13] Realism is important, however, with the avowed expression of this school's position as 'post-sovereign realism'.[14] The focus on social processes that determine security is driven by a desire to modify realism, rather than replace it. By adopting constructivism, 'it will sometimes be possible to maneuver [sic] the interaction among actors and thereby curb security dilemmas'.[15] Constructivism, reflexively engaging with realism, is clearly aimed at using the power of knowledge and understanding to temper and alter realism—in a way, this is similar to the mission adopted by Wendt. Ultimately, however, the Copenhagen school's mission is to improve realism, in an effort to transform security relationships and, in an ideal world, to make realism redundant. In the final analysis, realism's dominance would be removed by embracing it. At this point, the Copenhagen bridge between constructivism and realism falls short of becoming constructivist realism. Its mission is not to place realism in an intersubjective context, which facilitates sound and beneficial analysis—even though its approach makes this possible. Rather, its purpose in embracing realism is to demonstrate that it is not necessarily an inherent or 'natural' position, whatever its strengths and merits, but a phenomenon or philosophy that is constituted and, because it is constituted, is also changeable. Once realism has a change-able character—so the logic of the Copenhagen school continues—realism, while a present reality at the point of departure, might be transformed out of existence.

In contrast, others who have sought to bring constructivism and realism together have not had the eventual aspiration of removing real-ism from the scene. These scholars have embraced the two with a sense of using the combination to improve knowledge and understanding of the world around us with a theoretical or epistemological prism that might be more flexible than traditional realism, as well as more in line with strategic, political and social needs in many respects, thus enabling adaptation and change in a changing world. This was certainly an aspi-ration in Gow's initial treatment of the idea in 2004, which sought to offer an intellectual mechanism that would allow adjustment to, and facilitate understanding of, questions of peace and security, as well as force and justice, in the twenty-first century—discussion of which, in draft form, prefigured Freedman's 'Premature Constructivist' article.[16] However, that initiative was overlooked by others, in the main.[17]

There was more recognition, though less than there might have been, for J. Samuel Barkin's examination of the compatibility and use-fulness of the two approaches in something he termed 'realist construc-tivism', in the *International Studies Review*.[18] Realist constructivism was later developed into a book, by the same name.[19] The greater attention came through a set of response and reflection articles published subse-quently in the same journal, openly using the phrase 'bridging the gap', and with a brief editorial by Patrick Thaddeus Jackson.[20] These responses shared Barkin's mission, while varying sufficiently to make Barkin himself respond in terms of plural 'realist constructivisms'.[21]

Barkin originally made the same point as Gow: that constructivism is a means, just as compatible with realism as with any other worldview and not in 'direct opposition' to it. It is, Barkin correctly asserts, 'mis-leading' to view constructivism as 'an IR paradigm' in the same way as realism and liberalism.[22] These paradigms reflect 'a set of assumptions about how politics work', whereas constructivism 'is a set of assumptions about how to study politics'.[23] The blending of the two, he argues, can actually serve as a corrective to critics' misperceptions of realism, regarding materialism and the place of morality (offering a good exposition of the place of morality in Morgenthau, along the way). He thus shows that realism and constructivism are not incompatible—rather, they can form a complementary general approach to the study of international politics. It is an approach that recognizes power, among other factors, but also offers understanding of how power is shaped and used. While embedded in a world of international relations theory, this is a point of connection both to strategy, as practice, and to Freedman's work, in practice, both of which are driven by the mechanics of constructivist realism at their heart. It is not a connection made by Barkin, of course, as his concerns are theoretical and with the realm of international politics, not the application of theory (consciously or unconsciously) in policy analysis, or policy itself, or in strategic action.[24]

As noted, this perspective led to further reflection by other scholars. Jackson and Daniel Nexon argue that power is embedded in social structures and so inheres in those very structures—yet those structures are, axiomatically, socially formed. Hence constructivism's utility is in allowing those social structures to be unpicked and understood.[25] For them, the point is to use constructivism to explain why power cannot be transcended in international politics (in contrast to most constructivists who adopt the approach with a view to overcoming it). In making this case, in their title and in one passing (but undeveloped) reference they raise a distinction between constructivist realism and realist-constructivism. They posit that Barkin, despite using the formulation 'realist constructivism', actually calls for 'constructivist realism', by which they mean 'a realism that takes norms and ideas seriously as objects of analysis'. They contrast this with realist-constructivism, in which not only the inversion of the two terms is important, but also the insertion of a hyphen: this, they contend, is 'a constructivism that involves a self-consistent set of arguments about why power cannot, in any way, be transcended in international politics'.[26] While there is a discussion about the relationships between the key terms, realism and constructivism, and their ordering (which I shall revisit below, briefly), that there is value in their conjunction is beyond question.

Jennifer Sterling-Folker sees power as embedded in social structures, but also founded in nature. She points to the claimed value of realist constructivism in allowing space for morality (as Barkin, and, indeed, Morgenthau, might argue). However, she shows considerable scepticism, in the end concluding that 'inadvertently' Barkin has advocated a 'combination in which classical realism assists liberal IR scholars in understanding why power keeps getting in the way of desirable normative structures', which 'threatens to keep us on the same old theoretical treadmill'.[27] In many respects, this is unfair and misses the very purpose in the realist constructivist agenda: to provide a means with which to research, interpret and understand international politics better, rather than to develop an end position that settles the ideological differences between realism and liberalism as dispositions.

Janice Bially Mattern shares Barkin's view that power matters, although this is an assumption with no reasons to back it, but adds the perspective that power has different forms and expressions, which depend on context and social institutions.[28] One strength of the realist constructivist approach in particular, therefore, is that it can capture and explain this variety. This underscores the value of the approach, to a large extent, as the focus is on research and outcomes.

The final contribution to the forum on Barkin's realist constructivism is somewhat different from the others. Richard Ned Lebow is less focused on the place of power and explaining power—although it remains important. Instead, he successfully builds on Barkin's start by showing how the realist and constructivist traditions can, and need to, work together both to investigate the 'modalities that govern the ends actors seek and the means they use to achieve these ends' and to explore 'the kinds of worlds in which liberal and realist assumptions give us the most analytical leverage'.[29] In doing this, he also extends Barkin's approach to Morgenthau's classical realism, adding references to Thucydides and Clausewitz, as well as classical Greek philosophy, in particular the notion of honour. Honour is one of three elements—the others are appetite (or interest) and fear—in that classical tradition. While realism can explain what happens when appetite and fear are at work, it is constructivism that can allow space for the construction, interpretation and interplay of honour with other factors. He follows the classical writers in seeing fear—and so the place for power—as having relevance when appetite and honour are not satisfied. The value of realist constructivism is to allow the importance of social identity to emerge and be explained—and also to allow the place of power (which might be better conceived as negative or material power) rooted in fear to be illuminated.

Evidently, from the work of the Copenhagen school, which embraced realism and constructivism while envisioning the eventual transcendence of realism, through the more consciously integrated work of Barkin, Gow and others discussed above, there is value in bringing the two together. Even if there might be some scepticism regarding which term has primacy, as well as differences over the exact relevance of power, these are discussions of how and why realist constructivism is relevant, not of whether the two terms are mutually exclusive.

Constructivist and realist

Recognizing that realism is not a natural phenomenon and that it is not fixed is contrary to the positions of both its proponents and its critics is also to recognize it as a social construction. While both realists and some of their opponents appear to believe that this undermines the concept, it actually reinforces it. Moreover, the constructivist interpretation allows greater adaptability and variety, enhancing the concept, as well as permitting appropriate place for aspects other than power, such as values. Simplistic and reified interpretations of the international environment need to be eschewed, following Sabrina Ramet (although she made the point from an adamantly idealist perspective). The 'othering' of realists and idealists as archetypes tends more to impair theory and generate only caricature.[30] We inhabit a complex world. In that context, a composite theoretical approach, conceived and applied with suitable sensitivity, is needed, which can embrace both the immanence of rules and the significance of change. The value of a framework that blends constructivism and realism seems unmissable. 'Constructivist realism' offers rich possibilities for approaching the study of power, values and practices in the changing global context, as the remainder of this section shows, with necessity at the core of analysis.

Constructivist realism, in many respects, only bears out features that realism always consisted of. Emphasizing the material, as many in traditional realism do, while offering an a priori basis for a would-be scientific methodology and worldview, in truth only helps to highlight a significant focal point for the attribution of value. Conventional realists and neorealists concentrate heavily on the material in some cases, because it is apparently believed to have an independent or intrinsic force. However, the significance of the material is that it can reveal the attribution of value—Barkin suggests that the emphasis on the material by some realists (or critical creators or realist straw men) is that it helps to make power 'measurable'.[31]

Freedman echoes this, noting that power may be attributed to entities and 'measured in terms of the more blatant indicators of military and economic strength'. But that is rarely enough: 'an ample stock of both did not guarantee favorable outcomes in all encounters' and 'the powerful did not always get their way'—context and the relationship between the relevant actors have to be taken into account.[32] It is the contexts and the interrelationships that count. Otherwise, Davids would never bring down Goliaths and, beyond this, secure triumphs. Freedman points out that David's success was dependent not only on his acuity with the sling and stone, but also on his killing Goliath to make sure of the outcome of that duel and, in addition, on moral factors—faithful adherence to God's will and the Philistines' acceptance of his victory over Goliath (whereas they could have regarded it as a matter of trickery requiring revenge).[33] This reflects the political-sociological understanding that permeates Freedman's work.

Despite his obvious concern with power, Freedman is clear that realism is limited. Indeed, he clearly is realist to the extent that he judges that power matters—as he notes, realism is a 'temperament to which strategic theorists have been presumed to be susceptible'.[34] However, in discussing the appropriation of Thucydides by realists, he makes clear both his rejection of that appropriation through processes of reduction and the beginnings of his scepticism regarding the narrowly cast and 'more doctrinaire' versions of realism and the supposedly rational, materially focused, self-interested mechanical theory that emerges. Thucydides, he maintains, while realistic in 'describing human affairs as he found them', was not a realist in the theoretical sense. The Greek historian, Freedman justly argues, 'did not suggest that men were bound to act on the basis of narrow self-interest or that they actually served their broader interests if they did'. Instead, Thucydides presented a more 'complex' picture, in which 'momentary strength' was susceptible to 'underlying weakness' and leaders had to deal with a variety of actors as they sought advantage; and even to the extent that Freedman recognizes that Thucydides acknowledged the importance of power—which Freedman certainly does not reject—it is linked to reputation and to the combined qualities of 'fear, honor and interest'.[35] As he develops his magisterial review of strategic thinking in all its forms, Freedman exposes not only the strong sociological aspects of good strategic analysis, but also the importance of psychological studies and, ultimately, of scripts as the starting points for strategic narratives—which narratives, nonetheless, are the intersubjective product of scripts meeting scripts and then extemporization and revision.[36]

In making this analysis, nothing conveys the constructivist sensibility more than Freedman's discussions of the sociology of power and, especially, the limitations of rational actor theory—a mechanistic approach linked to conventional realist understanding.[37] Rational choice theory, which borrowed from economics, posited that individuals make choices to maximize utility. In realist terms, the basic rational motivation was self-interest, served by material benefit, made possible by (and further making possible) the maximization of power. However, whereas economic affairs could be expressed in monetary—and so numerical—terms, free will, intuition, psychological disposition and sociability, among other things, also affected decisions. In contrast to the natural sciences, which the scientific positivists of political science and realism sought to emulate, laws could not be established—this was 'impossible when dealing with voluntary agents'. What might work normally—threats or inducements producing a particular response— 'could on occasion produce something quite different'.[38] Indeed, social and psychological experiments came to show that mature human behaviour did not conform to the theory that narrow self-interest was the motor for decision-making, with the exceptions of children and those with neurological disorders—meaning that rational actor theory and realism were predicated on the mentality of children and those with emotional health issues as the norm.[39] For those with more 'normal', adult qualities, factors such as reputation and cooperation were important. Strategy, whether in Thucydides' historical description of

271

actors in the Peloponnesian Wars or in contemporary engagement in matters of peace and security, required a more sophisticated approach, which took account of social factors, including both cooperation and interaction with others. Undoubtedly, the realist disposition might remain, but it needs to be understood in socially constructed and changing circumstances. Recognizing that realism is socially constructed does not make it a mere invention. Social construction occurs around points of value—whether these are material or spiritual or completely other, in some way. It occurs around that which counts.[40]

Structure in international and group life is the product of social processes of construction. In the twenty-first century security context, relationships and their patterns are complex. They are a product of state behaviour—acknowledging states as the dominant agents in international activity—and the behaviour of other social groups and processes in relation to international society. In general, that activity is predominantly shaped by the imperative to foster stability in the international system (and, in some cases, by actors who would, on the contrary, foster instability to suit their ambitions).[41]

The post-Cold War period revealed, more than ever, the importance of stability in international life and of the state as a core actor, even if other actors had gained importance above, below and beyond the state. Statehood remained central to violence in international society. Every violent conflict was about statehood, one way or another, whether this meant control of existing states and how they should be run, or the absence of central enforcing authority in such states, or the redistribution of territory, populations and resources within or across the boundaries of existing states, or changing the contours or status of those borders. Quasi-states, quasi-entities and quasi-structures emerged,[42] alongside the conventional state, which retained key importance as the key actor and so the leading focus for study in international life.

In the early post-Cold War period, the Yugoslav conflict gave ample evidence both of the salience of sub-state actors and transnational characters and of the way in which the interaction of actors shapes events, with one action begetting a reaction, and so forth. The conflict developed from being an important question for European security and stability, and a first test of the brand-new Conflict Prevention Centre of what was then the Conference on Security and Cooperation in

Europe.[43] It subsequently became a test of the nascent EU Common Foreign and Security Policy. As that test was fumbled, the conflict continued to become a trial of both UN diplomacy and UN peacekeeping. After this, international engagement with the South Slav combatants and interactions among themselves provided a harsh examination of European, transatlantic and East–West relations, as well as post-Cold War co-operative security initiatives. Finally, NATO's credibility and, with it, that of the US were critically challenged, ending in the use of force first to end armed hostilities in Bosnia and Hercegovina, and, then, in tackling Serbian atrocities in Kosovo. Taken as a whole, the handling of the Yugoslav conflict demonstrated that it was possible for international action to be instrumental in ending the conflict and generating arrangements for peace that had to be underpinned by the same type of engagement and commitment. Without commitment to the follow-on, securing agreement was likely to be futile. The interaction of actors and existing structures with the events in the former Yugoslavia and their own actions, shared interests and values resulted in an international use of force and full engagement, each decision governed by necessity, paving the way for further necessary action when what had gone before proved not enough to achieve success.[44]

Sub-state actors in internal armed conflicts became more prominent and other non-state, or in some cases quasi-state, actors saliently appeared on the international stage. Sometimes, these were transnational bodies. They were often non-governmental or quasi-governmental. Sometimes they were sponsored by states, yet kept an independent character. The dominant example, in the first decades of the twenty-first century, became al-Qa'ida. Meanwhile, other phenomena, given meaning by social contexts but independent of them, became highly significant, including environmental degradation, climate change and the impact of highly integrated global financial markets. All of this required new approaches to state sovereignty. This did not make states or sovereignty irrelevant. Rather, they confirmed the continuing centrality of the state, as soon as discussion moved beyond the superficial. The reason for attention to be paid to any of these issues at all lay in their impact on certain states, groupings of states, capacities of states, or the very meaning of the state. The panoply of non-state actors and phenomena that emerged gained attention because they affected the state. New thinking on the protection offered by the traditional mutual recognition mechanism between holders of sovereign rights only served, in the end, to reinforce the state in one way or another. The order and stability that states needed required amendments to the traditional interpretations of, and protections offered by, sovereignty.

In this context, there was a problem with the stance taken by conventional realists, such as John Mearsheimer.[45] Mearsheimer argues strongly that realism remains relevant and essential. He posits five theses to support this position. First, states are still the principal actors and they continue to operate under conditions of anarchy. Secondly, great powers (on which he retained a considerable fixation) continue to need—and possess—offensive military capacity. Thirdly, states can never be completely sure about the intentions of other states (he remains reluctant to acknowledge a significant place for other actors). Fourthly, great powers continue to insist on their survival. And, last, the state remains a relatively rational actor, capable of formulating strategies to guarantee that survival. In themselves, these propositions are far from unreasonable. The same can be said for Mearsheimer's projection from this basis. No one can know for sure how states and power might be aligned at any moment in the future. However, his approach cannot start to address the real challenges faced by states, including great powers, in the twenty-first-century security environment. The dominant threats and challenges, taking up perhaps 80 or 90 per cent of the policy agenda in the 2000s, do not begin to be covered by the Mearsheimer position—even if, sometimes, great power positions in the background are significant and powerful states can be a disruptive presence, as both the US in Iraq and Russia in Ukraine confirmed in their own ways. The disruption of international order and intrastate conflicts, such as those in the Yugoslav lands and Ukraine and many parts of Africa and Asia, as well as the operations of clandestine networks such as al-Qa'ida, aiming to disrupt and destabilize international order in general and Western societies in particular, have no place in that conventional realist analysis. However, constructivist approaches empirically do.[46]

As soon as it is acknowledged that threats and challenges stem less from states and more from non-state sources, including transnational or international ideological terrorist movements, then conventional realist logic cannot apply. While threats from other states could never be excluded, policymakers and serious academics had to face the real challenges of international security. To do otherwise would be negligent. It would also be quite unrealistic.

Tackling the genuine security challenges in the twenty-first century requires a perspective that can only be provided by social constructivism, involving strong empirical understanding of the appropriate agents and structures, infused with a strong dose of reality and recognition of power, described as a temperament by Berdal:[47] constructivist realism. However, to understand how to take value from that analysis requires the identification of a quality that can turn description into purposive analysis. That element is necessity—an attribute that might be applied to material factors or to ethical, emotional or reputational ones. Whichever variable, or combination of them, counts, the point is that they define a reality. Power and material need provide necessity for realists, while these factors consolidated in the structure of state interrelationships constitute necessity for neo-realism.

However, those versions of necessity do not apply to the twenty-first-century security context. Power, material interest and the structure of state relations sit alongside other variables in a web of contingency. Necessity provides a distinct alternative in constructivist realism, supplying a vital thread to make the greatest sense of the approach. Necessity sits at the heart of a constructivist realist approach, which acknowledges the importance of power (among other factors) but which is shaped by an understanding of social construction. Identifying threats, rogues and enemies is a social process. That process requires an empirical foundation and rationality. It is neither arbitrary nor contingent. Only necessity explains why political leaders take the difficult decisions surrounding security and the use of force, when otherwise they might well do all that they could to avoid taking action. Necessity is the defining element at the heart of decisions by political agents, in response to their various contexts and in relation to structures of which they find themselves a part. It is also at the core of the concept of constructivist realism. Construction produces structure. Structure can change as a result of processes of construction. Change results from need. People act when it is necessary, not because those holding a particular worldview wish it. This is an essentially realist point. Necessity marks out constructivist realist theory from constructivism more broadly. Necessity determines the social and intersubjective relations that constitute international security. Necessity might stem from material need—as it would in conventional realism. Equally, however, its source might lie in the realm of norms or emotions. It is even possible—if not likely—that a combination of material and moral factors will be at work. Whatever the case, it will be founded on need—as understood by the relevant actors—not contingency.

Conclusion

Strategy, in whichever idiom, is a product of constructivist realism, involving the reflexive admixture of input and reaction processes and the necessity of accepting empirical realities. Constructivist realism provides a prism with which to investigate and interpret flux and stasis in international politics. It both permits and demands attention to empirical matter,[48] even where perceptions are an issue regarding threats, as well as where threats might exist but be unperceived in practice while still perceptible in principle. The September 11 attacks on the United States provide a clear example here. At other moments, threats might be imperceptible to some actors, who will no doubt show strong scepticism, while others are able to identify them. To attribute value to the material should not mean excluding the value of the non-material. The constructivist realist embraces ideals and values, but not exclusively. Ideals contribute where they reflect a perceived need. Values are essential features of any reality. And, as the greatest realists such as Morgenthau realized, they need to be secured—and promoted. Constructivist realism captures this need. Its true usefulness and merit is that it facilitates interpretation of flux and change in the security sphere. It accounts for change and for new approaches to change, while maintaining its focus on necessity in international security. That has always been the essence of both practical politics and strategy—the ability and the capacity to absorb change and adapt while maintaining a sense of direction. Good strategy, looking to the future, and good scholarship, whether oriented to past, present or future, depend on this.

In terms of theory, acknowledging that realism is something constructed, and is not an essentialist material phenomenon that is discovered and not created, allows two developments. The first, as argued by Rankin and at least recognized by others, such as Freedman and Lebow, is that it paves the way for a more subtle and complex reading of realism, perhaps more in accordance with Morgenthau's original, in which various strands are recurrently interwoven. These strands, of course, include values and rules. Indeed, even in a conventional, narrow realist interpretation, where norms and rules are judged not to count, making and enforcing laws and standards, as the expressions of power, is a key element in the quest to maximize power for the purpose of physical survival. In many respects, this lies at the foundation of realism. The second development concerns greater flexibility. As situations change, understanding of both the world and the rules operating in it can shift accordingly. That adjustment is a social process. It involves intersubjective interaction. But at its heart are both the promotion and protection of physical security and values, and also the shaping of responses to what threatens them. Adaptation of this kind becomes possible when a constructivist realist lens is used—or, it might be said, a strategic approach.

Constructivist realism harnesses constructivism while acknowledging that there is merit in realism. The notion follows Wendt and others in giving place to ideals, values and social interaction. At the same time, it is realist to the extent that power, the material, and the possibility of self-interest (albeit hard to define precisely) are all recognized. But they are acknowledged as socially constructed—functions of social interaction. While there is probably little significant difference between a realist constructivist and a constructivist realist, in that each relies on both of these elements, distinctions can be perceived. These might lie in perspectives on the possibility of transcending power, as Jackson and Nexon posit. They might lie in the logic of starting with process and arriving at disposition—thus, a constructivist approach results in a realist understanding. This harmonizes with the realist constructivist perspective of Jackson and Nexon—the 'realist' describes the 'constructivist'. Conversely, the 'constructivist' might cast adjectival light on the 'realist'. This might be in the somewhat looser sense in which Jackson and Nexon see Barkin's view—a realism that allows space for values and norms (much as the father of political realism, Morgenthau, did). 'Constructivism' might also colour 'realism' in the sense that a disposition to recognize power is combined with a methodology, or at least a sensibility, which recognizes that power, like norms, is a function of social interaction, of the attribution of value, and that however embedded or reified it might become, there is always the possibility of adaptability and change. Necessity, as I have argued, lies at the core of such an approach.

This approach also makes evident that constructivist realism is not so much an oxymoron as an apparent oxymoron. Whereas an oxymoron is an apparent contradiction that actually makes sense—an understanding that would fit with the conventional views of both realists and constructivists in their silos on either side of an intellectual, philosophical and methodological divide—the truth is that, properly understood, as shown in the present chapter, there is not even an apparent contradiction. It may be better to judge the combination of these terms to be not an oxymoron but rather an apparent oxymoron, since there can be little real dispute that they are complete complements to one another when applied, as they are in Freedman's scholarship and practice—whether strategic analysis and history of policy, or strategic and policy practice. In the end, however, the application of the label matters little, where the work produced is informed, even implicitly, by the way of working it represents, and it stands on its own merits. Freedman's output, over the years, as well as good strategy with this approach at its core, confirms this.

15

FREEDMAN ON MACHIAVELLI

Philip Bobbitt

This chapter was originally presented as a lecture entitled 'Freedman
on Machiavelli', but somehow, in the transmission from my word pro-
cessor to the printers of the programme, the title changed to
'Freedman and Machiavelli'. One should not be too picky about these
things, but there is a substantial difference between the two titles.
'Freedman *on* Machiavelli' takes up a rich subject owing to Lawrence
Freedman's many reflections on the Florentine master, including those
that appeared in *Strategy: A History*.[1] 'Freedman *and* Machiavelli' suggests a slightly different focus on the two men and even hints that there
is something other than the formal relation between them of the first
title: it sounds as though they are in league somehow, and that the
political theorist and academic empire-builder who is Lawrence
Freedman may have some Machiavellian traits which his good-natured
demeanour and ready laugh do not advertise.

For, like Niccolò Machiavelli, Lawrence Freedman has led many
lives. Both men served as foreign policy advisers to the heads of their
respective governments, Machiavelli as principal national security

adviser to Piero Soderini, the Gonfaloniere of Florence, and Freedman as a foreign policy adviser to Prime Minister Tony Blair and an author of Blair's path-breaking address in Chicago in 1999. Both men were tasked to be official historians, Machiavelli having been commissioned by the Medici to write the *Florentine Histories* and Freedman as the author of *The Official History of the Falklands Campaign*. Both men held high government office, Machiavelli as the Second Chancellor to the Florentine Signoria and Freedman as a member of the Privy Council. Both men wrote about war, each describing its practice as an 'art'. Of course, there are also differences, but I imagine that the relationship between these two thinkers is deeper than the biographical. For each addressed a problem that emerged in the Renaissance and has not left mankind's preoccupations since: to what extent, and in what ways, can we rationally anticipate and shape the future to serve our ends?

In some respects, the conclusions of these two writers are quite similar, and this is captured by the description of Freedman as a 'constructivist realist'. The constructivist, I take it, is one who believes that

> international actors reproduce or alter systems through their actions. Any given international system does not exist because of immutable structures, but rather the very structures are dependent for their reproduction on the practices of the actors. Fundamental change of the international system occurs when actors, through their practices, change the rules and norms constitutive of international interaction …

> Fundamental changes in international politics occur when beliefs and identities of domestic actors are altered, thereby also altering the rules and norms that are constitutive of their political practices. To the extent that patterns emerge in this process, they can be traced and explained, but they are unlikely to exhibit predetermined trajectories to be captured by general historical laws, be they cyclical or evolutionary.[2]

The realist dissents from this view by holding that there are indeed some general laws that govern states. For example, realists

> claim that survival is the principal goal of every State. Foreign invasion and occupation are thus the most pressing threats that any State faces. Even if domestic interests, strategic culture, or commitment to a set of national ideals would dictate more benevolent or cooperative international goals, the anarchy of the international system requires that States constantly ensure that they have sufficient power to defend themselves and advance

their material interests necessary for survival ... Realists hold States to be rational actors.

This means that, given the goal of survival, States will act as best they can in order to maximize their likelihood of continuing to exist ... Realists assume that all States possess some military capacity, and no State knows what its neighbors intend precisely. The world, in other words, is dangerous and uncertain. In such a world it is the Great Powers—the States with most economic clout and, especially, military might, that are decisive.[3]

Machiavelli believed that political actors could alter the structures of action and meaning within which they operated—after all, he was the chief advocate of a neoclassical princely state that would replace feudal structures—but he also believed in certain immutable laws:

And it is easily recognized by those who consider present and ancient affairs that the same desires and passions exist in all Cities and people, and that they always existed. So that to whoever with diligence examines past events, it is an easy thing to foresee the future in any Republic, and to apply those remedies which had been used by the ancients, or, not finding any of those used, to think of new ones from the similarity of events. But as these considerations are neglected or not understood by those who govern, it follows that the same troubles will exist in every time.[4]

I have often thought that the image of the bicycle, had it been foreseen by his friend Leonardo, would have captured this dualism: that history moved by cycles, repeating itself endlessly, but it did move, making some choices impossible and opening up others—just as the bicycle wheel rotates in the same circular motion, bringing each point on the rim to a temporary prominence but, as it moves across a street, changing its position relative to the world that the wheel must traverse.

Like Machiavelli, Freedman has not devoted himself to describing ideal worlds towards which we must strive. I am inclined to think there is no more fatuous, if wistful, observation than that of G.B. Shaw, who famously remarked that 'most men see things as they are; I see things that never were, and ask, Why not?' For Freedman, as for Machiavelli, it is not only awfully hard to see things as they truly are; it is distracting and self-defeating to pretend to live in a world where the ordinary dynamics of human history and interaction have been suspended.

But if there are similarities between Freedman and Machiavelli, there are also differences, and these can be most clearly observed in those formulations of Machiavelli that Freedman himself expresses. Freedman calls our attention to the distinction between strategy and stratagems, a distinction that is important for Machiavelli. His stratagems of course are legendary, even notorious. For example, in discussing how to restore order to a city divided into factions whose conflicts have led to violence, Machiavelli writes that there are three ways:

> either to kill them as the Romans did, or to remove them from the City, or for them to make peace together under an obligation not to offend each other again. Of these three methods this last is the most harmful, less certain, and more useless; for it is impossible where much blood has run or other similar injuries inflicted that a peace made by force should endure; for seeing themselves together face to face each day, it is difficult that they should abstain from injuring each other, as new causes for quarrel can arise among themselves because of their intercourse every day. [The best method] is none other than to kill the leaders of the tumults. (Book 3, Chapter 27)

Or this famous passage:

> a Prince should inspire fear in such a fashion that if he do not win love he may escape hate. For a man may very well be feared and yet not hated … And if constrained to put any to death, he should do so only when there is manifest cause or reasonable justification. But, above all, he must abstain from the property of others. For men will sooner forget the death of their father than the loss of their patrimony.

Or his oft-quoted advice: 'Upon this, one has to remark that men ought either to be well treated or crushed, because they can avenge themselves of lighter injuries, of more serious ones they cannot; therefore the injury that is to be done to a man ought to be of such a kind that one does not stand in fear of revenge'.

Machiavelli's stratagems are well known, if not entirely well understood, because, ironically, he first became known outside his Florentine circle through a collection of 'maxims' drawn from his writings. But his grand strategy, his call for a neoclassical state in Italy, was ignored by his contemporaries and overlooked by subsequent commentators. This may be responsible for the paradox that while, as Freedman notes, Machiavelli is identified with the tactics of overcoming the enemy by deceit and cunning, he greatly admired the Roman Republic on which he wished to model an Italian republic, consolidating the Papal States with the city and possessions of Florence. As Freedman notes,

The most powerful dichotomy in all strategic thought was the one first introduced by Homer as the distinction between one seeking victory in the physical domain and the other in the mental, one relying on being strong and the other on being smart, one depending on courage and the other imagination, one facing the enemy directly and the other approaching indirectly, one prepared to fall with honor and the other seeking to survive with deception … Under the Romans, Homer's Odysseus morphed into Virgil's Ulysses and became part of a story of deceitful and treacherous Greeks … Heroes were sought who were more plain-speaking, honorable as well as brave in battle, less reliant on cunning and cleverness. Thus the Roman historian Livy wrote of the more traditionally minded Senators' distaste for a tendency toward 'an excessively cunning wisdom'. This was akin to 'Punic tricks and Greek craftiness, among whom it was more glorious to deceive an enemy than to conquer by force'. Romans would not wage war 'through ambushes and nocturnal battles, nor through feigned flight and unforeseen returns upon a careless enemy' … nor by 'craft or accident'.[5]

How can the identification of Machiavelli with guile and trickery be reconciled with his admiration for Livy? After all, Machiavelli's *Discourses* are *Discourses on the First Ten Books of Livy*. Partly, the answer is context. As in the celebrated passage about the lion and the fox:

> Because therefore a prince must sometimes practise the ways of the beasts, he should choose from among them the fox and the lion, for while the lion cannot defend himself from traps, the fox cannot protect himself from wolves. It is therefore necessary to be a fox in order to recognize traps, and a lion in order to frighten wolves: those who rely only on the ways of the lion do not appreciate this.[6]

But another partial explanation is that Machiavelli looked to the Roman Republic for a grand strategy, for a model for the state and not simply for stratagems.

Freedman characterizes Machiavelli in two ways, from which I would slightly dissent. Firstly, he describes Machiavelli's methods as 'empirical' and suggests that this is why he should be considered the father of political science. And secondly, Freedman claims that Machiavelli 'did not consider himself to be offering a new morality but rather a reflection on contemporary practical morality'.[7] In a very interesting way, these two ideas are connected.

Machiavelli is far from an empiricist, if by that is meant that he held that we have no source of knowledge save that which can be inferred from the data of experience. Seeing him this way, which of course many do, leads to the awkward conclusion that, as an empiricist, he was not a very good one. After all, many of the examples he gives are drawn from mythology, or from historical accounts that he either concocted, or knew to be false. It would be truer to say that Machiavelli was a rhetorician who used historical and mythological examples the way a lawyer uses precedents. He did not collect the data and then inductively arrive at a premise, which he then tested against data. Rather, he intuited conclusions he wished to persuade others of and made persuasive use of those examples he could show as supporting his conclusions, distinguishing away counter-examples.

This is important because Machiavelli is often thought, on the basis of the description of his work as empirical, to have been the first political scientist. Thus it has been said that what Galileo gave in his *Dialogue* and what Machiavelli gave in *The Prince* were really 'new sciences'. Just as Galileo's law of dynamics became the foundation of our modern science of nature, so, it is suggested, Machiavelli paved a new way to political science. I think I know what people have in mind when they say this; it is Machiavelli's resolute reliance on the actuality of politics as he knew it. A Galileo in the study of politics would distinguish between facts and dogma, in contrast to a normative vision of a political science. But Machiavelli does not in fact separate fact from morality,[8] even if he denies that observing the conventional moral virtues will always yield the most efficacious result for the state. Rather, he asserts a vigorous morality that comes with taking responsibility for the state. He is not trying simply to describe facts dispassionately, disinterestedly, but instead wants to move his readers to action; his approach is that of the historical rhetorician rather than the policy scientist.

This brings us to the second of Freedman's claims, that Machiavelli did not offer a new morality but merely wished to turn a gimlet eye on the prevailing moral behaviour in his time. In fact, Machiavelli's prince is not advised on how to comport himself for his own sake in the light of the corruption of his times, but rather to subordinate all indices of right behaviour to the one parameter of serving the state. It is not that, by following Machiavelli's suggestions, a prince will be a better prince; rather, the very notion of what it means to be a prince must change with the advent of a princely state.

We can see this point in one of Machiavelli's unacknowledged references to Cicero's *De Officiis*. Cicero urges that rulers cultivate the virtue of generosity, and that 'any suspicion of avarice must be avoided', and he observes that 'no vice … is more foul than avarice … particularly among leading men and those who control public affairs'.[9] Yet when Machiavelli takes up the qualities of 'liberality and meanness' in *The Prince*, he offers a very different view of the matter. Liberality is thought to be a good aspect of reputation; as a Christian, the prince should make his benefactions anonymously, but this will only win him a reputation for meanness; if, instead, the prince is overtly generous, this leads to higher taxes on his subjects and poverty for the community, which will offend the many who are taxed, while rewarding only the few who receive gifts. The result is that when danger ensues, the prince will be forced to adopt measures of austerity and thus be thought mean after all. So the prince—acting as a sovereign and not as a Christian—must be frugal and even miserly in order to enable him to be liberal, because by not taxing he gives to all and is really only ungenerous to the few who otherwise would have been the recipients of his bounty. Liberality is a wasting asset that leads either to poverty— which is the loss of the power to be liberal—or else, to avoid poverty, to rapacity, which leads to hatred, which in turn compromises the prince's power to govern. Machiavelli therefore concludes that it is permissible to have a reputation for being miserly, which may lead to reproach, because it does not endanger the state.

This is a subtle distinction and it has misled even some of the most reflective of Machiavelli's critics. Because he believed Machiavelli had detached ethics from politics, Leo Strauss concluded that he was 'a teacher of evil', counselling leaders to avoid the common values of justice, mercy and love in preference for cruelty, violence, fear and deception.[10] Even a more sympathetic reader like Benedetto Croce treats Machiavelli as a 'realist' who suspends ethics in matters of politics. Similarly, some defenders of Machiavelli simply take the view that moral values have little place in the particular kinds of decisions that political leaders must make, and it is therefore a sort of category mistake to assume otherwise.[11] But Machiavelli is in fact a moralist no less than Cicero, whose morals he turns upside down. It is just that the morality he urges on a prince, when he is acting on behalf of the people and not simply on his own behalf, subordinates the good of the prince to the good of the state. This view is closely related to Machiavelli's decisive preference for republics over principalities, for whether we ought to accept the subordination of our personal morality depends on the nature and purposes of the state.

Machiavelli was among the first to appreciate this distinction, and his argument that the moral imperatives for the official are different from those of the rest of us was a key insight at the birth of the modern state. Indeed, one can account for the timing of this insight by correlating it with the emergence of the state. Whereas feudal princes fused the personal with the political, Machiavelli saw that the state was by no means synonymous with the person of the prince and concluded that the head of a princely state has an obligation to govern in the light of this distinction.

Nevertheless, Freedman does see what seems to me the heart of the matter, that stratagems do not create a sustainable political legacy: the foundation of states lies in good laws and good armies. This relationship between strategy and law—between developments in warfare and corresponding developments in the constitutional order—represents an advance by Machiavelli over his chief precursor, Thucydides. Perhaps because Thucydides lived in an era of states and Machiavelli did not, the latter was drawn to the potential of a model that was, for Thucydides, simply a given.

This is one reason why—*contra* the usual realist assumptions—Machiavelli thinks the constitutional nature of the regime is so important in strategic affairs. Let me give one example. Machiavelli asks why Alexander's successors governed with such success over his conquests despite the fact that they lacked dynastic legitimacy or, indeed, any cultural affinity with their subjects. He proposes this answer: that all monarchies govern through one of two ways—either through an aristocracy of nobles or through ministers. If it is the former, the regime is highly vulnerable to conquest because there will always be some dissatisfied elements of the nobility who wish to enhance their stature and bring a certain legitimacy to rebellion. Such countries are easy to conquer but difficult to hold onto, for the same reason: the aristocracy can never be wholly satisfied and will breed new allies for new conquerors. In the latter case of the monarch who governs through ministers, the regime is hard to defeat. The governing class owes everything to the ruler and will fight tenaciously to defend the status quo. But should such a regime fall, the country is easily governed, for there are no natural opponents with any greater legitimacy than the new conquerors, so long as they had the foresight to destroy any dynastic claimants to the throne.

Freedman appreciates this, I think, and remarks, 'The most interesting aspects of his work, however, were less about dealing with an external enemy and more about sustaining loyalty and commitment internally'. But if the constitutional structures of states are overlooked by some realists as salient, so the recurring rules of the human condition—those laws that are too subtle and varied to be adequately foreseen but too powerful to be evaded—mitigate against the constructivist, and it would be a mistake to claim this title for Machiavelli. I am not sure whether Freedman fully describes Machiavelli's view when he quotes Machiavelli as observing: 'Fortune governs one-half of our actions, but even so she leaves the half more or less in our power to control'.[12] Even in this area of apparent control, it would be necessary to adapt to circumstances. Free will suggests the possibility of fitting events to an established character; Machiavelli suggested that the character would be shaped by events.

This is a complex matter with which Machiavelli grappled throughout his life and it has important implications for his constitutionalism. It is true that he strongly endorsed free will and also that he attributed 'one-half' of our fates to Fortune. Early in his life, he describes Fortune as a powerful river that, with sufficient ingenuity, might be channelled through bulwarks and canals to serve the purposes of man. But he did not believe that our characters are shaped by or could be adapted to the times, and hence he was led to his ultimate conclusion that our fates are a matter of chance.

> If one could change one's character with the times and with events, [one's good] fortune would continue, [but] one cannot deviate from that path toward which nature inclines each of us ... [Soderini] always acted with patience and humility. When the times were in accord with his approach, he and Florence prospered, but when things changed and he had to put aside his patience and humility, he did not know how to do this so that, along with his native city, he lost his position.[13]

Machiavelli came to this conclusion by asking himself how leaders of very different characters could thrive and prosper. Each of the principal actors on the European stage enjoyed a time of historic success, yet each differed profoundly in character from the others, just as profoundly in fact as Alexander VI differed from his enemy, Giuliano della Rovere, who became Pope Julius II and destroyed Alexander's son Cesare. Each leader follows his nature—one proceeds cautiously like Emperor Maximilian, another impetuously like Julius II, another cunningly like Emperor Ferdinand—and for a time each will succeed, while the commands of his temperament are in accord with the demands of the situation.

> For one can see that men ... proceed in different ways: one by caution, another by impulsiveness; one through force, another through guile; one with patience, another with its opposite; and each one can achieve his goals with his means. And we can also observe that, in the case of two cautious men, for example, one achieves his goal while the other does not; and, likewise, two men may equally prosper though using two different means, the one being cautious and the other impetuous: this is explained by the character of the times that either suits or does not suit the chosen way of acting.[14]

What was needed was the ability to anticipate and adapt to the changing demands of Fortune: 'I also believe that the man who shapes his plans and methods to comport with the temper of the times will triumph and, likewise, that the man who sets his course of action out of harmony with the times will come to grief'.[15] The difficulty is that a man cannot change his 'way of proceeding' because this derives from his individual nature. 'No man', Machiavelli wrote, 'is so wise that he knows how to adapt his own nature ... both because he cannot deviate from the path to which his nature inclines him, and also because he cannot be convinced to abandon a well-known path that has always brought him success by his following it."[16]

This inflexibility is a fatal vulnerability for feudal realms. While they may achieve greatness for a period, because they are tied to the will of a single person such dominions inevitably will fail. Collective leaderships, like the oligarchies of Venice and the Florentine Signoria, could mitigate this problem, but they introduced other difficulties such as indecision, procrastination, diffusion of command and responsibility, and, perhaps worst of all, the danger of violent faction. Machiavelli had a solution: while his predecessors had thought of *virtù* as a trait of the individual, Machiavelli conceived of a collective *virtù* that would be found in the character of the people. Resolution and self-reliance on their part would permit the society to marshal the ruthlessness of the public to replace leaders whose particular gifts did not serve the times with those persons whose natures were better suited to current events.

This brings me to my final observation about Freedman on Machiavelli. In *Strategy: A History*, Freedman renders exquisitely a Miltonic Satan as the embodiment of the Machiavellian prince. He taxes Satan who:

> despite appearing to be modeled on Machiavelli's ideal prince, [falls short] … He stuck with a strategy that had already brought him failure, in part by claiming that it was almost successful … [Ultimately he failed because, though] he may seem to be a free agent, boldly innovating his future, he is instead a slave to his own nature.[17]

From a Machiavellian point of view, there is much to note in this description. First, there is no contradiction between being Machiavelli's ideal prince and falling short of ideal behaviour; indeed, this was precisely the case with Cesare Borgia, a demonic figure if ever there was one. Nor is it surprising that Satan was unable to abandon the strategy that had almost brought him success. This is true of all of us; it is even true of great powers which, for example, continue to invest in carrier battle groups, despite their increasing vulnerability, because they won the Second World War. Finally, it is not that Satan is not a free agent because he is confined by his nature; that, alas, is the quality of freedom which, however irksome, constrains us to be innovative, to find ways to accommodate and act within our constraints. Machiavelli believed that human nature is constant through time, but manifests itself according to the historical context; because contexts change unpredictably, no person can be sure of success, which depends on the synchrony of temperament and character with the ever-shifting demands of the time. Thus history is both cyclical—because every context returns in time—and irreversible, because human interaction with its contexts brings about change.

Does that make Machiavelli a constructive realist? Perhaps it does. It strikes me as an apt description of Lawrence Freedman. But what about Milton? I think he should have the last word as we enter a period when our enlightenment by both Niccolò Machiavelli and Lawrence Freedman will be sorely tested.

> They, therefore, as to right belonged
> So were created, nor can justly accuse
> Their Maker, or their making, or their fate,
> As if Predestination overruled
> Their will, disposed by absolute decree
> Or high foreknowledge. They themselves decreed
> Their own revolt, not I. If I foreknew,
> Foreknowledge had no influence on their fault,
> Which had no less proved certain unforeknown.
> So without least impulse or shadow of fate,
> Or aught by me immutably foreseen,
> They trespass, authors to themselves in all,
> Both what they judge and what they choose; for so
> I formed them free, and free they must remain
> Till they enthrall themselves.

16

STRATEGIC SCRIPTS AND NUCLEAR DISARMAMENT

Matthew Harries and *Benedict Wilkinson*

From their genesis, nuclear weapons have provoked two instinctive reactions. First, the enormous power that nuclear weapons possess, as well as the horrible effects of radiation, makes their use essentially unthinkable by any rational and moral human being. But secondly, and equally important, the existence of this awesome destructive power, and especially its ability to deter a potential aggressor, have changed the nature of war irrevocably and, as a result, the very foundation of international politics. Both reactions are implicit in the line from the Bhagavad Gita which Robert Oppenheimer famously found drifting into his thoughts as he watched history's first nuclear explosion in the New Mexico desert on 16 July 1945: 'Now I am become Death, the destroyer of worlds'.

These two instincts underpin what William Walker calls the 'logic of disarmament' and the 'logic of armament'.[1] To the disarmers, if nuclear weapons are unthinkably destructive, it follows that they must be abolished. The threat of inflicting mass murder, so the argument runs, is no way to run the world. To the armers, it is precisely these threats that hold the promise of a more peaceful global order. No leader, however aggressive, would be foolhardy enough to contemplate launching an all-out war against a nuclear-armed country if he or she was convinced that nuclear punishment would surely follow. Yet, rather than solely inspiring either armament or disarmament, the two instinctive reactions have tended to coexist, even in the same camps.[2] Those committed to nuclear disarmament, especially, have been capable of feeling both horror and awe, and this has done much to shape the nature of disarmament advocacy throughout the nuclear age.

The quest to abolish nuclear weapons has produced a multiplicity of treaties and diplomatic initiatives, popular movements and protests, and has had profound effects on the politics of a number of countries. After a lull in attention caused by the declining salience of nuclear issues after the Cold War, and active damage to its prospects caused by the Bush administration's distrust of multilateral diplomacy, the goal of nuclear abolition re-entered the international political discourse at the beginning of the Obama administration. In part, this derived from fears that the nuclear non-proliferation regime could collapse unless greater attention was paid to its disarmament component; but, in part, it also stemmed from a perception that nuclear risks might now be too great to control indefinitely in an age of terrorists and regional nuclear-armed belligerents.

In response to this, a 'gang of four' prominent statesmen—Henry Kissinger, William Perry, George Shultz and Sam Nunn—wrote a series of op-eds in the *Wall Street Journal*, beginning in 2007, calling for 'reassertion of the goal of a world free of nuclear weapons'.[3] They were joined in this by British politicians in the multilateral arena,[4] and, most important of all, by President Barack Obama. Obama's speech on 5 April 2009 in Prague recommitted the United States to the goal of abolishing nuclear weapons and set a wide-ranging agenda for progress in tackling all nuclear threats. These elite-level initiatives were matched by a flurry of academic and think tank papers, books and seminars, and by the establishment of a high-profile campaigning organization, Global Zero.

Yet beneath the surface of this renewed global interest in nuclear disarmament lay a profound contradiction in the approaches taken by different stakeholders in the movement for zero. And it is a contradiction best explained by identifying two distinct courses—or as we, in the mould of Lawrence Freedman, term them, 'strategic scripts'—for nuclear disarmament. In this chapter, we begin by describing the concept of scripts as mental frameworks for understanding particular situations and for identifying responses to those situations. The second section then proceeds to apply the concept of strategic scripts to the nuclear weapons context. The final, concluding section provides some reflections on whether the two instinctive disarmament reactions—'stable reductions' and 'delegitimization'—can be reconciled or whether international efforts for nuclear disarmament will be left to a process of 'muddling along'.

The aim of this chapter, therefore, is not only to explain the contradictions inherent in approaches to disarmament, but also to elucidate further the concept of strategic scripts which was developed by Freedman. In our view—and, for transparency, we should say that we both worked on strategic scripts as doctoral students under Freedman's supervisory eye—the concept has potential value for both theory and politics. For theory, scripts can be deployed in order to understand the strategic dilemmas and choices that face political leaders, generals, political movements, global conglomerates and radicals alike. For politics and policy, an understanding of the concept has the potential to improve the strategist's ability to write better strategic scripts. Such an understanding can contribute to a fuller recognition of the cognitive processes at work in formulating strategy, an appreciation of the importance of the internal credibility of scripts and, potentially, the writing of better stories and the realization of better strategies. We hope that such an outcome will be attainable by those who read this chapter.

Strategic scripts

In *Strategy: A History*, Freedman developed the idea of 'strategic scripts' as a way of thinking about the narrative aspects of strategy.[5] In order to understand the concept fully, it is useful to trace it back to its origins in the fields of transactional psychology and artificial intelligence. Here, Roger Schank and Robert Abelson developed the concept of scripts as a way of thinking about how both humans and machines (might) understand the world around them. They argued that, in order to navigate a complex world, humans rely on their knowledge of scripts. For Schank and Abelson, a script is a mental structure which describes 'a predetermined, stereotyped sequence of actions that define a well-known situation'.[6] Scripts come in many shapes and sizes. Some can be quite generalized and therefore only weakly predictive, while others are highly specified and thus highly predictive or even, on rare occasions, infallible:

> In its weak sense, [a script] is a bundle of inferences about the potential occurrence of a set of events … In its strong sense, it involves expectations about the order as well as the occurrence of events. In the strongest sense of a totally ritualized event sequence (e.g., a Japanese tea ceremony), script predictions become infallible—but this case is relatively rare.[7]

Scripts are therefore stereotypical sequences of actions which typically take place in everyday situations. Walk into a café or a restaurant, for example, and the appropriate script will suggest a series of actions to be performed by different actors: asking for a menu, bringing a menu, ordering food, cooking the food, eating the food, asking for the bill, and so on. Scripts therefore describe patterns of typical behaviour in stereotypical situations. But they also serve as a receptacle for new information as it is learned. As Schank put it:

> Scripts are a kind of 'memory structure'. They serve to tell us how to act without our being aware that we are using them … They serve as a kind of storehouse of old experiences of a certain type in terms of which new experiences are encoded. When something new happens to us in a restaurant which tells us more about restaurants, we must have some place to put that new information so that we will be wiser next time.[8]

Freedman extends the concept of scripts to the world of strategy. As in artificial intelligence and psychology, he suggests, strategic scripts are rules of thumb about particular scenarios. They 'explain how individuals enter into new situations, give them meaning, and decide how to behave'.[9] Based on the work of cognitive psychologists like Daniel Kahneman, Freedman proceeds to identify two types of script: subconscious or System 1 scripts and deliberative or System 2 scripts.[10] The first type is an 'internalized foundation for attempts to give situations meaning and suggest appropriate responses'.[11] These scripts are largely stereotypical, providing intuitive readings of a situation and suggesting essentially automatic, instinctive responses. System 1 scripts, as Freedman argues:

often serve as substitutes for original thought or consideration of the particularities of situations. While they may be validated if acted upon, they may turn out to be wrong ... [or] may result in predictable behavior and miss variations in the context that should demand original responses.[12]

System 2 strategic scripts, by contrast, are the product of 'effortful' thought and deliberation; they require conscious consideration, the recognition of a range of factors, actors and constraints in a given situation, and the identification of multiple possible actions. Although they may have their origins in System 1 scripts or may be influenced by the decision-maker's knowledge of analogous situations or personal experience, 'they take the present as a starting point and project forward'.

For Freedman, then, strategic scripts are cognitive structures that allow strategists to form expectations about how a sequence of events might unfold, making it possible to select a potentially successful course of action. They sit at the heart of strategic decision-making because they aid the interpretation of a situation, identify suitable actions or reactions, and provide expectations about the likely sequence of events and the likely outcome of that sequence.

For Freedman, it is useful to think about scripts as 'stories told in the future tense'. Scripts, in essence, are stereotypical narratives, with all the associated characters, plots and denouements; they describe the way in which situations evolve and conclude.[13] In this sense, Freedman observes, constructing a strategic script often involves starting with 'imaginative fiction but with an aspiration to nonfiction'.[14] The narrative aspect of scripts is important because it reflects their role in strategy more generally. Freedman points out that the purpose of a script is not simply:

> to predict events *but to convince others to act in such a way that the story will follow its proposed course*. If it fails to convince the inherent prediction will certainly be wrong. As with other stories, these must relate to the audience's culture, experience, beliefs and aspirations. To engage they must ring true and survive examination in terms of their internal coherence and consistency ('narrative probability'). They must also resonate with the historical and cultural understandings of their intended audience ('narrative fidelity'). The main challenge for strategic narratives lies in their potentially brutal encounter with reality.[15]

This is why there is a difference between scripts and plans. Unlike plans, scripts can and must incorporate elements of uncertainty and improvisation. Whereas plans provide a step-by-step process in which each effect is logically and necessarily derived from its preceding cause, strategic scripts allow for unanticipated reactions and the random impact of unexpected events. This is why strategic scripts have an 'unfinished quality': after the first move, there is no guarantee that others will behave as the script predicts; unanticipated events may disrupt the plot or send it in a different direction; new, previously unaccounted-for actors might emerge to send the story in a completely different direction. This, of course, is the crucial challenge for strategists: they have to make predictions about how other parties will respond to particular actions in particular situations. Indeed, the thrill and frustration of creating strategy are generated by the capricious art of prediction: as Yogi Berra, the eminently wise and wry baseball player put it, 'it is hard to make predictions—especially about the future'.

The nuclear context

All this can be fruitfully applied to nuclear disarmament, where there are two readily identifiable scripts. The first can be called 'stable reductions'. Its primary assumption is that nuclear weapons, by their nature—although their nature makes them undesirable to retain in the long term—are valuable instruments of strategy: deterrence is a real phenomenon, to be managed. In this script, the need for nuclear deterrence may eventually fade away, but, while it exists and while nuclear weapons still exist, traditional concerns of nuclear strategy must be taken seriously. The language of deterrence and nuclear strategy, in this script, is a reflection of reality rather than a political act in itself.

This implies a number of assumptions for the way in which disarmament should proceed. First, if states use nuclear weapons to maintain their security, then disarmament will tend to proceed only at the rate at which this deterrent role declines or other instruments emerge to act as substitutes for nuclear deterrence. In other words, disarmament is possible, and desirable, but only when nuclear weapons are less useful in today's world; and, in theory, there may need to be some compensation for the absence of nuclear deterrence. The compensation might come in the form of hardware (advanced conventional weapons to fill previously nuclear roles, or ballistic missile defences to remove the threat from others' arsenals) or in the form of political changes in the processes for managing international security (reform of the United Nations Security Council, advanced dispute resolution, and so on).

Secondly, and related to this, the relative balance of nuclear forces is important, and increasingly so, as nuclear arsenals grow smaller. A state with a significantly larger arsenal might, in time of crisis, seek to launch a pre-emptive first strike, removing the opponent's ability to retaliate. With smaller nuclear arsenals, the number of weapons that would constitute a significant asymmetry could be quite small; in that case, the risk of first strike instability would grow as disarmament advanced. This makes the detail of disarmament agreements complicated and difficult to negotiate: there are even issues as basic as definition (what constitutes an 'operational' nuclear weapon, for example). Relatively modest reductions in nuclear forces may therefore take significant amounts of time and effort to conclude. In addition, individual states will struggle to take the lead in disarmament without some means of ensuring that others will join them. By the same token, non-universality seriously threatens the disarmament process; although it is incumbent on the states with the largest arsenals to move first, the absence of one or more states from a global disarmament process will halt the initiative as a whole.

Thirdly, cheating on nuclear disarmament agreements matters. If nuclear deterrence is a powerful instrument of statecraft, anything that allows one state to wield it unopposed would put others under severe threat. This problem is especially serious as it relates to the end state of total nuclear disarmament, where one could imagine chronic instability if states could not entirely trust each other not to restart nuclear weapons programmes covertly. The incentive in such a world would be to launch a pre-emptive strike against nascent nuclear facilities or, instead, for a number of states to attempt to rebuild small nuclear arsenals. This means that meaningful disarmament would have to be verified to a high degree of confidence, which poses serious technical and political challenges.

Because of these assumptions, which are inherent in the script, the route to nuclear abolition proposed by the script can only be slow, incremental and consensual. It is slow because the nature of relations between states changes slowly. It is incremental because each step in the process relies on trust and confidence built by the previous step, and because large steps bring a risk of instability. It is consensual in the sense that it is a process that must be managed principally by the possessors of nuclear weapons in concert (although this is not to say that non-nuclear states have no role to play at all), according to the demands of mutual stability. The archetype of this disarmament script is the Prague speech; more detailed elaborations can be found in such non-governmental reports as that of the International Commission on Nuclear Non-proliferation and Disarmament (ICNND), convened by the Australian and Japanese governments. It is also the script to which, broadly speaking, the 'gang of four' subscribe.[16]

Although the route to abolition varies in certain details according to the proponent, some basic ingredients can be identified. First, there would be a further round of arms reductions between the two largest nuclear powers, the United States and Russia—which will bring into play the thorny questions of how to deal with tactical and non-deployed nuclear weapons, and the implications of developments in ballistic missile defence and strategic conventional capabilities. While these are taking place, there should be a commitment by the other nuclear-armed states not to increase their arsenals. During either this period or the next, it will also be necessary to bring into force the Comprehensive Nuclear Test Ban Treaty and to negotiate a Fissile Material Cut-off Treaty.

Subsequently, it will be necessary to bring others into a multilateral reductions process—here problems include how, if at all, to set a fair ratio between the arsenals of the larger and smaller powers, and how to verify disarmament among more than two powers. At the same time, the problem of managing security for those states currently under the United States' nuclear umbrella will have to be confronted: first, by eliminating from the strategy of extended deterrence any kind of forward-deployed system, instead relying on 'central deterrence'; and, secondly, by seeking alternatives to nuclear deterrence itself.

If all this can be done, the world will have reached a point where several states have small nuclear arsenals (although it is conceivable that one or two might already have taken unilateral decisions to disarm completely). This is what the ICNND report calls the 'minimization point', at which there might need to be a phase of consolidation, to maintain stability and to allow for negotiations on the very difficult final reductions to take place.[17] At this point it will be necessary to confront a range of complex issues on the road to total abolition, including a stringent verification regime for warhead dismantlement, tightened non-proliferation controls, and probably international management of the nuclear fuel cycle.

The second disarmament script is that of 'delegitimization'. This script assumes that the value ascribed to nuclear weapons is a political construct: change the way in which nuclear weapons are perceived, and you can achieve disarmament. The means to do this are inherent in the nature of the weapons: namely, the appalling violence that their use entails. Deterrence is a myth,[18] so this script proclaims, an ad hoc construct to justify the possession of nuclear weapons and not sufficient to outweigh their barbarity. Once international society is convinced that the possession and threat of use of nuclear weapons are inherently illegitimate, states will no longer be able to justify their continued existence.

The implications of this position tend to be the inverse of those of the deterrence script. First, disarmament will advance as the belief system that supports nuclear deterrence is deconstructed; hence no direct substitute for deterrence need be found. The task for disarmers, in other words, is not primarily to persuade nuclear-weapon states that the ends of nuclear deterrence can be achieved by other means, but rather to persuade them that nuclear deterrence itself is fatally flawed. Disarmament can and should progress, therefore, separately from changes in the context of international security or developments in other weaponry.

Secondly, the primary value of disarmament agreements is the norm that they establish. This does not necessarily lead to demands for a complete prohibition on nuclear weapons, but it tends in the end to do so. Disarmament treaties, according to this script, are the manifestation of political will generated through advocacy, rather than detailed agreements on the practicalities necessary to allow disarmament to take place. Their value lies in the process of 'reframing' the discourse around nuclear weapons en route to a treaty, more than stability or trust built through treaty provisions.[19]

Lastly, the disarmament process need not be coordinated or consensual—indeed, it may be more effective if it is not. It need not be coordinated in the sense that progress on delegitimizing nuclear weapons can take place without waiting for the agreement of any particular subset of nuclear weapons possessors. It need not be consensual, similarly, in the sense that the primary mechanisms for disarming the nuclear powers through delegitimization are likely to be shame, criticism and eventually legal recourse—rather than persuasion or self-controlled negotiation.

The route to abolition proposed by this script, therefore, deals in political absolutes, allows for more dramatic steps, and takes much of the responsibility for progress out of the hands of the weapons possessors. In contrast to the 'stable reductions' script, which envisages a complex sequence of steps, 'delegitimization' calls for a relatively simple process. A sustained political campaign should be undertaken to establish an international consensus that the possession and use of nuclear weapons are inherently illegitimate. Such a consensus should then be mobilized to pressure individual governments in their domestic political arenas, but, more important, to rally support for universal legal prohibitions—most likely first of the use of nuclear weapons, and then of their possession (although the most ambitious versions foresee prohibiting both at the same time).

This script has manifested itself in perennial calls, particularly at Non-Proliferation Treaty (NPT) Review conferences, for negotiations on a nuclear weapons convention. But in recent years the script has been given more fluent expression through its co-option of the language of humanitarian disarmament. This language found its way into the 2010 NPT Review Conference final document and was followed by the establishment of an initiative on the humanitarian effects of nuclear weapons, beginning with a diplomatic conference hosted by the Norwegian government, in 2013, and followed by meetings in Mexico and Vienna, in 2014 and 2015. The initiative used scrutiny of the practical humanitarian effects of a nuclear detonation to make the implicit (and often explicit) case that nuclear weapons are inherently illegitimate. NGOs and, increasingly, states within the initiative saw it as a route to achieving a legal prohibition, following a model established in the prohibition of land mines and cluster munitions, which took place outside existing disarmament forums and without waiting for weapons possessors to take the initiative. And they got their wish: the UN General Assembly voted in October 2016 to open negotiations, in 2017, for a treaty banning nuclear weapons outright.

These ideal types are of course complicated by the fact that the language of each script can be adopted by those who have different goals in mind. There is a narrow gap, for example, between the argument for caution in the pace and nature of nuclear reductions and the argument for no reductions at all. The deterrence script can easily be used to profess generalized support for the disarmament aspiration while resisting all meaningful action. At the same time, the delegitimization script is a handy tool for would-be proliferators to divert attention from their own behaviour and to undermine the normative power of the non-proliferation regime. Iran, for example, has been an enthusiastic proponent of world disarmament on the grounds of the inhumanity of nuclear weapons, particularly at moments of diplomatic pressure over its own non-proliferation non-compliance.[20] Last, the delegitimization script also correlates more broadly with states' exercises in transformational rhetoric about the structure of international politics. That is to say, it is the most effective way in the nuclear arena for unempowered states to argue for a reordering of the international hierarchy, regardless of their substantive belief in disarmament itself.

Even notwithstanding these cross-currents, however, the fundamental problem that advocates of nuclear disarmament face is that each script on its own lacks persuasive power, and the two scripts tend to contradict each other too much to act in combination. In terms of persuasive power, the deterrence script quite obviously suffers from a lack of emotional appeal. A multi-decade staged process of international agreements does not tend to light a fire in the hearts of political campaigners—and in the absence of public pressure it is difficult to see where the incentive for change might come from. Along the same lines, the necessarily slow progress of disarmament according to this model is likely to lead to accusations of prevarication and bad faith. As Borrie rightly puts it: 'The more the NPT nuclear weapon states dismiss humanitarian concerns, the more they contribute to the framing that activists have sought to construct of a nuclear weapons control regime that currently fails to serve its own long-term objective of elimination because it is insufficiently radical and progressive, and is dominated by problem states'.[21]

For its part, the delegitimization script cannot provide a convincing answer to the concerns of those states (significant in number) that stress nuclear weapons as a core part of their security. In East Asia, in particular, extended nuclear deterrence is a high-profile part of strategies to preserve national sovereignty in the face of an expanding and assertive nuclear-armed neighbour; it is also, arguably, a powerful tool of non-proliferation in its own right. In the case of Japan, at least, it cannot be said that this reliance on nuclear deterrence is maintained because the legitimacy of the weapons is left unquestioned. These states are essentially being asked to take a leap into the dark of a kind never before seen in international politics—far different from a decision to abandon landmines or cluster munitions, which, although they were defended to an extent on grounds of utility, never came close to the perceived strategic significance of nuclear weapons.

The delegitimization script is also vulnerable to the accusation that it is least effective against non-democratic states, which are the most resistant to international norms and are currently taking the most concrete actions to undermine disarmament: China, for example, is in the process of enthusiastically modernizing and expanding its nuclear arsenal. Finally, the absolutism of the delegitimization script encourages an absolutist political dynamic, in which the achievement of even modest steps towards disarmament becomes contingent on support for the final goal of nuclear abolition, which itself is vulnerable to charges of utopianism. The limited disarmament good of New START, for example, was made much harder to achieve in the US political arena because Congressional opponents of the treaty were able to attack it as a symbol of President Obama's naive aspirations, rather than focusing on its very modest substance.

Reconciliation?

The next logical step after identifying these two scripts is to ask whether they might be reconciled. This is not entirely unthinkable, especially if they can be applied with different weight in different contexts. The delegitimization script excels in generating political energy, which the stable reductions script is sometimes able to harness. The Comprehensive Test Ban Treaty (CTBT) serves as a good example. The CTBT was a totem of the anti-nuclear movement for several decades before it was opened for signature, in 1996, and was the result in part of focused campaigning in the early 1990s by NGOs committed to delegitimizing nuclear weapons.[22] Yet it was accompanied by stringent verification provisions, and its entry-into-force mechanism, which requires the treaty's ratification by 44 key states, is an implicit acceptance of the idea that disarmament must not encourage imbalance, thereby threatening stability.

However, the success of negotiating the CTBT was the high-water mark for multilateral disarmament. The treaty's ratification was defeated by the US Senate in 1999, and the UN machinery failed subsequently to negotiate a Fissile Material Cut-off Treaty (a subject still subject to desultory debates in the Conference on Disarmament today). Coordinated multilateral reductions in nuclear arsenals are deemed not to be feasible until the US and Russia bring their numbers down significantly, but the two nuclear superpowers have gone no further than the modest reductions contained in the New START treaty and have failed to open new negotiations on the next steps. In this atmosphere of stagnation, the gap between the two scripts has widened. The 'humanitarian impacts' initiative has abandoned any effort to find interim disarmament steps, while the NPT's five nuclear weapon states have convened talks among themselves, labelled the 'P5 process', which are pushing the mantra of incrementalism to the point of parody—the P5 process's signal (public) achievement from six years of work up to 2015 was the writing of a common glossary of nuclear terms.

If they cannot be reconciled, then, the two scripts appear to be reduced to their mean—namely, an effort to 'muddle along'. Nuclear disarmament gains may be possible: countries may decide, especially for financial reasons, to reduce or do away with their arsenals; and events might intervene (as they did in the field of chemical weapons, where Syria was forced to accede to the Chemical Weapons Convention). But the prospects for a coordinated and sustained movement towards disarmament look grim.

Part of the reason for this somewhat sombre prediction is that there is an inherent difficulty in both scripts, which essentially boils down to their narrative aspects. Both tell particular 'stories' about disarmament. The stable reductions script says that disarmament can happen, but only as nuclear weapons lose their deterrent role and only if a relative balance between states can be maintained. Or, to phrase the story slightly differently, nuclear states need to agree to disarm in a coordinated, synchronized manner based on mutual trust that other states are reducing their stockpiles at a similar rate or that some new technology has come onto the market which replaces the need for nuclear weapons. The delegitimization script is based on a single assertion: that nuclear weapons have the potential to create such appalling destruction that their use is beyond consideration by rational and moral political leaders. At first glance, this story *appears* to be quite short—as we phrased it earlier: deterrence is a myth; simply change the way in which nuclear weapons are perceived and you can achieve disarmament. Indeed, the brevity of the delegitimization story may be why it is able to generate political and popular support with greater effect than the 'stable reductions' script. But, on more careful inspection, this script contains numerous implicit steps which need to be completed, not least the daunting prospect of changing international society's perception of the strategic value of nuclear weapons.

Both scripts, then, tell very long stories. One talks of a coordinated, internationally validated process of disarmament by nuclear powers which will take place over decades; the other of effecting an immediate change in deeply ingrained political attitudes across the international community. These may well be compelling stories about how nuclear disarmament must happen and they may well be sufficiently persuasive to drive people to action in pursuit of a nuclear weapon-free world. Indeed, that is precisely the attraction of stories, as scholars such as Nicholas Nassim Taleb have argued. Stories, he argues, help humans to make sense of the world around them, to distil it into ready frameworks for interpretation and understanding: 'we like stories, we like to summarize, and we like to simplify'.[23] Charles Tilly similarly argued that stories provide:

> vivid, compelling accounts of what has happened, what will happen or what should happen … cementing people's commitments to common projects, helping people make sense of what is going on, channelling collective decisions and judgments, spurring people to action they would otherwise be reluctant to pursue.[24]

However, the problem with both nuclear disarmament stories—and what troubled both Tilly and Taleb about stories more generally—is that they imply causality where it is weak or absent and they smother the role of luck and the unpredictable (or, in Taleb's language, black swans). As Freedman himself suggests, in strategy:

there is only one action that can be anticipated with any degree of certainty, and that is the first move of the central player for whom the strategy has been devised. Whether the plot will unfold as intended will then depend on not only the acuity of the starting assumptions but also whether other players follow the script or deviate significantly as they follow a script of their own.[25]

The difficulty for both nuclear disarmament scripts is twofold. In the first place, both scripts propound long stories with equally lengthy cause-effect structures. The problem here is that it only takes one player—the US Senate, say, or an encircled autocrat—to stray from the sequence of events described by the script for the whole narrative to fall apart. The longer the story, the greater likelihood that other players will deviate from the allotted sequence, leaving political objectives unattained. In the second and related place, both scripts are extremely rigid; they leave little in the way for improvisation or flexibility, and thus there is no room to adapt to changing political contexts, the emergence of new players or the impact of unpredictable events.

While two competing scripts—stable reductions and delegitimization—coexist uneasily, nuclear disarmament looks set to be a process of 'muddling along' rather than a coordinated, systematic path to disarmament. While the strategists may look to utopian futures in which their political objectives are obtained as their scripts foretold, the reality is that nuclear disarmament is likely to be an uneven and untidy process of getting to the next stage in a slightly better or, at least, no worse position than if one had no strategy at all. In this sense, nuclear disarmament resembles what Freedman sees as the nature of strategy more broadly—rather than being a three-act play in which all threads of the narrative are firmly resolved, it is actually a form of soap opera. Like soap operas in which plots unfold, new characters emerge, old characters depart but no definitive conclusion is ever reached, strategy is ongoing. As Freedman himself puts it,

Even when the desired end point is reached, it is not really the end. The enemy may have surrendered, the election won, the target company taken over, the revolutionary opportunity seized, but that just means that there is now an occupied country to run, a new government to be formed, a whole new revolutionary order to be established, or a distinctive sets of corporate activities to be merged. Here the dramatist can leave the next stage to the reader's imagination, or take a breathing space before she starts on the sequel so that the story is picked up after the passage of time, perhaps even with many new characters. Strategists have no such luxury.[26]

PART 5

CONTEMPLATIONS

17

CONFESSIONS OF A PREMATURE CONSTRUCTIVIST

Lawrence Freedman

My title has no better justification than that it is one I have sought to use for some time.[1] It derives from an evocative article by Bernard Knox that was printed in 2001.[2] It described how from Cambridge Knox ended up in Spain as part of the International Brigades during the Civil War and what he did when he got there. It was this activity that got him labelled a 'premature anti-Fascist' in the US after the Second World War. Knox, who was to become a professor of Classics, claims to have been taken aback when he first heard the phrase. 'How', he wondered, 'could *anyone* be a *premature* anti-Fascist?' And:

> Could there be anything such as a premature antidote to a poison? A premature antiseptic? …. If you were not premature, what sort of anti-Fascist were you supposed to be? A punctual anti-Fascist? A timely one?'

In fact it was an FBI codeword for 'communist'. To have taken up arms early against the Fascists was to demonstrate disturbing political sympathies.

No such distinction attaches to being a premature constructivist. The connection between Knox's article and this lecture is tenuous though not entirely absent, for the relevance of the Cold War ideological struggle to our understanding of our scholarship, and how we should go about it, is at the core of my argument. I chart the move from the class struggle of the interwar years, when commitments seemed unavoidable, to the more disoriented setting of thirty years ago when the first British International Studies Association (BISA) conference was held, and then on to the end of the Cold War. I am afraid that this is a little autobiographical, although I certainly do not want to claim that my own political or intellectual journey is either representative or special. But I do know that things that bothered me as I moved through my undergraduate and graduate studies bothered many others.

The confessions, of which there are few, will come as something of a disappointment. I was a premature constructivist because constructivism describes how I have always tended to approach issues, though it was not a label I thought about until Peter Katzenstein offered it to me. Actually he described me as a realist constructivist, which if anything is slightly more sinister than a premature one. Even earlier than that, someone had observed that I was clearly dabbling in semiotics without realizing it. In both cases I felt like Molière's Monsieur Jourdain, who discovered that he had 'been speaking prose all my life, and didn't even know it!' So my constructivism was premature because I engaged in it without knowing. If only I had understood the need to give it a label, I might have made a name for myself as an innovative theorist. The approach, however, came rather naturally to anyone who had studied sociology over that period.

The sociology of knowledge

The sociology of knowledge is the most dangerous area of the social sciences to enter, requiring protective clothing and regular health checks. To refuse to enter damns you as a naive empiricist or a mindless eclectic. A lack of precautions takes you on a terrible journey towards epistemological despair. With your first steps you are struck at once by the limits of positivism and the dispiriting revelation that to call our studies 'science' does not necessarily make them so, at least as the term is understood by the natural scientists. Step further in and the air becomes thinner and the brain starts to pound. Are statements about any aspect of society at all valid? The very notion of an objective reality on which we are able to report has evaporated. Every statement, including this one, has been conditioned by social position and political ideology. What then is the point of so-called independent study and research? How are we to distinguish between good and bad work? Stagger forward and the language becomes more obscure as all meanings become signs and all concepts are contested. In the blur, knowledge transforms itself from input to output. What we know does not shape our worldview but our worldview shapes what we know. You began this journey supposing you could say useful things about society and politics; now you realize that such claims explain no more than the underlying political stance of the claimants or even factors for which no correction can be made, such as gender, sexual orientation, colour, class and creed.

Now you have been warned, we are ready to begin, taking the most perilous route as we explore the politics of the sociology of knowledge. There is one final health warning. I will by necessity refer to the very un-English category of 'intellectuals' to include people like us. This is because many of the debates to which I will refer involved people who were not employed by universities or research institutes. Moreover, the issue which I will be addressing has long been framed in terms of whether intellectuals acquire special political responsibilities because of their learning and erudition.

This story begins with the problem that the sociology of knowledge posed for scientific Marxism. Confidence in the contradictions of capitalism as being bound to result in class warfare and proletarian victory was a great source of reassurance, but this left nagging doubts about the purpose of political activism, especially as it was Marx who had urged the move from merely interpreting society to changing it. If the course of history was to be accelerated, this required developing an advanced revolutionary consciousness among the working classes. For the intellectuals, who supplied a good proportion of the political activists, this provided them with an opportunity and a challenge. The resultant debates within Marxism were particularly intense and fruitful during the economic and political aftershocks of the First World War, with intellectual-activists such as Rosa Luxemburg, Georg Lukács, Antonio Gramsci and of course Leon Trotsky to the fore. Even those who were not Marxists were drawn in, if only to explain why they were avoiding direct affiliation and total commitment to the class struggle and seeking a form of detachment that might allow a greater analytical objectivity. On these debates great life choices depended— the sort made by my premature anti-Fascist, Bernard Knox.

A non-Marxist who made a major contribution was Karl Mannheim. Before he fled to Britain—and the LSE—to escape the Nazis, Mannheim had been taught in Hungary by Lukács. Lukács made his name through his analysis of 'false' consciousness as an objective consequence of the class situation. Such consciousness was grounded, he insisted, in the economic set-up and so was not 'arbitrary, subjective nor psychological'.[3] Mannheim, by contrast, saw the impact of social context on thinking, yet also took a more pragmatic view of knowledge, and looked well beyond the falsity or otherwise of consciousness. His work demonstrates a tension between an appreciation of the social construction of knowledge and recognition that this does not render it wrong or mean that understanding cannot be improved through a deeper engagement with social processes. Though he believed that sociology offered the best means of grasping the totality of social processes, and so could become 'the master science of political practice', he could never quite pin down what sort of political practice this might mean.[4]

Mills, Bell and Chomsky

Mannheim in turn influenced the American C. Wright Mills, who was by far my favourite sociologist during my undergraduate days. Although he died aged 45 in 1962, Mills provides a link between the intense debates of the interwar years, often conducted in the dense abstractions of German philosophy, and the emerging New Left of the US in the 1960s. Like Mannheim, Mills believed that it was the task of sociology to connect private troubles with social and political structures. If an individual was unemployed, that was a private trouble; if 20 per cent of the population was unemployed, that was a structural issue and thus a task for sociology. He was fascinated by the structures of power: how it was in modern corporate America that the elite no longer needed brute force or coercion to sustain its power but could instead rely on manipulation. His most lasting contribution came with *The Sociological Imagination*,[5] in which he derided what he saw to be the two false paths of mainstream sociology. On the one hand there was Grand Theory, whose self-importance he famously deflated with translations of pages of the obscurantist prose of Talcott Parsons into a few lines, and on the other there was Abstracted Empiricism, full of microscopic studies that remained marginal to the big questions of the day. His own creed was established in an appendix on intellectual craftsmanship. He was certainly not against facts and acknowledged that they could be better established through painstaking research. He believed a sense of history essential because that was how one could gather the direction in which events were moving, and, having studied Mannheim carefully, he was determined that his interest in the origins of knowledge should guide his work without overwhelming it.

Unlike Mannheim's, his style was direct and refreshing, though the line between analysis and knockabout polemics was regularly blurred. One piece of advice was that 'any writing that is not imaginable as human speech is bad writing'. Mills did follow Mannheim in believing that sociology could be the master discipline of politics, that the sociological imagination could feed the political imagination. 'Before you are through with any piece of work, no matter how indirectly on occasion', he insisted, 'orient it to the central and continuing task of understanding the structure and the drift, the shaping and the meanings, of your own period, the terrible and magnificent world of human society in the second half of the twentieth century'. Mills was particularly concerned with the nuclear arms race and put some effort into explaining how the military component of the policy elite was pushing the country towards a catastrophic Third World War.

Mills was an unattached radical. He had all but given up on workers' movements and was instead looking to students as the new agents of change, which perhaps helps explain why he was so popular on the campuses of the 1960s, especially as the Freedom Rides into the segregationist South and then the burgeoning campaign against the Vietnam War gave this notion credibility. But in Eisenhower's America, in which he wrote his best work, revolutionary consciousness was not high. One of the most challenging books as the 1950s turned into the 1960s, which appalled Mills, was Daniel Bell's *End of Ideology*, which suggested that the great battles which had divided Western societies in the past had been resolved in a melange of markets and planning, welfarism and liberal democracy.[6]

For Bell, the logic of the new situation was that social scientists would become almost technical experts, devoted to dealing with the second-order problems that had not yet quite been solved. As the political context become more intense as a result of Vietnam, Bell's judgement on the End of Ideology looked increasingly out of touch (a fate that Fukuyama's *End of History* suffered almost three decades later). The critiques of mainstream social science, which had even been relabelled 'behavioural science' to avoid any hint of socialism, took on a harder edge.

Bell was a natural target for Noam Chomsky's withering critique of the irresponsibility of intellectuals in a famous article in the *New York Review of Books* in February 1967,[7] which was also a centrepiece of his trenchant *American Power and the New Mandarins*.[8] I suppose it is another confession that this book also made a big impression on me as a student. Though Chomsky's academic distinction lay elsewhere, he is now among the most read single figures on the international affairs of our time and, according at least to the magazine *Prospect*, the world's top public intellectual. His remorseless critique of American foreign policy has now acquired something of a routine and at times self-parodying quality, but its initial impact was huge.

The original article was not just about exposing the falsehoods and rationalizations spread by the intellectuals supporting and in some cases conducting the war—the New Mandarins in question—but about how they had allowed themselves to get into this position. The problem was not that ideology was dead but that intellectuals had become too comfortable to retain an interest in 'converting ideas into social levers for the radical transformation of society'. The 'free-floating intellectuals of the past' were being replaced by 'scholar-experts'. Those who had already achieved power and affluence, or who sensed that they could achieve them by 'accepting society' as it is and promoting the values that are 'being honored in this society', had made a Faustian bargain that required them to abandon moral sensibility. Meanwhile, their claims to expertise were fraudulent. This, Chomsky believed, had been exposed by Vietnam:

> If there is a body of theory, well-tested and verified, that applies to the conduct of foreign affairs or the resolution of domestic or international conflict, its existence has been kept a well-guarded secret. In the case of

Vietnam, if those who feel themselves to be experts have access to principles or information that would justify what the American government is doing in that unfortunate country, they have been singularly ineffective in making this fact known. To anyone who has any familiarity with the social and behavioral sciences (or the 'policy sciences'), the claim that there are certain considerations and principles too deep for the outsider to comprehend is simply an absurdity, unworthy of comment.

The implication of Chomsky's critique was that the intellectuals must rediscover their vocation as social critics and challenge the very foundations of mainstream thinking. He did so in the direct, forceful prose of a pamphleteer and as a dogged empiricist, collecting facts that exposed the lies and crimes of the policy elite. Chomsky is notoriously impatient with critics who challenge him on sources and evidence, yet there is an undoubted problem when the course of advocacy is so clearly set and the facts are then expected to fit.

Dissent in the East: Kołakowski

While Chomsky was protesting on the steps of the Pentagon a different sort of dissent was being heard within the Soviet bloc. One of the leading voices arguing for basic political rights was Leszek Kołakowski, who in 1968 was expelled from Poland for his trouble, eventually to move to All Souls in Oxford. In the 1950s Kołakowski had been the closest there had been to a New Left intellectual in the Soviet bloc. As a student of religious doctrine in Poland, he quickly came to see the parallels with the malign influence of Stalinist doctrine as an enforced and bureaucratized system of thought that allowed for no challenge and no admission of error. His 1956 essay *What is Socialism?*, censored by the authorities, contained a list of things which socialism should not be, but clearly was in Poland at the time. This included 'a state whose government always knows the will of the people before it asks them' and 'thinks freedom amounts to obedience to the state'.[9] This was a year of political upheaval in Poland and Hungary, and Nikita Khrushchev's speech to the Twentieth Party Congress. In acknowledging the Stalinist terror, Khrushchev caused chaos and confusion in the ranks of the international communist movement from which it never recovered. This meant that Marxism as an approach to both scholarship and poli-

315

tics increasingly began to develop in the West independently of the communist party line, in many cases as part of the 'New Left'. Although this was something of a liberation, it did not stop the increasing divergence between radicals in the West who still focused on issues of inequality and militarism and those in the East who were by now more preoccupied with basic political rights.

Kołakowski made his views clear on the perils of state socialism, but he did not renounce Marxism and remained a member of the party. In 1957 C. Wright Mills visited Poland and met Kołakowski, and adopted him as a kindred spirit from the other side of the Iron Curtain. Although Mills was not a Marxist, he acknowledged the actual and potential contributions of the tradition, independent of the baleful consequences of the Soviet experience. The two men conferred about how Marxism might eventually be assimilated into Western thought without having constantly to assert its singularity. When the next year, 1958, Mills spoke of his 'contempt for the indifferent professors and smug editors who so fearlessly fight the cold war' in the US, he added for good measure 'the cultural bureaucrats and hacks, the intellectual thugs of the official line who have abdicated the intellect in the Soviet bloc'. In asserting this equivalence of contempt for the servants of the two blocs who threatened the world with a nuclear disaster, he added that 'Leszek Kołakowski will understand where I stand'.[10]

By the time he left Poland, however, Kołakowski was taking a more jaundiced view of Marxism and Marxists. He did not see an equivalence between the struggles in his country and elsewhere for basic political rights and those in the West who already had their rights to exercise and were doing so in a way which could be construed as letting his oppressors off the hook.

Another leading light in the post-1956 New Left, also in touch with Mills but this time from Britain, was the Marxist historian E.P. Thompson. Thompson retained a vigorous and sentimental attachment to the Marxist tradition, or perhaps more accurately a Marxist tradition all of his own. This combined a vision that was generous and humane with deep suspicion of alternative forms of Marxism, especially perverse continental imports. In 1973, Thompson lamented in an open letter that, while in 1956 he and Kołakowski had both been communist revisionists, now Kołakowski was giving succour to anti-communists who opposed all that they once stood for.[11] Kołakowski's reply was withering, charging Thompson with empty assertions of the possibility of goodness and a reluctance to recognize that the problems exhibited by the states claiming to be socialist were more than the errors of Stalinism. There was no evil associated with capitalism—'exploitation, imperialism, pollution, misery, economic waste, national hatred, and national oppression'—that these countries had not achieved. Worse, they added some of their own, including economic inefficiency and 'above all, the unrestricted role of the omnipotent bureaucracy, a concentration of power never known before in human history'.[12]

Détente and doubts in the '70s

We have now reached 1975, the year of the first BISA conference. What I have tried to do thus far is argue that the sociology of knowledge was from the start about the political role of intellectuals. At the start, after the First World War, the issue was the extent to which intellectuals should affiliate themselves to class-based parties. The decline of the ideological zeal that once animated these parties meant that this issue lost its salience and the intellectuals either contented themselves with second-order tasks or railed against the stultifying complacency of mainstream social science and its celebration of the status quo. With civil rights and Vietnam, a political voice was rediscovered and social science acquired a critical edge. Part of this edge involved a direct challenge to the more obnoxious government policies of the time, but it also led to a demand to look at the underlying assumptions which informed policy and the biases that appeared to be built into the established structures of power. In the West this led to campaigns against bad policies; in the East, however, it led to campaigns against bad systems.

The foundation of BISA came halfway between the end of the Second World War and 2005. For a number of reasons, not all apparent at the time, this was a turning point in contemporary international affairs. One reason, we might have argued, was that the Cold War had just concluded. Of course, we now know that the Cold War did not really conclude until 1989, but in the mid-1970s it was already being spoken of in the past tense. The year 1975 saw the surge of treaty-making and confidence-building activities, collectively known as 'détente', which had begun in the late 1960s, more or less complete its course with the adoption in Helsinki of the Final Act of the Conference on Security and Cooperation in Europe (CSCE). This confirmed the durability of the status quo, dividing Europe into the three distinct spheres of NATO, the Warsaw Pact, and the Neutral and Non-Aligned. With Berlin sorted and everyone promising not to attempt to change borders through military means, the risk of a hot war seemed to be drastically reduced. If there was no risk of a hot war, could we really talk about a Cold War? After all, when things got tense again, Fred Halliday wrote about a second Cold War.[13]

Related to the sense of calmer great power relations was the embarrassing American exit that year from Vietnam. The Vietnam syndrome, if that refers to a reluctance to risk lives and commit resources to foreign wars, was already established. The previous decade's image of American aggression, messing up the Third World out of a paranoid fear of communism, gave way to an image of a fallen giant, traumatized by the Watergate scandal, suffering, like all Western countries, under the harsh economic conditions of the time and clearly not up for a fight. The loss of Indochina to communism combined with the impact of the 1973 Arab–Israeli War and the subsequent hike in fuel prices led to the US gaze, certainly in relation to military policy, shifting from East Asia to the Middle East where it has remained ever since. Prior to the mid-1970s, the big tests for US foreign policy outside of Europe had been Asian—China, Korea and then Vietnam. Afterwards, they were in the Middle East—Iran, Lebanon and Iraq.

Against this broad geopolitical background different sorts of changes were under way. The study of international affairs was inevitably influenced by the big problems of the day, but they were also influenced by the wider intellectual currents of the time. Two in particular seem to me to be important. The first relates to the exhaustion of the left after the heady days of the student revolutions and the general militancy of the early 1970s. The enthusiasms of the earlier period had been stifled by the dead hand of sectarian Marxism. The early radicalism of the 1960s lacked theory and focus and Marxists could provide both. Discussions of strategy became dogged by close examination of sacred texts which those who did not know their Marx from their Foucault found to be something of a turn-off. As significant, the great moral battles of the 1960s either had been won or no longer seemed so clear-cut. Bourgeois politics, after all, had seen the Americans extract themselves from Vietnam and Nixon driven from office, while the miners had done for Edward Heath in Britain. It was possible to argue that much could be done within the system. More seriously, it was by no means clear that the left had good answers to, or even good analysis of, the problem of stagflation then confronting Western countries. The collectivist solutions to which socialists were naturally inclined were at one level at odds with the logic of the 1960s, which in the social and cultural sphere at least stressed the value of individual freedom. Moreover, there was a developing economic critique of contemporary capitalism, which came from the right more than the left, stressing the importance of individualism and free markets and objecting to the overbearing power of the state. The libertarian aspects of the 1960s challenged traditional conservative values, especially those which stressed self-discipline and family life and deplored drug-taking and extramarital sex. Certainly they also challenged racism, homophobia and, surprisingly belatedly, sexism. But they were not at all inconsistent with an anti-statist economic policy.

Furthermore, the question of greater human rights at home raised questions of human rights abroad. This again had always been one of the fault lines in the New Left. Exciting as May 1968 had been in Paris, August 1968 in Czechoslovakia was even more challenging and, to its participants, more dangerous. In this sense also, 1975 was a turning point, though again its full significance was not fully appreciated at the time, for 'basket three' of the Helsinki Final Act gave for the first time legitimacy to those who argued that the denial of human rights breached a central requirement of European security. The European left was profoundly ambivalent towards this development. In principle, of course, all favoured greater human rights for all, but there was anxiety that taking this agenda too far would risk the gains of détente and the consequent stabilization of international affairs. Nobody had pretended, for example, that the Vietnamese communists were democrats in any Western sense, but their excuse was that they were nationalists, and that gave them the right to fight imperialists. The evidence of what this might mean in practice, in Vietnam and even more terribly Cambodia, only became apparent during the latter part of the 1970s.

The Soviet Union, as events in Czechoslovakia and also Poland had demonstrated, was seen as deeply repressive, but the argument was that its power had to be recognized and that the suppression of the rights of Central and East Europeans was a small price to pay for the avoidance of a catastrophic third world war.

Social science and politics

I now want to rewind back to the 1960s and consider how very broadly the conduct of social—or, more specifically, political—science was influenced by these developments and how, much more narrowly, they affected me. The challenge posed by C. Wright Mills was to pull social science back towards difficult and even dangerous topics. The political radicals may have assumed that once this was done, and done honestly, then the conclusions would fall into place, but need this have been so?

The developing critique had three parts to it. The first came directly from the radicals. The status quo had been celebrated while outward superficialities had been mistaken for enduring qualities of the American system as if it represented a pinnacle of political and economic development. The second part of the critique was that this was in part the responsibility of mainstream theory and methods, and, in particular, the futile attempt to mimic the natural sciences, which narrowed the field of study and provided an excuse to avoid normative issues. At this point Thomas Kuhn's work on the structure of scientific revolutions was making an impact, demonstrating that even the laws of science were socially constructed and sustained through the politics of the scientific profession as much as the scientific method.[14] As no amount of experimental data could explain everything, theories—or paradigms—were developed that provided the best possible interpretations of the data available and could sustain the greatest consensus in the scientific community, until they were undermined as anomalies started to appear in the evidence that could not be explained by the prevailing paradigm.

Kuhn was not saying that paradigms were impervious to evidence. The drama comes from the interaction between the evidence and the paradigm. This gets to the third point, which was the importance of underlying assumptions and the consequent need to look beyond what the economist Kenneth Galbraith had described in his book *The Affluent*

Society as the 'conventional wisdom', that is those 'ideas which are esteemed at any time for their acceptability'.[15] The same arguments were at work in political science as in sociology. Critics charged that political science had become political silence, as it had passed quickly by the civil rights movement and paid scant attention to economic inequalities. It had become a way of failing to achieve science while avoiding that dangerous subject, politics.[16] It had limited itself by dealing only with the conspicuous and measurable. Perhaps it was possible to say some interesting things about why people with certain opinions behave, for example in elections, but not so much about why they held these opinions. There was little sense of the historical or social conditions that made patterns of behaviour recur to the point where they were claimed as virtual laws. Power was evaluated only in its surface manifestations—to be judged only by who won or lost when an issue got to the fore, rather than its underlying structures. Peter Bachrach, in a famous 1962 article with Morton Baratz, addressed the question of how the sociologist's view of power being wielded by an elite (as Mills had argued) could be squared with the pluralist view in political science that power was much more diffusely held and its exercise denied any group domination. There were, they argued, 'two faces of power':

> Of course power is exercised when A participates in the making of decisions that affect B. But power is also exercised when A devotes his energies to creating or reinforcing social and political values and institutional practices that limit the scope of the political process to public consideration of only those issues which are comparatively innocuous to A. To the extent that A succeeds in doing this, B is prevented, for all practical purposes, from bringing to the fore any issues that might in their resolution be seriously detrimental to A's set of preferences.[17]

They argued for study of the 'mobilization of bias' in institutions and dismissed the objection that this was a fruitless approach because it involved looking at 'unmeasurable elements' as if, because they could not be measured, they were unreal. To take this stand meant that the pluralists were vulnerable to the same charge they had levelled against the elitists: 'their approach to and assumptions about power predetermine their findings and conclusions'.

This fundamental insight carried a message both methodological and political that was radical in two senses. The political radicalism lay in warning that the American political system had not solved the problem of power; the methodological radicalism lay in urging scholars to dig deep, to look at agenda-setting, the way that issues were defined before they were decided, how political victories became institutionalized in the routines of organizations and to consider what was taken for granted in the background, as well as what was disputed in the foreground.

Nuclear weapons and neocons

As a student I bought into this completely—and I still do. Here I should confess that I have never taken an undergraduate or postgraduate course in either international relations or international history. My interest in nuclear issues was stimulated by Roger Williams's course on the politics of science and technology while I was an undergraduate at Manchester. This led to the case studies I chose for my later graduate work, but in this instance my interest was less in the strategic choices facing governments than in the way that scientific expertise was used to structure these choices. At this stage, if I had to describe myself it would have been as a political sociologist, and for that reason I had been engrossed by the debates I have just been describing.

My paper at the first BISA conference was a critique of Graham Allison's work on bureaucratic politics, which, it seemed to me, had borrowed directly from pluralist study of domestic American politics and brought it into foreign policy analysis. For my part, I was applying the sort of critique that flowed from Bachrach's work.[18] This paper was, as is often the case, a discarded chapter from my thesis, which was also completed in 1975. The topic was the way that the US assessed the Soviet strategic threat, which seemed to me to be a good way to explore the underlying mindset that influenced foreign policy and led me to employ what would now be called a constructivist approach.[19]

Although intelligence agencies are in principle dedicated empiricists, I was also considering their forward projections. On the basis of what they knew, say, in 1956 (which was not a lot), how did they project forward to 1961 or 1966? This mattered because decisions on future weapons programmes, with lead times of a decade at least, were supposed to anticipate the future threat. Because they could not, I was able to demonstrate that the institutional biases of the agencies affected their projections. Practitioners and students of intelligence alike were fully aware of the consequences of fragmentary information and the need to speculate, and also the challenges and temptations this created. In this context a constructivist approach was not, as we say in the fields of epistemology and cognition, 'rocket science'. In arguing that intelligence estimates emerged out of a political process and explaining how worst-case thinking might take hold, my thesis showed traces of my earlier radicalism, but to be frank they were no more than traces.

As the nuclear debate picked up during the late 1970s, I found myself on what was considered to be the liberal side of the argument, critical of those who exaggerated the Soviet threat and sought technical fixes to what seemed to me at the time intractable though intriguing problems of nuclear deterrence. Mutual Assured Destruction appeared to describe a terrible condition not a strategic choice. In this, I was at odds with the group already known as 'neocons'. Yet there was something in their analysis that gave me pause for thought. Neoconservatism was an outgrowth of splits within the Democratic Party, with the traditionalist Cold War wing horrified by what they saw as the anti-defence and essentially appeasing attitudes of the McGovernite wing. Anti-militarism is a traditional left-wing virtue, at least in the West, and after Vietnam there was an understandable distrust of any allegations that the military and its supporters might make about Soviet threats. The neoconservatives' arguments, to start with, were undoubtedly based on the conviction that arms control attempts were folly and that the Soviet Union was still committed to advancing its totalitarian ideology by force if necessary. The conviction that national security was in peril became a consistent theme of this political tendency and was consistently overdone. But even if one did believe that the balance of terror was a contribution to a war-preventing stability, as I did, this was hardly a satisfactory basis for security. It also carried high political costs. Here the charge was that, whatever the Soviet Union might do in the future as its military power continued to grow, its existing power was sufficient to lead the West to stifle objections to its abhorrent current practices. This was an issue that came to the fore over the question of the linkage between the right of Soviet Jews to emigrate and the trade agreement, and also President Ford's unwillingness to meet Alexander Solzhenitsyn when he was in Washington. When President

Carter wished to demonstrate that he was taking the US on a new moral course in foreign policy, it was human rights he stressed, even though he did not, at least initially, buy into the neocons' national security agenda.

The anti-nuclear movement

This aspect of the debate came to the fore at the end of the decade as a new European-wide anti-nuclear movement gained strength. This was in response to a series of nuclear decisions, most notably that taken by NATO, in December 1979, to introduce US missiles into five European countries, which was followed almost immediately by the Soviet invasion of Afghanistan, raising international tension by a number of notches. Thinking I was on the left, I had used a set of arguments to challenge the anti-deterrence notions of the right, their exaggerated political claims and fascination with technical fixes promised by new weapons systems. I felt unable to take a different approach just because the next set of simplistic critiques came from the left, this time with exaggerated claims about Western motives and a belief that fewer weapons, as a result of disarmament, could have a transformative political effect.

The most prominent of the anti-nuclear groups was the European Nuclear Disarmament campaign (END). To the fore was E.P. Thompson, now playing the Chomsky role, with a brilliant pamphleteering style and withering scorn (I recall being described as a 'compliant cowboy', a label that fortunately failed to stick).[20] In line with his sympathies, Thompson damned Eastern Stalinism as much as Western militarism and lumped them together as part of a common 'exterminism'. In this respect he ensured that END avoided the equivocation of the CND of two decades earlier, in which there was a definite communist influence and therefore often a reluctance to condemn the workers' bomb with the same fervour as the capitalists'. Instead, the END appeal, drafted by Thompson, proposed a nuclear-free zone from Poland to Portugal to be achieved through dissolution of the blocs. This approach was profoundly misleading, assuming that the blocs had a malign equivalence, an equal capacity for dissolution, which could be achieved through nuclear disarmament, or that after dissolution a benign harmony would spread across Europe and bind it together.[21]

In this once again it was the leading Central and Eastern European intellectuals who challenged Thompson most directly. Václav Havel accepted what he called a 'prerational' sympathy with those who put the general good ahead of private interest. But he was as ever sensitive to the political use of language and warned how the rhetoric of 'peace' had been so abused by Soviet propaganda as to be treated with the deepest scepticism. Meanwhile, he insisted:

> The cause of the danger of wars is not weapons as such but political realities … No lasting, genuine peace can be achieved by opposing this or that weapons system because such opposition deals only with consequences, not with reasons.

To Adam Michnik, writing from a Polish prison, the idea that 'arms are more important than people' was part of a 'Soviet pattern of thinking'.[22]

After the Cold War

In the event, the Cold War concluded with the implosion of European communism, with disarmament negotiations as something of a sideshow. This story began with communist intellectuals gearing themselves to undermining the false consciousness of the masses, but at the end it was anti-communist intellectuals speaking out for bourgeois freedoms that were to the fore in the Velvet Revolution. The ideological struggle, which had been at the heart of the Cold War, had a clear victor, whose proponents were imbued with classic liberalism. It made the final end run, having left the pacemaking for years to socialists. Moreover, this proved to be a truly transformational ideology, adopted by the people, which served as the basis of European unity. As it was the ideology of the most powerful countries, and with the counter-ideology having evaporated, there seemed few barriers to taking the good message to those suffering under less enlightened regimes.

Yet, in doing so, it became apparent that alternative ways of thinking were extraordinarily resilient. Recent conflicts have had cultural as much as economic roots, with questions of ethnicity, religion and language at their heart, and intellectuals have often played a dangerous role as the constructors of divisive identities. Sometimes they did this as part of the backlash of communism's failure, in an attempt to substitute nationalist themes for socialist ones. The views they promoted were exactly of the sort that the intellectuals of the past had deplored and had seen it as their task to expose as dangerous mystifications, detracting from true class consciousness. Liberals also saw the risks of either dooming their adherents to subjugation or else inciting violent conflict with people with whom they really had a lot in common. Is it the duty of the scholar to point this out and work to change beliefs and forms of behaviour? Or, does this compromise scholarship while patronizing its objects, especially at a time when we are discouraged from 'privileging' our beliefs over others' and encouraged to celebrate cultural diversity?

At any rate, given the frustrations of past purveyors of a true consciousness, what hope is there to provide guidance from outside? As conflict takes hold, opinions harden and group solidarity becomes a political imperative. Divisive structures demonstrate great resilience once established. Warning against primordial concepts of ethnicity, and demonstrating how forms of ethnicity are social constructions, make them sound easier to change than if they were physical facts. This is less helpful politically than one might hope. These constructs are not fragile but are often remarkably robust. Deconstructing the enemy can be a tough call.

The ethnic nationalists of the 1990s could, along with the communist philosophers of the 1920s or the 'peace' campaigners of the 1960s and 1980s, claim a form of political leadership based on their intellectual grasp of events and their consequent capacity to raise the consciousness of ordinary people. But without the class—or ideological or national—struggle that provides a ready means of demonstrating political commitment, intellectuals struggle to make themselves heard against a cacophony of voices. In addition there is also the question of whether such a leadership role, including leading campaigns against particularly obnoxious policies of an otherwise legitimate government, is compatible with scholarship. As Hedley Bull observed in the introduction to *The Anarchical Society*, good scholarship is likely to be subversive of all causes, good or bad.[23]

Yet, particularly when debates are intense, political distance is hard to achieve. Even innocuous statements are seized upon as being loaded with ideological meaning or are apt to be seized on by activists as evidence of where your sympathies really lie. As citizens we can use our knowledge to make contributions. In particular, it seems to me that we can offer context. We can explore the background and unspoken assumptions of political protagonists, and explain how their thought patterns have been shaped by the conflicts of years past, perhaps reflecting the legacies of otherwise forgotten academic scribblers. We can challenge propensities to dubious reasoning through analogy and the abuse of sources of evidence. We can note how worldviews have become embedded in the culture of institutions, or carelessly developed and bowdlerized through media commentary. To neglect all this because it is hard to measure or to be absolutely sure of its correctness, to meet exacting standards of falsifiability, is to deny access to vital avenues of analysis and important contributions to political life. If you take precautions, of which self-awareness is the most important, epistemological despair can be avoided and useful knowledge can be generated. Understanding how this knowledge is socially constructed need not lead to a loss of confidence in its validity. Last, as important as the construction of knowledge is its effective communication. Here we can recall that two of BISA's key founders—Alastair Buchan and Susan Strange—were both former journalists. I am not sure how much they worried about the theory of language, but they sure knew how to use it.

18

OBSERVATIONS ON WHITEHALL AND ACADEMIA

Sir David Omand

It was Lawrence Freedman who came to call on me in the Cabinet Office, as I prepared to retire from the post of UK Security and Intelligence Coordinator, to suggest that I might join him at King's College as a visiting professor in the Department of War Studies. With some trepidation about how my former colleagues on the inside would react, I settled down to research and write the book on security and intelligence that I wish I had had available to read when I first came into contact with the world of secret intelligence. In my own writings on national security,[1] wearing my King's College War Studies hat, I have stressed the need to learn to live with strategic surprises. Certainly in the fields covered by the Joint Intelligence Committee (JIC) the past record of insiders anticipating trouble by predicting its outbreak (including Czechoslovakia in 1968, the Yom Kippur War in 1973, the Chinese attack on Vietnam in 1978, the Soviet invasion of Afghanistan in 1979, Iran-Iraq in 1979, and the invasion of the Falkland Islands in 1982) is patchy at best. Academics might have done just as well. But as Michael Goodman, one of the professors in the Department of War

Studies at King's College London, has observed in his work on the official history of the JIC: the intelligence community no more has a crystal ball than anyone else, but it does come into its own in supporting policymakers with very rapid assessments of rapidly unfolding situations and detailed source analysis to enable a crisis to be understood and managed.[2]

What Whitehall says it wants above all from academia is 'impact'. Academia must show, in the words of the Research Councils UK, the 'demonstrable contribution that excellent research makes to society and the economy', including 'increasing the effectiveness of public services and policy through significant advances in understanding, method, theory and application'.[3] In the fields of study of social sciences and public policy, Whitehall says explicitly that it is looking for three things:[4] 'instrumental contributions', influencing the development of policy, practice or service provision, shaping legislation, and altering behaviour; 'conceptual contributions' to the understanding of policy issues and reframing debates; and 'capacity building' through technical and personal skills development.

In practice, the Whitehall preferences for working with academia tend largely to the instrumental, and the immediately instrumental at that. The pace is relentless, with the time for reflection compressed close to zero and the number of policy officials continuing to fall, while the resources to invest in tomorrow's potential issues are lacking. The policy–academic relationship will be explored in the rest of the present chapter, looking first at what Whitehall—the policy world—wants, what tends to be provided and, then, examples of the relationship at work.

What Whitehall wants

Threatening clouds can gather quickly out of a clear sky. In such circumstances, Whitehall has, of course, its own expertise on which to call that should not be underestimated and its own professional cadres, with military, diplomatic, scientific, medical, economic and statistical expertise foremost among them. Nonetheless, often the up-to-date knowledge that is needed in a hurry is to be found outside. Then the search is on for an expert in academia who can advise on the epidemiology of human-to-human transmission of a new strain of bird flu, on the language use of tribes in Yemen, or some other state teetering on the edge, on sayings in the Hadith cited in an incendiary blog, or to provide a cross-bearing on whether there really is a weakness in the mathematics of some elliptic curve-derived cryptosystem in common use, and so on. Whitehall recognizes deep expertise and values access to it, but only when it decides it needs it and on the terms of engagement that it decides.

The late Sir Michael Quinlan coined his own syllogism to describe the problem: what you can predict/expect, you prepare for, and what you prepare for, you deter/avoid/mitigate; therefore, the really testing situations that you will experience are those that you have not prepared for. It is in such situations that having outside expertise to bring fresh thinking can be most valuable. It was a sign of recognition of that truth that, when I was in the Cabinet Office, we set up with the assistance of the Royal Society standing panels of academics in different areas of expertise who would be prepared, at no notice in the event of an unforeseen serious emergency threatening the life of the nation, to come into the Cabinet Office briefing rooms and provide advice.

Successive government chief scientists, to their great credit, have done much over the last twenty years to try to popularize horizon scanning and 'futures' work among policy officials, not so much to reduce the likelihood of surprise, but more accurately to learn to live better with the inevitability of surprise.[5] The natural but unscientific desire to make long-term predictions about essentially unknowable events has been replaced by curiosity about examining the evidence about individual future trends themselves. A measure of the potential that such work might deliver can be seen from the arrangements recently made to improve connections to academia and to provide swift-flowing channels through which advice can actually reach the most senior levels. There is ministerial oversight of the 'futures' programme and high-level Whitehall support from an advisory group (CSAG) chaired by the Cabinet Secretary himself, with the government chief scientist and the principal permanent secretaries, to examine the potential implications for policy of future threats or scenarios. One level down, the chair of the Joint Intelligence Committee runs a Whitehall-wide group to coordinate the work of the relevant communities of interest. In these communities are to be found specific advisory groups drawing widely from across academia and representatives of, for example, the Royal Society, the academic institutions and universities, and major global businesses.

What academics might seek to provide

Organization of advising. Commissioning from academia deeper work on possible long-term developments of interest is one way of preparing better for the future, without falling into the trap of imagining that one can predict the course of future events, let alone base national strategy on assumptions about a future that follows a predictable path. An example worth recalling is the paper commissioned by the policy staff in the Ministry of Defence (MoD) from King's War Studies on what might be expected as the former Yugoslavia threatened to descend into violence and anarchy. The resulting paper drew lessons from the collapse, as I recall, of the Roman, Byzantine, Austro-Hungarian and British empires and was a sobering guide to what happens when the centre cannot hold.

My own model of the intelligence analytic process, of situational awareness, explanation and estimation, has a fourth component, strategic notice. Planning the future of the UK intelligence community needs, for example, to have a good feel for possible future developments in the nature of the demands for intelligence (such as the emergence of new terrorist groups or shifts in state power), in the technological environment (such as the 'internet of everything' and in advanced robotics in warfare), and in development of social attitudes to privacy (such as changes in the acceptability of the national and international legal structures in which intelligence activity has to be carried out).

Casting the net widely across academia will add value when looking at possible developments in specific threat vectors (such as in the potential for more flexible design of cyber weapons or measuring the spread of knowledge of synthetic biology capable of being used to design bioweapons). Without having some ideas in mind, at least of a possible set of pictures that might have been found on the missing lid of the jigsaw puzzle box, the chance of analysts sensibly connecting disparate pieces together when they come to hand is remote. The idiom 'failure to connect the dots' is in common use to describe so-called intelligence fail-ures.[6] But dots can, with imagination, be connected in many patterns, often dependent on the 'framing' of the problem by the analyst. Without at least some hypotheses in mind to be tested against the evidence, Whitehall has little hope of 'connecting the dots' when the first emer-gence of such possibilities begins to be detected. The founder of scientific intelligence, Professor R. V. Jones, however, coined a warning of what he termed 'Crabtree's Bludgeon': 'No set of mutually consistent observa-tions can exist for which some human intellect cannot conceive a coher-ent explanation, however complicated'. And, we might append today, taking particular care that it is not just the politically expedient explana-tions of the fragmentary evidence that emerge.

Structure of advice. Inevitably, I suspect, the focus of such 'futures' work will end up being more about avoiding crises or being prepared to manage mid-term threats rather than identifying long-term opportuni-ties and considering how to best position the nation to take advantage of them should they emerge, a bias that is naturally all too readily reflected in everyday official advice to government. It takes great imagination and an optimistic cast of mind, sadly often lacking in much of the public service today, to identify new potential opportunities or even to see a threat as a national opportunity.

At least this conceptual approach to looking into the middle distance by academia may help Whitehall identify where policies may not be robust enough against changes in different future environments. As an example, a common thread of advice from academics to the planners in the MoD has been the need to ensure that future equipment pro-grammes would support capabilities needed in a wide variety of future scenarios. Such flexibility has its cost, the outcome might be a lower level of fielded effort—but with the advantage of knowing that the result is robust against a larger number of possible futures. Another example would be the use of simple games theoretic concepts to exam-ine different possible anti-terrorist protective security investment strategies. Thus a minimax approach would concentrate expenditure on minimizing the maximum harm a terrorist group might be able to inflict, identifying and hardening a small number of potential very sen-sitive targets, such as sites where nuclear materials are stored. A maximin approach, on the other hand, would focus on maximizing the general minimum level of security that might be offered to the general public, for example when using mainline railway stations. The trade-offs come from the high assurance in the former case, but at a level of expenditure and inconvenience that cannot be widely applied; and the limited protection offered in the latter case, though it may be affordable in ways that affect a large proportion of the public.

How deep the advice reaches

What Whitehall generally finds harder is to absorb the outcome of academic research into more fundamental issues around policy effectiveness where the findings challenge accepted wisdom. Keynes's saying that the difficulty lies not so much in developing new ideas as in escaping from old ones is certainly apposite in relation to getting a large institution to recognize that old concepts have become time-expired and should no longer be part of current doctrine or taught as such. Such cases in the defence and security domain are often associated with rapid technical change. As was pointed out by academics many years ago,[7] the growth rate of productivity due to the adoption of innovative ideas is governed by the rate of investment to incorporate them, and that in turn depends upon the animal spirits of the investors.

When funds for investment are in short supply, the mood is bearish and old ways of doing business persist along with the old equipment. It is then not easy to follow the advice of Admiral Jackie Fisher: 'The design of fighting ships must follow the mode of fighting instead of fighting being subsidiary to and dependent on the design of ships'.[8] I recall the efforts in the MoD during the Defence Review of 1981, in the latter part of the Cold War, to persuade the Royal Navy that a world war, if one were to start, would end with at least a limited nuclear release to restore deterrence and was not likely to require Atlantic convoy escorts over a prolonged period; to persuade the army cavalry regiments to champion the attack helicopter; and to persuade fast jet pilot leadership in the Royal Air Force to invest in remotely piloted vehicles. Each of these causes had its champions among the younger officers, and, interestingly, the senior officers closest to front-line responsibility were mostly sympathetic to them, but the moment of inertia of conventional thinking within a large organization should not be underestimated.

Examples of the impact of advice

Terrorism. An example of the power of a concept, risk management, from my own time as a permanent secretary, was when I started in the Cabinet Office after 9/11 to develop the UK counterterrorism strategy, CONTEST. The strategic aim endorsed by the Cabinet was to reduce the risk from international terrorism so that people could go about their normal lives, freely and with confidence. The underlying strategic logic was that the risks to society of a terrorist attack could be decomposed into the likelihood of terrorists attempting an attack, the vulnerability of society to that form of attack, the initial impact should the terrorists succeed, and the length of disruption to normal life that would then ensue before normality could be restored. Each of these factors can be reduced by selective government measures (in the case of reducing likelihood, both by increasing the capacity to uncover and disrupt terrorist networks and by preventing the radicalization of another generation of recruits; reducing vulnerability through protective security measures for air travel, public buildings, etc.; and reducing initial impact and disruption through investing in and training together the emergency services).

The power of the idea of national risk mitigation, to which all could contribute, took hold readily across Whitehall, local government, the armed forces, police, intelligence community, industry and civil society itself. No doubt that is one reason why the CONTEST strategy is still in force over ten years from its inception. That strategy of denying the terrorists what they most seek in terms of disruption of normality distinguished the UK from the US adoption of a risk elimination strategy through a war metaphor, aimed at destroying al-Qai'da. The distinction can still be seen in the very different interpretations of international law taken by the US administration and by the British government over such matters as when and where lethal force can be used against terrorists, whether by armed drones or special forces.

A related example is the popularization, as part of UK counterterrorism strategy, of the concept of resilience. Originally taken from the academic study of materials, it is the ability of a body to absorb an impact, or blow, and to bounce back into shape, with the amount of energy absorbed in the impact being a measure of the damage to the internal structures of the material. The metaphor could be applied readily to societies facing disruptive challenges (as they are euphemistically called in Whitehall). The value of deliberately investing in the resilience of the national critical infrastructure (energy, telecoms, finance, etc.) quickly caught on.

Later dialogue on the development of the concept between academia (including the King's War Studies department) and Whitehall identified the psychological resilience of a population under attack as a key determinant of how much damage could be expected. That led to policies such as building up social capital (another borrowing from academia) through encouragement and engagement of civil society voluntary organizations, such as local Red Cross or St John Ambulance or Mothers' Union branches, that would provide some of the essential glue holding communities together at times of great stress. One great advantage of such approaches was the impact of relatively modest initiatives and the wide variety of circumstances—civil contingencies as well as malign attack—in which the investment would produce an ample dividend. The great crash of 2008 cut off many lines of funding, but the power of the idea of resilience seems to have staying power—although one day it too will no doubt have to give way to another concept more apt to the circumstances of the time.

Operational analysis. It is in such debates that the academic world can play such a useful role in articulating the case for change, pointing to developments overseas, and providing some of the evidence to help weigh the arguments, for it is rare that there are not also rational views on the other side of an argument for change. The record of trying to use the quantitative methods of operational analysis, as often advocated by defence academics, to model defence problems is mixed, however. The analyses generated, for example, in the 1970s and 1980s at the defence operational analysis establishment at West Byfleet had only limited impact in influencing procurement decisions,[9] largely because the assumptions for scenario modelling could always be challenged by those whose favoured programmes did not come out on top. True, research findings often provide complex data that are hard to reduce to the simplicities of 'what works'. And the more that 'evidence-based policy' is championed from academia, the greater the temptation for political advisers to interpret that as 'look, we already have the policy, what we need academia to do is provide the evidence to support it and guide its implementation'. My experience when I moved to the Home Office was that civil departments have an even harder time than defence in turning external research into policy, given the closeness of media scrutiny and the greater party-political sensitivity of the topics. Officials will look to academia for ideas; but special advisers may be more inclined to look to think tanks. These are also a valuable source of thinking and also often a waypoint to academia. The risk is that the choice of a preferred think tank will reflect a pre-existing political outlook.

I recall, in 1980, meeting John Nott at the airport as his new private secretary when he returned from his last Far East trip as Trade Secretary to become Defence Secretary. He had not wasted the flight and waved a clutch of academic papers critical of British defence policy that he had obtained at the High Commission and on which he now demanded departmental views. His mind was already turning to the need for an internal defence review. External critiques were certainly plausible but, without the knowledge only available on the inside, they lacked conclusions that were capable of being translated into detailed investment priorities once the interests of allies and of industry (and of electoral politics) had been taken into account. At the level of strategic thinking, Prime Minister Thatcher, Foreign Secretary Carrington and Nott himself were all agreed on the overriding importance of not undermining NATO's cohesion at an important period for the Alliance following the Soviet invasion of Afghanistan and the continuing arms control negotiations with the Soviet Union over intermediate nuclear forces following the deployment of the Soviet SS20. Lawrence Freedman's subsequent judgement stands:

> Defence policy prior to April 1982 can be seen as following NATO orthodoxy by concentrating on land and air forces capable of blocking a conventional invasion of West Germany, backed up by a nuclear deterrent. Therefore, the most significant feature of the Falklands War was that it was fought well out of the NATO area and with the Royal Navy the lead service. It was precisely the war for which Britain was planning least.[10]

Getting the story straight

At least a familiarity with the relevant concepts and arguments that academia is good at articulating, desirably with some practice in deploying them at international gatherings and speaking to academic and think tank audiences, makes it easier for a secretary of state to have the confidence to delve under the surface of a superficially polished Whitehall argument. Much of the art of administration lies in detecting not only what needs to be done but also when the time is ripe to expound a new explanatory narrative to justify the steps to be taken. The elements of such narratives are often to be found being tossed around academic debate before they emerge as part of the political conversation.

A sense of historical continuity helps when it comes to the difficulties of detecting when that tipping point has arrived and investment programmes need to be rebalanced. I used to remind the defence planners about the Admiralty debates over steam versus sail and iron versus wood or, for the army, carbines versus swords or horses versus tanks. As Bagehot complained in 1867:

> The naval art and the military art are both in a state of transition; the last discovery of today is out of date, and superseded by an antagonistic discovery tomorrow … In their foolish constructive mania the Admiralty have been building when they ought to have been waiting; they have heaped a curious museum of exploded inventions; but they have given us nothing serviceable.

To give the staffs the reassurance that they are in the line of historical succession of the pioneering thinkers of their service is to empower them to be bold.

Institutional structures too carry historical baggage and can crucially influence the outcome of debates within a Whitehall ministry. Academia has been influential in shaping the controversies, lasting a century, around the role and organization of an MoD. A guide to the early steps on that journey (certainly drawn on by this author in his work on the 1980s and 1990s reorganizations of MoD)[11] was provided by the first head of the King's Department of War Studies, Sir Michael Howard, in his influential paper, *The Central Organisation for Defence*,[12] followed by other critiques and commentaries on the subsequent vagaries of defence organization, many of them by former insiders writing from the outside.[13]

Academia has also has provided an apt language to analyze such factors in terms of the psychodynamics of organizations and the emotional life within them. Within the MoD since its earliest days in the 1950s there have been tensions among the views of the naval, military and air staffs and their champions—the single-service chiefs, and between them as a group and the central defence or 'purple' staffs and their champion, the Chief of Defence Staff. The direction of travel has for the last half century been towards being able to give the secretary of state a united defence outlook, against a persistent undertow of single-service currents. Notable milestones were the creation of the post of Chief of Defence Staff to serve as the chair of the Chiefs of Staff Committee (1959), becoming the principal military adviser to the government (after the controversies of the 1981 defence review) and being the military representative on the National Security Council (after the Iraq and Afghanistan campaigns, 2010). A significant step was the creation of a Permanent Joint Headquarters in 1996 (incorporating lessons after the first 1991 Gulf War) led by a commander joint operations, drawn from any of the three services at three-star level (lieutenant general and equivalent), responsible for planning and executing UK-led joint and multinational operations; exercising operational command of the UK forces assigned to multinational operations led by others; and, significantly in the latest set of changes, providing 'politically aware' military advice to the MoD.[14]

Advice, politics and money. Politics rightly always has to be a defining factor in Whitehall debates. Freedman has always understood this, and he rejected the view sometimes held by senior ranks in the armed forces that national security is somehow above politics and above petty considerations of national budgeting. A justified case for spending more can always be made (and perhaps never more so than now), but the opportunity cost too has political—and, potentially, national security—implications. The ideas from industry and academia for new ways of spending money may be interesting and vibrant with potential, but the electorate has to be convinced of the case for taking the money from other programmes. Ideally, political leaders will take the lead on such matters in the light of their assessment of the threat, and not just navigate through the rear-view mirrors of focus groups and today's Twitter statistics.

Defence has not suffered in the past quite as badly as civil departments from the toxic combination of media witch-hunting and party-political manoeuvring that has characterized much recent debate over policy. A rough consensus among most parliamentarians on the broad lines of defence policy, and an admiration for the armed forces (and a distinct unwillingness to be seen to be criticizing them), helped prevent the sort of sniping commonly directed at, for example, the prison service, the police service and Home Office border and immigration staffs.

Problems are nevertheless bound to arise when research results conflict with the currents of political populism. That the provision of access to television in cells can be shown in research findings to improve prisoner behaviour is unsurprising (not least given the rise in time spent in cells due to overcrowding and staff shortages and the ability it then provided to the prison governors to sanction bad behaviour in a way that prisoners really would want to avoid). But that is not how the popular media would report it. Finding an absence of research spending by the Home Office to support penal policy was 'the biggest initial shock which has come to me', declared Rab Butler on taking over that office in 1957.[15] He wanted to be a reforming Home Secretary and wanted the evidence on which to base policy. He created strong links with academia and for many years Whitehall could boast a world-class criminology department inside the Home Office before the institutional vandalism in 2007 that broke the old Home Office, one of the great departments of state, into a ministry of justice and a continental-style 'ministry of the interior' or 'ministry of state security'. The media can be guaranteed to jump on any opportunity to portray ministers as soft on criminals and on punishment for crime.

Another example of Whitehall and academia at cross-purposes (pun intended) was the acrimonious dispute over the relative risks of so-called soft drugs and alcohol that resulted in the sacking in 2009 by the Home Secretary of the chair of the Advisory Council on the Misuse of Drugs (ACMD). A 'concordat' in the shape of a revised Code of Practice for Scientific Advisory Committees then had to be drawn up with the assistance of the Government Chief Scientific Adviser to regulate the relationship between ministers and academics when the latter are being used as external advisers. The 2011 version of code[16] includes the injunction: 'Whether acting proactively or reactively, Scientific Advisory Committees should expect to operate free of influence from the sponsor department, officials or Ministers, and remain clear that their function is wider than simply providing evidence just to support departmental policy'. Nevertheless, the Police Reform and Social Responsibility Act 2011 removed the previous legal requirement for the ACMD to have scientists and other defined professionals on the committee. Any academic invited to advise government would be well advised to establish in advance the rules of engagement, including the right to publish the results of research.

Ideas in and out of government

War of ideas. Whitehall is not exempt from Keynes's famous warning:

> The ideas of economists and political philosophers, both when they are right and when they are wrong, are more powerful than is commonly understood. Indeed, the world is ruled by little else. Practical men, who believe themselves to be quite exempt from any intellectual influences, are usually slaves of some defunct economist. Madmen in authority, who hear voices in the air, are distilling their frenzy from some academic scribbler of a few years back.

Today it is the strength of will of the 'practical men' to get those things done that are valued most; the relevance of the conceptual categories and narratives they use to drive implementation of policy is under-examined. Policy and its execution cannot be safely separated, a lesson Professor Michael Howard had drawn from his study of the mistakes made by the over-centralized and remote German high command structure (OKW) in the later stages of the Second World War, analysis that was influential in defining the responsibilities of the UK Chief of Defence Staff and his relationship to the heads of the single services.[17]

The practical virtues have been in much demand to adapt the public service to modern circumstances, not least to the potential of information and communications technology. Very necessary, but an inadvertent consequence, has been the relative increase in the influence of political advisers at the cost of downplaying the role of the senior civil servant in the policy formulation process (using that terminology to distinguish it from the policy 'making' role that lies with the elected government of the day). The explosion of modern communications has long meant that Bagehot's ideal is impractical: 'Recent experience seems, however, to show that in all great administrative departments there ought to be some one permanent responsible head through whom the changing Parliamentary chief always acts, from whom he learns everything, and to whom he communicates everything'.[18] Such a channel would quickly become a cause of delay that ministers and their special advisers would easily navigate around. But at least on the key policy issues the permanent secretary and senior officials have to be deeply engaged with the secretary of state.

Academia, because organized knowledge is its stock in trade, has generally been able to adapt faster than Whitehall over the last decade to the opportunities offered through the internet to share data and findings between scholars, to facilitate ad hoc collaborations, and to systematize knowledge. What academia and Whitehall do share is a natural inclination to become stove-piped organizations (departments for Whitehall and faculties for academia), having then to overlay mechanisms for working cross-boundary (czars and endless committees for Whitehall and interdisciplinary institutes for academia).

Whitehall is also vulnerable (and the ministerial advisers especially) to fashions in ideas about public policy and how to 'deliver' (itself a valuable concept, even if politically laden through its overuse by New Labour). Recently the worlds of microeconomics and applied and cognitive psychology have found favour, with revealed preferences, focus groups, 'nudge' units, fast and slow thinking, and the power of noticing as just a few conceptual examples.

A partially digested academic idea can of course be dangerous. The Chilcot Inquiry released into the public domain the policy paper that one of its members, Lawrence Freedman, had provided to Prime Minister Tony Blair to help with the preparation of a major speech he was to give in Chicago on 22 April 1999 on liberal interventionism.[19] Freedman noted that the principle of non-interference had long been considered 'basic to international order' and was 'not one that we would want to jettison too readily'. Still, he added, it 'must be qualified in important respects'. As discussed in earlier chapters in this volume, the real challenge, he argued, was to decide whether to intervene and what tests would have to be satisfied when making the decision: tests that Freedman then set down in his paper. In the subsequent event, the decision to join the US invasion of Iraq in 2003 did not appear to the Chilcot inquiry to satisfy those tests, so the specific influence of the paper can be overemphasized, although the thrust of the argument was certainly, to judge from the evidence given by Tony Blair to the Chilcot Inquiry, absorbed.

A relevant question for this chapter is whether such an insightful paper would have had that effect if written from the inside. The answer is probably that, yes, it could have been penned by any number of officials. But as research at King's College into the problems of delivering forecasting and warning advice has concluded from studying several cases, the evidence is that it does matter who is delivering the advice, and not just the content of the advice itself.[20]

As Beatrice Heuser remarks in chapter 6 of this book, the Blair Chicago speech does not mark the end of an evolution in thinking about when a war can be considered justified, but it can be regarded as a rediscovery of older traditions of 'just war' thinking. Her observation links to that of Mats Berdal that a central and recurring theme to emerge from Freedman's work is his insistence on the importance of ensuring—whenever, and in whatever capacity, the use of military power is contemplated—that military actions are aligned to wider political purposes. The comparison with the Obama doctrine of 'strategic patience'[21] will no doubt provide material for scholars for years to come.

Whitehall has, however, always been wary of attaching academic labels to policy. Those who seek to influence thinking in the MoD and the armed forces have to remember that these are practical people, with guns. Casual use of words like 'discourse' and 'signifiers' will have them reaching for their metaphorical revolvers. I would not therefore advise the Political Director of the FCO or the Director General Security Policy of the MoD in their roles of attending the Chiefs of Staff Committee to attempt to get the chiefs to appreciate, for example when considering different options for further military action against the so-called Islamic State in the Levant (ISIL) in Iraq and Syria, whether the paper before them comes from a realist constructivist or a constructivist realist stance (nor whether Lawrence Freedman is best described as either). As Mats Berdal cogently argues in chapter 8 of this book, the analytical strength of a constructivist approach should be in understanding processes and dominant interpretations and that is something military officers, diplomats and senior civil servants can relate to, in plain English.

Armistice of ideas. Sometimes, thankfully, Whitehall officials' need for fresh thinking coincides with the ability of academia to inspire it. This chapter has already drawn attention to some notable examples of the work of King's College. Since 2008, War Studies' researchers have published 213 books and well over 1,000 research papers in peer-reviewed journals or edited volumes, as well as gathering a rising volume of research income, not least from Whitehall. The subject focus on 'war' demands work that is not confined to any one discipline, but rather requires eclectic, wide-ranging and reflective approaches to research, drawing on numerous disciplines. Within war studies, different multidisciplinary centres are deliberately organized to provide foci for Whitehall (and wider) interest, through the Centre for Defence Studies (CDS), the Centre for Science and Security Studies (CSSS), the European Centre for Energy and Resource Security (EUCERS), the International Centre for the Study of Radicalisation and Political Violence (ICSR), the King's Centre for Military Health Research (KCMHR), the Marjan Centre for Conflict and Conservation, and the Research Centre in International Relations (RCIR) and several others. It is evident that, in terms of instrumental contributions, as called for by Whitehall, there is much going on.

The academic advantage. Academics have, by the nature of their calling, to allocate time to reading to keep up with their chosen field and related disciplines and to attend conferences to explore and defend their ideas with their peers. That was a feature of the defence policy environment a decade or more ago, when Lawrence Freedman, Michael Clarke or John Gearson could be found accompanying official delegations to staff talks and seminars with their opposite numbers from the defence ministries of NATO nations or to boost the UK voice at stiftung conferences. But that has quickly become a luxury today for the hard-pressed civil servant in any key role, given the pressure of internet connectivity with the expectation of instant responses and the hollowing out of Whitehall policy staffs. Only when retired did I have time to become fully aware of the literature on intelligence studies and intelligence history and of the active networks of scholars working in those fields. I confess that at least some of this literature would have been useful to have read as a practitioner when in government service.

My experience, like that of others with whom I have raised the subject in preparing this chapter, is that the ability of a university to accept former officials and officers and those on sabbaticals—giving them the intellectual space to reflect, research, write and, if they wish, teach and supervise—does significantly change the attitude of Whitehall to academia and vice versa. That had been the case with defence studies for some years (the Centre for Defence Studies was set up in King's in 1990 with an initial ten-year MoD grant, in part precisely to initiate such links).

The field of intelligence studies in which I now work is a relatively recent addition to war studies. The secrecy that traditionally surrounds intelligence activity might have been expected to give rise to some suspicion in Whitehall when King's came to expand its coverage of intelligence studies at the university (including the delivery of a specialized master's-level course). The presence of faces familiar from the past must have been some reassurance, including the presence of Lawrence Freedman himself, fully security-cleared for his role as official historian of the Falklands campaign (and for the last six years a member of the Chilcot Inquiry).

Reflecting that attitude of Whitehall to the King's corner of academia, Dr Michael Goodman, then a reader in the department, was appointed as the official historian of the Joint Intelligence Committee (JIC) and given complete access to all of the top secret papers of the committee over its years of existence and those of the principal Whitehall departments. Volume I of the JIC history, which takes the story up the Suez debacle of 1956, has recently been published, revealing much that was previously under-researched about its origins, a good war record, and the development of intelligence during the Cold War into a vital part of the UK national security machine.

Following the report by Lord Butler into intelligence on weapons of mass destruction in 2004, it was to King's that the Cabinet Office turned with a contract to develop and deliver accredited master's-level courses in intelligence analysis to improve the professionalism of newly hired analysts as well as career analysts seconded from the secret agencies, the Joint Terrorism Analysis Centre, Defence Intelligence, and the Cabinet Office Assessments Staff supporting the JIC and now officers from different branches of law enforcement. It has been personally rewarding to take a leading role in this 'formation' of many of the brightest young minds on whom British intelligence will depend in the years to come and who need to be able to see through an outside perspective the challenges and opportunities they will have to grapple with in their working lifetimes, not least the advances in technology and the need to secure public support for and confidence in their mission. The teaching staff has been multidisciplinary from the outset with a mix of academics and senior retired officers from the intelligence and policy community in Whitehall, further thickening the strands connecting Whitehall and academia. At the end of 2016, some 25 of these courses at the master's level had been given. International interest has been high,[22] and the formula is being exported to Norway, Sweden, France and Germany. King's has also designed and delivered courses at a similar level for the police officers working on the Channel programme to counter Jihadist radicalization in the European community, as part of the government's 'Prevent' programme, and for officials working on counterterrorism in the Foreign Office.

Conclusion

Whitehall has thus certainly benefited from (in the words of the Economic and Social Research Council) capacity-building by the universities. The largest and longstanding contribution of the War Studies Department to capacity-building in government has been the responsibility given by MoD to King's College London to design and deliver the academic content of staff officer training at the Joint Services Command and Staff College (renewed in 2011 for a further ten years). For the three armed services, this means that all of their senior officers of the future will continue to have experienced at the hands of King's academics a robust training both in military history and in contemporary security studies drawn from the cutting edge of research. In parallel, officers from all three services study for master's degrees, including through modern distance learning technology that enables officers to combine study with operational duties. Since 2008, the Centre for Defence Studies has developed research concentrations in areas of critical concern for Whitehall policymakers: examples include maritime policy, the role of private security companies, air power, defence procurement, terrorism and counterinsurgency, and ethics and war, as well as providing regional expertise in African and Asian security, Turkish studies and the Maghreb. High-level work by King's College researchers helped the US and UK governments to develop their positions on nuclear non-proliferation for the G8 nuclear summit. Theo Farrell, when at King's, conducted extensive field research himself into the war in Afghanistan, resulting in several high-level campaign reviews for ISAF: for COMISAF (McChrystal, 2010, and Dunford, 2013), and the first command assessment of ISAF joint command (IJC) for COMIJC (Rodriguez, 2010), producing significant policy impact.

It is fair to presume that input from institutions like the Centre for Defence Studies, or other parts of the War Studies grouping at King's College London, in some way influenced the thinking behind the Strategic Defence and Security Review 2015—and that something similar would be the case in the future. It is a good sign that such academic input is genuinely sought. The contribution that outside experts can generally make to such exercises is the debate within a 'safe space' where officers and officials can hear academics rehearse the arguments among themselves and can come to understand more deeply the issues involved without the constraints of a defensive brief that must be followed or having to avoid ideas that might be deemed too subversive of the present order.

There are many current topics in the fields of defence, security and intelligence policy that can benefit from even closer collaboration and interchange between academia and Whitehall. A short list would include terrorism and asymmetric warfare, the future effectiveness of the NATO deterrence strategy, the security implications of climate change and large-scale migration, the governance of the internet and global norms for cyber surveillance and cyber attack, and autonomous weapons systems and robotics on the battlefield.

On all such issues there is no monopoly of understanding or expertise inside or outside Whitehall, and good government policy towards them will continue to depend on the robustness of the links between Whitehall and academia, of the kind that Lawrence Freedman has so encouraged. From his perch now as emeritus professor, he will no doubt continue to be quietly instrumental in shaping significant parts of Whitehall thinking. I write 'quietly', since I suspect he subscribes to one of my laws for the public service, that the rate of progress with a new idea within Whitehall is in inverse proportion to the amount of personal credit one wants from it. His latest venture into developing Whitehall (and wider) self-awareness through the concept of 'strategic scripts' has gained traction, as is well discussed in chapters in this volume, and this should help officials puncture the lazy use of shallow analogies with Munich, Pearl Harbor, Suez or, more recently, the decision to join the invasion of Iraq in 2003.

Searching for a description of what will be needed, I came across this passage by Keynes. He was addressing the economics profession inside and outside of government, but I think it fits Lawrence Freedman and those he has inspired as well:

> He must contemplate the particular, in terms of the general, and touch abstract and concrete in the same flight of thought. He must study the present in the light of the past for the purposes of the future. No part of man's nature or his institutions must be entirely outside his regard. He must be purposeful and disinterested in a simultaneous mood, as aloof and incorruptible as an artist, yet sometimes as near to earth as a politician.[23]

19

REFLECTIONS ON THE FREEDMAN SCHOOL

James Gow

Good ideas and better ways of doing things do not necessarily prevail, whether in life or in the realm of scholarship and thinking. They certainly do not necessarily become well known and used, at any given time. Academic life, as with all other spheres, is subject to 'fads and fashions'.[1] The great physicist Ludwig Boltzmann committed suicide in 1906, 'isolated and defeated',[2] in desperation that his formula to explain entropy, which theorized the reality of atoms and proved their existence, ran counter to, and was not accepted by, the contemporary scientific world, even at the start of the twentieth century, as 'anti-atomic doctrines' dominated and appeared to have won the debate. Yet he died on the eve of the atomic ascendancy: J. J. Thomson and Ernest Rutherford proved not only that atoms were real, but also that they had inner worlds, when the latter split the atom in 1917. With that, the intellectual fashion changed. Rutherford became the father figure of nuclear physics, a new field or school of thought.

The creation of a school of thought rests not only on the merit of the thought involved, as the preceding snippet from the history of nuclear physics shows—though in a case such as Rutherford's, the thinking and the evidence clearly made a major difference. Other factors always play a role. These can include intellectual fashion and 'group think' (the cause of Boltzmann's despair), recognition and awards, research funding and, notably, the appointment of 'acolytes' to academic and other relevant positions.[3]

These are all characteristics that apply to Lawrence Freedman, whose 'acolytes' are many, knowingly or not, and whose success on all other counts is undoubted. Yet, for all the success and all the 'acolytes' spread across the academic and practitioner worlds of strategy and policy, there is no name to the school of thought associated with this work—although there surely is a school. Freedman's work has inherent quality—just as Boltzmann's theory of entropy was correct and had intrinsic value, even if the foundation of a new school of thought in nuclear physics would only come after his death and be led by others. Freedman's work has certainly been recognized. But the full scope of his achievement and the characteristics of a school remain unacknowledged.

The present 'reflection' attempts to address two gaps that emerged in the Freedman project, as it approached its end: Freedman and the policy world, and sceptical challenges to his approach. In the present volume, various versions of Freedman and his work have been explored, as well as more theoretical reflections around constructivism and our subject's whimsical comment (repeated in his chapter) that he could have started a school of thought in international relations if only he had known at the time. This collection of studies reflects both the pluralism in Freedman's work and that of the scholars who have engaged with his thought and work (although it would no doubt have benefited from more contributions from women). The volume incorporates perspectives and approaches from across the span of the strategic studies–politics–history–international relations field. From the personal perspective, this is a rich and stimulating album that bridges a range of discourses about power, order, interests, ideas and values. It also manages to cover major tropes in Freedman's catalogue: national security policy and strategy; nuclear policy and deterrence; US and UK foreign and security policy; the Falklands War; Iraq and the Middle East; ethics and humanitarian intervention; terrorism; philosophy, social theory and scripts; and, of course, the phenomenon of war itself.

Yet, as noted, in all of this two gaps emerged. The first of these, notwithstanding the contributions by Gearson and Omand, is Freedman's relationship to the policy world and the focus on the person himself and some of the qualities that shape this particular academic in the policy world.[4] The second is a sceptical approach to Freedman's work and its potential problems as well as the challenges to the work. In what follows I shall consider these gaps and hope that my reflections will persuade readers that there is in fact a school of thought around Freedman.

The person in the policy world

Freedman's relationship to policymaking and his impact on the broader security policy community are among the most telling and distinctive aspects of his success. Alongside the scholarly achievements, his roles in working with the policy community and in changing the way in which that community thought about security are remarkable feats, as was the expansion of war studies, both intellectually and institutionally, under his leadership. Freedman has been relatively unusual in being publicly known for his involvement (or some of it) in the policy world. Two examples are especially prominent. His (informal) advice to Prime Minister Tony Blair, in the 1990s, is one of them (though it is greatly overstated by most of those who comment on it—he was involved in many discussions, but the Chicago speech was the only example of real influence—an overstatement which probably makes him uncomfortable). The other example is his membership of the Iraq Inquiry, led by Sir John Chilcot.[5] Serving as one of three academic (out of a total of ten) expert advisers to Secretary of State George Robertson for the pioneering 1998 Strategic Defence Review and as official historian of the Falklands campaign also involved clearly public roles, but these are far less known or recalled. However, he undoubtedly was a welcome figure quietly and privately giving advice—or, at least, being a sounding board—to secretaries of state, junior ministers and also senior officials from the time of the Cold War and the Falklands War through to his retirement. In some respects, this involvement was peculiar. To some, especially those less familiar with either Freedman or the UK system, this might seem even more unusual than it was in reality. While many academics in the US swap ivory towers or the Ivy League for government roles, before returning to the academy, it is not at all common for academics in the UK to be embraced by the policy community—certainly in the sphere of security studies. Of course, the two modes of government are quite different, and there is little expectation in the UK that academics will become practitioners in government.

Those differences also make clear that Freedman's role in relation to government is not at all equivalent to that of any US scholar entering government. Even Freedman's well-known inclusion in Blair's discussions and his contribution to Blair's approach was not, as such, a formal role (and, as already noted, was greatly exaggerated by commentators) while his formal roles were met with far less public attention. For the most part, Freedman's roles in the world of policy have been informal—and, as such, he is not unique, but in line with those of many before him and in his time, including some contributors to this volume, notably his doctoral mentor, Michael Howard.[6] The informality in the role that he played was extremely important, above all because not being formally employed meant that he could exercise shadowless independent judgement; similarly, never being a political appointment meant that he could always work with whoever happened to be in office. What sets Freedman apart, perhaps, is the extent to which he has played this role—many who have been consulted have done so for relatively short periods, perhaps while an official who favoured them held a particular post or while a particular politician or party was in office. Freedman's distinction is to have been involved for over thirty years, no matter which colour of government or which particular officials were in place.

This distinguished role—even if it is not what some would imagine it to be—over so long a period owes much to the man himself and his work. Two personal qualities, aside from scholarship, are important in understanding why this has been so. One is Freedman's exceptional judgement—while not always right, of course, he has the capacity to process complex information and arrive at a sound judgement of a situation swiftly. This is a precious aspect that other scholars with great intellectual calibre have lacked in similar roles, especially when free of a particular ideological or political bent. The other attribute is his humility, backed by his humanity. While an academic star, his feet are always on the ground and he is friendly and personable, making it easy, even for those who might be intimidated, to work with him.

Of particular significance must surely be Freedman's relationship with Sir Michael Quinlan over thirty years. Quinlan was a supreme mandarin who became First Permanent Under-Secretary in the Ministry of Defence, had one of the finest minds and was a most eloquent communicator (the present volume, for any strengths it might have, is all the poorer for missing a contribution from this greatly missed subtle intelligence). Those interactions included occasional dinner discussions on nuclear theology, defence and security policy, the changing world around them, and also, of course, how to respond. It is no doubt a pity that no record of these discussions exists—they must have been fascinating occasions, tackling issues of theology (nuclear, but perhaps also the genuine article, with one a liberal Jew and the other a devout Roman Catholic),[7] as well as the policy issues of any particular moment. To a large extent, this helps to explain Freedman's wider influence. The trust built in this relationship, it seems to me, was important in leading to other things—it was shared both within the Ministry of Defence and across government, because of the esteem Quinlan inspired, and outside it, as Quinlan implicitly embraced discussion with those who worked with Freedman, simply because they did so. These two patterns of trust or, at least, initial credit helped to broaden the horizons, in my experience and observation, of both those in policy departments and those in the academic security studies field, especially members of the King's family, in relating to each other.

Indirectly, as a result of the strong relationship and respect between Freedman and Quinlan, understandings of defence and security began to be broadened officially; the Centre for Defence Studies was launched as a research and innovation initiative under the wings of Freedman and the Department of War Studies at King's College London; Freedman was able to persuade King's to invest in new appointments and in the expansion of the war studies programme, including the introduction of a new undergraduate degree; and eventually, among many other things, the Department of Defence Studies was created as a sibling to that of War Studies, but based at the Joint Services Command and Staff College, providing academic education for those being trained as staff officers. When Freedman was appointed to King's in 1982, the Department of War Studies was a mere cottage industry of four and a half people. By 1990, with the creation of the new BA degree and the Centre for Defence Studies, there were twelve and a half academics (although the half was, by now, a different individual and for a different reason). By 2016, with enormous growth in war studies and the emergence of defence studies, the established faculty counted over one hundred, to which a community of adjunct and visiting scholars, as well as over two hundred research students, had to be added. Of course, by this point, Freedman had retired as Vice Principal at King's and had long left the direction of the Department of War Studies behind. But no one doubted that his influence would remain strong long into the future. Freedman was responsible, in many respects, for an 'intellectual juggernaut',[8] expanding horizons and, of course, the King's estate.

Questioning Freedman's approach

Those intellectual horizons have expanded and study at King's has flourished because the range of questions to be covered by war studies is endless. It may be no fault of Freedman's that the expansion of the field and the flourishing of war studies under his leadership are far from reaching their end. So far, to the extent that war studies can be regarded as a discipline, it is one that has been shaped in particular ways—or, in line with Freedman's approach, 'constructed' in a certain way. However, this 'way' is not unproblematic and has been brought into question. Although the contributions to this volume have been broadly positive in their approach to Freedman's work—despite the avowed intention to produce a research volume on his work, rather than a simple celebration of it, and the invitation to contributors to write as inspired, including disapprovingly, if that was the perspective taken—it is reasonable to address some of the possible difficulties with his opus. The following paragraphs, therefore, note and reflect on some of the less positive views that could be taken—concerning war studies as a field, Freedman's association with the policy world, and the potentially problematic impact of his work.

War studies is a field of study rather than a discipline, as conventionally cast. But it can be regarded as a discipline—and, indeed, is, for official purposes, at least on documents underpinning the programmes at King's. So far as the existing coverage goes, the discipline of war studies is a particular construction. Just as film studies as a discipline— the core matter that new students master and scholars contest—came to be shaped rather more around theory and socio-psychological approaches to moving images than, say, technical and scientific or, even, more formal compositional factors,[9] so war studies has been largely shaped around the expanding agenda set by Freedman. In *War*, a 'reader' with insightful essays by a range of scholars, he selected authors to address the causes, conduct and experience of war, as well as strategic thought, the military and society, and ethics.[10] This is a perfectly reasonable and acceptable way in which to approach the topic, of course. However, it is one to which contemporary security issues or foreign and diplomatic policy and defence and security policy can be—and were—immediately added. It is an interdisciplinary eruption that potentially has no bounds. Yet this version of war studies, launched beyond Howard's baseline in history and ethics by Freedman, successful as it is institutionally and intellectually, has been subject to significant dissenting critique.

Whether as a putative discipline or as a field wanting for disciplinary character, war studies as framed in Freedman's sphere has been challenged, as such, for not being truly formed as a discipline, by Tarak Barkawi and Shane Brighton, both part-products of King's.[11] While acknowledging that war studies in the Freedman mould at King's is world-leading, they take its interdisciplinarity to lack coherence.[12] Using somewhat disparaging terminology that makes the Freedman version of war studies sound like something from communist East Germany, they write that 'the actually existing study of war amounts to a grab bag of disparate topics cobbled together from a variety of disciplines and sources'.[13] While not discounting the need for research and education in the various ways embraced by Freedman's version of war studies, they seek a discipline framed in what they call the 'ontology' of war—interrogating its very essence as a phenomenon, rather than contingencies affecting it or produced by it. This is, of course, a major challenge—and it is not one eschewed at King's (indeed, it is a concern of my own and one to which all war studies undergraduates at King's are introduced). It is, as Barkawi and Brighton note, a challenge taken up by Karl von Clausewitz, the great soldier-philosopher who sought to understand war both as a phenomenon and as a product of his own early nineteenth-century historical moment, when great change was afoot.[14] In the world of war studies, they judge, this essence of war is largely missing—everything researched and taught is contingent. At best, in their view, the Freedman approach relies on a common use of the word 'war'.

There is surely merit in this challenge: a fundamental of any field of inquiry is to define the subject of study. Yet it seems that the most likely ways to do just that relate to identifying and labelling the subject's characteristics. That might well bring us back to the Freedman approach. Certainly, just as the existence of atoms could be theorized from other observed phenomena—as Boltzmann did from entropy—war can be studied theoretically from an analysis of its epiphenomena. Similarly, manifestation of phenomena owing to a source, or showing something else harder to identify in practice, is a key epistemology in cosmology, where the existence of objects can be inferred from, and those objects studied by virtue of, observation and interrogation of phenomena (for example, 'invisible' objects in deep space are identified by gravitational pull, say, and studied in relation to the observed objects when that pull indicates the existence of another body). In a sense, the intangible can be explored though examination of its tangible manifestations. Or, to take another approach to the same kind of problem, a phenomenological approach to inquiry, in which all aspects around a topic are studied, may be a more productive form of investigation or education than abstractly trying to delve into its core.[15] Thus, while there is merit in the Barkawi–Brighton approach, equally—or, perhaps, preponderantly—merit remains in the approach developed by Freedman, recognizing that interpretation of war is, in any context or aspect, constructed.

The meta-critique delivered by Barkawi and Brighton could also translate into a questioning of Freedman in terms of his proximity to policy and the impact of his work. While some have challenged his position ideologically, as he notes in chapter 17, I shall approach these issues hypothetically in the present discussion. In effect, I am creating straw people not so much to knock them down as to indicate the existence of other perspectives on Freedman. Of course, as will be evident, I do challenge these positions.

Proximity to power, whether political, religious or financial, has always been a problematic issue for scholars. Many take the view that knowledge should be pure and for its own sake. For these academics, association with government in any way means being tainted. For others, who might welcome, if not espouse, the King's College London mission to produce knowledge and understanding 'in the service of society', there may be a question of ensuring independence—after all, especially if funding is involved, it might be easy to play the paymaster's tune. However, it is in reality quite possible to maintain integrity and independence if the scholar has the appropriate ethical disposition—which is not to say that others will necessarily perceive the matter that way. Moreover, those involved in policy will usually want and, in any case, benefit from strong independent and critical input—as David Omand writes in chapter 18, policymakers do not want to be told what they already know; they want challenges or new knowledge that improves what they know. In this sense, something that could be seen as a problem, when practised with strong self-limitation and integrity, as in Freedman's case, becomes a virtue. Sound judgement protects against any Mephistophelean temptation.

The value of sound judgement, to develop and exemplify this view of working close to the policy world, can be seen by discussion of specifics. While there is not scope here—nor inclination—to discuss UK involvement in the 2003 US-led action over Iraq, this controversial event is a topic that can be used to illustrate the point. Some might see the calamitous aftermath of Washington's action—and British involvement in it—as a consequence of the Chicago speech, making it also an impact of Freedman's thought and work. A scholar of this view might therefore regard the Chicago speech as problematic, a script (in Freedman's term) that led to what turned out to be a disastrous military adventure (as well as other troubled interventions, such as in Libya, it might be added). The form of liberal enlightenment envisaging humanitarian intervention, saving lives and making the world a better place at work here, it might be argued, paid its true dividend in Iraq and the catastrophe of unintended consequences there. In this view, the hell of Iraq followed a route paved with good humanitarian intentions, all owing to the Chicago speech.

There are, however, two major problems with any such position. The first of these, most obvious to anyone actually familiar with either the Chicago speech or Freedman's note that was used for it, is that Iraq did not conform to the terms of the doctrine, even as Blair espoused it. To the extent that the 'doctrine of international community', as it was called, was novel, its content was not. It was soundly based in the just war tradition, in which each of its five tenets could be found with little effort. By that measure, debate will continue for many years regarding the first point—'are we sure of our case?' (to which the answer would probably be that some were only too sure, but not on the basis of complete evidence and sound assessment). On the third point—whether there were practical (meaning also with a reasonable and proportionate probability of success) military operations that could be 'sensibly and prudently' undertaken—the answer might well be that, as the record showed, defeating Iraq's armed forces and removing the Saddam Hussein regime were certainly achievable and at a relatively limited cost, but the utter failure to prepare for any kind of adequate follow-up for years of occupation failed the test. On the fourth point—preparedness to stay for the long term—there can be little doubt that this was not met. Indeed, one of the central reasons for the lack of proper planning for the follow-on (or, rather, for non-adoption of such planning as had been made) was a short-termist self-delusion in important minds in Washington DC (which Blair's UK followed on trust, it would seem) that the US would succeed militarily in removing Saddam Hussein from power, that Iraqis as a whole would welcome this, and that the US would be able to leave behind a 'new' Iraq after a 90-day transition. This was woefully misguided and, even as the US was forced to remain in Iraq for years afterwards, both there and in Afghanistan an impatient hurry was evident to leave and declare 'done' missions that, in truth, remained unfinished. The fact that, despite officially 'leaving', engagement continued for years afterwards on an indefinite basis (albeit at reduced levels) was testimony to this. Thus, a critic laying the embarrassment and debris of Iraq at Freedman's feet would be mistaken in doing so. It was not the doctrine that spawned these disasters, but a failure to take note of it and follow its precepts.

Not only could Freedman not be 'blamed' in principle for the Iraq misadventure in relation to the 'doctrine of international community', but in practice he could be seen to have attempted to avoid, or at least, mitigate some of the worst consequences. That is, in other words, he made attempts to ensure that, implicitly at least, the terms of the 'doctrine' were followed. In this context, he warned against the short-termism of Washington's approach to its longstanding and major partners and allies, as it needed coalitions beyond operational requirements. And he sought to ensure that Blair had been made aware of the possible consequences of the impending Iraq action. To this end, he used his influence to arrange a seminar for Blair where he himself and five other high-calibre scholars, specialists on Iraq and on international affairs and military-political matters, made clear what the likely aftermath of the action would be and of the need for adequate follow-on in the long term.[16] Thus, not only in principle but also in practice, had Freedman's judgement been more influential (alongside that of the others he brought in), further questions might have been asked and some of the worst consequences of the action might have been avoided (though the armed campaign against Iraq would have gone ahead, come what may).

In the end, it is this type of integrity that also meant that Freedman could be trusted to be part of the Iraq Inquiry into events in which he had played a small part. To those who saw him as part of the Blair problem, he should have been automatically disqualified—here was a policy insider who was perceived to have formed the policy itself and was being tasked to be poacher-turned-gamekeeper. The truth was that, problematic as it might be at the level of perception, the independence of mind and soundness of judgement inherent in all Freedman's activities made him right, it could be said, for each of these roles. To this might be added the measure of his scholarly approach.

Conclusion

As even a relatively superficial skim of Freedman's works shows, the range of his thinking and writing is vast. Despite its breadth, there is a methodological, social and philosophical coherence to it. That breadth and also the coherent methodological thread running through it are evident throughout the present volume and the wider project that it reflects. Yet very little in that volume of writing addressed either the ideas or approaches that might be negatively critiqued in Freedman's work, or the importance of the person in the policy world. This absence of 'Freedmanbashing' meant a need to introduce and examine some sceptical thinking in relation to the Freedman or war studies approach.[17] The present volume has gone some way towards introducing scepticism to Freedman's approach—although the Introduction also concludes by observing that even his critics recognize his importance and contribution. It has also offered a personal perspective not only on Freedman's methodological approach and intellectual disposition, but also on the personal qualities and characteristics that facilitated his work with the practitioner worlds, in particular those of policy and defence education, as well as in building the realm of war studies.

Theory, scholarship and practical influence are the qualities that testify to Freedman's achievements in taking the kernel left by Michael Howard and cultivating it into a strong, sturdy and fine tree of many branches and rich fruit that is the inheritance he left at King's on retirement, as well as around the world in the number and quality of scholars inspired by him. That tree and those many branches are reflected in this book and the themes it has covered (even if, inevitably, other themes could have been included). This is a set of intellectual agendas that Michael Howard welcomes in his Foreword to the volume. A great supporter of this project to explore his successor's scholarship and achievements, he notes that the version of war studies with which he began was limited and he recognizes the way in which the subject and its intellectual scope have expanded to reflect the 'huge and terrifying questions' that fall 'within the remit of war studies'.

As a student of war, Freedman blends sociology, political philosophy, history, international relations and policymaking. All this provides sound foundations for studying the field that is probably his core realm: strategy—the business of generals and political leaders, which lies at the heart of war and also, as he has shown, other spheres of activity.[18] Not only is Freedman a strategic analyst, he is a strategist as well—one who has contributed to strategic thinking in government and who has applied strategic understanding to academic institutional growth in his role as a Vice Principal at King's. In all of this, two important dimensions of his work are ethics and construction. There can be no strategy without the complex negotiation of rights and wrongs presented by difficult situations that constitutes ethics. That complex negotiation is itself one part of the interactive and intersubjective process of social construction at the core of strategy. This was evident in the writing of the great philosopher of war, Clausewitz, and his consideration of the duel between opponents, the interplay of reason, chance and passion, and the need for policy to be continuously linked to developments at the military level and to adjust, if necessary, to the empirical realities of the struggle with the enemy—the core insight defining his genius (even if constructivism as a term was not part of his lexicon). Strategy, an ethical sphere of action involving social construction, as well as the conceptualization of action in relation to empirical realities, lies at the heart of Freedman's work.

20

CONCLUSION

James Gow and *Benedict Wilkinson*

Lawrence Freedman's oeuvre is vast and his legacy has already been recognized around the world, both inside the academy and outside it. Some of that work has been considered in the present volume, although by no means all of it. Its sheer scope and size mean that it would not have been realistic to attempt to explore it all. The contributions to this volume have, however, addressed some of the highlights in the Freedman canon, as well as casting light into some of the less well-known corners of his thought and work. In particular, we have attempted to extend reflection on the relationship between theory and practice that runs through them and to foster an integrated under-standing of Freedman's scholarship, seeking to discern whether an identifiable approach could be said to exist.

To that end, in the Introduction, we posed a series of questions regarding the character of Freedman's work. In particular, we asked if there was a sum to the various parts of his work, a coherence that might constitute a school of thought. Freedman is clearly a figure of considerable influence. But is there anything distinctive in his approach, a way of working, a methodology or a school of thought? As Freedman's work on strategic scripts developed, so the project shifted a little to accommodate the idea of scripts. Ultimately, we have sought to address three core problems. To what extent does constructivist realism constitute a theoretical prism that gives coherence to Freedman's (and the war studies) approach to questions of peace and security, defining a school of thought? To what extent does strategic scripturalism offer a sustainable theoretical framework that captures the Freedman and war studies approach and, so, underpins a school of thought? Is there some other theoretical approach that can be said to characterize Freedman's approach? Finally, the overarching question, which each of these others addresses: is there a cohesive school of thought that originates with Freedman, is evident in his approach, and combines theoretical strength and scholarly recognition with tangible impact on the real world aspects of peace and security?

In this book, we have presented the investigation of Freedman's contribution to scholarship and practice in five parts, each providing material with which to answer those questions. In this Conclusion, we answer those questions in five sections, each devoted to one of those areas. We begin with strategy, before moving on to ethics and principles in conflict. The third part concerns the chapters on history and policy. In the fourth, we explore theory. Lastly, the fifth section is concerned with overarching contemplations of our subject's scholarly approach and his nimble crossing of the academic–policy divide and back— including Freedman's own consideration of his approach. Inevitably, there was overlap between the chapters in different sections as authors followed the subject's work in crossing boundaries and integrating analysis. There is overlap because, while authors treat strategy and other dimensions separately, the reality is that aspects such as ethics and social theory inhere in strategy itself, for example. In this sense, the chapters are individual contributions. But, in the Conclusion, we draw on them to answer the core questions posed regarding each of the five areas, emphasizing the integrated coherence and the disposition or methodological thread in each section.

Strategy

The first set of chapters deals with strategy and deterrence. This is the longest standing focus of interest for Freedman and the one for which he is best known by many. Indeed, in his Foreword to this volume, Michael Howard suggests that Freedman's *The Evolution of Nuclear Strategy* is the only book of continuing relevance on its topic and that all the other works in the catalogue of nuclear strategy and its evolution have been relegated to dustier corners of libraries. While it might be an exaggeration to call it the 'only' book of continuing relevance on the topic—Freedman himself would surely counsel students to read Brodie and Schelling, at a minimum—it is, indeed, the definitive study on this topic, enriched among other things by the ever-present feeling of just how awful, in all senses, nuclear weapons are and that, despite its fascination as a subject of academic scrutiny, this is a 'disagreeable topic'.[1] This decidedly humane aspect in Freedman's writing on the subject contrasts strongly with some contributions to the literature on nuclear strategy, such as Herman Kahn's almost arithmetical ladder of 'escalation' to the point of mutual destruction,[2] and the nuclear planners who became obsessed with narrow and somewhat esoteric discussions of throw-weight and 'tactical' use of nuclear weapons (apropos of which Freedman pointed out that the use of labels such as 'strategic' and 'tactical' in relation to nuclear weapons was an absurdity, resting on a false understanding of those qualifying words).[3] Yet, Freedman captures the essence of nuclear deterrence better than anyone else, contending that credibility rests on a major assumption that, unlike any time in the past, something existed that would not actually be used, but that nuclear deterrence nonetheless remained viable—indeed, ineluctable—as policy.

At the core of Freedman's success in capturing the combined absurdity and sense of nuclear deterrence is the sound grounding that his work has in the wider realms of strategy and warfare—as well as later work on deterrence itself.[4] He explores and explains how nuclear weapons thinking initially—and for a long time—simply emerged from the realm of so-called strategic bombing and was seen as nothing more than a version of that phenomenon, which had become so destructive already during the Second World War, just with bigger, ever more powerful bombs. As he puts it, the 'terms of the debate on the strategic significance of the new technology were thus set by the existing debate on the value of strategic bombardment'.[5] This strength is developed in Freedman's treatment of the debates that followed the later realization that nuclear weapons had important, qualitative differences from other munitions and were not simply bigger, and more powerful, versions of old weapons. Freedman's discussion of the important 1950s work on 'limited war' by Osgood and Brodie is, above all, a core discussion of warfare. Chapters 7 and 8, which deal with the debate on limited warfare in the late 1950s, constitute a consummate discussion of war itself. They are essential reading for any student of the topic. They are also, along with the remainder of the book, a living embodiment of Freedman's approach, blending a constructivist sensibility with a realist disposition.

These are qualities that emerge in the contributions to the first section of the present book, which engages with those parts of Freedman's repertoire that deal with strategy. In chapter 1, Robert Ayson argues that strategy constitutes an 'intellectual system', in which 'actions and expectations are interrelated'. For Ayson, ideas and actions have meaning and effect in 'a wider context in which other related parts need to be taken into consideration'. Like Freedman, he emphasizes the importance of the social settings to illuminate how deterrence works and what it means. For Ayson, echoing Freedman, strategy is about human choices, in given situations, rather than about fate and predestination. And for this reason, the strategist has to assess his own options, as well as those of others, and how these influence one another. Ayson's analysis suggests that strategy is an inherently social activity that can never be separated from its social context.

In chapter 2, Jan Willem Honig expands the social theme, as he interrogates strategy and warfare, in particular the themes of 'limited war' and influence, which permeate Freedman's work. He argues that war is what 'we and our militaries make of it', paraphrasing Alexander Wendt's constructivist version of anarchy in international society. Honig explores the notion of 'comfortable' and 'uncomfortable' wars, using four paintings to illustrate the vision of 'comfortable' war that emerged in the nineteenth century, which he contrasts with 'uncomfortable' warfare—warfare that is 'limited' or small and in which the application of violent means is just one instrument among many. By 'comfortable', Honig means that societies and militaries accept the idea of war that is very violent and for national survival, or some other necessary reason that justifies its awfulness. In contrast, the idea of 'limited war' with 'limited means' as a way of influencing enemies and opponents proves to be 'uncomfortable' because it does not fit the prevailing intellectual and cultural template—to say nothing of the practical issues that many 'limited wars' have faced, from Vietnam to the twenty-first century. The social construct of war as being inclined towards 'total war' replaced the earlier construct of more 'limited war'. As the realities of both the nuclear age and the post-Cold War world bring a different structure to international life, the kinds of military operations that can and must be undertaken remain well outside Western societies' comfort zones. Violence is a necessary part of war, but the kind of war faced, which has generated a 'consistently unhappy experience', has 'failed because it threatened to take war's established construct out of its comfort zone'. That conclusion, in itself, reinforces the constructed character of warfare and the salience of interaction and interrelationships, bounded by the realities of physical and social force.

In chapter 3 Patrick M. Morgan also focuses on the social aspects of strategy, arguing for the importance of relationships in strategy and, particularly, in the understanding of deterrence. Deterrence, in its essence, is predicated upon a social relationship—the one deterring and the one to be deterred. Morgan emphasizes the importance of alliance and cooperation in generating the means for 'actively managing international security'. He argues that, following Freedman's work on 'deterrence' in the post-Cold War context, ever-greater interaction and interdependence might instil a stronger sense of international community, in which more traditional and 'relatively primitive' notions of deterrence, risky as they might be, can be developed. However, he notes that this strategic aspiration relies on international, especially transatlantic, social cohesion. This was a property that weakened in the twenty-first century, triggering new threats from new kinds of opponent. That made the need for a sophisticated and social strategy for managing international security all the more necessary. Such a management project is made possible only by a blend of scripts that fits a social context, in which those scripts shape and are shaped by interaction.

Richard Falkenrath examines strategy and deterrence in practice, in chapter 4. He traces the shift from deterrence by 'punishment' to deterrence by 'denial' in Washington's conduct of the Global War on

Terror. The former rested on an assumption that the consequences of an action would be such that an actor would refrain, for fear of the 'punishment' that might follow. The latter may carry messages of consequences that might follow, but these are delivered by taking action that removes the choices or capabilities available to opponents—in the given context, the Islamist terrorists challenging the US. Both approaches, he notes, rest on credibility. But these are more complex in the realm of counterterrorism, where there is a relationship with an opponent who, from the perspective of the US authorities, whether national or local (both familiar to the author, who worked in counterterrorism roles for the US government and the New York Police Department), has no obvious 'return to sender' address. This means that threats to punish can have questionable credibility. In this context, denial, whether by physical intervention where that proves to be possible or by surveillance, offers a more realistic way of deterring and preventing terrorist attacks. Yet the advanced means available to the US, whether unmanned aerial strikes on terrorist targets or electronic surveillance, are deeply problematic in liberal democratic societies, in which critics question the ethics of each approach. However, there would likely be even bigger questions if governments failed to act. Once again, the analysis reinforces the importance of understanding the interaction of ideas and environments, each influencing and constraining the other.

Thus, each of these four chapters dealing directly with strategy captures the elements that define Freedman's scholarship. This is the essence of a realist constructivist approach, grounded in an understanding of scripts and the vital interaction of ideas, actions, opponents and environments. Ayson shows the importance of understanding social context in the iterative and interactive world of strategy, and also the relationship between ideas and empirical realities. Honig, Morgan and Falkenrath not only reinforce this but, in addition, introduce elements of scripturalism and constructivist interaction. In doing so, they highlight the social, constructed and yet realist character of strategy.

Ethics and humanitarian intervention

The ethical filament in Freedman's treatment of nuclear strategy runs through all that he has written. In the 1990s, it became a major focus, not only in academic work on the Iraq and ex-Yugoslavia conflicts,[6] for example, but in highly influential policy work. His paper on 'just intervention', drawing largely on the tenets of just war theory, underpinned UK Prime Minister Tony Blair's famous 1999 Chicago speech, which outlined a 'doctrine of international community'.[7] The nub of both Blair's doctrine and Freedman's input comprised five points that reflected a modern interpretation of just war theory: to be sure of one's case; to have exhausted diplomatic options; to ensure that sensible military options are available, prudently to be taken; to ensure also that there is sufficient commitment in the long term to make sense of whatever immediate action is taken; and to establish that there is sufficient 'national interest' (however that might be defined) to warrant taking action (a late twentieth-century gesture to democratic politics based on heavy news media scrutiny and focus group research, perhaps). Although the Iraq adventure four years later was, in some senses, an extension of the same internationalist thinking, it also failed the test set in the doctrine by omitting to make suitable provision for the follow-on and the long term—something that Blair himself acknowledged in his memoir.[8] This ruined Blair's reputation and obscured the insight and inspiration that the Chicago speech generated. Nonetheless, the speech itself and the international community it both addressed and projected are landmarks in the history of international affairs. The blend of security thinking and ethics reflected Blair's personal position. Freedman's input, certainly, reflected both a core ethical perspective and emphatic intellectual weight.[9]

The chapters in Part 2 treat Freedman's association with ethics and principles. In chapter 5, Mervyn Frost extends the analysis of strategy and international security in the twenty-first century, and the ethical problems Western liberal polities face in managing international security and confronting enemies in asymmetric warfare. He focuses on the notion of 'ethical leverage', which encapsulates the way in which the opponents of liberal Western societies can turn errors, or unjust violence, by Western forces against the West itself. This is a world in which power is levered through 'ethical criticism'. Wherever a Western liberal actor can be portrayed as acting in a manner inconsistent with its own standards, it will be damaged strategically. There are things that states and individuals 'ought not to do if they wish to maintain their ethical standing and the associated influence and power that go with it'. This is because it is the 'flouting' of the West's international norms that 'provides the only source of international power for the weaker party in such wars'.[10] This conjunction of strategy and ethics epitomizes the balance between power and both ethics and social construction found in Freedman—and, in a sense, lies at the heart of the large parts of the Chilcot Report (the Iraq Inquiry Report)[11]—significantly drafted by Freedman—which was published after seven years, just as the final manuscript for this book was being completed, and which was set to have lasting, historic impact (in the UK, at least).

Frost's combination of strategy and ethics paves the way for Beatrice Heuser's review of just war thinking from ancient times to the late twentieth century. In chapter 6, she engages with the 'problematic phenomenon' of the 'judicialization' of war. The phenomenon emerges from the application of the laws of war and international humanitarian law to the conduct of armed operations—instruments that make the potential identification or suspicion of wrongdoing all the easier and more likely. This generates a need for 'action within legal constraints which more often than not will limit military options, indeed, frequently eliminating the technically most effective ones', and ultimately leaving soldiers' having to 'fight with one arm tied behind their backs'. However, Heuser points out that constraints on the reasons for—and the conduct of—warfare 'can be traced throughout recorded European history'. In tracing that history, she argues that Blair's Chicago speech, informed by Freedman's thinking, did 'not mark the end of an evolution'. Rather, she avers, it was the 'full rediscovery of older traditions' that paved the way for further developments in relation to notions of justice and human rights in international politics, and notions of humanitarian action, in particular—even if we might note that those developments were uneven and, in some cases, foundered on the rocks of realism. Likewise, these failures and tensions are taken up by Richard Caplan, in the immediately subsequent chapter, and also that chapter's successor by Mats Berdal.

Caplan takes up the focus on humanitarian issues, noting that states—Western ones, at least—have given increased weight to human rights and humanitarian norms 'as matters of international concern', while after 1990 the UN Security Council frequently characterized that concern as justifying its authorization of legally binding enforcement measures to tackle humanitarian crises under Chapter VII of the UN Charter. Caplan traces how these concerns were also developed outside the UN Security Council framework, following Blair's Chicago speech and the contemporaneous NATO action over Kosovo, as the UK government and others sought to reconcile effectiveness in protecting human rights and international humanitarian law 'with the need for legitimacy of process'. This gave rise to international commissions and resulted, among other things, in the emergence of the Responsibility to Protect (R2P) doctrine. He notes that the adoption of this doctrine also coincided with a period in which there appeared to be a general decline in mass atrocities—although certainly not their absence or elimination, as events in Syria and elsewhere confirmed. Yet R2P, he suggests, had little real effect—it cannot be shown to have caused the decline in mass atrocities, only to have echoed it. Further, he notes that where action was in question, the Responsibility to Protect was not prominent. Regarding Libya, for example, Caplan notes that only France mentioned the notion in international discussions about threats to the peace and the need to protect civilians, which produced UN Security Council resolutions that placed responsibility with the Libyan authorities, not the UN or some 'international community'. Thus, the promise of R2P and an age of humanitarianism failed to emerge, even if the post-Cold War period will surely be noted for the growth of action in this sphere—and the way is paved for future development. This is an exposition of the constructivist role of ideas and values, their iteration through scripts and their grounding for future developments—but, also, the way in which they are tempered by (constructed, but fixed) realities.

In chapter 8, Mats Berdal develops an analysis of humanitarian intervention in the post-Cold War era, a period which witnessed a 'growing tendency … for the use and the threat of use of military force in international relations to be justified, whether wholly or in part, on humanitarian grounds'. He explores the problems and achievements arising from the use of armed force in pursuit of humanitarian goals, in particular, examining Freedman's writing on the topic and his contribution to the field, arguing that this work reveals an author who rejects the traditional 'dichotomies' in international relations scholarship.

Despite his focus on war, force and strategy, for which he might be assumed to fall into a 'realist paradigm', Freedman's work on what Berdal calls New Interventionism, with the Chicago speech contribution at its core, suggests that it is 'misleading and unhelpful' to 'delineate sharply' different existing schools of thought or paradigms—the longstanding dichotomy between realism and idealism 'is a false one'.

In a contribution that extends Caplan's reflection on the Responsibility to Protect and humanitarian intervention into detailed discussion around these issues, the author notes that Freedman himself 'draws a vital distinction between "realism as an unsentimental temper" and realism as a "theoretical construction"'. The former informs Freedman's scholarly work, his policy advice and his personal morality as an engaged citizen, Berdal argues. Liberal values are important for Freedman and their universality is to be asserted, but that does not mean being naively oblivious to 'dangers and difficulties' inherent in seeking to act to promote them, intrinsically and—citing Freedman's reflections on abuse in Iraq—as standards against which Western governments should be judged.

The four chapters in this section all deal with ideas and values in relation to warfare and the conduct of military operations. Heuser's catalogue of precedent and change not only builds on Frost's chapter and shares with it implicit relevance to the Chilcot Report, but it also implicitly commends the value of the constructivist approach, allowing for ideas and change, yet always bounded by empirical realities and the possibilities of context. The chapters on the practice of humanitarian intervention by Caplan and Berdal reflect these same trends, each emphasizing and examining the balance between ideas and values, on one hand, and the avenues and dead ends of context, on the other, that runs through Freedman's work. In Berdal's construction, this work reveals the meeting point of idealist perspective and 'realist disposition'. This is the blend of constructivism and realism, as well as the meeting of scripts and political contexts, that hallmarks Freedman.

History and policy

The blend of strategic judgement and ethical intelligence runs through another strand of Freedman's work—diverse histories and policy studies of particular problems. This class of books and its range may, in part, explain why the coherence in Freedman's work is not always recognized, even if the consistent quality is.[12] His studies on the Falklands War are, it is almost too obvious to write, landmarks, with his official history of that conflict being one of the publisher's most successful individual books.[13] His work on the Gulf conflict of 1990–1 is a mainstay of the literature, capturing the massive detail of an enormous historical and policy event in lucid perspective.[14] His treatment of *Kennedy's Wars* was rightly acclaimed, as it investigated the inner workings and decision-making of the short-lived US presidency of John F. Kennedy in connection with Berlin, Vietnam and Cuba, winning the US Council on Foreign Relations Arthur Ross Prize Silver Medal.[15]

His later book on the US and the wider Middle East, *A Choice of Enemies*, not only revealed an unmatched authority across the range of US security challenges in that troubled region, but was also awarded the Lionel Gelber Prize and the Duke of Westminster's Medal for Military Literature in 2009. This is a book that starts, fleetingly, with the sense that the US had managed to find itself with a specific choice of enemies at the same time in the 2000s under President George W. Bush—Iraq, Iran and al-Qa'ida. It develops, however, as a profound study of the range of issues facing US policy in a wider Middle East that has no fixed boundaries, as temporal factors make Afghanistan and Pakistan, or the western Maghreb, or parts of sub-Saharan Africa fall within its embrace as a policy concern. It finishes, overwhelmingly, as an exploration of Washington's internal dilemmas, over whether its priorities should focus on upholding the sovereign state order or promoting democratic change. Each could be used to promote stability, but the dilemma is: which would promote the greater stability, in the long and short runs, or what kinds of stability, and at what costs? It is this that constitutes the real policy choice for the US and, as Freedman pointed out, it is a dilemma that Washington still finds itself unable to resolve in any satisfactory manner.

He concludes by saying that, as things currently stand for the US, 'the challenge is to revive their diplomatic skills, learning how to work with the local political grain without losing a sense of purpose and principle', and pushing the countries and peoples of the region towards 'positive engagement with the rest of the world'.[16] As with all of

Freedman's policy and historical analysis, this monumental volume offers a command of rich empirical detail, seasoned with humble and sound judgement embedded in a realistic perspective, framed by interpretation based on social interaction. This is a world in which one actor's words and deeds influence those of one or more others in an evolving web, where choices frame future choices, but where nothing is necessarily predestined or set in stone—just made more or less difficult by previous strata of speech and action.

Informed and inspired by Freedman's interpretations of words and deeds and of social interaction, the authors in the third section engage with history and policy at key moments. In the first of these, Jeffrey Michaels draws on Freedman's examination of the Kennedy administration in *Kennedy's Wars* and his introduction of the 'strategic scripts' concept to analyze Washington's role in the 1963 military coup that deposed Ngo Dinh Diem as President of South Vietnam and saw him and his brother murdered the following day. Michaels deploys the notion of scripts to counter prevailing interpretations which view the American hand as shaping these events directly. On the contrary, in Michaels's analysis, the US role was one of many factors and, at best, indirect: because of Kennedy's 'indecision', framed in a script that read in effect 'not to support a coup, but not to thwart one either' (thus confirming Freedman's analysis), although he did not choose to overthrow Diem, his ambivalence produced the same outcome. Moreover, Michaels points out that, while Washington had discussed the possibility of a coup and the likelihood that it would happen with or without pulling the strings, there was no thought that Diem would be killed. There was an assumption and contingency planning to fly Diem into exile, if the coup happened. There was no script for the situation that actually emerged. Ironically, this gave rise to a script, Michaels posits, in which US policymakers ever since have used the Diem 'analogy' to deter 'discussion about overthrowing friendly governments whose leadership is viewed as problematic'.

Julian Thompson explores the operational legacy of the Falklands War, through the lens of organizational and operational innovations. Thompson takes Freedman's official history of the conflict and its assessment of the legacy of the conflict as his point of departure. Based on the premise that the conflict was the first British naval operation in decades, Thompson identifies a range of innovations—including the establishment of a War Cabinet, the appointment of an overall in-the-atre commander, the requirement for an amphibious capability—that can be linked to the success of the Falklands campaign. But, he notes with some chagrin, the legacy of the Falklands War has been lost. 'What', he asks, 'remains of the operational legacy of the Falklands War?' His answer is 'very little'. Scripts might have been written but, without a nurturing social environment, it might be said, they are lost and shredded.

David Dunn examines the effects of the Global War on Terror on US engagement with the world, in chapter 11. His departure point is a comment by Freedman that Donald Rumsfeld's legacy as US Secretary for Defense was comparable with that of Robert McNamara and that where the latter begat the 'Vietnam syndrome'—the persistent reluctance to become involved in overseas wars—the former would leave behind the 'Iraq syndrome': 'the paralysing belief that any large-scale US military intervention abroad is doomed to practical failure and moral iniquity'. Dunn inspects the American use of force discourse under President Barack Obama, arguing that the effects of Iraq are more profound even than Freedman indicated. Rather than questions of civil-military relations and the qualities and conditions needed for military success, in the Obama era the use of force itself was ever more in doubt: rather than how and when it was wise to intervene and to do so effectively, under Obama the issue became whether it could 'ever be effective to intervene at all'. Obama has reduced the US commitment to engage militarily in the world (notwithstanding the engagement with international Islamist terrorism that continued), and, in 'limiting US commitment to fighting for core interests and formal allies, the Obama administration is breaking with the main post-war tradition of US foreign policy'. This, in turn, Dunn justly continues, 'will also make US leadership in the use or threat of force that much more difficult'. He concludes that 'America's appetite for risk in the form of the use of force has been blunted by its experience in Iraq'. Obama's position is characterized as 'unhelpful' in embracing and embodying the 'implications of the limitations of American power'. It is hard not on feel that this US 'risk aversion' risks failing both the US and the world.

In the last chapter in Part 3, John Gearson explores the evolution in Britain's approach to national security in the post-Cold War period, including the development of academic provision for defence and military education. These are areas that Freedman pioneered, and both his work and practice lay at the core of both. Gearson charts the shifts in approach from terrorism in the City of London, through the advent of strategic defence reviews, eventually to a National Security Strategy. He notes the way in which defence education formed part of this package of change and concludes that the 'policy-focused work of the war studies group at King's College London, educated and inspired by Lawrence Freedman over three decades, contributed to some of the innovations and new thinking'.

Gearson's chapter exposes the way in which the interaction of values and circumstances combines in a way that allows real differences to be made in the world, whether the educational or the security policy aspects of it. It is a story marked by a series of scripts, iteratively deployed in processes of social engagement and construction that produced important change. If Gearson's chapter tends to emphasize the way in which the interaction of ideas, events and contexts can make differences positively, the other three chapters in the section show how the tale of scripts and social environments is not straightforward. Michaels's analysis demonstrates both how the absence of a script to follow can shape events, more for ill than benefit, and also how the narrative emerging from such a situation can become the script with which subsequent challenges are met. Thompson confirms that even the development of a strong script in relation to events is no guarantee of effect, as the operational legacy scenario post-Falklands unravelled almost unnoticed. Worse still, Dunn's chapter shows how the iterative pattern of social reception of scripts and adaptations in response to situations can generate unintended or unhelpful narratives, as the Vietnam syndrome script transposed to the Iraq syndrome narrative identified by Freedman, but with an even more negative line in the script than Freedman had reported. This line—informed by assumptions that correlate with the analysis in Frost's contribution earlier in the book—potentially leaves the US somewhat neutered by a powerful but intended script line, in which the successful use of force for extended purposes is almost impossible, conveying a message of risk aversion and disengagement understood by a variety of international audiences. Scripts, social construction and the realist's temperament suffuse these four accounts of history and policy, illustrating the methodological thread that characterizes Freedman's approach.

Theory

The fourth part of the book moves beyond the practical requirements of the policy world and addresses some of the more theoretical and philosophical aspects of Freedman's work, although some of these have clearly surfaced contingently in the preceding chapters, as just noted. The importance of language and stories is a significant element that runs throughout Freedman's work. It is a focus that gained considerable prominence in the 2000s and underpinned his salient and influential *The Transformation of Strategic Affairs* and the colossal *Strategy: A History*. In the former, winning is about narrative, not sheer brute force.[17] In this concise volume, Freedman emphasizes the importance of cultural aspects and that the source of victory in contemporary conflicts lies in 'strategic narratives'.[18] Defining narratives as 'compelling story lines which can explain events convincingly and from which inferences can be drawn', he argues that these are essential for the vitality of cultural networks where dispersed or diverse groups cohere around given stories. They are important for framing issues and the responses to them. Stories in this sense are the constructs through which information is interpreted and understood. As such, he notes, effective narratives work because they appeal to the values, interests and prejudices in a target audience, but they can fall apart where they rest on false or weak information (although this is not necessarily the case).

For Freedman, then, the secret to successful strategy lies in narratives. It was this thinking that paved the way for 'strategic scripts', a concept which he propounds in *Strategy*. *Strategy* is a rich and wide-ranging work, encapsulating a lifetime's study and reflection, in addition to four years' new research, including developing the notion of 'scripts'. It is no surprise that it covers each of the areas discussed in the previous sections of our book. But it also reaches beyond them to what are, for Freedman, largely uncharted waters: from biblical episodes to the contemporary era, Freedman examines strategy and its use in different contexts, demonstrating equal command of military, political, business, management and economic contexts. One of the most notable parts in the book, for example, is the contrast between Ford and General Motors in their strategic approaches and why the latter was more successful.[19] The ethical dimension—the importance of acting justly and not acting unjustly, as the complex issues of wrong and right are negotiated—runs throughout the analysis. This is clear from the outset in the discussion of biblical episodes, where it is vital to have God on one's side, but also important to understand that, while that is a necessary condition of success in those interpretations, it is never sufficient.[20]

In the first of four chapters concerned with the theoretical dimensions of Freedman's output, the importance of classical sources and a social approach to understanding questions of international security is developed by Richard Ned Lebow, alongside the concepts of trust and deterrence, all important in Freedman's scholarly world, especially his *Strategy: A History*. In chapter 13 Lebow turns to classical sources to inform analysis of trust as a factor in diplomacy and international relations. Lebow begins with Sophocles and Plato, linking trust to friendship, and viewing both trust and society as co-constitutive phenomena—in similar fashion to Freedman's discussion of scripts in *Strategy*. While 'deterrence and realist models of international relations assume that trust is in short supply', following the great figures of ancient Greece, Lebow avers that trust will be more widespread 'the more robust the society is'. He explores the importance of honour and reputation in a way that makes Dunn's interpretation of the Obama administration all the more troubling, as well as offering further echoes of Freedman's analysis in *Strategy*. He concludes, after Plato, that trust 'comes from friendship and the demonstrable willingness to do things for friends that have nothing to do with one's own goals'. Treating others as friends begets trust and builds security through co-constitutive interaction, where it can be achieved. When we treat others as friends, not as means to an instrumental end, trust is built. This applies to societies and states as well as to individuals. It is a function of social context.

James Gow investigates the theoretical element that runs through Freedman's scholarship and the world of strategy—constructivist realism—the implicit theoretical mechanism that underpins Freedman's scholarship and practice—and, as he argues, constitutes the essence of good strategy. Drawing on Freedman's own 'confession' of constructivist tendencies and his *Strategy* in particular, Gow argues that whether realism and constructivism are seen as 'dispositions, theories or meth-odologies', a form of analysis that combines them presents a 'distinc-tive and beneficial' approach to the study of issues of war and peace—one that runs throughout Freedman's work and is consciously present in *Strategy*, where social theory is favoured and rational actors are demolished. The author discusses each concept, including the con-structed character of realism, and attempts to bring them together, arguing that 'necessity' is the quality that 'sits at the heart' of a con-structivist realist approach. Here, the socially generated character of issues and sober acknowledgement that power (and other empirical realities) can combine to offer an approach with which flux and stasis in international society and international security may be profitably studied in policy-friendly ways. He concludes that the seeming oxymo-ron of the constructivist realist compound is no more than that—it does not represent an apparent contradiction as, in the end, properly understood, they are complementary to one another—and so there is not even the apparent contradiction that would make it an oxymoron. Indeed, they are complements that operate at the core of strategy and of policy in practice (and, therefore, are needed for scholarship relating to them). In the end, 'the label matters little', he muses, when the work itself is driven by this same approach and stands the tests of cri-tique, as do both good strategy and Freedman's scholarship.

In chapter 15, Philip Bobbitt also invokes the 'constructivist realist' notion, as he links Freedman's work to that of one of the greatest political philosophers in history, Niccolò Machiavelli. Bobbitt muses over whether 'constructivist realist' is an apposite term for the two thinkers, speculating that the unchanging sense of human nature inter-acts with ever-changing context, and that humans have to adapt to new circumstances as best they are able—but with the limitations imposed on them both by their own characteristics and by the situations they face. These reflect the dynamic at work in any notion of constructivist realism. Bobbitt notes significant biographical parallels—both advised political leaders, both were official historians, both were loved by fam-ily and friends and were devoted fathers, and both won fame for their writing on war. However, he maintains that it is the similarities and complementarities in their thinking that are more profound reasons to associate them, as both wrestle with the challenge of understanding the

ways in which and the extent to which it is possible rationally to anticipate and shape the future to serve our ends. He sees parallels, but also
differences, which stem from Freedman's own treatment of Machiavelli
in *Strategy*—although it is likely that Freedman and Bobbitt are actually
in the same space, broadly. Certainly, Bobbitt's analysis brings out the
importance of the moral factor for both writers and their engagement
with classical sources and literary sources as vehicles for illustrating
and investigating the problems of power, or war and peace.

In the last chapter in this section, Matt Harries and Benedict
Wilkinson span Freedman's earliest focus on nuclear weapons and his
development of strategic scripts as an analytical tool over three decades
later. They discuss the way in which opposing logics of disarmament
and armament coexisted in relation to nuclear weapons. They deploy
the notion of strategic scripts to explain the contradictions 'inherent'
in approaches to nuclear disarmament, developing the concept of strategic scripts as they do so. Scripts, they maintain, can help theorists to
explore the strategic choices and dilemmas with which political, military and business leaders are faced. Equally, they can assist policymakers to focus understanding of the utility of scripts and, beyond this, to
improve their own scripts, fostering internal credibility and improving
their position vis-à-vis others. They show how the notion of scripts can
be used to explore and even to promote nuclear disarmament. They
identify two scripts, one of 'stable reduction', the other of 'disarmament', each of which serves to frame thinking: the scripts in question
are 'mental frameworks for understanding situations and for identifying
responses to those situations'. These scripts and the interactions they
generate facilitate understanding of the way in which opposite instinctive reactions and, stemming from these, scripts about nuclear weapons
coexist. The narratives they generate, however, also confirm the fragile
character of scripts as either an analytical or a strategic tool—they are
all too vulnerable, in a world of social interaction, to the effects of any
one actor's deviation from the script. These are unending scripts
prompting never-ending narratives—while in real life strategy there is
always the next phase or a new beginning.

The four chapters in this section clearly emphasise and elaborate on
Freedman's theoretical themes. Lebow alludes to Freedman's use of classical sources, which are both scripts handed down to successor genera-

tions and, at the same time, examples of the manner in which scripts operate in socially co-constitutive ways. Lebow uses this approach to show its relevance to diplomacy and, especially, to the place that scripts have in shaping trust in that social and socially constructed domain. Both Gow and Bobbitt engage with the constructivist realist theory that characterises Freedman and his work. The former discusses the nature of this notion and exposes its utility. The latter shows how it characterises not only Freedman's work, but also that of Machiavelli. As he explores parallels and smaller differences in their work, Bobbitt emphasises both the greatness of these writers and the salience of their approaches. In the final chapter in this section, Harries and Wilkinson further develop the importance of social interaction at the core of the Freedman, or constructivist realist, approach in a chapter that draws on and draws out the explanatory and the practical value of scripts, as developed by Freedman. Among other things, the authors show not only the explanatory power of scriptural analysis but, even more, its capacity to explain the coexistence of opposing logics and apparent contradictions in the world of nuclear deterrence. They also, however, confirm the fragility of scripts, both in practice and for the analyst (confirming, in a sense, the analyses by Thompson and by Dunn, in particular, earlier in this volume). As part of a world of social interaction, any script is subject to the context in which it is received and responses to it, including counter-scripts and, back to the core balance in Freedman's approach, the realities of the empirical world, including power and force. This is the essence of a school of thought that deserves recognition.

Reflections and conclusions

Section five comprises more reflective contemplations of Freedman's contribution. These are less research-driven pieces, albeit they are still informed by research. They are also enlightened by personal experience and thought. The first of them is an updated version of an article by Freedman himself (and, suitably, one of his favourites). In the chapter, he explores his self-reflective characterization as a 'premature constructivist' and notes that Peter Katzenstein once called him a 'realist constructivist' (a term that crops up elsewhere in the volume, in particular in Gow's exploration of the parameters and utility of such a notion in chapter 14). Freedman examines the sociology of knowledge and the importance of intellectual leadership and language, and, most important, argues that understanding how knowledge is socially constructed 'need not lead to a loss of confidence in its validity'. This concluding point in the confession of a premature constructivist is the starting point for strategists, scriptural scholars and constructivist realists—all versions of the same intellectual approach described and espoused by Freedman, and all appropriate to students of war and peace.

In the second of the reflective pieces in this section of the book, David Omand explores a key facet of Freedman's life as an academic—namely, his work with policymakers and the scholarly connections between King's College London and Whitehall that he developed. Linking back to his own career, Omand examines the utility of academic research to policymakers, concluding that much of it has the potential to be of value. However, he notes, part of the problem is that the pace of life for politicians and civil servants is 'relentless', and that the need for experts is often driven by unanticipated events. Picking up on this theme, he praises the work of the Department of War Studies and the Defence Studies Department at King's for their research and teaching. For Omand, this relationship can have genuine benefits, be it concerning the concept of risk management that informed his own thinking in the formulation of the wider CONTEST strategy or the ideas of resilience that permeated his thinking on counterterrorism strategy. Not that the relationship between academia and policy is always easy, particularly when evidence bases go against political will, as was the case with 'soft' drugs. Nonetheless, Omand concludes by recognizing the role played by Freedman in pioneering links between Whitehall and the academy, particularly since such a role requires the academic to be as 'aloof and incorruptible as an artist, yet sometimes as near to earth as a politician'.

In the last of the three contemplations, Gow offers reflections, sometimes informed by personal perspective, on Freedman's contribution and the nascent elements of a school of thought that is relevant to both academic and policy realms, as well as introducing a more sceptical and critical approach to the subject's scholarship. He considers Freedman's engagement with the policy world and why this has managed to be both extensive and successful, as well as its outcomes. He also introduces discussion of possible challenges to Freedman's work to temper the positive mood dominating the volume and to signal a balancing perspective, although he also concludes by indicating the weaknesses of such challenges.

These final meditations strengthen the sense of a school of thought informed by a distinctive approach. Freedman's own contribution identifies more than anything else that the approach is one he owns and has developed—and one that, as this book has broadly shown, has considerable analytical value. One element of the virtue of Freedman's approach is that there can be great confidence in the validity of knowledge, even if it is understood that such knowledge is inevitably socially constructed (in contrast to many students, who keenly seize on the idea that knowledge is socially constructed to infer that it has no validity and that everything, then, can be relativized). This is central to the Freedman school of thought—social constitution of knowledge and understanding is not abstract invention, but occurs in relation to empirical realities. Those realities both generate ideas and values and temper them.

The balance between ideational and material realities also inhabits David Omand's consideration of the relationship between academic research and the policy world, where social context is a salient factor—policy world processes tend to be immediate, whereas research frames are longer-term. This makes it all the more remarkable that Freedman and war studies have, at times, produced work that carries weight, and certainly interest, in the policy world. This also translates into relationships with defence education, where the same unusual blend of independent incorruptibility and political practicality is vital—as is the research that underpins it. Moreover, these activities and relations exemplify the role of scripts in shaping and interacting with contexts. They also embody the way in which new knowledge and new realities may come to be co-constituted as a result. This is a world that reflects a way of thinking.

That way of thinking is both critiqued and confirmed in Gow's final reflection. He examines Freedman's special relationship with the policy world as well as considering the sceptical challenges that can be made to Freedman's scholarly corpus. He also reflects on the question of there being a school of thought and identifies the elements of such a school that emerge in the course of this book. This is an approach that is evident throughout Freedman's oeuvre and also in the wider harvest of research at King's (and, to a lesser extent, elsewhere, of course) conducted on the same basis. This is the blend of scripturalism and constructivism, on one side, with realism, on the other, that is the hallmark of the nascent school and the way in which it is germane in both academic and policy domains.

Conclusion

Overall, this book and what we informally called the 'Freedman project' have pointed to the value of Freedman's approach—and, in doing so, they have allowed us to show the coherence that confirms the substance of that approach and its theoretical elements. The contributions in the preceding pages engage with their subject's thought in ways that foster integrated understanding of his scholarship—with the coda that although they have done so, the work remains unfinished. Nonetheless, the theoretical underpinning for Freedman's work is clear, as is the way in which this and the scope of war studies, as developed by and beyond Freedman, move towards the identification of a discrete school of thought.

It is our belief, as editors, that there is the necessary intellectual distinction in Freedman's scholarship and approach to warrant the elevation of his work into the ranks of significant thinkers. The material in this book provides considerable evidence to support this, even though we approached this research study as an open inquiry, testing the suspicion that there was something that constituted a school of thought, but posing questions, including the overarching one concerning the existence of a school. In doing this, we also identified the four broad areas in which Freedman's contribution stands out. However, authors were free, against this background, to determine both topic and approach when writing on, investigating, testing, critiquing, developing and extending both Freedman's work and that of his academic home. The mission involved engaging with research at the frontiers of knowledge, but often with deep relevance to the 'real world'. In a similar vein, the notion that Freedman might be a 'constructivist realist' was raised in the initial idea for this project as an area to be investigated and one towards which we tend—as would Freedman himself. As the project evolved, the complementary notion of strategic scripts was also incorporated. But these perspectives certainly did not bind the authors in the volume, who were invited to address the relevant aspects of Freedman's work as they saw fit and, if appropriate, to challenge these perspectives, the idea of any coherent approach, and even the sense that Freedman's work deserved intellectual recognition. Broadly, the chapters in the book support those perspectives and judgements—just as several authors make greater and smaller nods in this direction in their contributions, with the only significant 'challenge' offered in Gow's rumination in chapter 19, where critical perspectives are embraced and addressed. Even then, the result is to reinforce the salience of Freedman's approach and underline the importance of understanding how social interaction and processes define a body of work related to making a difference in the world.

Freedman's work has focused much of the time on strategy, and this, in itself, plays a part in why he has been so influential not only among scholars but in the policy world, while building something of an academic empire at King's College London. Strategy involves the blending of theory and practice. It is this transition from the intellectual and conceptual to application to make a difference in practice, inherent in strategy, that marks Freedman's record. It is also at the heart of informing his scholarly work. Strategy requires conceptualization of an approach to a challenge that embraces all the available and relevant empirical data, in the first instance, but then the flexibility and adaptability to take account of changes in that empirical reality. Those changes are inevitable because strategy is interactive. One party conceives of action in relation to the realities of a situation, the other party does the same from its own perspective, and once action has started, each has to take account of and respond to the moves of the other. Strategy is, therefore, a social process. This is the context for his later career focus on scriptural analysis—that is, that strategic scripts are required for good strategy, but, in an open-ended real world improvisation, these change with necessity. It is at the heart of Freedman's use of social theory balanced by a strong sense of the relevance of power and the clear-headed recognition that realities count.

Recognizing the importance of social context and constitutive interaction is vital. They inform Freedman's analysis throughout its span. This includes his examination of political thought, his assessment of the deficiency of rational actor and game theories, the success of Martin Luther King and the US civil rights movement, reflections on world wars, the Vietnam conflict and the Arab Spring, humanitarian intervention and ethics, and, of course, strategy. They are at the core of Freedman's novel discussion of constructivist realism and 'strategic scripts', and the way scripts provide 'a way of addressing the problem about how individuals enter into new situations, give them meaning, and decide how to behave'.[21] Because strategic situations are interactive, however, the scripts with which an actor enters a new situation may well need appraisal and revision, in the face of events and counter-scripts, if success is to be achieved: 'following established scripts risks strategic failure'. It is in responding to situations and developing new 'scripts' which are plausible, credible and appropriate both to audiences and to circumstances that the prospect of success lies—even if, because the nature of both strategic narratives and interpretation is open-ended, success, or its sustainability, is never guaranteed for the strategist.

The outcrop of strategic scripturalism in Freedman's later work is both a part of this and a discrete aspect in its own right. And all of his work turns around the study of strategy that is informed by these ideas or approaches. Nor, despite the absence of any neat theoretical formula, are the authors, including the editors, bound by any sense that such a formula is needed to explain, justify or bring coherence to this rich body of work. We do believe, however, that this book suggests a way forward—and trust that those reading it fairly will agree—in method, disposition and application, towards the further development of a distinctive approach.

There are clearly aspects of Freedman's work that are shared by those who have worked with him, for him and in his light. Something is undeniably associated with him, as recognition around the world confirms. There might not be—and might never be—'Freedmanites' as such (probably, quite fortunately). But, it is he who gives definition to this approach around the world—those working with him are always recognized in part for the association with Freedman and, de facto, constitute a 'school' reflecting that thought and certainly the broad approach born of it. The engagement in this volume of outstanding scholars and scholar-practitioners suggests a shared interest in this issue and, perhaps, some of Freedman's predilections. By exploring this approach, the authors in this project have marked out elements of Freedman's distinctive intellectual contribution, his approach and his research in his endeavour to make a difference in the real world, something in which he has succeeded where other scholarly approaches have failed. This approach lacks the identity of a 'school' of thought—it is not labelled as such. Yet, under the leading influence of Freedman for thirty years (in the wake of Michael Howard), a distinctive working method—a school of thought, an approach—has been pioneered, but not given a name. It has been open, multidisciplinary and interdisciplinary, reflecting the way in which war touches every aspect of human experience.

Several aspects of this 'school' were already set in place by Howard: the reality that no single discipline can catch war's multifaceted nature; the sense that war is a grim and, at its very core, controversial phenomenon, where dispassionate analysis is at a premium (which is far from saying that those analyzing it should somehow be disengaged or uncaring); and making contributions that count in this sphere. This last aspect requires avoiding obscure, scholastic language infused with technical or quasi-scientific jargon. This template set by a liberal historian with a conservative disposition embraced political and moral philosophy in particular. What Freedman has brought to it and developed brilliantly is a sense of the social science debate and an interest in applying its approaches. While Howard certainly recognized that the way political and military leaders thought about the world affected their decisions and behaviour, Freedman has added the intellectual apparatus to extend this. The insight of a strategist was married to the application of social scriptural theory. His knowledge of social and political theory and the sociology of knowledge expanded the intellectual scope and breadth of research and education at King's, and beyond. The foundation laid by the liberal with a conservative disposition has been transformed into an academic castle by the constructivist with the realist's temper.

NOTES

INTRODUCTION

1. Paul Kennedy, 'Success Stories: a Reader's Guide to Strategy' (review of *Strategy: A History* by Lawrence Freedman, Oxford University Press, 2013, 768 pp), *Foreign Affairs*, 93:5, 2014.
2. This book results from a research project funded by the Harry Frank Guggenheim Foundation, 'Constructivist Realism: A Theory of International Relations and International Security—the Work and Career of Professor Sir Lawrence Freedman' (James Gow, King's College London, 2013, $40,000).
3. A select bibliography appears at the end of this book, indicating just part of Freedman's expansive output.
4. Only the great John Erickson springs to mind as having retained firm roots in the UK but also having been recognized as a major figure in US security policy circles.
5. One indication of this standing is the 2014 REF in the UK, where King's research power made it no. 1 in the field, judged to have more world-leading or internationally excellent research than any other university. See http://www.kcl.ac.uk/sspp/news/newsrecords/2014/war-studies-ref.aspx (accessed 24 May 2016).
6. The peer review process for this volume made clear how strongly different versions of Freedman and his work exist, with reviewers seemingly familiar with one version—his work on nuclear strategy, his work on humanitarian intervention or, perhaps, his histories of policy decisions and diplomacy, or even his policy-linked work itself. The Introduction has been shaped in light of this in an attempt to ensure the range of his work is noted. Chapter 19, containing reflections on Freedman's life and work by Gow, is also a response to issues raised in the peer review process.

7. Anecdotally, over coffee in early 2016, as this book was being finalized, Freedman volunteered that the Chicago speech was almost the only thing people were interested in—which might be a surprise to the peer reviewer who wrote that the connection between humanitarian intervention and Freedman escaped them.

8. *Kennedy's Wars: Berlin, Cuba, Laos and Vietnam*, New York: Oxford University Press, 2002, won the US Council on Foreign Relations Arthur Ross Prize Silver Medal; *A Choice of Enemies: America Confronts the Middle East*, Toronto: Doubleday Canada, 2008, won both the Lionel Gelber Prize and the Duke of Westminster's Medal for Military Literature in 2009.

9. In his critical but positive review essay on Freedman's *Strategy: A History* in *Foreign Affairs*, Paul Kennedy suggests that the answer to this question is that Freedman's thinking will last: the work will 'stand close to books by Clausewitz, Jomini and Mahan, and not far from … Michael Howard'. Kennedy, 'Success Stories'.

10. See chapter 19 by Gow, in the present book.

11. See chapter 17 by Freedman, in the present book.

12. The theoretical matters necessarily introduced here are revisited and developed in chapter 14 by Gow, which is devoted to exploration of the constructivist realist notion.

13. Of course, Falkenrath was also a student of Freedman's, breaking the mould by completing his PhD dissertation at such speed that his supervisor had to prove his qualities as strategist and tactician to obtain a suspension of regulations—without which, supervisor and student would have been waiting eighteen months from completion to examination.

1. STRATEGIC THEORY AS AN INTELLECTUAL SYSTEM

1. See Lawrence Freedman, *Strategy: A History*, New York: Oxford University Press, 2013, and compare pp. 82–3, 85–95 (Clausewitz) and 160–73 (Schelling).

2. Lawrence Freedman, 'Has Strategy Reached a Dead-end'?, *Futures* (April 1979), 127–8.

3. For the subsequent book, see Robert Ayson, *Thomas Schelling and the Nuclear Age: Strategy as Social Science*, London: Frank Cass, 2004.

4. Lawrence Freedman, 'Strategic Stability/Superiority: The US View', in Carl G. Jacobsen (ed.), *Strategic Power: USA/USSR*, Basingstoke: Macmillan, 1990, pp. 170–1.

5. Lawrence Freedman, 'Confessions of a Premature Constructivist', *Review of International Studies*, 32:4 (October 2006), 692.

6. See Freedman, *Strategy: A History*, p. 608.

7. See the early portions of Lawrence Freedman, *Deterrence*, Cambridge: Polity Press, 2004.

8. Lawrence Freedman, *The Transformation of Strategic Affairs*, Adelphi Paper 379, Abingdon: Routledge for IISS, 2006, p. 42.

9. Freedman, *Strategy: A History*, 162, where he is quoting from Schelling's *The Strategy of Conflict*.

10. Freedman, *The Transformation of Strategic Affairs*, p. 9.

11. Freedman, *Strategy: A History*, p. 7.

12. Lawrence Freedman, 'Escalation and Quagmires: Expectations and the Use of Force', *International Affairs*, 67:1 (January 1991), pp. 27–8.

13. Ibid., p. 28.

14. Lawrence Freedman, 'A Theory of Battle or a Theory of War?', *Journal of Strategic Studies*, 28:3 (2005), p. 435.

15. Freedman, *The Revolution in Strategic Affairs*, Adelphi Paper 318, Oxford University Press for IISS, 1998, p. 76.

16. Freedman, *The Transformation of Strategic Affairs*, pp. 9–10.

17. Lawrence Freedman, *The Evolution of Nuclear Strategy*, London: Macmillan, 1981, p. 180.

18. Freedman, 'Has Strategy Reached a Dead-end?', p. 128.

19. Lawrence Freedman, 'Logic, Politics and Foreign Policy Processes: A Critique of the Bureaucratic Politics Model', *International Affairs*, 52:3 (July 1976), p. 448.

20. Ibid., pp. 448–9.

21. Ibid., pp. 449.

22. Clausewitz, *On War*, Howard and Paret translation, cited in Freedman, 'Escalators and Quagmires', p. 22. For a similar connection, see Freedman, *Strategy: A History*, p. 94.

23. Ibid., p. 170.

24. Lawrence Freedman, 'The Changing Forms of Military Conflict', *Survival*, 40:4 (Winter 1998/9), p. 42.

25. Freedman, *Strategy: A History*, p. 88.

26. Lawrence Freedman, 'Terrorism as a Strategy', *Government and Opposition*, 42:3 (2007), p. 318.

27. Ibid., p. 324.

28. Professor Lawrence D. Freedman, 'Indignation, Influence and Strategic Studies', Inaugural Lecture in the Chair of War Studies, King's College London, 22 November 1983, 14. The author is grateful to Professor Desmond Ball, an Australian contemporary of Lawrence Freedman's, for providing a copy of this published address.

29. Lawrence Freedman, *Kennedy's Wars: Berlin, Cuba, Laos and Vietnam*, Oxford University Press, 2000, xii.

30. Ibid., xiii–xx.
31. Freedman, 'Indignation, Influence and Strategic Studies', p. 14.
32. Bernard Brodie, *War and Politics*, New York: Macmillan, 1973, p. 452.
33. For the argument that this is how their relationship might best be understood, see Robert Ayson, 'Strategic Studies', in Chris Reus-Smit and Duncan Snidal (eds.), *The Oxford Handbook of International Relations*, Oxford: Oxford University Press, 2008, pp. 558–75.
34. Lawrence Freedman, 'Strategic Studies and the Problem of Power', in Lawrence Freedman, Paul Hayes and Robert O'Neill (eds.), *War, Strategy, and International Politics: Essays in Honour of Sir Michael Howard*, Oxford: Clarendon Press, 1992, p. 294.
35. Freedman, *Strategy: A History*, p. 7.
36. Freedman, 'Strategic Studies and the Problem of Power', p. 291.
37. Lawrence Freedman, *US Intelligence and the Soviet Strategic Threat*, London and Basingstoke: Macmillan, 1997, p. 198.
38. Ibid., p. 185.
39. Freedman, 'Confessions of a Premature Constructivist', p. 690.
40. Ibid.
41. Freedman, 'Logic, Politics and Foreign Policy Processes', p. 445.
42. Freedman, *Strategy: A History*, 626.
43. Ibid., p. 627.
44. Michael Howard quoted in Freedman, 'Strategic Studies and the Problem of Power', p. 279.
45. Lawrence Freedman, 'Arms Control: Thirty Years On', *Daedalus*, Winter 1991, p. 71.
46. Ibid.
47. Freedman, *Strategy: A History*, p. 622.
48. Ibid., p. 17.

2. UNCOMFORTABLE VISIONS: THE RISE AND DECLINE OF THE IDEA OF LIMITED WAR

1. The ideas presented in this chapter form part of a book I am writing under contract with Cambridge University Press, entitled *Winning Wars: The Invention of Strategy and the Making of Modern Warfare*.
2. I wish also to recall that Professor Freedman was instrumental in helping me win a John D. and Catherine T. MacArthur Postdoctoral Fellowship early on in my career; this was meant to investigate the issues also discussed here, for which I was not entirely ready at the time.
3. P. Fain (ed.), *Mémoires du baron Fain, premier secrétaire du cabinet de l'empereur*, Paris: Plon, 1908, 39–40. See also Colonel (Jean-Baptiste) Vachée, *Napoléon en campagne*, Paris: Berger-Levrault, 1913, 65–8.

4. For the Italian part of the project, see Anne Godlewska, Marcus R. Létourneau and Paul Schauerte, 'Maps, Painting and Lies: Portraying Napoleon's Battlefields in Northern Italy', *Imago Mundi*, 57:2 (2005), 149–63. The battle paintings and maps of Italy can be found as part of Godlewska's online project at https://www.jstor.org/stable/40233993 (last accessed 7 February 2017). On French military mapmaking in general, see Anne Godlewska, *Geography Unbound: French Geographic Science from Cassini to Humboldt*, Chicago: University of Chicago Press, 1999, and the classic account by (Colonel) Henri-Marie-Auguste Berthaut, *Les Ingénieurs-géographes militaires, 1624–1831*, 2 vols, Paris: Imprimerie du Service Géographique de l'Armée, 1902.

5. One can see the changing evaluation of battle and the growing interest in singular decisiveness in retrospect also, for example in the designs of the Arc de Triomphe in Paris. Begun under Napoleon in 1806 and completed only under Louis-Philippe in 1836, the battle inscriptions (a novel idea in themselves at the time) are subject to a process of categorization and reduction. See the designs in the book by the monument's first inspector, J.D. Thierry, *Arc de Triomphe de l'Étoile*, Paris: Firmin Didot, 1845.

6. Christopher Prendergast, *Napoleon and History Painting: Antoine-Jean Gros's 'La Bataille d'Eylau'*, Oxford: Clarendon Press, 1997, p. 145.

7. Charles Esdaile, *Napoleon's Wars: An International History, 1803–1815*, New York: Viking, 2008, 283. For a slightly lower casualty estimate of the 'grisly and indecisive' battle, see David G. Chandler, *The Campaigns of Napoleon*, Vol. 2: *The Zenith, September 1805*, London: Folio Society, 2002, 172.

8. http://classes.toledomuseum.org:8080/emuseum/view/objects/asitem/199/233/displayDate-asc?t:state:flow=e71d1a97-dba1-48ca-a246-47b62f305db1(last accessed 7 February 2017).

9. Prendergast, *Napoleon and History Painting*, p. 7.

10. Ibid., pp. 164–5.

11. *Hinterlassene Werke des Generals Carl von Clausewitz über Krieg und Kriegführung*, Vol. 1: *Vom Kriege*, Part 1, Berlin: Dümmler, 1832, xviii.

12. I trace these forms of institutionalizing war as violence more fully in *Winning Wars*.

13. For biographical details and the reception of the painting, see François Robichon, *Édouard Detaille: un siècle de gloire militaire*, Paris: Bernard Giovanangeli and Ministère de la Défense, 2007, 21–4. Other important evidence is to be found in the hugely popular panoramas which Detaille and Alphonse de Neuville painted of major Franco-Prussian War battles, which also depict death as omnipresent on the battlefield, reproduced in ibid., pp. 36–49. Strikingly, the fragments preserved

and on display in the Musée de l'Armée in Paris are of dead French and German soldiers.

14. For the soul-searching this issue nonetheless caused, see Jan Willem Honig, 'Clausewitz's *On War*: Problems of Text and Translation', in Hew Strachan and Andreas Herberg-Rothe (eds.), *Clausewitz in the Twenty-First Century*, Oxford: Oxford University Press, 2007, pp. 57–73.

15. Colonel C. E. Callwell, *Small Wars: Their Principles and Practice*, 3rd edn, London: HMSO, 1906, 85, 90 and 97. The first and third quotes are from chapter titles indicating their importance.

16. Jan Willem Honig, 'The Idea of Total War: From Clausewitz to Ludendorff', in *The Pacific War as Total War: Proceedings of the 2011 International Forum on War History*, Tokyo: National Institute for Defence Studies, 2012, pp. 29–41. See https://www.researchgate.net/publication/301220150_'The_Idea_of_Total_War_From_Clausewitz_to_Ludendorff' (last accessed 7 February 2017).

17. R. R. Palmer, 'Frederick the Great, Guibert, Bülow: From Dynastic to National War', in Edward Mead Earle (ed.), *Makers of Modern Strategy: Military Thought from Machiavelli to Hitler*, Princeton: Princeton University Press, 1943, pp. 49–74.

18. For similar understandings, which were famous in their day and beyond, see John U. Nef, *War and Human Progress: An Essay on the Rise of Industrial Civilization*, Cambridge, MA: Harvard University Press, 1950; Quincy Wright, *A Study of War*, Chicago: Chicago University Press, 1942; and Johan Huizinga's 1938 *Homo Ludens*, London: Routledge & Kegan Paul, 1949, as well as his earlier 1919 *Waning of the Middle Ages*.

19. Michael Howard, *War and the Liberal Conscience*, 2nd edn, London: Hurst, 2008.

20. Quoted in Brian Bond's biography, *Liddell Hart: A Study of His Military Thought*, London: Cassell, 1977, 6. Liddell Hart's liberalism is the leitmotiv in Azar Gat, *Fascist and Liberal Visions of War: Fuller, Liddell Hart, Douhet and Other Modernists*, Oxford: Clarendon Press, 1998.

21. B.H. Liddell Hart, *Paris, or the Future of War*, London: Kegan, Paul, 1925.

22. B.H. Liddell Hart, *Sherman: Soldier, Realist, American*, Boston: Dodd, Mead, 1929, p. 430.

23. Gat, *Fascist and Liberal Visions of War*, 160, claims that the publisher chose the 'Decisive Wars' title.

24. B.H. Liddell Hart, *The Decisive Wars of History: A Study of Strategy*, London: Bell, 1929, pp. 153–4.

25. Bond, *Liddell Hart*, pp. 167–8, notes the contradiction.

26. *Blitzkrieg* was a product of substantial myth-making and invention after

the fact. See Karl-Heinz Frieser, *Blitzkrieg-Legende: Der Westfeldzug 1940*, 2nd edn, Munich: Oldenbourg, 1996. See also John Mearsheimer, *Liddell Hart and the Weight of History*, Ithaca, New York: Cornell University Press, 1988 and Azar Gat, *British Armour Theory and the Rise of the Panzer Arm: Revising the Revisionists*, Basingstoke: Macmillan, 2000.

27. Lawrence Freedman, *The Evolution of Nuclear Strategy*, London: Macmillan, 1981, pp. 91–119, esp. pp. 97–100.

28. In March 1946, *Harper's Magazine* published an article he had submitted under the title 'Can War Be Limited?' as 'War, Limited'.

29. On the contemporaneous invention of the term see Lawrence Freedman, 'On the Tiger's Back: The Concept of Escalation', in Roman Kolkowicz (ed.), *The Logic of Nuclear Terror*, Boston: Allen & Unwin, 1987, pp. 109–52.

30. Thomas C. Schelling, *Arms and Influence*, New Haven: Yale University Press, 1966.

31. Fred Kaplan, *The Wizards of Armageddon*, New York: Simon & Schuster, 1983, pp. 334–5.

32. Lawrence Freedman, 'Vietnam and the Disillusioned Strategist', *International Affairs*, 72:1 (1996), p. 143.

33. Quoted in Lawrence Freedman, *Kennedy's Wars: Berlin, Cuba, Laos, and Vietnam*, New York: Oxford University Press, 2000, p. 100. Italics in original.

34. Robert Ayson, *Thomas Schelling and the Nuclear Age: Strategy as Social Science*, London: Frank Cass, 2004, p. 36.

35. See Honig, 'Clausewitz's *On War*', 68; Bond, *Liddell Hart*, p. 99.

36. *The U.S. Army and Marine Corps Counterinsurgency Field Manual, U.S. Army Field Manual No. 3*, Chicago: University of Chicago Press, 2007, p. 294.

3. REFLECTIONS ON LAWRENCE FREEDMAN'S 'DETERRENCE'

1. Lawrence Freedman, *Deterrence*, Cambridge: Polity Press, 2004, p. 6.

2. Bernard Brodie (ed.), *The Absolute Weapon*, New York: Harcourt Brace, 1946, p. 31.

3. This premise is one reason the Cold War deterrence apparatus has only gradually been reduced and shows few signs of disappearing soon.

4. Freedman, *Deterrence*, p. 4.

5. Ibid., pp. 4–5.

6. Ibid., pp. 67–8.

7. Peter J. Katzenstein, 'Introduction', in Katzenstein (ed.), *The Culture of National Security: Norms and Identity in World Politics*, New York: Columbia University Press, 1996, p. 5.

8. Freedman, *Deterrence*, p. 69.

9. To a realist, states are likely to internalize norms that are in the national interest or beneficial in other ways, not because they enjoy wide support from international 'society' or the global 'community'.

10. Freedman, *Deterrence*, p. 30.

11. In effect, this is internalizing at the point where a norm is emerging, rather than where a fully established norm or set of norms is the anchor around which respect coalesces. And the learning is partly rational or cost-benefit-driven on the basis of past confrontations, not just absorption of socially acceptable mores. See Lieberman, Elli, *Reconceptualizing Deterrence: Nudging Toward Rationality in Middle Eastern Rivalries*, New York: Routledge, 2012.

12. Mercer, Jonathan, 'Rationality and Psychology in International Politics', *International Organization*, 59 (Winter 2005), pp. 77–106; 'Emotion and Strategy in the Korean War', *International Organization*, 67 (Spring 2013), 221–52; 'Emotional Beliefs', *International Organization*, 64 (Winter 2010), pp. 1–31. Freedman takes note of Mercer's work in *Deterrence*, pp. 53–4.

13. A good example pertaining to deterrence is the emergence of the principle that a government must uphold its citizens' welfare, and that when it abandons this duty in favour of deliberately contributing to citizens' harm, state sovereignty can be breached on behalf of the sovereignty the citizens ultimately represent, to protect them from atrocities or other egregious harm.

14. It is seldom noted that one of the most conflictual elements in today's international politics is regime legitimacy.

4. DETERRENCE AND DEMOCRACY: REFLECTIONS ON AMERICAN POST-9/11 HOMELAND SECURITY

1. 'Authorization for Use of Military Force (2001 S.J.Res. 23)', https://www.govtrack.us/congress/bills/107/sjres23 (last accessed 6 February 2017).

2. The use of force against Anwar al-Awlaki, the US-Yemeni citizen killed in a drone strike in 2011, is a case in point.

3. These terms were adopted by Glenn Snyder, *Deterrence and Defense: Toward a Theory of National Security*, Princeton: Princeton University Press, 1961.

4. Richard Ned Lebow, 'Deterrence: A Political and Psychological Critique', in Paul C. Stern et al. (eds.), *Perspectives on Deterrence*, New York: Oxford University Press, 1989, p. 25.

5. See, for example, Lawrence Freedman, *Deterrence*, Cambridge: Polity, 2004.

6. Wyn Bowen, 'Deterrence and Asymmetry: Non-State Actors and Mass Casualty Terrorism', *Contemporary Security Policy*, 25:1 (2004), p. 59.

7. Lawrence Freedman, 'Terrorism as a Strategy', *Government and Opposition*, 42:3 (2007), pp. 314–39.

8. Jerrold M. Post, *The Mind of the Terrorist: The Psychology of Terrorism from the IRA to al-Qaeda*, Basingstoke: Palgrave Macmillan, 2007.

9. J.M. Post, 'Terrorist Psycho-Logic: Terrorist Behavior as a Product of Psychological Forces', in Walter Reich (ed.), *Origins of Terrorism: Psychologies, Ideologies, Theologies, States of Mind*, Washington, DC: Woodrow Wilson Center Press, 1998.

10. Marc Sageman, *Understanding Terror Networks*, Philadelphia: University of Pennsylvania Press, 2004; Marc Sageman, *Leaderless Jihad: Terror Networks in the Twenty-First Century*, Philadelphia: University of Pennsylvania Press, 2008.

11. Robert Trager and Dessislava Zagorcheva, 'Deterring Terrorism: It Can Be Done', *International Security*, 30:3, p. 108.

12. Freedman, *Deterrence*, p. 39.

13. For a sense of some of these operations and their impact, from a critical journalistic perspective, see 'Highlights of AP's Pulitzer Prize-winning Probe into NYPD Intelligence Operations' available at http://www.ap.org/media-center/nypd/investigation (accessed 8 July 2014). The 'Demographics Unit' that led these activities was closed in 2014, with Associated Press claiming some of the credit for this, as well as legal cases prompted by its reporting. See 'New York Police Disband Unit that Spied on Muslims', available at http://bigstory.ap.org/article/new-york-police-end-muslim-surveillance-program (accessed 8 July 2014).

14. 'US National Security Strategy 2002' from John Stone, *Military Strategy: The Politics and Technique of War*, London and New York: Continuum, 2011.

5. ETHICS IN ASYMMETRICAL WAR

1. Lawrence Freedman, *The Evolution of Nuclear Strategy*, New York: St. Martin's Press, 1981.

2. Lawrence Freedman, *Strategy: A History*, Oxford University Press, 2013.

3. Freedman, *The Evolution of Nuclear Strategy*.

4. International Commission on Intervention and State Sovereignty, *The Responsibility to Protect*, Ottawa: International Development Research Center, 2001.

5. Richard N. Haass, *War of Necessity: War of Choice*, New York: Simon & Schuster, 2009, Introduction.

6. International Commission on Intervention and State Sovereignty, *The Responsibility to Protect*.

7. For an analysis of the structure of power in such wars, see the excellent article by Emanuel Adler, 'Complex Deterrence in Asymmetric-Warfare Era', in T.V. Paul, Patrick M. Morgan and James J. Wirtz (eds.), *Complex Deterrence: Strategy in a Global Age*, Chicago: Chicago University Press, 2011, obiter.

8. Steven Lukes, *Power: A Radical View*, London: Macmillan, 1974.

9. For early discussion of this topic see Andrew J.R. Mack, 'Why Big Nations Lose Small Wars: The Politics of Asymmetric Conflict', *World Politics*, 27: 2 (January 1975), pp. 175–200, and Ivan Arreguin-Toft, 'How the Weak Win Wars: A Theory of Asymmetric Conflict', *International Security*, 26:1 (Summer 2001), pp. 93–128.

10. On the processes of radicalization, see the work done by the International Center for the Study of Radicalization and Political Violence at King's College London: http://icsr.info/ (accessed 6 February 2016).

11. David Whetham (ed.), *Ethics, Law and Military Operations*, Basingstoke: Palgrave Macmillan, 2011, pp. 10–24.

12. Ibid.; David Fisher, *The Morality of War*, Oxford: Oxford University Press, 2011; David Rodin, *War and Self Defence*, Oxford: Oxford University Press, 2002; Charles Guthrie and Michael Quinlan, *Just War: The Just War Tradition: Ethics in Modern Warfare*, London: Bloomsbury, 2007; Nigel Biggar, *In Defence of War*, Oxford: Oxford University Press, 2013.

13. David Omand, 'Ethical Guidelines in Using Secret Intelligence Services', *Cambridge Review of International Affairs*, 19:4 (December 2006), 613–28.

14. Richard B. Bilder, 'Speaking Law to Power: Lawyers and Torture', *American Journal of International Law*, 98:4 (October 2004), pp. 689–95.

15. Gary Marx, 'An Ethics for the New Surveillance', *The Information Society*, 14:3 (1998), p. 174.

16. An example of profile development may be viewed in Tim Sorrick, 'Political Violence Prevention: Profiling Domestic Terrorists', *Small Wars Journal*, 6 June 2013, p. 1.

17. These came to light after the Edward Snowden leaks in June 2013 about the processes used by the US intelligence services to monitor cyber communications worldwide.

18. These policies that offend against international law and the settled ethical constraints in international practice are often justified by using arguments that refer to the *exceptional* circumstances that surround

these conflicts. On such arguments, see Giorgio Agamben, *State of Exception*, tr. Kevin Attell, Chicago: University of Chicago Press, 2005.

19. This, of course, is the proper aim of positivist social science. See the discussion of positivist approaches to social science in D. Marsh and G. Stoker (eds.), *Theory and Methods in Political Science*, Basingstoke: Palgrave, 2002, chapter 10.

20. When discussing practices people somewhat loosely refer to the 'rules of the game'. However, this is misleading because many practices are not games. One should rather write of 'rules of the practice'.

21. On social practices in general, see Charles Taylor, *Philosophy and the Human Sciences: Philosophical Papers*, Vol. 2, Cambridge: Cambridge University Press, 1985; Theodore R. Schatzki, *Social Practices: A Wittgensteinian Approach to Human Activity and the Social*, Cambridge: Cambridge University Press, 1996; Stephen B. Turner, *The Social Theory of Practices: Tradition, Tacit Knowledge and Presuppositions*, Chicago: Chicago University Press, 1994; Phil Hutchinson, Rupert Read and Wes Sharrock, *There Is No Such Thing as a Social Science [Electronic Resource]: In Defence of Peter Winch*, Directions in Ethnomethodology and Conversation Analysis, Aldershot and Burlington, VT, Ashgate, 2008.

22. These are well accounted for within the so-called English school approach to the study of international relations. There are ongoing disputes about detail among adherents to this approach, but there is agreement on the core tenet about the existence of a society of sovereign states. There is a large literature on the English school, but a good discussion of recent issues is to be found in Cornelia Navari and Daniel M. Green (eds.), *Guide to the English School in International Studies*, Guides to International Studies, Chichester, West Sussex and Malden, MA: Wiley Blackwell, 2014.

23. Nowadays, whether an entity is to be recognized as a sovereign state in this practice is determined by the United Nations.

24. For more on the practice of sovereign states, see Mervyn Frost, *Ethics in International Relations: A Constitutive Theory*, Cambridge: Cambridge University Press, 1996, chapter 5.

25. Imagine that John punches James in the face. John's assertion that it was not an act of aggression is not on its own conclusive proof of whether it was, or was not, an act of aggression. We only establish what was done by taking into account, among many other things, what both parties said had happened, by looking into the surrounding circumstances of the punch, and by examining the history of the relationship between the two people.

26. This was achieved for some years, for example, by the Lord's Resistance Army in parts of northern Uganda, Southern Sudan and the Democratic Republic of the Congo.

27. A good example of the kind of self-restraint required to avoid grant-ing ethical leverage to terrorist groups is provided by the way in which the Norwegian government and people reacted to the terrorist attacks by Anders Behring Breivik on 22 July 2011: setting off a car bomb in downtown Oslo killing eight people, and then opening fire on a group of young people on the island of Utøya, killing a further 69. At every point in the reaction by the government and the people, the response was to endorse in rhetoric and in deed the core values of our inter-national practices. Similar restrained reactions endorsing international ethical standards have been demonstrated by the international com-munity's engagement in Libya and most recently in Syria.

6. THE RISE, FALL AND RESURGENCE OF 'JUST WAR' THINKING FROM CICERO TO CHICAGO

1. Special thanks to Dr Stephen Neff of the University of Edinburgh and Dr Ruvi Ziegler from the University of Reading for their very help-ful comments; all mistakes remaining are entirely my own.
2. 'The Blair Doctrine', Transcript, 22 April 1999, *PBS Newshour* avail-able at http://www.pbs.org/newshour/bb/international-jan-june99-blair_doctrine4–23/ (accessed 15 May 2015).
3. Lawrence Freedman, 'Chicago Speech: Some Suggestions', 3, available at www.iraqinquiry.org.uk/news/100118-freedman.aspx (accessed 28 January 2016).
4. For an important impartial analysis of the rights and wrongs of NATO intervention in the Kosovo case, see James Gow: 'The War in Kosovo, 1998–1999', in Charles Ingrao and Thomas A. Emmert (eds.), *Confronting the Yugoslav Controversies: A Scholars' Initiative*, 2nd edn, West Lafayette, IN: Purdue University Press, 2013.
5. *Le Monde*, 7 Dec. 2012.
6. Plato, *Alcibiades*, quoted in Cian O'Driscoll: 'Rewriting the Just War Tradition: Just War in Classical Political Thought and Practice', *International Studies Quarterly*, 59 (2015), p. 3.
7. Aristotle: *Rhetoric to Alexander*, quoted ibid.
8. Ibid., p. 2.
9. Cicero, *De Officiis*, pp. 14–15.
10. Thanks to Augustine of Hippo, in whose work this specific fragment is copied, we know that Cicero said this in his *De Re Publica* (54 BCE), tr. Niall Rudd, *The Republic and The Laws*, Oxford: Oxford University Press, 1998, p. 69.
11. Cicero, *Philippics*, quoted in Stephen Neff, *War and the Law of Nations*, Cambridge: Cambridge University Press, 2005, p. 18.
12. Terence (Publius Terentius Afer, second century BCE) is quoted by

Vitoria, *De Indis Relectio Posterior, sive de Iure Belli*, 2.1 section 21, in Francisco de Vitoria: *Political Writings*, tr. Jeremy Lawrance, Cambridge: Cambridge University Press, 1991, p. 307.

13. John Rich, 'Warfare and External Relations in the Middle Roman Republic', in Beatrice Heuser and Anja Victorine Hartmann (eds.), *War, Peace and World Orders in European History*, London: Routledge, 2001, pp. 62–71.

14. Onosander, *Onosandri Strategeticus sive de Imperatoris Institutione*, Paris: Saugrain, 1599, Book 4, ed. and tr. Wm Oldfather, Loeb Classical Library, New York: G.P. Putnam's Sons, 1923.

15. O'Driscoll, 'Rewriting the Just War Tradition', p. 8.

16. Neff: *War and the Law of Nations*, p. 36

17. Henrik Syse, 'The Platonic Roots of Just War Doctrine: A Reading of Plato's Republic', *Diametros*, 23 (March 2010), p. 113.

18. For example, Christine de Pizan, *Le Livre du corps de policie*, I.9, ed. Angus J. Kennedy, Paris: Honoré Champion, 1998, p. 15.

19. Neff, *War and the Law of Nations*, 32f; O'Driscoll, 'Rewriting the Just War Tradition', p. 4f.

20. Cicero, *De Officiis*, pp. 14–15.

21. Neff, *War and Law of Nations*, p. 32f.

22. *Gai Institutiones or Institutes of Roman Law by Gajus*, ed. E.A. Whittuck, tr. Edward Poste, Oxford: Clarendon Press, 1904.

23. Justinian, *The Digests of Justinian*, trs. Henry Monro, 2 vols., Cambridge: Cambridge University Press, 1904, 1909.

24. Hans-Henning Kortüm, *Transcultural Wars from the Middle Ages to the 21st Century*, Berlin: Akademie Verlag 2006.

25. Neff, *War and the Law of Nations*, p. 65.

26. Gratian, *Decretum* (Corpus Iuris Canonici: *Decretum*, Causa XXIII, Quaest. I, VIII).

27. James Turner Johnson, *Just War Tradition and the Restraint of War: A Moral and Historical Inquiry*, Princeton, NJ: Princeton UP, 1981, p. 127.

28. John Gillingham, 'Women, Children and the Profits of War', in Janet L. Nelson, Susan Reynolds and Susan M. Johns (eds.), *Gender and Historiography: Studies in the Earlier Middle Ages in Honour of Pauline Stafford*, London: Institute of Historical Research, 2012, pp. 61–74.

29. Giovanni de Legnano, *Tractatus de Bello, de Represaliis et de Duello* (1360), ed. and tr. Thomas Erskine Holland, Oxford: OUP for the Carnegie Institution, 1917, chs. cxxvii–clxvii; Honoré Bonet or Bouvet, *L'Arbre des batailles*, Paris: Jehan du Pré, 1493, chs. lxxxv–c.

30. Christine de Pizan, *Livre des fais d'armes et de chevalerie* (1410), ed. and tr. Sumner Willard and Charity Cannon Willard, *The Book of Deeds of Arms and of Chivalry*, University Park, PA: Pennsylvania University

Press, 1999, chs. xvi–xxi; Christine de Pizan, *Le Livre des faits et bonnes mœurs du roi Charles V le Sage*, II.iv, ed. and tr. Eric Hicks and Thérèse Moreau, Paris: Stock, 1997, p. 117.

31. Vitoria, *De Iure Belli*, 3.1, sec. 37, in *De Indis Relectio Posterior, sive de Iure Belli*, 3.1, reprinted as Vitoria, *Political Writings*.

32. Ibid.

33. Lagnano, *Tractatus de Bello*.

34. Quoted in Geoffrey Best, *Humanity in Warfare*, London: Weidenfeld and Nicolson, 1980, p. 73.

35. Jean Blanot, 'Rex Franciæ in regno suo princeps est, nam in temporalibus superiorem non recognoscit', in his *De Actionibus* (1256).

36. Legnano, *Tractatus de Bello*.

37. Vitoria, *De Iure Belli*, 2.1, sec. 20; Bertrand de Loque, *Deux traités: l'un de la guerre, l'autre du duel*, 1588, Lyon: Iacob Rayoyre, 1589; Balthazar Ayala, *De Iure et Officiis Bellicis et Disciplina Militari*, Douai: Ioannes Bogardus, 1582, I.2.34ff, I.3.

38. William Fulbecke, *The Pandectes of the Laws of Nations*, London: Thomas Wight, 1602, p. 34a; see also Johnson: *Ideology, Reason*, p. 177.

39. Quoted in Neff, *War and the Law of Nations*, 7.

40. Quoted ibid., p. 131.

41. Emeric de Vattel, *Le Droit des gens, ou Principes de la loi naturelle*, Leyden: La Compagnie, 1758, Book 3, *De la guerre*.

42. August Rühle von Lilienstern, *Handbuch für den Offizier: zur Belehrung im Frieden und zum Gebrauch im Felde*, Vol. 2, Berlin: G. Reimer, 1818.

43. Carl von Clausewitz, *On War*, tr. Michael Howard and Peter Paret, Princeton: Princeton University Press, 1976, I.1. and I.2, p. 75, p. 90.

44. Neff, *War and Law of Nations*, 154, 202–24. This supposed equality of sovereign states is not a feature of the Treaty of Westphalia, as some American political scientists try to make us believe.

45. Quoted in Neff, *War and the Law of Nations*, 167.

46. On this subject, see Jan Martin Lemnitzer, *Power, Law and the End of Privateering*, Houndsmills, Basingstoke: Palgrave Macmillan, 2014.

47. Best, *Humanity in Warfare*, p. 163.

48. Ibid., p. 156f.

49. Quoted ibid., p. 166.

50. Ibid., pp. 173–6.

51. To distinguish overall American policies, institutions and interests from those of individual states of the US (such as Texas and Connecticut), Americans tend to use 'national' as a synonym for 'public', or for the adjective continental European languages derived from 'state' (e.g. *étatique*, *staatlich*), which English lacks. Britain did the same previously—it used to have a 'Public Record Office' while it has recently followed

the American example in renaming this 'The National Archives', much to the dismay of Scottish and Welsh nationalists.

52. On the German roots of realism, see Jan Willem Honig, 'Totalitarianism and Realism: Hans Morgenthau's German Years', *Security Studies*, 5:2 (1995), pp. 283–313.

53. For example Gen Giulio Douhet, *Probabili aspetti della guerra futura*, in Gen. Giulio Douhet, *Il dominio dell'aria*, Verona: A. Mondadori, 1932, 216; Memorandum of General Sir Hugh Trenchard, printed in Jeremy Thin, 'The Pre-History of Royal Air Force Area Bombing, 1917–1942', MA thesis, University of Canterbury, NZ, 2008, 141–4, available at http://www.google.co.uk/url?sa=t&rct=j&q=&esrc=s&source=web &cd=3&ved=0CC4QFjAC&url=http%3A%2F%2Fir.canterbury.ac.nz% 2Fbitstream%2F10092%2F1740%2F1%2Fthesisfulltext.pdf&ei=a_q_ U8nuBOPH7Abl-4DgCg&usg=AFQjCNEpTr55t0mecB0b44DjqA4uG THWdA&bvm=bv.70810081,d.ZGU (accessed 11 July 2014).

54. James F. Willis, *Prologue to Nuremberg*, New York: Greenwood Press, 1982.

55. Neff, *War and the Law of Nations*, p. 211.

56. League of Nations Covenant, Article 10.

57. Treaty between the United States and Other Powers Providing for the Renunciation of War as an Instrument of National Policy. Signed at Paris, 27 August 1928; ratification advised by the Senate, 16 January 1929; ratified by the President, 17 January 1929, Article I.

58. Charter of the United Nations, Chapter I, Article 1 and Chapter VII, Article 51.

59. See, for example, Jonathan Riley-Smith, *What Were the Crusades?*, 4th edn, Basingstoke and New York, 2009; and Bertrand de Loque, *Deux traités* (1589), excerpts translated by Beatrice Heuser (ed.), *Strategy Makers: Thoughts on War and Society from Machiavelli to Clausewitz*, Santa Barbara, CA: ABC-Clio for Praeger, 2010, p. 54.

60. R.J. Rummel, *Democide: Nazi Genocide and Mass Murder*, New Brunswick, NJ: Transaction Publishers, 1992.

61. 'All Members shall refrain in their international relations from the threat or use of force against the territorial integrity or political independence of any state'.

62. Charter of the United Nations, Chapter VII.

63. This report has curiously been withdrawn from the UN website in 2013, but can still be found on http://iis-db.stanford.edu/pubs/ 20806/A_More_Secure_World_.pdf, (accessed 26 Sept. 2013).

64. The Blair Doctrine'.

65. http://www.pbs.org/newshour/bb/international-jan-june99-blair_doc-trine4-23/ (accessed 15 May 2015).

66. See, for example, Rotem Giladi, 'Reflections on Proportionality, Military Necessity and the Clausewitzian War', *Israeli Law Review*, 45:2 (July 2012), pp. 323–40.

7. HUMANITARIAN INTERVENTION: LESSONS FROM THE PAST FEW DECADES

1. *Military Intervention in Europe*, Oxford: Blackwell for Political Quarterly, 1994.
2. See for instance, UN Security Council Resolutions 232 (1966) and 418 (1977).
3. Christopher Greenwood, 'Is There a Right of Humanitarian Intervention?' *The World Today* 49:2 (1993), 34–40.
4. Chicago speech. See 'UK Paper on International Action in Response to Humanitarian Crises', *British Yearbook of International Law 2001*, pp. 695–6.
5. International Commission on Intervention and State Sovereignty (ICISS), *The Responsibility to Protect: Report of the International Commission on Intervention and State and Sovereignty*, Ottawa: International Development Research Centre, 2001: United Nations Secretary General, 'A More Secure World: Our Shared Responsibility', Report of the Secretary-General's High Level Panel on Threats, Challenges and Change, 2004.
6. 'In Larger Freedom: towards Development, Security and Human Rights for All', Rreport of the United Nations Secretary-General, UN Doc. A/59/2005 (2005).
7. 2005 World Summit Outcome Document, UN Doc. A/Res/60/1 (2005), paras 138–40.
8. Interactive Thematic Dialogue of the United Nations General Assembly on the Responsibility to Protect, 23 July 2009 http://www.unorg/ga/president/63/interactive/responsibilitytoprotect.shtml
9. Cited in Roger Cohen, 'How Kofi Annan Rescued Kenya', *New York Review of Books* 55:13 (14 August 2008).
10. Thomas M. Franck and Georg Nolte, 'The Good Offices Function of the UN Secretary-General', in Adam Roberts and Benedict Kingsbury (eds), *United Nations, Divided World*, 2nd edn., Oxford: Clarendon, 1993, 143–82.
11. Gareth Evans, 'Ethnopolitical Conflict: When is it Right to Intervene?', *Ethnopolitics*, 10:1 (2011), 120.
12. Alex J. Bellamy, 'The Responsibility to Protect: Five Years On', *Ethics and International Affairs*, 24:2 (Summer 2010) pp.143–69.

13. United Nations Security Council, 'Statement by the President of the Security Council', UN Doc. S/PRST/2008/4, 6 February 2008.

14. Bellamy, 163.

15. Marie-Eve Loiselle, 'The Normative Status of the Responsibility to Protect after Libya', *Global Responsibility to Protect*, 5:3 (2013), 317–41.

16. Evans, 122.

8. 'REALISM AS AN UNSENTIMENTAL INTELLECTUAL TEMPER': LAWRENCE FREEDMAN AND THE NEW INTERVENTIONISM

1. S/RES/1973, 17 March 2011.

2. S/RES/1270, 22 October 1999, para. 14.

3. The first reference to the New Interventionism appears to have been made in James Mayall (ed.), *The New Interventionism, 1991–1994*, Cambridge: Cambridge University Press, 1996.

4. Andrew Hurrell, *On Global Order: Power, Values, and the Constitution of International Society*, Oxford: Oxford University Press, 2007, p. 57.

5. Lawrence Freedman, 'The Counterrevolution in Strategic Affairs', *Daedalus*, 140:3 (2011), p. 7.

6. Ibid., p. 2.

7. UNDP, *Human Development Report 1994*, New York: Oxford University Press, 1994. For an unsurpassed critical analysis of the history of the concept, see S. Neil MacFarlane and Yuen Foong Khong, *Human Security and the UN*, Indianapolis: Indiana University Press, 2006.

8. *Our Global Neighbourhood: Report of the Commission on Global Governance*, Oxford: Oxford University Press, 1995, p. 78.

9. *Human Development Report 1994*, p. 22.

10. James Mayall, 'Introduction', in *The New Interventionism*, pp. 3–4.

11. Freedman, 'The Age of Liberal Wars', *Review of International Studies*, 31:1 (2005), p. 97.

12. 'Reflections on Intervention', 26 June 1998, Kofi Annan, *The Question of Intervention: Statements by the Secretary-General*, New York: United Nations Department of Public Information, 1999, p. 5.

13. Lawrence Freedman, 'The Age of Liberal Wars', p. 102.

14. S/1999/957, 8 September 1999.

15. *Kosovo*, Foreign Affairs Committee, 4th Report, Vol. 3, London: The Stationery Office, 2000, p. 138.

16. Adam Roberts, 'NATO's "Humanitarian War" over Kosovo', *Survival*, 41:3 (1999).

17. For a flavour of that debate, see Albrecht Schnabel and Ramesh Thakur (eds.), *Kosovo and the Challenge of Humanitarian Intervention*, Tokyo: UNU Press, 2000.

18. 'The Responsibility to Protect: Report of the International Commission on Intervention and State Sovereignty (ICISS)', Ottawa: IDRC, 2001, pp. 32–3.
19. Ibid.
20. Ibid., p. xi.
21. '2005 World Summit Outcome Document', A/RES/60/1, para. 139.
22. Lawrence Freedman, 'Chicago Speech: Some Suggestions', 3, http:// www.iraqinquiry.org.uk/media/96209/1999-04-16-Memo-Freedman-to-Powell.pdf (last accessed 7 February 2017).
23. Ibid.
24. Ibid., 3. The tests proposed, all of which were incorporated into Blair's speech, were: 'Are we sure of our case? Have we exhausted all diplomatic options? Are there military operations that we can sensibly and prudently undertake? Are we prepared for the long-term? Do we have national interest involved?'
25. Freedman, 'The Age of Liberal Wars', p. 98.
26. Lawrence Freedman, *The Transformation of Strategic Affairs*, Oxford: Oxford University Press, 2006, p. 40.
27. Freedman, 'The Age of Liberal Wars', p. 104.
28. Ibid.
29. Ibid., 95.
30. Edward C. Luck, 'The Responsibility to Protect: Growing Pains or Early Promise?', *Ethics and International Affairs*, 24:4 (Winter 2010).
31. Ramesh Thakur, 'UN breathes life into "responsibility to protect"', *Toronto Star*, 21 March 2011 (available at www.thestar.com/opinion/editorialopinion/2011/03/21/un_breathes_life_intoresponsibility_to_protect.html).
32. Ibid.
33. Lord Hannay, House of Lords Debate on Libya, 1 April 2011 (www.publications.parliament.uk/pa/ld201011/ldhansrd/text/110401–0001.htm).
34. 'Ban Ki-moon Address to Sofia Platform', 12 May 2011.
35. 'General Assembly Debate on R2P: Statement by China, 12 July 2011', (http://www.globalr2p.org/media/files/china1.pdf) (accessed 6 February 2017).
36. Michael Akehurst, 'Humanitarian Intervention', in Hedley Bull (ed.), *Intervention in World Politics*, Oxford: Clarendon Press, 1984, 99.
37. David D. Kirkpatrick and Kareem Fahim, 'Qaddafi warns of assault on Benghazi as U.N. vote nears', *New York Times*, 17 March 2011.
38. Panel Discussion, during 'War and Peace, 2003–2014', UNU-UNESCO Conference, Paris, February 2014. See also Michael Clark, 'The Making of Britain's Libya Strategy' in Adrian Johnson and Saqeb

Mueen, *Short War, Long Shadow—The Political and Military Legacies of the 2011 Libya Campaign*, Whitehall Report 1–12, RUSI, p.8

39. S/RES/1970 (2011), 26 March 2011.
40. Edward C. Luck, 'Building a Norm: The Responsibility to Protect Experience', in Robert I. Rotberg (ed.), *Mass Atrocity Crimes: Preventing Future Outrages*, Washington: Brookings Institution Press, 2010, p. 109.
41. S/RES/2149, 10 April 2014. The new mission, the UN Multi-dimensional Integrated Stabilization Mission in CAR (MINUSCA), will eventually consist of some 12,000 peacekeepers, making it one of the largest active UN field operations.
42. S/RES/2150 (2014), 16 April 2014.
43. Ibid.
44. Freedman, *The Transformation of Strategic Affairs*, p. 8.
45. Lawrence Freedman, *The Revolution in Strategic Affairs*, Oxford: Oxford University Press, 1998, p. 68.
46. Freedman, 'The Counterrevolution in Strategic Affairs', 1.
47. 'The Use of Force in Intervention Operations', Presentation, International Institute for Strategic Studies, 1994.
48. Rupert Smith, 'The Security Council and the Bosnian Conflict: A Practitioner's View', in Vaughan Lowe, Adam Roberts, Jennifer Welsh and Dominik Zaum (eds.), *The Security Council and War: The Evolution of Thought and Practice since 1945*, Oxford: Oxford University Press, 2008, p. 445.
49. Nicholas Morris, 'Humanitarian Intervention in the Balkans', in Jennifer M. Welsh (ed.), *Humanitarian Intervention and International Relations*, Oxford: Oxford University Press, 2004, p. 99.
50. Freedman, *The Revolution in Strategic Affairs*, pp. 14–17.
51. Lawrence Freedman, 'International Security: Changing Targets', *Foreign Policy*, 110 (Spring 1998), p. 60.
52. Freedman, *The Transformation of Strategic Affairs*, p. 41.
53. Lawrence Freedman, 'On War and Choice', *The National Interest*, 107 (May/June 2010).
54. The tendency has been reinforced by the fact, noted by Gerard Prunier in relation to African conflicts, that humanitarian action has had the 'advantage' for the international community of being 'highly visible for the media and [thus able to] provide world public opinion with a low-cost alternative to real political action'. Gerard Prunier, *Africa's World War*, Oxford: Oxford University Press, 2009, p. 347.
55. Freedman, 'On War and Choice', p. 17.
56. MONUC was renamed the UN Stabilization Mission in the DRC (MONUSCO) in 2010. In the following, I use MONUC in referring to the activities of both.
57. Philip Windsor, 'IR: The State of the Art', in Mats Berdal (ed.), *Studies*

in International Relations: Essays by Philip Windsor, Brighton: Sussex Academic Press, 2002, p. 19.

58. Ibid.
59. Freedman, 'International Security: Changing Targets', p. 54.
60. 'Report of the Secretary-General's Internal Review Panel on United Nations Action in Sri Lanka', November 2012, para. p. 74.
61. Ibid.
62. Ibid.
63. On this, see reflections on the ICC's role by John Holmes, UN Under-Secretary-General for Humanitarian Affairs from 2007 to 2010, in John Holmes, *The Politics of Humanity*, London: Head of Zeus, 2013, especially pp. 371–6.
64. Freedman, *The Transformation of Strategic Affairs*, 37.
65. Ibid., 35–6.
66. Leszek Kołakowski, 'The Self-Poisoning of the Open Society', in *Modernity on Endless Trial*, Chicago: University of Chicago Press, 1990, p. 163.
67. Freedman, 'The Age of Liberal Wars', p. 107.
68. 'Introduction', *The Security Council and War*, p. 3.
69. Windsor, 'IR: The State of the Art', p. 18.
70. Freedman, 'International Security: Changing Targets', p. 54.
71. Peter Wilson, *The International Theory of Leonard Woolf: A Study on Twentieth-Century Idealism*, Basingstoke: Palgrave Macmillan, 2003, p. 217.

9. ESSENCE OF INDECISION: COUP SCRIPTS, NGO DINH DIEM, AND THE KENNEDY ADMINISTRATION

1. Lawrence Freedman, *Kennedy's Wars: Berlin, Cuba, Laos and Vietnam*, New York: Oxford University Press, 2000, pp. 362–97.
2. Lawrence Freedman, *Strategy: A History*, New York: Oxford University Press, 2013, pp. 607–29.
3. Memorandum of a Conversation, 26 August 1963, 12 p.m., Declassified Documents Reference System [DDRS].
4. Thomas L. Ahern, Jr., *CIA and the Generals: Covert Support to Military Government in South Vietnam*, CIA Center for the Study of Intelligence, October 1998, p. 143.
5. Memorandum from Lansdale to Douglas, 15 November 1960, *Foreign Relations of the United States (FRUS), 1958–1960 Volume I, Vietnam*, Doc. 238.
6. Memorandum from Wood to Anderson, December 2, *1960, FRUS, 1958–1960 Volume I, Vietnam*, Doc. 256.
7. This point is also highlighted in Moya Ann Ball, 'A Case Study of the

Kennedy Administration's Decision-Making Concerning the Diem Coup of November, 1963', *Western Journal of Speech Communication*, 54:4 (1990), pp. 557–74.

8. Memorandum of a Conference with the President, 29 August 1963, 12 noon, DDRS.

9. Memorandum of a Conference with the President, 6 September 1963, *FRUS, 1961–1963 Volume IV, Vietnam, August–December 1963*, Doc. 66.

10. Cable from Harkins to Taylor, 30 October 1963, in Neil Sheehan, Hendrick Smith, E.W. Kenworthy and Fox Butterfield, *The Pentagon Papers*, Gravel Edition, Vol. 2, pp. 784–5.

11. Memorandum of a Conference with the President, 27 August 1963, 4 p.m., DDRS; Memorandum of a Conference with the President, 28 August 1963, 12 p.m., DDRS.

12. Memorandum of a Conversation, 26 August 1963, 12 p.m., DDRS.

13. Telegram from Embassy in Vietnam to Department of State, 29 August 1963, *FRUS, 1961–1963 Volume IV, Vietnam, August–December 1963*, Doc. 12.

14. Memorandum of a Conference with the President, 28 August 1963, *FRUS, 1961–1963 Volume IV, Vietnam, August–December 1963*, Doc. 1.

15. See for instance: Memorandum of Conversation, 26 August 1963, DDRS.

16. Michael R. Adamson, 'Ambassadorial Roles and Foreign Policy: Elbridge Durbrow, Frederick Nolting, and the U.S. Commitment to Diem's Vietnam, 1957–61', *Presidential Studies Quarterly*, 32 (2002), pp. 229–55.

17. Memorandum of Conference with the President, 29 August 1963, 12 noon, DDRS; Memorandum of a Conference with the President, 6 September 1963, *FRUS, 1961–1963 Volume IV, Vietnam, August–December 1963*, Doc. 66.

18. Telegram from Embassy in Vietnam to the Department of State, 13 September 1963, *FRUS, 1961–1963 Volume IV, Vietnam, August–December 1963*, Doc. 102.

19. Henry Cabot Lodge, *The Storm Has Many Eyes: A Personal Narrative*, New York: W.W. Norton and Company, 1973, p. 209.

20. Memo from Galbraith to Kennedy, 21 November 1961, Digital National Security Archive, accessed 25 July 2013.

21. Paper Prepared by Robert H. Johnson, 28 November 1961, *FRUS, 1961–1963, Volume I, Vietnam 1961*, Doc. 292.

22. Memo from Mendenhall to Rice, 16 August 1962, *FRUS, 1961–1963, Volume II, Vietnam 1962*, Doc. 268.

23. See for instance: Memo from Hilsman to Rusk, 30 August 1963, *FRUS, 1961–1963 Volume IV, Vietnam, August–December 1963*, Doc. 25.

24. Memo of a Conference with the President, 28 August 1963, *FRUS, 1961–*

1963 Volume IV, Vietnam, August–December 1963, Doc. 1; Memorandum of a Conference with the President, 29 August 1963, 12 noon, *FRUS, 1961–1963 Volume IV, Vietnam, August–December 1963*, Doc. 15.

25. Ambassador Joseph A. Mendenhall, Interview on 11 February 1991, The Association for Diplomatic Studies and Training, Foreign Affairs Oral History Project, 1998.

26. Memo from Hilsman to Rusk, 30 August 1963, *FRUS, 1961–1963, Volume IV, Vietnam, August–December 1963*, Doc. 25.

27. Stanley Karnow interview with Lucien Conein, 1981. Transcript available at http://openvault.wgbh.org/catalog/vietnam-3abc7d-interview-with-lucien-conein-1981 (accessed 6 February 2017).

28. Cablegram from Lodge to Bundy, 30 October 1963 cited in Sheehan et al., *The Pentagon Papers*, pp. 226–9.

29. Memorandum of Conference with the President, 27 August 1963, 4 p.m., DDRS.

30. Memorandum of Conference with the President, 28 August 1963, 12 p.m., DDRS.

31. Memorandum prepared by McCone, 13 September 1963, *FRUS, 1961–1963 Volume IV, Vietnam, August–December 1963*, Doc. 105.

32. John Prados (ed.), *The White House Tapes: Eavesdropping on the President*, New York: The New Press, 2003, 97–8.

33. Ibid., p. 101.

34. Ibid., p. 102–3.

35. Ibid., p. 112.

36. Telegram from Harkins to Taylor, 30 October 1963, *FRUS, 1961–1963 Volume IV, Vietnam, August–December 1963*, Doc. 247.

37. Cable cited in Harold P. Ford, *CIA and the Vietnam Policymakers: Three Episodes 1962–1968*, CIA Center for the Study of Intelligence, 1998, 38.

38. Sheehan et al., *The Pentagon Papers*, New York: Bantam Books, 1971, pp. 182–3.

39. Prados, *The White House Tapes*, p. 112.

40. Memorandum of a Conference with the President, 28 August 1963, DDRS.

41. Memorandum of Conversation, White House, 26 August 1963, DDRS.

42. Prados, *The White House Tapes*, p. 111.

43. Telegram from Embassy in Vietnam to Department of State, 29 August 1963, *FRUS, 1961–1963 Volume IV, Vietnam, August–December 1963*, Doc. 12.

44. The Kennedy–Lodge correspondence is cited in Anne Blair, *Lodge in Vietnam: A Patriot Abroad*, New Haven, CT: Yale University Press, 1995, 46.

45. Telegram from Lodge to Department of State, 30 October 1963, *FRUS, 1961–1963 Vol. IV, Vietnam, August–December 1963*, Doc. 242.

46. Telegram from Bundy to Lodge, 30 October 1963, *FRUS, 1961–1963 Volume IV, Vietnam, August–December 1963*, Doc. 249.

47. Stephen G. Rabe, *The Most Dangerous Area in the World: John F. Kennedy Confronts Communist Revolution in Latin America*, Chapel Hill, NC: University of North Carolina Press, 1999, p. 122.

48. Telegram from Department of State to Embassy in Vietnam, 1 November 1963, *FRUS, 1961–1963 Volume IV, Vietnam, August–December 1963*, Doc. 264.

49. Circular Telegram from Department of State to All Diplomatic Posts, 2 November 1963, *FRUS, 1961–1963 Volume IV, Vietnam, August–December 1963*, Doc. 277.

50. Memorandum of the Record of Discussion at the Daily White House Staff Meeting, 4 November 1963, *FRUS, 1961–1963 Volume IV, Vietnam, August–December 1963*, Doc. 288.

51. Freedman, *Kennedy's Wars*, p. 397.

10. THE OPERATIONAL LEGACY OF THE FALKLANDS WAR

1. Lawrence Freedman, *The Official History of the Falklands Campaign, Vol. 2: War and Diplomacy*, 2nd edn, Abingdon, Routledge, 2007, 729. It is important that the second edition is referred to as it contains new and revised material inserted after the publication of the first edition.

2. Ibid., p. 730.

3. Ibid., p. 730.

4. Christopher Meyer, *DC Confidential*, London: Weidenfeld and Nicolson, 2005.

5. Author's conversation with the late Baroness Thatcher.

6. Freedman, *The Official History*, pp. xxix–xxxii.

7. Under the terms of ATP 8, the amphibious group commander in charge of all the amphibious ships and their escorts (commander amphibious task group—COMATG in modern terminology) is in overall command of the amphibious operation until, with the agreement of the commander landing force (CLF), command is 'chopped' to the latter on completion of the amphibious phase of the operation. This well-established operating procedure seems to have been overlooked by Fieldhouse and his staff, if indeed they were aware of it.

8. Christopher L. Elliott, *High Command: British Military Leadership in the Iraq and Afghanistan Wars*, Oxford: Oxford University Press, 2014.

9. Jonathan Bailey, Richard Iron, and Hew Strachan (eds.), *British Generals in Blair's Wars*, Oxford: Oxford University Press, 2013; and Hew

Strachan, *The Direction of War: Contemporary Strategy in Historical Perspective*, Cambridge: Cambridge University Press, 2013.

10. Strachan, *The Direction of War*, pp. 79–80.
11. Bailey et al., *British Generals in Blair's Wars*, p. 6.
12. Ibid., p. 9.
13. Ibid., p. 6.
14. Private information.
15. Bailey et al., *British Generals*, p. 341.
16. The author was one of seven lieutenant-colonel-equivalent assistant secretaries to the Chiefs of Staff (COS) Committee in 1970–1. These officers from all services, under the secretary to the COS, took the minutes at COS meetings and processed the mass of papers by which the majority of the chiefs' business was done out of committee.
17. Strachan, *The Direction of War*, p. 24.
18. Ibid., p. 24.
19. Bailey et al., *British Generals*, p. 341.
20. Elliott, *High Command*, p. 137.
21. Ibid., pp. 175–9.
22. Bailey et al., *British Generals*, p. 341.
23. Ibid., p. 341.
24. Private information.
25. Written evidence to the House of Commons Defence Committee.
26. Lincoln Paine, *The Sea and Civilization: A Maritime History of the World*, London: Atlantic Books, 2014, p. 9.
27. Admiral of the Fleet Sir Henry Leach and Leo Cooper, *Endure No Makeshifts: Some Naval Recollections*, London: Leo Cooper, 1993, p. 225. Also in conversation between Sir Henry Leach and the author.
28. There is disagreement about whether this was said and when. But Bush himself mentioned it in a speech when he awarded Thatcher the Medal of Freedom.

11. THE IRAQ SYNDROME REVISITED: AMERICA'S USE OF FORCE DEBATE UNDER OBAMA

1. Lawrence Freedman, 'Rumsfeld's Legacy: The Iraq Syndrome?' *Washington Post*, January 8, 2005. See http://www.washingtonpost.com/wp-dyn/articles/A58318-2005Jan8.html (last accessed 7 February 2017).
2. On the numbers, see http://www.archives.gov/research/military/vietnam-war/casualty-statistics.html. On the controversy, see for example Geoff Simons, *Vietnam Syndrome: The Impact on US Foreign Policy*, London: Palgrave, 1998 (last accessed 1 January 2016).

3. Reagan's forceful interventions in Grenada, Lebanon and Libya were all 'hit and split' operations.

4. See Richard Lock-Pullan's *US Intervention Policy and Army Innovation: From Vietnam to Iraq*, London: Routledge, 2006.

5. See Lawrence Freedman, *A Choice of Enemies, America Confronts the Middle East*, London: Phoenix, 2008, p. 148.

6. See Lock-Pullan, *US Intervention Policy*.

7. See for example, George C. Herring, 'America and Vietnam: The Unending War', *Foreign Affairs*, Winter 1991/92 (www.foreignaffairs. com/articles/vietnam/1991–12–01/america-and-vietnam-unending-war) (last accessed 1 January 2016).

8. Lawrence Freedman, 'The Third World War', *Survival*, 40:4 (Winter 2001), p. 70.

9. Ibid., p. 80.

10. See David Hastings Dunn, 'Myths, Motivations and "Misunderestimations": The Bush Administration and Iraq', *International Affairs*, 79:2 (March 2003), pp. 279–97.

11. See George W. Bush's Second Inaugural Address, and its call for a 'Freedom Agenda', at http://www.npr.org/templates/story/story. php?storyId=4460172 (last accessed 1 January 2016).

12. See https://www.govtrack.us/congress/bills/107/sjres23 (last accessed 1 January 2016).

13. Freedman, 'Rumsfeld's Legacy'.

14. See Lock-Pullan, *US Intervention Policy*; and Bob Woodward, *Bush at War*, New York: Simon and Schuster, 2004.

15. See Steven Erlanger and Sheryl Gay Stolberg, 'Surprise Nobel for Obama stirs praise and doubts', *New York Times*, 9 October 2009. See http://www.nytimes.com/2009/10/10/world/10nobel.html (last accessed 1 January 2016).

16. See Toby Harnden, 'How Barack Obama beat Hillary Clinton', *Daily Telegraph*, 4 June 2008. See http://www.telegraph.co.uk/news/politics/local-elections/2076258/How-Barack-Obama-beat-Hillary-Clinton.html (last accessed 1 January 2016).

17. Spencer Ackerman, 'The Obama Doctrine', *The American Prospect*, April 2008, www.prospect.org/cs/articles?article=the_obama_doctrine (last accessed 1 January 2016).

18. Todd Heisler, 'Years after campaign began, a different world', *New York Times*, 17 January 2009.

19. The White House, National Security Strategy, 27 May 2010. See www. whitehouse.gov/sites/default/files/rss_viewer/national_security_strategy.pdf (last accessed 1 January 2016).

20. Henry Kissinger, 'Obama's foreign policy challenge', *Washington Post*, 22 April 2009.

21. See Hilary Rodham Clinton, *Hard Choices*, New York: Simon and Schuster, 2014, pp. 231–8.
22. David E. Sanger and Elaine Sciolino, 'Iran strategy: Cold War echo', *New York Times*, 30 April 2006.
23. See Adam Quinn, 'The Art of Declining Politely: Obama's Prudent Presidency and the Waning of American Power', *International Affairs*, 87:4 (July 2011), pp. 803–24.
24. In meetings Gates would ask, 'Can I just finish the two wars we're already in before you go looking for new ones?' He did not believe it was a 'vital national interest'. See Robert M. Gates, *Duty: Memoirs of a Secretary at War*, Croydon: WH Allen, 2014, 511–15. See also Ryan Lizza, 'The consequentialist', *New Yorker*, 2 May 2011, http://www. newyorker.com/magazine/2011/05/02/the-consequentialist   (last accessed 1 January 2016).
25. The phrase was first used in an interview by an unnamed Obama administration official. See Lizza, 'The consequentialist'.
26. See, for example, Abigail Hauslohner, 'Lawless Libya: The growing list of unsolved murders', *The Independent*, http://www.independent. co.uk/news/world/africa/lawless-libya-the-growing-list-of-unsolved-murders-8970830.html (last accessed 1 January 2016).
27. Michael Crowley, 'Watch out for missile blowback', *Time*, 2 June 2014, p. 17.
28. Anne Gearan and Karen DeYoung, 'Obama's "red line" warning to Syria on chemical arms draws criticism', *Washington Post*, 21 August 2012.
29. 'President Obama's September 10th Speech on Syria', *Washington Post*, http://articles.washingtonpost.com/2013–09–10/politics/41939044_ 1_chemical-weapons-poison-gas-sarin-gas (last accessed 1 January 2016).
30. Leon Panetta, *Worthy Fights*, New York: Penguin, 2014), p. 450.
31. He continues, 'The power of the United States rests on its word, and clear signals are important both to deter adventurism and to reassure allies that we can be counted on. Assad's action clearly defied President Obama's warning; by failing to respond, it sent the wrong message to the world'.
32. Indeed, Russian support for UN Security Council Resolution 2118 was groundbreaking in several respects. Most significantly, it was the first time that the Russians had permitted any resolution on Syria to pass the Security Council. Given that the Russians presented this as their initiative, it also allowed Moscow to reclaim a role that it has long sought, to return to being an effective and influential player in great power politics. The resolution, adopted unanimously on

27 September at ministerial level, also broke new ground in that the Council agreed 'that the use of chemical weapons anywhere constitutes a threat to international peace and security'. This language goes beyond the Chemical Weapons Convention, which only prohibits the use of chemical weapons between states. And although the Russians explicitly refused to allow the Resolution to fall under Chapter VII of the UN Charter, which would imply automatic threat of force in return for non-compliance, the fact that it was passed at all did lay the legal foundations for enforcement measures should they be considered necessary at a later date. The passage of 2118 also strengthened the role of the UN in the conflict and increases the possibility of a move towards negotiations in Geneva aimed at a ceasefire and political transition in Syria.

33. David Ignatius, 'Obama is criticized for right result on Syria', *Washington Post*, 18 September 2013, http://articles.washingtonpost.com/2013–09–18/opinions/42183785_1_chemical-weapons-barack-obama-the-united-nations (last accessed 1 January 2016).

34. See 'Efforts of the United Nations and the Organization for the Prohibition of Chemical Weapons to Accomplish the Elimination of Syrian Chemical Weapons' at http://www.state.gov/t/isn/rls/rm/2014/223973.html (last accessed 1 January 2016).

35. See 'Kerry says "raw data" points to new Syria chemical strikes', http://www.nti.org/gsn/article/hagel-holds-off-endorsing-claims-new-syria-chemical-strikes/?mgs1=0216fTodlO.

36. See, for example, Michael Gerson, 'On foreign policy, Obama was "behind the curve"', *Washington Post*, 11 January 2016, www.washingtonpost.com/opinions/obamas-inner-circle-has-few-kind-words-for-the-former-boss/2016/01/11/ddd67742-b892–11e5–829c-26ff-b874a18d_story.html; and Max Boot, 'The US strategy against the Islamic State must be retooled. Here's how', *Washington Post*, 14 November 2014, www.washingtonpost.com/opinions/the-us-strategy-against-the-islamic-state-must-be-retooled-heres-how/2014/11/14/7972e50c-6b8a-11e4-a31c-77759fc1eacc_story.html (last accessed 1 January 2016).

37. Joe Klein, 'Obama and Syria: Stumbling toward Damascus', *Time*, 11 September 2012. He continues, 'It has been one of the more stunning and inexplicable displays of presidential incompetence that I've ever witnessed'.

38. Interestingly, by contrast Russia and Assad were strengthened by the episode. Russia has gained influence in Syria, the region and the UN as the power that was able to blunt the American sword. It was able to protect its ally, Syria, and therefore its interests in Syria, namely the Tartus

naval base (Russia's only military base outside the former USSR), and its position in the anti-Western Shiite Crescent. It is also able to aid Assad, and its role in any eventual peace process will have been strengthened. For President Assad the immediate threat of military force has gone, and he is now an important interlocutor in his own chemical disarmament process. Far from being someone whom the US would not engage with diplomatically, Assad is now legitimized as the leader who will facilitate the destruction of his chemical arsenal.

39. See Panetta, *Worthy Fights*, p. 449.

40. Ibid.

41. Richard Haass, 'A foreign policy flirting with chaos', *Wall Street Journal*, 29 April 2014.

42. Michael Chertoff, 'The U.S. must stand behind its security obligations', *Washington Post*, 16 April 2014, see http://www.washingtonpost.com/opinions/the-us-must-stand-behind-its-security-obligations/2014/04/16/111c379c-c4cd-11e3-bcec-b71ee10e9bc3_story.html (last accessed 1 January 2016).

43. Remarks by the President at the United States Military Academy Commencement Ceremony, http://www.whitehouse.gov/the-press-office/2014/05/28/remarks-president-west-point-academy-commencement-ceremony. Hereafter 'West Point speech' (last accessed 1 January 2016).

44. 'President Obama, in his West Point speech, binds America's hands on foreign affairs', *Washington Post*, http://www.washingtonpost.com/opinions/president-obama-in-his-west-point-speech-binds-americas-hands-on-foreign-affairs/2014/05/28/f3db48fe-e66d-11e3-a86b-362fd5443d19_story.html (last accessed 1 January 2016).

45. 'Remarks by the President'.

46. 'Remarks of the President'.

47. See William Kazer, 'Chinese general says U.S. foreign policy has "erectile dysfunction" problems', *Wall Street Journal*, see http://blogs.wsj.com/chinarealtime/2014/06/02/chinese-general-says-u-s-foreign-policy-has-erectile-dysfunction-problems/ (last accessed 1 January 2016).

48. See http://www.pewresearch.org/key-data-points/u-s-foreign-policy-key-data-points/ (last accessed 1 January 2016).

49. Steve Luxenberg, 'Bob Woodward book details Obama battles with advisers over exit plan for Afghan war', *Washington Post*, 29 September 2010, www.washingtonpost.com/wp-dyn/content/article/2010/09/21/AR2010092106706_pf.html (last accessed 1 January 2016).

50. Lawrence Freedman, 'Obama's speech and fretting allies', http://

warontherocks.com/2014/05/obamas-speech-and-fretting-allies/ (last accessed 1 January 2016).

51. Michael Gerson, 'Obama's global war on straw men', *Washington Post*, 3 June 2014, http://www.deseretnews.com/article/865604381/ Obamas-global-war-on-straw-men.html?pg=all (last accessed 1 January 2016).

52. Freedman, 'Obama's speech'.

53. Gerson, 'Obama's global war'.

54. Sam Jones, 'Masterly Russian operations in Ukraine leave Nato one step behind', *Financial Times*, http://www.ft.com/cms/s/0/a5829d60-ed48–11e3–8a1e-00144feabdc0.html?siteedition=uk#axzz34KJxi6At (last accessed 1 January 2016).

12. BRITAIN'S JOURNEY TO A NATIONAL SECURITY APPROACH AND THE EVOLUTION OF A DEFENCE ACADEMY

1. Peter Hennessy, *The Secret State: Preparing for the Worst 1945–2010*, London: Penguin, 2010.

2. Christopher Andrew, *Defence of the Realm: The Authorized History of MI5*, London: Allen Lane, 2009, p. 845.

3. Private information.

4. Thomas Hobbes, *Leviathan* (1651), Harmondsworth: Penguin, 1968; John Locke, *Two Treatises of Government* (1689), New York: Cambridge University Press, 1960.

5. David Cameron and Nick Clegg, foreword to *The Coalition: Our Programme for Government*, London: Cabinet Office, May 2010, p. 7.

6. Nick Ritchie, 'Rethinking security: A Critical Analysis of the Strategic Defence and Security Review', *International Affairs*, 87:2 (2011), 355–76, p. 359.

7. Cabinet Office, *The National Security Strategy of the United Kingdom: Update 2009*, Security for the Next Generation', June 2009, Cm 7590, 5, https://www.gov.uk/government/uploads/system/uploads/attachment_data/file/229001/7590.pdf (last accessed 12 Nov. 2015).

8. *Security for the Next Generation—The NSS: Update 2009*, 4.

9. Mohammad Sidique Khan, leader of London suicide attackers, video broadcast, *Al Jazeera*, 1 September 2005.

10. Emma Rothschild, 'What is security?', *Daedalus*, 124:3 (Summer 1995), 53–98, p. 70.

11. Mohammad Sidique Khan, leader of London suicide attackers, video broadcast, *Al Jazeera*, 1 September 2005.

12. Defence Committee, 'Re-thinking defence to meet new threats', www.publications.parliament.uk/pa/cm201415/cmselect/cmdfence/512/51206.htm (last accessed 24 Jan. 2016).

13. National Commission Report into National Security (2009), 99, www.ippr.org/files/images/media/files/publication/2012/01/shared-responsibilities_security-final_June2009_1704.pdf?noredirect=1 (last accessed 25 Nov. 2015).

14. He warned that national security might be undermined if their departmental budgets were significantly cut in the forthcoming SDSR. Malcolm Chalmers, *RUSI Briefing: The 'Missing Links' in SDSR Financing Organized Crime, Migration and Diplomacy*, London: RUSI, Sept. 2015, 2.

15. Arnold Wolfers, 'National Security as an Ambiguous Symbol', *Political Science Quarterly*, 67:4 (December 1952), 67.

16. Lawrence Freedman, 'The Revolution in Strategic Affairs', *Adelphi Paper 318*, London: OUP/IISS, April 1998, 9–10.

17. DAC for CT Peter Clarke, 'Learning from Experience: The Inaugural Colin Cramphorn Memorial Lecture', *Policy Exchange*, 2007, p. 20.

18. Andrew, *Defence of the Realm*, p. 804.

19. Ibid., p. 805.

20. Hennessy, *The Secret State*, p. 375.

21. TSO, *The Strategic Defence Review of 1998*, House of Commons 138, 1997 (1998), p. 5 (hereafter, SDR).

22. *SDR*, p. 5.

23. Daniel Korski, 'Memo to the Defence Committee' (June 2009), para. 7, in House of Commons Defence Committee, 7th Report of Session 2009–10, *The Comprehensive Approach: The point of war is not just to win but to make a better peace*, House of Commons 224 [Incorporating HC 523–i, ii, iii and iv, Session 2008–09], 18 March 2010, Ev. 141.

24. David Omand, *Securing the State*, London: Hurst, 2010, p. 63.

25. Omand, *Securing the State*, p. 63.

26. Ibid., 64.

27. This is based on personal experience when researching and presenting a paper for the MoD.

28. Joint Committee on the National Security Strategy, available at www.parliament.uk/business/committees/committees-a-z/joint-select/national-security-strategy/role/ (last accessed 10 Jan. 2016).

29. TSO, *The Strategic Defence Review: A New Chapter*, Cm 5566, vol. 1, July 2002.

30. The Defence Committee discovered significant numbers of the reservists in the London and other metropolitan districts (the most likely to need to be called out) were already deployed in Afghanistan and on other operations. House of Commons Defence Committee, *A New Chapter to the Strategic Defence Review* (Sixth Report of Session 2002–03) House of Commons 93–1, 5 May 2003.

31. House of Commons p. 557, 2002–03.

32. Korski, 'Memo to the Defence Committee', para. 3, Ev. 140.

33. John Gearson and James Gow, 'Security, Not Defence, Strategic, Not Habit: Restructuring the Political Arrangements for Policy Making on Britain's Role in the World', *Political Quarterly*, 81:3 (July–Sept. 2010), p. 414.

34. Andrew Rathmell, 'Planning Post-Conflict Reconstruction in Iraq: What Can We Learn?', *International Affairs*, 81:5 (2005), 1013–38, p. 1030. This is not to overlook that the US's National Security structures did not prevent these lessons being overlooked as well, of course.

35. Theo Farrell, 'The Dynamics of British Military Transformation', *International Affairs*, 84:4 (2008), 777–807, pp. 793–4.

36. Pauline Neville-Jones (chairman), *An Unquiet World: Submission to the Shadow Cabinet*, London: National and International Security Policy Group, July 2007, p. 9.

37. TSO, *CONTEST: The United Kingdom's Strategy for Countering Terrorism*, Cm 8123, July 2011, p. 10.

38. Robert Raine, 'Reflections on Security at the 2012 Olympics', *Intelligence and National Security*, 30:4 (2015), pp. 422–33.

39. Alan Hubbard, 'Sebastian Coe: "London 2012 has been beyond my wildest dreams"', *The Independent*, 12 August 2012, www.independent.co.uk/news/people/profiles/sebastian-coe-london-2012-has-been-beyond-my-wildest-dreams-8034865.html (last accessed 16 Nov. 2015).

40. Anthony Seldon and Peter Snowdon, *Cameron at 10*, London: William Collins, 2015, p. 223.

41. Raine, 'Reflections on Security', p. 432.

42. The 'success' of London 2012 security is now being used to seek to assist other Olympic organizers and export UK capability/expertise overseas with a UKTI Security Export Strategy including a 'Major Event Security' section connecting the UK's domestic security record to its diplomatic engagements—a British 'national security approach' in action? UKTI/Home Office, 'Increasing Our Security Exports: A New Government Approach', June 2014, https://www.gov.uk/government/uploads/system/uploads/attachment_data/file/328120/UKTI_Security_Exports_Brochure_update.pdf (last accessed 16 Nov. 2015).

43. 'It was right to set out the strategic framework and get it widely agreed: a published strategy and a common concept of operations. They provided the glue that this massive, multi-agency operation needed. They ensured there were a common purpose and a common vocabulary. And publishing these documents widely made sure that they were enforceable'. Raine, 'Reflections on Security', p. 432.

44. Ibid., p. 433.

45. UKTI/Home Office, 'Increasing Our Security Exports: A New Government Approach', June 2014, https://www.gov.uk/government/uploads/system/uploads/attachment_data/file/328120/UKTI_Security_Exports_Brochure_update.pdf (last accessed 16 Nov. 2015).

46. Raine, 'Reflections on Security', p. 433.

47. Sir John Sawers, 'The Limits of Security', *The War Studies 2015 Annual Lecture*, King's College London, 16 February 2015.

48. GPO, National Commission on Terrorist Attacks upon the United States, *The 9/11 Commission Report*, Washington: GPO, July 2004, p. 399.

49. Korski, 'Memo to the Defence Committee', para. 4, Ev. 140.

50. Gearson and Gow, 'Security, Not Defence', p. 416.

51. Lawrence Freedman, *The Politics of British Defence*, London: Macmillan, 1999, p. 95.

52. David Cameron evidence to JCNSS, quoted in KCL/Institute of Government, *The NSC* (2015), p. 32.

53. Evidence to Joint Committee on the National Security Strategy, *First Review of the National Security Strategy*, Session 2010–2012, HC1384, 16, referring to Q94.

54. Lawrence Freedman, *Strategy: A History*, New York: Oxford University Press, 2012.

55. Richard Betts, 'Is Strategy an Illusion?', *International Security*, 25:2 (2000), 6.

56. Hew Strachan, 'Strategy and contingency', *International Affairs*, 87:6 (2011), 1281–8.

57. Hal Brands and Patrick Porter, 'Why Grand Strategy Still Matters in a World of Chaos', *The National Interest*, 10 Dec. 2015, http://nationalinterest.org/feature/why-grand-strategy-still-matters-world-chaos-14568 (first accessed 20 Jan. 2016).

58. 'Jane Barder interviewing Sir Anthony Parsons', FCO Oral History Programme Transcript, 25–8, https://www.chu.cam.ac.uk/media/uploads/files/Parsons_Anthony.pdf (accessed 11 May 2015).

59. Mark Phillips, 'Policy-Making in Defence and Security', *RUSI Journal*, 157:1 (2012), pp. 28–35.

60. Michael Welkin, 'Ch. 11: Educating for national security', in G. Marcella (ed.), *Affairs of State: The Interagency and National Security*, London: SSI, December 2008, p. 474.

61. Omand, *Securing the State*, p. 9.

62. Wolfers, 'National Security', p. 67.

63. Welkin, 'Ch. 11: Educating', p. 447.

13. TRUST AND INTERNATIONAL RELATIONS

1. Lawrence Freedman, *Strategy: A History* New York: Oxford University Press, 2012, p. 4.

2. James Coleman, *Foundations of Social Theory*, Cambridge, MA: Harvard University Press, 1990, 300–7, pp. 743–4.

3. Jean Cohen, 'Trust, Voluntary Association and Workable Democracy: The Contemporary American Discourse of Civil Society', in Mark E. Warren (ed.), *Democracy and Trust*, Cambridge: Cambridge University Press, 1999, pp. 208–48.

4. Ronald Inglehart, 'Trust, Well-Being and Democracy' and Russell Hardin, 'Do We Want Trust in Government?' in Warren (ed.), *Democracy and Trust*, pp. 88–120, pp. 22–41.

5. Emile Durkheim, *The Division of Labor in Society*, tr. W.D. Halls, New York: Macmillan, 1984, pp. 229–30; Marcel Mauss, *The Gift: The Form and Reason for Exchange in Archaic Societies*, tr. W.D. Halls, New York: Norton, 1990 [1925]).

6. Robert Axelrod and W.D. Hamilton, 'The Evolution of Cooperation', *Science*, 211:4489 (1981), 1390–6; Robert Axelrod, *Evolution of Cooperation*, New York: Basic Books, 1984.

7. Richard Ned Lebow, 'Beyond Parsimony: Rethinking Theories of Coercive Bargaining', *European Journal of International Relations*, 4:1 (1998), pp. 31–66.

8. Richard Ned Lebow and Janice Gross Stein, *We All Lost the Cold War*, Princeton: Princeton University Press, 1994, chs. 2–6.

9. Robert Axelrod and Douglas Dion, 'The Further Evolution of Cooperation', *Science*, 242 (9 December, 1988), pp. 1385–90; Martin Nowak and Karl Sigmund, 'A Strategy of Win-Shift, Lose-Stay That Outperforms Tit-for-Tat in the Prisoner's Dilemma Game', *Nature*, 364 (1993), pp. 56–8; David Kraines and Vivian Kraines, 'Evolution of Learning among Pavlov Strategies in a Competitive Environment with Noise', *Journal of Conflict Resolution*, 39 (1995), pp. 439–66; Jianzhong Wu and Robert Axelrod, 'Coping with Noise: How to Cope with Noise in the Iterated Prisoner's Dilemma', *Journal of Conflict Resolution*, 39 (March 1995), pp. 183–9.

10. Robert Axelrod, *The Complexity of Cooperation: Agent-Based Models of Competition and Collaboration*, Princeton: Princeton University Press, 1997, p. 30.

11. Matthew Evangelista, 'Turning Points in Arms Control', in Richard K. Herrmann and Richard Ned Lebow (eds.), *Ending the Cold War: Interpretations, Causation, and the Study of International Relations*, New York: Palgrave, 2004, pp. 83–106.

12. Mikhail Gorbachev, *Memoirs*, New York: Doubleday, 1995; Anatoliy Chernayev, *My Six Years with Gorbachev*, University Park, PA: Penn State University Press, 2000; Archie Brown, *The Gorbachev Factor*, Oxford: Oxford University Press, 1996; and the essays by Archie Brown, Richard K. Herrmann, Matthew Evangelista, Jacques Lévesque, James Davis and William C. Wohlforth, and George Breslauer and Richard Ned Lebow, in Herrmann and Lebow (eds.), *Ending the Cold War*.

13. Henry Farrell and Jack Knight, 'Trust, Institutions and Institutional Change: Industrial Districts and the Social Capital Hypothesis', *Politics and Society*, 31:4 (2003), pp. 537–66.

14. Mark Suchman, 'Managing Legitimacy: Strategic and Institutional Approaches', *Academy of Management Review*, 20 (1995), pp. 571–610.

15. Christian Reus-Smit, *American Power and World Order*, Cambridge: Polity Press, 2004.

16. Martha Finnemore and Stephen J. Toope, 'Alternatives to "Legalization": Richer Views of Law and Politics', *International Organization*, 55:3 (2001), pp. 743–58, make this argument in the context of compliance with international law.

17. Richard Ned Lebow, *A Cultural Theory of International Relations*, Cambridge: Cambridge University Press, 2008.

18. James Madison, 'Federalist Number 10', in Alexander Hamilton, James Madison and John Jay, *The Federalist Papers*, Baltimore: Johns Hopkins University Press, 1981.

19. David C. Kang, 'Hierarchy and Legitimacy in International Systems: The Tribute System in Early Modern East Asia', *Security Studies*, 19:4 (2010), pp. 591–622; Zhang Feng, *Chinese Hegemony: Grand Strategy, International Institutions, and Relationality in East Asian History*, forthcoming.

20. Warren (ed.), *Democracy and Trust*, on the debate over the necessity of trust for democracy.

21. James Madison, 'Federalist Number 51'.

22. Mlada Bukovansky, Ian Clark, Robyn Eckersley, Richard Price, Christian Reus-Smit and Nicholas J. Wheeler, *Special Responsibilities: Global Problems and American Power*, Cambridge: Cambridge University Press, 2012; Simon Reich and Richard Ned Lebow, *Goodbye Hegemony! Power and Influence in the Global System*, Princeton: Princeton University Press, 2014.

23. Ivo K. Daalder and James M. Lindsay, 'An alliance of democracies: our way or the highway', *Financial Times*, 6 November 2004, http://www.brookings.edu/research/opinions/2004/11/06globalgovernance-daalder (accessed 1 January 2014).

24. Michael Dobbs and John M. Goshko, 'Albright's personal odyssey shaped foreign policy beliefs', *Washington Post*, 6 December 1996, A25;

Madeleine K. Albright, Interview on NBC-TV 'The Today Show' with Matt Lauer, Columbus, Ohio, 19 February 1998; Daniel Deudney and G. John Ikenberry, *Democratic Internationalism: An American Grand Strategy for a Post-Exceptionalist Era*, New York: Council on Foreign Relations, 2012, p. 1.

25. Reich and Lebow, *Goodbye Hegemony!* for an elaboration of this claim.

14. THE ESSENCE OF STRATEGY: CONSTRUCTIVIST REALISM AND NECESSITY

1. Lawrence Freedman, 'Confessions of a Premature Constructivist', in the present volume.

2. A tiny exception here is James Gow, *Defending the West*, Cambridge: Polity, 2004, which appeared a year before Freedman's original 'Confessions of a Premature Constructivist' lecture at the 2005 BISA Annual Conference; it was when he was kindly reading drafts of that volume for me that Freedman pointed out that Katzenstein had once labelled him as a 'realist constructivist', that he had always been informed by a sociological approach, and that doing this was so obvious, he thought, that he had assumed it to be unremarkable.

3. The father of political realism was Hans J. Morgenthau, whose work is far richer and more subtle than many assume, or give credit for— indeed, the full interpretation of Morgenthau as, in effect, a constructivist remains to be made, although Ned Lebow has made a creditable start. See Hans J. Morgenthau, *Politics among Nations: The Struggle for Power and Peace*, New York: McGraw-Hill, 1993; Richard Ned Lebow, *The Tragic Vision of Politics: Ethics, Interests and Orders*, Cambridge: Cambridge University Press, 2003; other major figures succeeding Morgenthau include Kenneth N. Waltz, *Theory of International Politics*, Reading, MA: Addison Wesley, 1979, and John Mearsheimer, *The Tragedy of Great Power Politics*, New York: Norton, 2001.

4. For a limited number of surveys of the variety of views encompassed by liberalism, idealism and their variants, see, for example: Michael P. Doyle, *Ways of War and Peace: Realism, Liberalism, and Socialism*, New York: W.W. Norton and Co., 1997; Joshua S. Goldstein, *International Relations*, 3rd edn, New York: Longman, 1999, ch. 3; Tim Dunne, 'Liberalism', in John Baylis and Steve Smith, *The Globalization of World Politics: An Introduction to International Relations*, Oxford: Oxford University Press, 2001; Scott Burchill, 'Liberalism', in Scott Burchill et al., *Theories of International Relations*, 2nd edn, London: Palgrave, 2001.

5. See Burchill et al., *Theories of International Relations* and Steve Smith, Ken Booth and Marysia Zalewski (eds.), *International Theory: Positivism and Beyond*, Cambridge: Cambridge University Press, 1996.

6. Hugo Grotius, *De Jure Belli ac Pacis*, tr. Francis W. Kelsey, Oxford: Clarendon Press, 1925; Hedley Bull, *The Anarchical Society: A Study of Order in World Politics*, London: Macmillan, 1977.

7. Alexander Wendt, *The Social Theory of International Relations*, Cambridge: Cambridge University Press, 1999.

8. Ibid., p. xiii.

9. See Smith, 'Reflectivist and Constructivist Approaches to International Theory', in Baylis and Smith (eds.), *Globalization*, ch. 11.

10. Alexander Wendt, 'Anarchy Is What States Make It: The Social Construction of Power Politics', *International Organization*, 46:2 (1992).

11. See Reus Smit, 'Constructivism', in Burchill et al., *Theories*, 222–3, and Smith, 'Reflectivist', in Baylis and Smith (eds.), *Globalization*, ch. 11.

12. George Schöpflin, *Nations, Identity, Power*, London: Hurst, 2000.

13. Barry Buzan, Ole Weaver and Jaap de Wilde, *Security: A New Framework for Analysis*, Boulder: Lynne Rienner, 1998, p. 30.

14. Buzan et al., *Security*, 47 n.7.

15. Ibid., p. 31.

16. Gow, *Defending the West*, ch. 2.

17. One exception to this, of which I am aware, is a substantial paper presented at the International Studies Association Convention in 2010: Matthew A. Williams and Jack Covarrubias, 'A Realist-Constructivist Approach to Policy: Maintaining Power within a Viable Security Community', Prepared for Presentation at the Annual Convention of the International Studies Association in New Orleans, Louisiana, 17–20 February 2010, 28 and 49; available at http://citation.allacademic.com//meta/p_mla_apa_research_citation/4/1/4/2/1/pages414212/p414212–1.php (accessed 25 July 2014).

18. J. Samuel Barkin, 'Realist Constructivism', *International Studies Review*, 5:3 (2003), pp. 325–34. This article was written around the same time as the Gow chapter, but the latter was already completed for publication.

19. J. Samuel Barkin, *Realist Constructivism*, Cambridge: Cambridge University Press, 2010.

20. Patrick Thaddeus Jackson, 'Bridging the Gap: Toward a Realist-Constructivist Dialogue', *International Studies Review*, 6:2 (2004), pp. 337–52.

21. J. Samuel Barkin, 'Realist Constructivism and Realist Constructivisms', *International Studies Review*, 6:2 (2004), p. 349.

22. Ibid., 325.

23. Ibid., 338.

24. Mats Berdal, in his contribution to the present volume, however, does note the connection between international politics theory and

Freedman's work combining both a disposition tempered by a sense of power, or realities, and the role of values in practice.

25. Patrick Thaddeus Jackson and Daniel H. Nexon, 'Constructivist Realism or Realist Constructivism?', *International Studies Review*, 6:2 (2004), pp. 337–41.

26. Ibid., 338.

27. Jennifer Sterling-Folker, 'Realist-Constructivism and Morality', *International Studies Review*, 6:2 (2004), p. 343.

28. Janice Bially Mattern, 'Power in Realist Constructivist Research', *International Studies Review*, 6:2 (2004), p. 333, p. 346.

29. Richard Ned Lebow, 'Constructive Realism', *International Studies Review*, 6:2, p. 346.

30. Sabrina P. Ramet, 'The United States and Europe: Toward Greater Cooperation or a Historic Parting? An Idealist Perspective', in Sabrina Ramet and Christina Ingebretsen (eds.), *Coming In from the Cold War: Changes in US–European Interactions since 1980*, Lanham, MD: Rowman and Littlefield, 2002.

31. Barkin, 'Realist Constructivism', p. 329.

32. Freedman, *Strategy*, p. 372.

33. Ibid., 20–1.

34. Ibid., 30.

35. Ibid., 31.

36. Ibid., 607ff.

37. At the end of the 1990s, an important review of the field of international relations indeed concluded that the major rift was between 'rationalism' and 'constructivism'. Peter Katzenstein, Robert O. Keohane and Stephen Krasner, 'International Organization and the Study of World Politics', *International Organization*, 50:4 (1999).

38. Freedman, *Strategy*, p. 580.

39. Ibid., p. 595.

40. In providing a brief introduction to the notion of social constructivism, this is a position acknowledged by Terry Terrif, Stuart Croft, Lucy James and Patrick M. Morgan, *Security Studies Today*, Cambridge: Polity, 1999.

41. This is a point developed with empirical examination in Gow, *Defending the West*.

42. The term 'quasi-state entity' is coined by Ernst Dijxhoorn, *Quasi-state Entities and International Criminal Justice: Legitimising Narratives and Counter-Narratives* New York: Routledge, 2017.

43. The Conference on Security and Cooperation in Europe became the Organization for Security and Cooperation in Europe on 1 January 1995.

44. See James Gow, *Triumph of the Lack of Will: International Diplomacy and the Yugoslav Crisis*, London and New York: Hurst & Co. and Columbia University Press, 1997, pp. 298–9.

45. John Mearsheimer, *The Tragedy of Great Power Politics*, New York: Norton, 2001.

46. Joseph S. Nye, *The Paradox of American Power*, New York: Oxford University Press, 2002 points out that the final report of a commission on national security led by two former US Senators warned that there would be attacks on American soil in which large numbers of people might die.

47. Mats Berdal, '"Realism as an Unsentimental Intellectual Temper": Lawrence Freedman and the New Interventionism', ch. 8 in the present volume. This provides an alternative, less theoretical but essentially similar, way of understanding Freedman's work.

48. Chris Mackmurdo spent considerable time as a sounding board and springboard for ideas, in the original development of my thinking on this topic, including the intriguing and correct observation that the problems here might be informed by an understanding of the dialogue between John Locke and George (Bishop) Berkeley—on which, see the discussion by Bryan Magee and Michael Ayers in Bryan Magee (ed.), *The Great Philosophers*, London: BBC, 1987, Dialogue 6.

15. FREEDMAN ON MACHIAVELLI

1. Lawrence Freedman, *Strategy: A History*, New York: Oxford University Press, 2012.

2. Rey Koslowski and Friedrich V. Kratochwill, 'Understanding Change in International Politics: The Soviet Empire's Demise and the International System', *International Organization*, 48:2 (March 1994), p. 215.

3. Anne-Marie Slaughter, 'International Relations, Principal Theories', in R. Wolfrum (ed.), *Max Planck Encyclopedia of Public International Law*, New York: Oxford University Press, 2011, para. 4 (available at https:// www.princeton.edu/~slaughtr/Articles/722_IntlRelPrincipalTheories_ Slaughter_20110509zG.pdf and http://opil.ouplaw.com/view/10.1093/ law:epil/9780199231690/law-9780199231690-e722?rskey=J4F7b8&re sult=1&prd=OPIL (both accessed 11 July 2014).

4. The quotations from Machiavelli are taken from my own work, *The Garments of Court and Palace: Machiavelli and the World That He Made*, London: Atlantic Books, 2013, and are the work-product of my collaboration with the Italian Renaissance scholar and novelist Lisa Hilton-Moro, but she bears no responsibility for my authorial decisions. This is further explained in *Garments*, p. 188.

5. Freedman, *Strategy*, p. 42.
6. Niccolò Machiavelli, *The Prince*, ch. 14: as quoted in Bobbitt, *Garments*.
7. Freedman, *Strategy*, p. 50.
8. But see Leo Strauss, *Thoughts on Machiavelli*, Chicago: University of Chicago Press, 1958.
9. Marcus Tullius Cicero, *On Duties*, ed. E.M. Atkins, tr. Miriam T. Griffin, Cambridge: Cambridge University Press, 1991 (*De Officiis*, Book 2, chs. 58, 77).
10. Strauss, *Thoughts*, pp. 9–10.
11. Cary J. Nederman, 'Niccolò Machiavelli', in *Stanford Encyclopedia of Philosophy* (Fall 2009 edition), ed. Edward N. Zalta, https://plato.stanford.edu (last accessed 7 February 2017).
12. Freedman, *Strategy*, p. 51.
13. Machiavelli, 'Letter to Giovan Battista Soderini', 1506 *Discourses*, Book 3 Ch. 9, see Bobbitt, *Garments*.
14. Machiavelli, *The Prince*, ch. 25, as quoted in Bobbitt, *Garments*.
15. Nederman, 'Niccolò Machiavelli'.
16. Ibid.
17. Freedman, *Strategy*, p. 63.

16. STRATEGIC SCRIPTS AND NUCLEAR DISARMAMENT

1. William Walker, *A Perpetual Menace: Nuclear Weapons and International Order*, London and New York: Routledge, 2012, p. 4.
2. Lawrence Freedman, *The Price of Peace: Living with the Nuclear Dilemma*, London: Macmillan, 1988, pp. 13–14.
3. 'A World Free of Nuclear Weapons', *Wall Street Journal*, 4 January 2007.
4. Margaret Beckett, 'A World Free of Nuclear Weapons?', Keynote Address to the Carnegie International Non-Proliferation Conference, Washington, DC, 25 June 2007; Des Browne, 'Laying the Foundations for Multilateral Disarmament', Speech to the Conference on Disarmament, Geneva, 5 February 2008.
5. Lawrence Freedman, *Strategy: A History*, New York: Oxford University Press, 2013, p. xiv.
6. Roger Schank and Robert Abelson, *Scripts, Plans, Goals, and Understanding: An Inquiry into Human Knowledge Structures*, Hove, East Sussex: Psychology Press, 1977, p. 41.
7. Robert Abelson, 'Psychological Status of the Script Concept', *American Psychologist*, 36:7 (1981), p. 717.
8. Roger C. Schank, *Tell Me a Story: A New Look at Real and Artificial Memory*, New York: Scribner, 1990, pp. 8–9.
9. Freedman, *Strategy: A History*, p. 619.

10. Daniel Kahneman, *Thinking, Fast and Slow*, London: Penguin, 2012.

11. Freedman, *Strategy: A History*, p. 620.

12. Ibid.

13. Ibid., xiv.

14. Ibid., 620.

15. Ibid., 621.

16. There has been a flurry of academic inquiries into a managed disarmament process along these lines: see e.g. George Acton and James Perkovich (eds.), *Abolishing Nuclear Weapons: A Debate*, Washington, DC: Carnegie Endowment, 2009, and James Acton, *Deterrence during Disarmament: Deep Nuclear Reductions and International Security*, London: IISS Adelphi Book no. 417, 2011.

17. *Eliminating Nuclear Threats: A Practical Agenda for Global Policymakers*, Report of the International Commission on Nuclear Non-Proliferation and Disarmament, Canberra and Tokyo, 2009, pp. 73–5.

18. See Ken Berry, Patricia Lewis, Benoît Pélopidas, Nikolai Sokov and Ward Wilson, *Delegitimizing Nuclear Weapons: Examining the Validity of Nuclear Deterrence*, Monterey: Monterey Institute for International Studies, May 2010; and Ward Wilson, 'The Myth of Nuclear Deterrence', *The Nonproliferation Review*, 15:3 (November 2008).

19. See John Borrie, 'Humanitarian Reframing of Nuclear Weapons and the Logic of a Ban', *International Affairs*, 90:3 (2014).

20. See, for example, Statement by President Mahmoud Ahmadinejad to the 2010 Non-Proliferation Treaty Review Conference, New York, 3 May 2010.

21. Borrie, 'Humanitarian Reframing', p. 643.

22. As discussed in Rebecca Johnson, *Unfinished Business: The Negotiation of the CTBT and the End of Nuclear Testing*, New York and Geneva: UNIDIR, 2009.

23. Nassim Nicholas Taleb, *The Black Swan: The Impact of the Highly Improbable*, London: Penguin, p. 64.

24. Charles Tilly, 'The Trouble with Stories', in Charles Tilly (ed.), *Stories, Identity and Political Change*, New York: Rowman and Littlefield, p. 258.

25. Freedman, *Strategy: A History*, p. 622.

26. Ibid., 634.

17. CONFESSIONS OF A PREMATURE CONSTRUCTIVIST

1. This chapter is a newly edited and amended version of 'Confessions of a Premature Constructivist', *Review of International Studies*, 32:4 (2006), which was a transcript of a plenary lecture given at the 40th anniversary conference of British International Studies Association, University

of St Andrews, December 2005. The author and the editors are grateful to the journal and to Cambridge University Press for permission to revise and publish in the present form.

2. Bernard Knox, 'Confessions of a Premature Anti-Fascist', *Los Angeles Times*, 23 July 2001. This was based on a lecture originally given at New York in July 1998.

3. Georg Lukacs, *History and Class Consciousness*, London: Merlin Books, 1967 [1920].

4. Karl Mannheim, *Ideology and Utopia*, London: Routledge, 1936. On Mannheim, see Colin Loader, *The Intellectual Development of Karl Mannheim*, Cambridge: Cambridge University Press, 1985.

5. C. Wright Mills, *The Sociological Imagination*, New York: Oxford University Press, 1959.

6. Daniel Bell, *The End of Ideology: On the Exhaustion of Political Ideas in the Fifties*, New York: The Free Press, 1960, republished Cambridge, MA: Harvard University Press, 2000.

7. Noam Chomsky, 'The Responsibility of Intellectuals', *New York Review of Books*, 23 February 1967.

8. Noam Chomsky, *American Power and the New Mandarins*, New York: New Press, 1969. This was republished in 2002.

9. I first came across Kołakowski in some collected essays, Leszek Kołakowski, *Marxism and Beyond: On Historical Understanding and Individual Responsibility*, London: Pall Mall, 1969.

10. C. Wright Mills, *The Causes of World War Three*, London: Secker and Warburg, 1958, 128–9.

11. 'Open Letter to Leszek Kołakowski' first appeared in the 1973 *Socialist Register*. It was republished in E.P. Thompson, *The Poverty of Theory and other Essays*, London: Merlin Press, 1978.

12. Kołakowski's reply, 'My Correct Views on Everything' was printed in the 1974 *Socialist Register*. It is the title essay of his collected essays, *My Correct View of Everything*, South Bend, IN: St Augustine's Press, 2005.

13. Fred Halliday, *The Making of the Second Cold War*, London: Verso, 1983.

14. Thomas Kuhn, *The Structure of Scientific Revolutions*, Chicago: University of Chicago Press, 1962.

15. John Kenneth Galbraith, *The Affluent Society*, London: Hamish Hamilton, 1958.

16. J. Peter Euben, 'Political Science and Political Silence', in Philip Green and Sanford Levinson (eds.), *Power and Community: Dissenting Essays in Political Science*, New York: Random House, 1970.

17. Peter Bachrach and Morton S. Baratz, 'Two Faces of Power', *American Political Science Review*, 56:4 (1962), pp. 947–52.

18. Lawrence Freedman, 'Logic, Politics, and Foreign Policy Processes: A Critique of the Bureaucratic Politics Model', *International Affairs*, 52 (1976), pp. 434–49.

19. Lawrence Freedman, *US Intelligence and the Soviet Strategic Threat*, London: Macmillan, 1978.

20. E.P. Thompson and Dan Smith (eds.), *Protest and Survive*, London: Penguin, 1980; Edward Thompson, 'Notes on Exterminism, The Last Stage of Civilization', *New Left Review*, 1:121 (May–June 1980).

21. Lawrence Freedman, 'A Criticism of the European Nuclear Disarmament Movement', *Armament and Disarmament Information Unit Report*, 2:4 (1980), pp. 1–4.

22. See George Weigel, 'Light from the East: Peace, Freedom, and the Civil Society', *American Purpose*, 1:3 (March 1987).

23. Hedley Bull, *The Anarchical Society*, London: Macmillan, 1977.

18. OBSERVATIONS ON WHITEHALL AND ACADEMIA

1. Sir David Omand, *Securing the State*, London: Hurst and New York: Oxford University Press, 2010, 209–51.

2. Michael S. Goodman, 'The Dog That Didn't Bark: The JIC and Warning of Aggression', *Cold War History*, 7:4 (Nov. 2007), 529–51.

3. www.esrc.ac.uk/funding-and-guidance/impact-toolkit/what-how-and-why/what-is-research-impact.aspx (last accessed 4 Feb. 2015).

4. The Economic and Social Research Council (ESRC) even has an 'impact toolkit' to help academics tailor their research proposals to the needs of the outside world, at least as defined by Whitehall, www.esrc.ac.uk/research/ (last accessed 5 Feb. 2015).

5. Efforts have been made to create a government-wide network of officials who are sympathetic to horizon scanning work and to build up expertise in its methodologies, see https://www.gov.uk/government/groups/horizon-scanning-programme-team (last accessed 5 Feb. 2015).

6. A good example is in President Obama's description of the failure to prevent the 'underpants bomber', Omar Farouk Abdulmuttalab, from boarding a transatlantic airliner, see www.thefreelibrary.com/ Obama%3a+US+intelligence+ %27failed+to+connect+dots%27-a0215899059 (last accessed 6 Feb. 2015).

7. Wilford E. G. Salter, *Productivity and Technical Change*, Cambridge: Cambridge University Press, 1960.

8. Sir Reginald H. Bacon, *Life of Lord Fisher*, London: Hodder and Stoughton, 1929, Vol. I, 172

9. Renamed in 1991 as the Defence Operational Analysis Centre and later subsumed into the Defence Research Agency and then DSTL.

10. Lawrence Freedman, *The Politics of British Defence 1979–1998*, London: Macmillan 1999, p. 83.

11. Cm 9315, *The Higher Organisation of Defence*, London: HMSO, 1984.

12. Michael Howard, *The Central Organisation for Defence*, London: Royal United Services Institute, 1970.

13. Such as two academic contributions from former insiders R. Hastie-Smith, *The Tin Wedding: A Study of the Evolution of the Ministry of Defence*, London: RCDS Seaford Papers, 1974, and Michael D. Hobkirk, 'Defence Organisation and Defence Decision-Making in the UK and the US', in L. W. Martin (ed.) *The Management of Defence*, London: Macmillan, 1976.

14. As described by MOD, see https://www.gov.uk/the-permanent-joint-headquarters (last accessed 6 Feb 2015).

15. Sir Leon Radzinowicz, *Adventures in Criminology*, London: Routledge, 1999, p. 172.

16. The Code can be found at https://www.gov.uk/government/uploads/system/uploads/attachment_data/file/278498/11–1382-code-of-practice-scientific-advisory-committees.pdf (last accessed 10 Feb 2015).

17. Annexed to Howard, *The Central Organisation*.

18. Walter Bagehot, *The English Constitution*, London: Fontana, 1894 edn, p. 218.

19. Lawrence Freedman, 'Chicago Speech: Some Suggestions', 3, available at http://www.iraqinquiry.org.uk/media/96209/1999-04-16-Memo-Freedman-to-Powell.pdf#search=freedman (last accessed 7 February 2017).

20. Chiara de Franco and Christoph O. Meyer (eds.), *Forecasting, Warning and Transnational Risks*, London: Palgrave Macmillan, 2011, p. 242–9.

21. Most clearly described in the 2015 *US National Security Strategy*, www.whitehouse.gov/sites/default/files/docs/2015_national_security_strategy.pdf (last accessed 9 Feb. 2015).

22. Michael S. Goodman and Sir David Omand, 'Analysts Training, CIA', *Studies in Intelligence*, 52:4 (2008), pp. 1–12.

23. John Maynard Keynes, 'Alfred Marshall, 1842–1924', *Economic Journal*, September 1924.

19. REFLECTIONS ON THE FREEDMAN SCHOOL

1. Lawrence Freedman, *Strategy: A History*, New York: Oxford University Press, 2013, p. 560.

2. Jacob Bronowski, *The Ascent of Man*, London: Book Club Associates in association with the BBC, 1977, p. 351.

3. Freedman, *Strategy*, p. 576.

4. The section relating to the policy world, in particular, and this final

reflection, throughout, are privileged by personal experience over 25 years, which significantly informs them at times. This is not, of course, unproblematic, I grant. It is, however, appropriate, and is why the label 'reflection' is used, in part. As well as the problem of possible prejudice, I risk making errors. Although I believe I have not, if this itself is a mistake, my apology is already present.

5. Although Iraq features in the foregoing chapters, there was no attempt to include Freedman's role in the Iraq Inquiry, as, even as this book was being finished, he was still working against the deadline for the million-word-plus report that the Inquiry would produce on all aspects of the 2003 Iraq adventure, before and after. This was destined to be a thankless task, inevitably, as the thorough, detailed and richly balanced work addressing what particular people knew and did not know at the time (rather than anything seen with subsequent knowledge or hindsight) was unlikely to satisfy anyone—except, perhaps, the purist scholars. Nonetheless, Freedman and his colleagues reached a conclusion in the report, published as the manuscript for the present book in its final stages, that charged former Prime Minister Tony Blair with sufficient personal responsibility that many observers were surprised and satisfied with, even if the report stopped short of judging him to have acted unlawfully, or to have lied. The Report of the iraq Inquiry, Report of a Group of Privy Counsellors Ordered by the House of Commons to be Printed on 6 July 2016, avialble at http://www.iraqinquiry.org.uk/the-report/ (accessed 7 February 2017).

6. Personally, it is interesting, however, to imagine—and this is pure speculation—what might have happened had the British Labour Party chosen David Miliband to be leader, not his brother Ed: while no one, of course, can know what would have happened otherwise for sure, there is a strong chance that David would have won the general election, where his brother calamitously lost it, in which case he might have given Freedman greater involvement, though not necessarily a formal role, and only if the Iraq Inquiry role permitted. Of course,

7. Both Freedman and Quinlan were among groups of Jewish and Roman Catholic intellectuals invited to a dinner with the Anglican Archbishop of Canterbury at Lambeth Palace to discuss nuclear issues. This must have been a memorable occasion and, whatever influence they might have had on the Archbishop, the influence the two of them had on each other was great.

8. I must acknowledge one of the peer reviewers here.

9. See Richard Dyer, 'Introduction to Film Studies', in John Hill and Pamela Church Gibson (eds.), *The Oxford Guide to Film Studies*, New York: Oxford University Press, 1998, ch. 1.

10. Lawrence Freedman (ed.), *War*, Oxford: Oxford University Press, 1994.

11. Unfortunately, by the time I gently suggested to Shane Brighton to contribute a 'friendly critique', it was far too late to be feasible. Mea culpa. Otherwise, he could have contributed a more sophisticated and developed challenge—and I might not have been writing these short paragraphs discussing the challenge.

12. Tarak Barkawi and Shane Brighton, 'Powers of War: Fighting, Knowledge, and Critique', *International Political Sociology*, 5:1 (2011), 26–143; and Barkawi and Brighton, 'Conclusion: Absent War Studies? War, Knowledge and Critique', in Hew Strachan and Sibylle Scheipers (eds.), *The Changing Character of War*, Oxford: Oxford University Press, 2011, pp. 524–42.

13. Barkawi and Brighton, 'Powers of War', p. 130.

14. Carl von Clausewitz, *On War*, tr. J.J. Graham, introduction and notes by Colonel F.N. Maude, introduction to the new edition by Jan Willem Honig, New York: Barnes and Noble, 2004.

15. For educational use of this approach, see http://www.phenomenaleducation.info/phenomenon-based-learning.html (accessed 10 February 2016).

16. *Independent on Sunday*, 25 January 2015.

17. While we would have happily embraced more sharply negative analyses (the contributions presented in this volume are certainly not simply plaudits and praise), it is surely a reflection of the esteem with which the various contributors hold the person and the work, as, in all probability, is their willingness to engage with this project. Of course, as noted in the Preface, it is also partly a function of practicalities and timing regarding at least one contributor, who would have been more outwardly sceptical, as his record already made clear.

18. Freedman, *Strategy*.

20. CONCLUSION

1. Lawrence Freedman, *The Evolution of Nuclear Strategy*, 3rd edn, Basingstoke: Palgrave Macmillan, 2003, p. xii.

2. Herman Kahn, *On Escalation*, New York: Praeger, 1965.

3. Freedman, *Evolution*, ch. 7.

4. *Deterrence*, Cambridge: Polity, 2004.

5. Freedman, *Evolution*, p. 21.

6. Lawrence Freedman and Efraim Karsh, *The Gulf Conflict*, London: Faber, 1992; Lawrence Freedman (ed.), *Military Intervention in European Conflicts*, Oxford: Blackwell, 1994.

7. 'The Blair Doctrine', Transcript, 22 April 1999, *PBS Newshour* available at http://www.pbs.org/newshour/bb/international-jan-june99-blair_doctrine4–23/ (accessed 1 February 2017); an edited video of Tony Blair delivering the speech is available at www.econclubchi.org/speakers (accessed 10 August 2014). Freedman, in a letter to Sir John Chilcot for the Iraq Inquiry concerning his involvement with Blair's Private Secretary Jonathan Powell about the speech, gave the following weblink for the transcript of the speech: http://www.econclubchi.org/Documents/Meeting/1afd70f3–4eb6–498d=b69b-a5a75b1.pdf; however, this link was not available in August 2014. Freedman's letter to Chilcot is available at http://www.iraqinquiry.org.uk/media/96241/2010-01-18-Letter-Freedman-to-Chilcot.pdf#search=freedman%20letter (accessed 1 February 2017) and accompanies a copy of his memo to Jonathan Powell about the Chicago speech, which includes the key points made by Blair: 'Chicago Speech: Some Suggestions', available at http://www.iraqinquiry.org.uk/media/42664/freedman-powell-letter.pdf (accessed 10 August 2014).

8. 'In retrospect, applying those tests to Iraq shows what a finely balanced case it was'. Tony Blair, *A Journey*, London: Hutchinson, 2010, p. 248.

9. The events from Kosovo to Iraq, and the emergence of the Blair Doctrine, also serve to illustrate Freedman's integrity and sound 'political' judgement, working closely with government (as he did with successive UK governments from the early 1980s onward), but never being seduced by the association with political power, nor losing intellectual and political independence—as his later involvement in the Iraq Inquiry also testifies.

10. This is what has been called 'the power of wrongdoing' elsewhere—James Gow, *War and War Crimes: Military, Legitimacy and Success in Armed Conflict*, London: Hurst and New York: Columbia University Press, 2012, p. 133.

11. The Iraq Inquiry, *The Report of the Iraq Inquiry*: *Report of a Committee of Privy Counselllors*, HC264, London: HMSO, Ordered by the House of Commons to be printed on 6 July 2016, available at http://www.iraqinquiry.org.uk/media/246416/the-report-of-the-iraq-inquiry_executive-summary.pdf (accessed 8 July 2016).

12. This category of Freedman's work, as he would probably acknowledge himself, is 'top down' and focused on strategic decision-making and the exercise of power, rather than being 'bottom up' studies of history as experienced by those living through it.

13. Lawrence Freedman, *The Official History of the Falklands Campaign: The Origins of the Falklands War: Vol. 1*, London: Routledge, 2007; *The Official*

History of the Falklands Campaign, Vol. 2: War and Diplomacy, London: Routledge, 2005.

14. Lawrence Freedman and Efraim Karsh, *The Gulf Conflict, 1990–91: Diplomacy and War in the New World Order*, London: Faber, 1993.

15. Lawrence Freedman, *Kennedy's Wars: Berlin, Cuba, Laos, and Vietnam*, New York: Oxford University Press, 2002.

16. Lawrence Freedman, *A Choice of Enemies: America Confronts the Middle East*, Toronto: Doubleday Canada, 2008, p. 511.

17. Lawrence Freedman, *The Transformation of Strategic Affairs*, Adelphi Paper 379, London: Routledge for the IISS, 2006.

18. Ibid., pp. 22–6.

19. Freedman *Strategy*, pp. 483–90.

20. Freedman, *Strategy*, p. 21.

21. Ibid., 619.

SELECT BIBLIOGRAPHY

(i) Authored Books, Edited Books, Articles and Chapters by Lawrence Freedman

A Choice of Enemies: America Confronts the Middle East, London: Weidenfeld and Nicholson, 2008.

A European Way of War, London: Centre for European Reform, 2004.

'A Theory of Battle or a Theory of War?' *Journal of Strategic Studies*, 28:3, 2005.

'Arms Control: Thirty Years On', *Daedalus*, Winter 1991.

Arms Control in Europe, London: RIIA, June 1981.

Arms Control: Management or Reform, London: RIIA, September 1986.

Arms Production in the United Kingdom: Problems and Prospects, London: RIIA, 1978.

Britain and Nuclear Weapons, London: Macmillan for Royal Institute of International Affairs, 1980.

Britain and the Falklands War, Oxford: Basil Blackwell, 1988.

Britain in the World with Michael Clarke, Cambridge: Cambridge University Press, 1991.

'Chicago Speech: Some Suggestions', 3, http://www.iraqinquiry.org.uk/media/96209/1999-04-16-Memo-Freedman-to-Powell.pdf (last accessed 7 February 2017).

'Confessions of a Premature Constructivist', *Review of International Studies*, 32:4, October 2006.

Deterrence, Cambridge: Polity Press, 2004.

'Escalation and Quagmires: Expectations and the Use of Force', *International Affairs*, 67:1, January 1991.

Europe Transformed, London: Tri-service Press, 1990.

'Has Strategy Reached a Dead-End?', *Futures*, 11, April 1979.

Independence in Concert: The British Rationale for Possessing Strategic Nuclear

Weapons, Nuclear History Program, with Martin Navias and Nicholas Wheeler, Occasional Paper 5, College Park: Center for International Studies, University of Maryland, 1989.

'Indignation, Influence and Strategic Studies', Inaugural Lecture in the Chair of War Studies, King's College London, 22 November 1983.

'International Security: Changing Targets', *Foreign Policy*, 110, Spring 1998.

Kennedy's Wars: Berlin, Cuba, Laos and Vietnam, New York: Oxford University Press, 2000.

'Logic, Politics and Foreign Policy Processes: A Critique of the Bureaucratic Politics Model', *International Affairs*, 52:3, July 1976.

Military Intervention in Europe, Oxford: Blackwell for Political Quarterly, 1994.

Military Power in Europe: Essays in Memory of Jonathan Alford, London: Macmillan, 1990.

Nuclear War and Nuclear Peace, with Edwina Moreton, Gerald Segal and John Baylis, London: Macmillan, l983; second edition, 1988.

'On the *Tiger's Back*: The Concept of Escalation', in Roman *Kolkowicz* (ed.), *The Logic of Nuclear Terror*, Boston: Allen and Unwin, 1987.

'On War and Choice', *The National Interest*, 107, May/June 2010.

Population Change and European Security, with John Saunders, London: Brassey's, 1991.

Scripting Middle East Leaders: The Impact of Leadership Perceptions on US and UK Foreign Policy, with Jeffrey Michaels, London: Bloomsbury, 2012.

Signals of War: The Falklands Conflict of 1982, with Virginia Gamba-Stonehouse, London: Faber and Faber, 1990.

Strategic Coercion, Oxford: Oxford University Press, 1998.

Strategic Defence in the Nuclear Age, London: IISS, Autumn 1987.

'Strategic Stability/Superiority: the US View', in Carl G. Jacobsen (ed.), *Strategic Power: USA/USSR*, Basingstoke: Macmillan, 1990.

'Strategic Studies and the Problem of Power', in Lawrence Freedman, Paul Hayes and Robert O'Neill (eds.), *War, Strategy, and International Politics: Essays in Honour of Sir Michael Howard*, Oxford: Clarendon Press, 1992.

Strategy: A History, Oxford University Press, 2013.

Super Terrorism: Policy Responses, London: Blackwells, 2002.

Terrorism, London: RIIA, October 1986.

'Terrorism as a Strategy', *Government and Opposition*, 42:3, 2007.

The Atlas of Global Strategy, London: Macmillan, 1985.

The Cold War, London: Cassell, 2001.

'The Age of Liberal Wars', *Review of International Studies*, 31:1, 2005.

'The Changing Forms of Military Conflict', *Survival*, 40:4, Winter 1998/9.

'The Counterrevolution in Strategic Affairs', *Daedalus*, 140:3, 2011.

The Evolution of Nuclear Strategy, London: Macmillan for International Institute for Strategic Studies, 1981; second edition, 1989; third edition 2003.

The Gulf Conflict 1990–91: Diplomacy and War in the New World Order, with Efraim Karsh, London: Faber, 1993.

The Military Threat, London: Greater London Area War Risk Study, GLAWARS Research Reports, 1986.

The Official History of the Falklands Campaign, Vol. 1 *Origins*, Vol. 2 *War and Diplomacy*, London: Routledge, 2005.

The Politics of British Defence Policy, 1979–1998, London: Macmillan, 1999.

The Price of Peace: Living with the Nuclear Dilemma, London: Firethorne, 1986.

The Primacy of Alliance: Deterrence and European Security, *Proliferation Papers* series, IFRI Security Studies Center, 46, March–April 2013.

The Revolution in Strategic Affairs, Adelphi Paper 318, Oxford University Press for IISS, 1998.

The South Atlantic Crisis of 1982: Implications for Nuclear Crisis Management, RAND/UCLA Center for the Study of Soviet International Behavior, May 1989.

'The Third World War', *Survival*, 40:4, Winter 2001.

The Transformation of Strategic Affairs, Adelphi Paper 379, Abingdon: Routledge for IISS, 2006.

The Treaty on Conventional Armed Forces in Europe: The Politics of Post-Wall Arms Control, with Catherine McArdle Kelleher and Jane M.O. Sharp, Baden-Baden: Nomos Verlagsgesellschaft, 1996.

The Troubled Alliance: Atlantic Relations in the 1980s, London: Heinemann, 1983.

US Nuclear Strategy: A Reader, with Philip Bobbitt and Gregory Treverton, London: Macmillan, 1989.

The West and the Modernization of China, London: RIIA, May 1979.

US Intelligence and the Soviet Strategic Threat, London: Macmillan, 1977, Reprinted 1986 with new foreword.

US Intelligence and the Soviet Strategic Threat, London and Basingstoke: Macmillan, 1997.

'Vietnam and the Disillusioned Strategist', *International Affairs*, 72:1, 1996.

War, Strategy and International Politics: Essays in Honour of Sir Michael Howard, with Paul Hayes and Robert O'Neill, Oxford: Clarendon Press, 1992.

War: A Reader, Oxford University Press, 1994.

(ii)   Authored Books, Edited Books, Articles and Chapters by Other Authors

Abelson, Robert. 'Psychological Status of the Script Concept', *American Psychologist*, 36:7, 1981.

Acton, George and James Perkovich (eds.). *Abolishing Nuclear Weapons: A Debate*, Washington, DC: Carnegie Endowment, 2009.

Acton, James. *Deterrence During Disarmament: Deep Nuclear Reductions and International Security*, London: IISS Adelphi Book no. 417, 2011.

Adamson, Michael R. 'Ambassadorial Roles and Foreign Policy: Elbridge

Durbrow, Frederick Nolting, and the U.S. Commitment to Diem's Vietnam, 1957–61', *Presidential Studies Quarterly*, 32:2, June 2002, 229–55.

Adler, Emmanuel. 'Complex Deterrence in Asymmetric-Warfare Era', in T.V. Paul, Patrick M. Morgan, and James J. Wirtz (eds.), *Complex Deterrence: Strategy in a Global Age*, Chicago: Chicago University Press, 2011.

Agamben, Giorgio. *State of Exception*, tr. Kevin Attell, Chicago: University of Chicago Press, 2005.

Ahern, Thomas L., Jr. *CIA and the Generals: Covert Support to Military Government in South Vietnam*, CIA Center for the Study of Intelligence, October 1998.

Akehurst, Michael. 'Humanitarian Intervention', in Hedley Bull (ed.), *Intervention in World Politics*, Oxford: Clarendon Press, 1984.

Arreguin-Toft, Ivan. 'How the Weak Win Wars: A Theory of Asymmetric Conflict', *International Security*, 26:1, 2001.

Axelrod, Robert. *Evolution of Cooperation*, New York: Basic Books, 1984.

———— *The Complexity of Cooperation: Agent-Based Models of Competition and Collaboration*, Princeton: Princeton University Press, 1997.

Axelrod, Robert and Douglas Dion. 'The Further Evolution of Cooperation', *Science*, 242:4884, 9 December 1988.

Axelrod, Robert and W.D. Hamilton, 'The Evolution of Cooperation', *Science*, 211:4489, 1981.

Ayala, Balthazar. *De Iure et Officiis Bellicis et Disciplina Militari*, Douai: Ioannes Bogardus, 1582.

Ayson, Robert. 'Strategic Studies', in Chris Reus-Smit and Duncan Snidal (eds.), *The Oxford Handbook of International Relations*, Oxford: Oxford University Press, 2008.

———— *Thomas Schelling and the Nuclear Age: Strategy as Social Science*, London: Frank Cass, 2004.

Ball, Moya Ann. 'A Case Study of the Kennedy Administration's Decision-Making Concerning the Diem Coup of November, 1963', *Western Journal of Speech Communication*, 54:4, 1990.

Barkawi, Tarak and Shane Brighton. 'Powers of War: Fighting, Knowledge and Critique', *International Political Sociology*, 5:2, 2010.

Barkin, J. Samuel. 'Realist Constructivism and Realist Constructivisms', *International Studies Review*, 6:2, 2004.

———— 'Realist Constructivism', *International Studies Review*, 5:3, 2003.

———— *Realist Constructivism*, Cambridge: Cambridge University Press, 2010.

Bayliss, John and Steve Smith. *The Globalization of World Politics: An Introduction to International Relations*, Oxford: Oxford University Press, 2001.

Beckett, Margaret. 'A World Free of Nuclear Weapons?', Keynote Address to the Carnegie International Non-Proliferation Conference, Washington, DC, 25 June 2007.

Bellamy, Alex J. 'The Responsibility to Protect: Five Years On', *Ethics and International Affairs*, 24:2, 2010.

Berry, Ken, Patricia Lewis, Benoît Pélopidas, Nikolai Sokov and Ward Wilson. *Delegitimizing Nuclear Weapons: Examining the Validity of Nuclear Deterrence*, Monterey: Monterey Institute for International Studies, May 2010.

Berthaut, Henri-Marie-Auguste and Jean Antonin Léon Bassot. *Les Ingénieurs-géographes militaires, 1624–1831*, 2 vols, Paris: Imprimerie du Service Géographique de l'Armée, 1902.

Best, Geoffrey. *Humanity in Warfare*, London: Weidenfeld and Nicolson, 1980.

Biggar, Nigel. *In Defence of War*, Oxford: Oxford University Press, 2013.

Bilder, Richard B. 'Speaking Law to Power: Lawyers and Torture', *American Journal of International Law*, 98:4, October 2004, 689–95.

Blair, Anne. *Lodge in Vietnam: A Patriot Abroad*, New Haven, CT: Yale University Press, 1995.

Blanot, Jean. *De Actionibus*, 1256.

Bobbitt, Philip. *The Garments of Court and Palace: Machiavelli and the World That He Made*, London: Atlantic Books, 2013.

Bond, Brian. *Liddell Hart: A Study of His Military Thought*, London: Cassell, 1977.

Bonet/Bouvet, Honoré. *L'Arbre des batailles*, Paris: Jehan du Pré, 1493.

Borrie, John. 'Humanitarian Reframing of Nuclear Weapons and the Logic of a Ban', *International Affairs*, 90:3, 2014.

Bowen, Wyn. 'Deterrence and Asymmetry: Non-State Actors and Mass Casualty Terrorism', *Contemporary Security Policy*, 25:1, 2004.

Brodie, Bernard, *War and Politics*, New York: Macmillan, 1973.

Brodie, Bernard (ed.). *The Absolute Weapon*, New York: Harcourt Brace, 1946.

Bronowski, Jacob, *The Ascent of Man*, London: Book Club Associates in association with the BBC, 1977.

Brown, Archie. *The Gorbachev Factor*, Oxford: Oxford University Press, 1996.

Bukovansky, Mlada, Ian Clark, Robyn Eckersley, Richard Price, Christian Reus-Smit and Nicholas J. Wheeler. *Special Responsibilities: Global Problems and American Power*, Cambridge: Cambridge University Press, 2012.

Bull, Hedley. *The Anarchical Society: A Study of Order in World Politics*, London: Macmillan, 1977.

Burchill, Scott, Andrew Linklater, Richard Devetak, Jack Donnelly, Terry Nardin, Matthew Paterson, Christian Reus-Smith and Jacqui True. *Theories of International Relations*, 2nd edn, London: Palgrave, 2001.

Buzan, Barry, Ole Weaver and Jaap de Wilde. *Security: A New Framework for Analysis*, Boulder, CO: Lynne Rienner, 1998.

Callwell, Colonel C.E. *Small Wars: Their Principles and Practice*, 3rd edn, London: HMSO, 1906.

Calvino, Italo. *Six Memos for the New Millennium*, London: Jonathan Cape, 1992.

Chandler, David G. *The Campaigns of Napoleon*, Vol. 2: *The Zenith, September 1805*, London: Folio Society, 2002.

Chernayev, Anatoliy. *My Six Years with Gorbachev*, University Park, PA: Penn State University Press, 2000.

Cicero, Marcus Tullius. *De Re Publica*, tr. Niall Rudd as *The Republic and The Laws*, Oxford: Oxford University Press, 1998.

——— *On Duties (De Officiis)*, ed. E.M. Atkins, tr. Miriam T. Griffin, Cambridge: Cambridge University Press, 1991.

Clausewitz, Carl von. *On War*, tr. Michael Howard and Peter Paret, Princeton: Princeton University Press, 1976.

Cohen, Jean. 'Trust, Voluntary Association and Workable Democracy: The Contemporary American Discourse of Civil Society', in Mark E. Warren (ed.), *Democracy and Trust*, Cambridge: Cambridge University Press, 1999.

Coleman, James. *Foundations of Social Theory*, Cambridge, MA: Harvard University Press, 1990.

Daalder, Ivo K. and James M. Lindsay. 'An alliance of democracies: our way or the highway', *Financial Times*, 6 November 2004, http://www.brookings.edu/research/opinions/2004/11/06globalgovernance-daalder (accessed 1 January 2014).

Deudney, Daniel and G. John Ikenberry. *Democratic Internationalism: An American Grand Strategy for a Post-Exceptionalist Era*, New York: Council on Foreign Relations, 2012.

Dijxhoorn, Ernst. *Quasi-state Entities and International Criminal Justice: Legitimising Narratives and Counter-Narratives* New York: Routledge, 2017

Douhet, Gen. Giulio. *Probabili aspetti della guerra futura*, reproduced in Gen. Giulio Douhet, *Il dominio dell'aria*, Verona: A. Mondadori, 1932.

Doyle, Michael P. *Ways of War and Peace: Realism, Liberalism, and Socialism*, New York: W.W. Norton and Co., 1997.

Dunn, David Hastings. 'Myths, Motivations and "Misunderestimations": The Bush Administration and Iraq', *International Affairs*, 79:2, March 2003.

Durkheim, Emile, *The Division of Labor in Society*, tr. W.D. Halls, New York: Macmillan, 1984.

Earle, Edward Mead (ed.). *Makers of Modern Strategy: Military Thought from Machiavelli to Hitler*, Princeton: Princeton University Press, 1943.

Esdaile, Charles. *Napoleon's Wars: An International History, 1803–1815*, New York: Viking, 2008.

Evangelista, Matthew. 'Turning Points in Arms Control', in Richard K. Herrmann and Richard Ned Lebow (eds.), *Ending the Cold War: Interpretations, Causation, and the Study of International Relations*, New York: Palgrave, 2004.

Fain, P. (ed.). *Mémoires du baron Fain, premier secrétaire du cabinet de l'empereur*, Paris: Plon, 1908.

Farrell, Henry and Jack Knight. 'Trust, Institutions and Institutional Change:

Industrial Districts and the Social Capital Hypothesis', *Politics and Society*, 31:4, 2003.

Feng, Zhang. *Chinese Hegemony: Grand Strategy, International Institutions, and Relationality in East Asian History*, Stanford, CA: Stanford University Press.

Finnemore, Martha and Stephen J. Toope. 'Alternatives to "Legalization": Richer Views of Law and Politics', *International Organization*, 55:3, 2001.

Fisher, David. *The Morality of War*, Oxford: Oxford University Press, 2011.

Ford, Harold P. *CIA and the Vietnam Policymakers: Three Episodes 1962–1968*, CIA Center for the Study of Intelligence, 1998.

Frieser, Karl-Heinz. *Blitzkrieg-Legende: Der Westfeldzug 1940*, 2nd edn, Munich: Oldenbourg, 1996.

———— *Mearsheimer, Liddell Hart and the Weight of History*, Ithaca, NY: Cornell University Press, 1988.

Frost, Mervyn. *Ethics in International Relations: A Constitutive Theory*, Cambridge: Cambridge University Press, 1996.

Fulbecke, William. *The Pandects of the Laws of Nations*, London: Thomas Wight, 1602.

Gajus. *Gai Institutiones, or Institutes of Roman Law by Gajus*, ed. E.A. Whittuck, tr. Edward Poste, Oxford: Clarendon Press, 1904.

Gat, Azar. *British Armour Theory and the Rise of the Panzer Arm: Revising the Revisionists*, Basingstoke: Macmillan, 2000.

———— *Fascist and Liberal Visions of War: Fuller, Liddell Hart, Douhet and Other Modernists*, Oxford: Clarendon Press, 1998.

Gearan, Anne and Karen DeYoung. 'Obama's 'red line' warning to Syria on chemical arms draws criticism', *Washington Post*, 21 August 2012.

Giladi, Rotem. 'Reflections on Proportionality, Military Necessity and the Clausewitzian War', *Israeli Law Review*, 45:2, July 2012.

Gillingham, John. 'Women, Children and the Profits of War', in Janet L. Nelson, Susan Reynolds and Susan M. Johns (eds.), *Gender and Historiography: Studies in the Earlier Middle Ages in Honour of Pauline Stafford*, London: Institute of Historical Research, 2012.

Godlewska, Anne. *Geography Unbound: French Geographic Science from Cassini to Humboldt*, Chicago: University of Chicago Press, 1999.

Godlewska, Anne, Marcus R. Le Tourneau and Paul Schauerte. 'Maps, Painting and Lies: Portraying Napoleon's Battlefields in Northern Italy', *Imago Mundi*, 57:2, 2005.

Goldstein, Joshua S. *International Relations*, 3rd edn, New York: Longman, 1999.

Gorbachev, Mikhail. *Memoirs*, New York: Doubleday, 1995.

Gow, James. *Defending the West*, Cambridge: Polity 2004.

———— *Triumph of the Lack of Will: International Diplomacy and the Yugoslav Crisis*, London and New York: Hurst and Columbia University Press, 1997.

———— *War and War Crimes: Military, Legitimacy and Success in Armed Conflict*, London and New York: Hurst and Columbia University Press, 2013.

Gratian. *Decretum* (Corpus Iuris Canonici: *Decretum*, Causa XXIII, Quaest. I, VIII).

Grotius, Hugo. *De Jure Belli ac Pacis*, tr. Francis W. Kelsey, Oxford: Clarendon Press, 1925.

Guthrie, Charles and Michael Quinlan. *Just War: The Just War Tradition: Ethics in Modern Warfare*, London: Bloomsbury, 2007.

Haass, Richard N. *War of Necessity: War of Choice*, New York: Simon & Schuster, 2009.

Holmes, John. *The Politics of Humanity*, London: Head of Zeus, 2013.

Honig, Jan Willem. 'Clausewitz's *On War*: Problems of Text and Translation', in Strachan, Hew and Andreas Herberg-Rothe (eds.), *Clausewitz in the Twenty-First Century*, Oxford: Oxford University Press, 2007.

———— 'The Idea of Total War: From Clausewitz to Ludendorff', in *The Pacific War as Total War: Proceedings of the 2011 International Forum on War History*, Tokyo: National Institute for Defence Studies, 2012, https://kcl-pure.kcl.ac.uk/portal/en/publications/the-idea-of-total-war-from-clause-witz-to-ludendorff(95527b6d-da0a-4f4c-ba11-179690c8d9c4)/export.html (last accessed 7 February 2017).

———— 'Totalitarianism and Realism: Hans Morgenthau's German Years', *Security Studies*, 5:2, 1995.

Howard, Michael. *War and the Liberal Conscience*, 2nd edn, London: Hurst, 2008.

Huizinga, Johan. *Homo Ludens*, London: Routledge and Kegan Paul, 1949.

Hurrell, Andrew. *On Global Order: Power, Values, and the Constitution of International Society*, Oxford: Oxford University Press, 2007.

Hutchinson, Phil, Rupert Read and Wes Sharrock. *There Is No Such Thing as a Social Science [Electronic Resource]: In Defence of Peter Winch*, Directions in Ethnomethodology and Conversation Analysis, Aldershot: Ashgate, 2008.

Jackson, Patrick Thaddeus. 'Bridging the Gap: Toward a Realist-Constructivist Dialogue', *International Studies Review*, 6:2, 2004.

Jackson, Patrick Thaddeus and Daniel H. Nexon. 'Constructivist Realism or Realist Constructivism?', *International Studies Review*, 6:2, 2004.

Johnson, James Turner. *Ideology, Reason, and the Limitation of War*, Princeton: Princeton University Press, 1975.

———— *Just War Tradition and the Restraint of War: A Moral and Historical Inquiry*, Princeton: Princeton University Press, 1981.

Johnson, Rebecca. *Unfinished Business: The Negotiation of the CTBT and the End of Nuclear Testing*, New York and Geneva: UNIDIR, 2009.

Justinian. *The Digests of Justinian*, tr. Henry Monro, 2 vols., Cambridge: Cambridge University Press, 1904, 1909.

444

SELECT BIBLIOGRAPHY

Kahn, Herman. *On Escalation*, New York: Praeger, 1965.

Kahneman, Daniel. *Thinking, Fast and Slow*, London: Penguin, 2012.

Kang, David C. 'Hierarchy and Legitimacy in International Systems: The Tribute System in Early Modern East Asia', *Security Studies*, 19:4, 2010.

Kaplan, Fred. *The Wizards of Armageddon*, New York: Simon & Schuster, 1983.

Katzenstein, Peter J. 'Introduction', in P. Katzenstein (ed.), *The Culture of National Security: Norms and Identity in World Politics*, New York: Columbia University Press, 1996.

Katzenstein, Peter, Robert O. Keohane and Stephen Krasner. 'International Organization and the Study of World Politics', *International Organization*, 50:4, 1999.

Kołakowski, Leszek. 'The Self-Poisoning of the Open Society', in *Modernity on Endless Trial*, Chicago: University of Chicago Press, 1990.

Kortüm, Hans-Henning. *Transcultural Wars from the Middle Ages to the 21st Century*, Berlin: Akademie Verlag, 2006.

Koslowski, Rey and Friedrich V. Kratochwill. 'Understanding Change in International Politics: The Soviet Empire's Demise and the International System', *International Organization*, 48:2, 1994.

Kraines, David and Vivian Kraines. 'Evolution of Learning among Pavlov Strategies in a Competitive Environment with Noise', *Journal of Conflict Resolution*, 39, 1995.

Lebow, Richard Ned. *A Cultural Theory of International Relations*, Cambridge: Cambridge University Press, 2008.

———— 'Beyond Parsimony: Rethinking Theories of Coercive Bargaining', *European Journal of International Relations*, 4:1, 1998.

———— 'Constructive Realism', *International Studies Review*, 6:2, 2004.

———— 'Deterrence: A Political and Psychological Critique', in Paul C. Stern, Robert Axelrod, Robert Jervis and Roy Radner (eds.), *Perspectives on Deterrence*, New York: Oxford University Press, 1989.

———— *The Tragic Vision of Politics: Ethics, Interests and Orders*, Cambridge: Cambridge University Press, 2003.

Lebow, Richard Ned and Janice Gross Stein. *We All Lost the Cold War*, Princeton: Princeton University Press, 1994.

Legnano, Giovanni da. *Tractatus de Bello, de Represaliis et de Duello* (1360), ed. and tr. Thomas Erskine Holland, tr. James Leslie Brierly, Oxford University Press for the Carnegie Institution, 1917.

Liddell Hart, B.H. *Paris, or the Future of War*, London: Kegan, Paul, 1925.

———— *Sherman, Soldier, Realist, American*, Boston: Dodd, Mead, 1929.

———— *The Decisive Wars of History: A Study of Strategy*, London: Bell, 1929.

Lieberman, Elli. *Reconceptualizing Deterrence: Nudging Toward Rationality in Middle Eastern Rivalries*, New York: Routledge, 2012.

Lock-Pullan, Richard. *US Intervention Policy and Army Innovation: From Vietnam to Iraq*, New York: Routledge, 2006.

Lodge, Henry Cabot. *The Storm Has Many Eyes: A Personal Narrative*, New York: W.W. Norton and Co., 1973.

Loque, Bertrand de, *Deux traités: l'un de la guerre, l'autre du duel*, Lyons: Iacob Rayoyre, 1589; excerpts translated in Beatrice Heuser (ed.), *Strategy Makers: Thoughts on War and Society from Machiavelli to Clausewitz*, Santa Barbara, CA: ABC-Clio for Praeger, 2010.

Luck, Edward C. 'Building a Norm: The Responsibility to Protect Experience', in Robert I. Rotberg (ed.), *Mass Atrocity Crimes: Preventing Future Outrages*, Washington DC: Brookings Institution Press, 2010.

———— 'The Responsibility to Protect: Growing Pains or Early Promise?', *Ethics and International Affairs*, 24:4, 2010.

Lukes, Steven. *Power: A Radical View*, London: Macmillan, 1974.

MacFarlane, S. Neil and Yuen Foong Khong. *Human Security and the UN*, Indianapolis: Indiana University Press, 2006.

Mack, Andrew J.R. 'Why Big Nations Lose Small Wars: The Politics of Asymmetric Conflict', *World Politics*, 27:2, 1975.

Madison, James. 'Federalist Number 10', in Alexander Hamilton, James Madison and John Jay, *The Federalist Papers*, Baltimore: Johns Hopkins University Press, 1981.

Magee, Bryan and Michael Ayers in Bryan Magee (ed.). *The Great Philosophers*, London: BBC, 1987.

Marsh, D. and G. Stoker (eds.). *Theory and Methods in Political Science*, Basingstoke: Palgrave, 2002.

Marx, Gary. 'An Ethics of the New Surveillance', *The Information Society*, 14:3, 1998.

Mattern, Janice Bially. 'Power in Realist Constructivist Research', *International Studies Review*, 6:2, 2004.

Mauss, Marcel. *The Gift: The Form and Reason for Exchange in Archaic Societies*, tr. W.D. Halls, New York: Norton, 1990 [1925].

Mayall, James (ed.). *The New Interventionism, 1991–1994*, Cambridge: Cambridge University Press, 1996.

Mearsheimer, John. *The Tragedy of Great Power Politics*, New York: Norton, 2001.

Mendenhall, Ambassador Joseph A. Interview on 11 February 1991, Association for Diplomatic Studies and Training, Foreign Affairs Oral History Project, 1998.

Mercer, Jonathan. 'Emotion and Strategy in the Korean War', *International Organization*, 67, Spring 2013.

———— 'Emotional Beliefs', *International Organization*, 64, 2010.

———— 'Rationality and Psychology in International Politics', *International Organization*, 59, 2005.

Michalski, Milena and James Gow. *War, Image and Legitimacy: Viewing Contemporary Conflict*, New York: Routledge, 2007.

Morgenthau, Hans J. *Politics among Nations: The Struggle for Power and Peace*, New York: McGraw-Hill, 1993.

Morris, Nicholas. 'Humanitarian Intervention in the Balkans', in Jennifer M. Welsh (ed.), *Humanitarian Intervention and International Relations*, Oxford: Oxford University Press, 2004.

Navari, Cornelia and Daniel M. Green (eds.). *Guide to the English School in International Studies*, Guides to International Studies, Chichester and Malden, MA: Wiley Blackwell, 2014.

Nederman, Cary J. 'Niccolo Machiavelli', in *Stanford Encyclopedia of Philosophy* (Fall 2009 edn), ed. Edward N. Zalta, http://plato.stanford.edu (last accessed 7 February 2017).

Nef, John U., *War and Human Progress: An Essay on the Rise of Industrial Civilization*, Cambridge, MA: Harvard University Press, 1950.

Neff, Stephen. *War and the Law of Nations*, Cambridge: Cambridge University Press, 2005.

Nowak, Martin and Karl Sigmund. 'A Strategy of Win-Shift, Lose-Stay That Outperforms Tit-for-Tat in the Prisoner's Dilemma Game', *Nature*, 364, 1993.

Nye, Joseph S. *The Paradox of American Power*, New York: Oxford University Press, 2002.

Omand, David. 'Ethical Guidelines in Using Secret Intelligence Services', *Cambridge Review of International Affairs*, 19:4, 2006.

Onosander. *Onosandri Strategeticus sive de Imperatoris Institutione*, Paris: Saugrain, 1599, Book 4, ed. and tr. W. Oldfather, Loeb Classical Library, New York: G.P. Putnam's Sons, 1923.

Palmer, R.R. 'Frederick the Great, Guibert, Bülow: From Dynastic to National War', in Edward Meade Earle (ed.), *Makers of Modern Strategy: Military Thought from Machiavelli to Hitler*, Princeton: Princeton University Press, 1943.

Pizan, Christine de. *Le Livre des faits et bonnes mœurs du roi Charles V le Sage*, II.iv, tr. and ed. Eric Hicks and Thérèse Moreau, Paris: Stock, 1997.

———— *Le Livre du corps de policie*, I.9, ed. Angus J. Kennedy, Paris: Honoré Champion, 1998.

———— *Livre des fais d'armes et de chevalerie* (1410), published as *L'Art de la chevalerie selon Végèce*, Paris: Antoine Verard, 1488.

Post, Jerrold M. 'Terrorist Psycho-Logic: Terrorist Behavior as a Product of Psychological Forces', in Walter Reich (ed.), *Origins of Terrorism: Psychologies, Ideologies, Theologies, States of Mind*, Washington, DC: Woodrow Wilson Center Press, 1998.

———— *The Mind of the Terrorist: The Psychology of Terrorism from the IRA to al-Qaeda*, Basingstoke: Palgrave Macmillan, 2007.

Prados, John (ed.). *The White House Tapes: Eavesdropping on the President*, New York: The New Press, 2003.

SELECT BIBLIOGRAPHY

Prendergast, Christopher. *Napoleon and History Painting: Antoine-Jean Gros's 'La Bataille d'Eylau'*, Oxford: Clarendon Press, 1997.

Prunier, Gerard. *Africa's World War*, Oxford: Oxford University Press, 2009.

Rabe, Stephen G. *The Most Dangerous Area in the World: John F. Kennedy Confronts Communist Revolution in Latin America*, Chapel Hill, NC: University of North Carolina Press, 1999.

Ramet, Sabrina P. 'The United States and Europe: Toward Greater Cooperation or a Historic Parting? An Idealist Perspective', in Sabrina Ramet and Christina Ingebretsen (eds.). *Coming In from the Cold War: Changes in US–European Interactions since 1980*, Lanham, MD: Rowman and Littlefield, 2002.

Reich, Simon and Richard Ned Lebow. *Goodbye Hegemony! Power and Influence in the Global System*, Princeton: Princeton University Press, 2014.

Reus-Smit, Christian. *American Power and World Order*, Cambridge: Polity Press, 2004.

Rich, John. 'Warfare and External Relations in the Middle Roman Republic', in Beatrice Heuser and Anja Victorine Hartmann (eds.), *War, Peace and World Orders in European History*, London: Routledge, 2001.

Riley-Smith, Jonathan. *What Were the Crusades?*, 4th edn, Basingstoke: Palgrave Macmillan, 2009.

Roberts, Adam. 'NATO's "Humanitarian War" over Kosovo', *Survival*, 41:3, 1999.

Robichon, François. *Edouard Detaille: un siècle de gloire militaire*, Paris: Bernard Giovanangeli and Ministère de la Défense, 2007.

Rodin, David. *War and Self Defence*, Oxford: Oxford University Press, 2002.

Rühle von Lilienstern, August. *Handbuch für den Offizier: zur Belehrung im Frieden und zum Gebrauch im Felde*, Vol. 2, Berlin: G. Reimer, 1818.

Rummel, R.J. *Democide: Nazi Genocide and Mass Murder*, New Brunswick, NJ: Transaction Publishers, 1992.

Sageman, Marc. *Leaderless Jihad: Terror Networks in the Twenty-First Century*, Philadelphia: University of Pennsylvania Press, 2008.

———— *Understanding Terror Networks*, Philadelphia: University of Pennsylvania Press, 2004.

Schank, Roger and Robert Abelson. *Scripts, Plans, Goals, and Understanding: An Inquiry into Human Knowledge Structures*, Hove: Psychology Press, 1977.

Schank, Roger C. *Tell Me a Story: A New Look at Real and Artificial Memory*, New York: Scribner, 1990.

Schatzki, Theodore R. *Social Practices: A Wittgensteinian Approach to Human Activity and the Social*, Cambridge: Cambridge University Press, 1996.

Schelling, Thomas C. *Arms and Influence*, New Haven: Yale University Press, 1966.

Schnabel, Albrecht and Ramesh Thakur (eds.). *Kosovo and the Challenge of Humanitarian Intervention*, Tokyo: UNU Press, 2000.

Schöplflin, George. *Nations, Identity, Power*, London: Hurst, 2000.

Sheehan, Neil, Hendrick Smith, E.W. Kenworthy and Fox Butterfield. *The Pentagon Papers*, Vol. 2, Boston: Beacon Press, 1971.

Simons, Geoff. *Vietnam Syndrome: The Impact on US Foreign Policy*, London: Palgrave, 1998.

Slaughter, Anne-Marie. 'International Relations, Principal Theories', in R. Wolfrum (ed.), *Max Planck Encyclopedia of Public International Law*, New York: Oxford University Press, 2011, https://www.princeton.edu/~slaughtr/Articles/722_IntlRelPrincipalTheories_Slaughter_20110509zG.pdf and http://opil.ouplaw.com/view/10.1093/law:epil/9780199231690/law-9780199231690-e722?rskey=J4F7b8&result=1&prd=OPIL (both accessed 11 July 2014).

Smith, Rupert. 'The Security Council and the Bosnian Conflict: A Practitioner's View', in Vaughan Lowe, Adam Roberts, Jennifer Welsh and Dominik Zaum (eds.). *The Security Council and War: The Evolution of Thought and Practice since 1945*, Oxford: Oxford University Press, 2008.

Smith, Steve, Ken Booth and Marysia Zalewski (eds.). *International Theory: Positivism and Beyond*, Cambridge: Cambridge University Press, 1996.

Snyder, Glenn. *Deterrence and Defense: Toward a Theory of National Security*, Princeton: Princeton University Press, 1961.

Sorrick, Tim. 'Political Violence Prevention: Profiling Domestic Terrorists', *Small Wars Journal*, 6, June 2013.

Sterling-Folker, Jennifer. 'Realist-Constructivism and Morality', *International Studies Review*, 6:2, 2004.

Stone, John. *Military Strategy: The Politics and Technique of War*, London: Continuum, 2011.

Strachan, Hew and Andreas Herberg-Rothe (eds.). *Clausewitz in the Twenty-First Century*, Oxford: Oxford University Press, 2007.

Strauss, Leo. *Thoughts on Machiavelli*, Chicago: University of Chicago Press, 1958.

Suchman, Mark. 'Managing Legitimacy: Strategic and Institutional Approaches', *Academy of Management Review*, 20, 1995.

Syse, Henrik. 'The Platonic Roots of Just War Doctrine: A Reading of Plato's Republic', *Diametros*, 23, 2010.

Taleb, Nassim Nicholas. *The Black Swan: The Impact of the Highly Improbable*, London: Penguin, 2008.

Taylor, Charles. *Philosophy and the Human Sciences: Philosophical Papers*, Vol. 2, Cambridge: Cambridge University Press, 1985.

Terrif, Terry, Stuart Croft, Lucy James and Patrick M. Morgan. *Security Studies Today*, Cambridge: Polity, 1999.

Thierry, J.D. *Arc de Triomphe de l'Etoile*, Paris: Firmin Didot, 1845.

Tilly, Charles. 'The Trouble with Stories', in Charles Tilly (ed.), *Stories, Identity and Political Change*, New York: Rowman and Littlefield, 2002.

SELECT BIBLIOGRAPHY

Trager, Robert and Dessislava Zagorcheva. 'Deterring Terrorism: It Can Be Done', *International Security*, 30:3, 2006.

Turner, Stephen B. *The Social Theory of Practices: Tradition, Tacit Knowledge and Presuppositions*, Chicago: Chicago University Press, 1994.

Vache, Colonel Jean-Baptiste. *Napoléon en campagne*, Paris: Berger-Levrault, 1913.

Vattel, Emeric de. *Le Droit des gens, ou Principes de la loi naturelle*, Book 3, 'De la guerre', Leyden: La Compagnie, 1758.

Vitoria, Francisco de. *De Iure Belli*, 3.1, Sec. 37, in *De Indis Relectio Posterior, sive de Iure Belli*, 3.1, reprinted as Vitoria, *Political Writings*, tr. Jeremy Lawrance, Cambridge: Cambridge University Press, 1991.

Walker, William, *A Perpetual Menace: Nuclear Weapons and International Order*, London and New York: Routledge, 2012.

Waltz, Kenneth N., *Theory of International Politics*, Reading, MA: Addison Wesley, 1979.

Wendt, Alexander. 'Anarchy Is What States Make It: The Social Construction of Power Politics', *International Organization*, 46:2, 1992.

———— *The Social Theory of International Relations*, Cambridge: Cambridge University Press, 1999.

Whetham, David (ed.). *Ethics, Law and Military Operations*, Basingstoke: Palgrave Macmillan, 2011.

Williams, Matthew A. and Jack Covarrubias. 'A Realist-Constructivist Approach to Policy: Maintaining Power within a Viable Security Community', Prepared for the Annual Convention of the International Studies Association in New Orleans, Louisiana, 17–20 February 2010, http://citation.allacademic.com//meta/p_mla_apa_research_citation/4/1/4/2/1/pages414212/p414212–1.php (accessed 25 July 2014).

Willis, James F. *Prologue to Nuremberg*, New York: Greenwood Press, 1982.

Wilson, Peter. *The International Theory of Leonard Woolf: A Study on Twentieth-Century Idealism*, Basingstoke: Palgrave Macmillan, 2003.

Wilson, Ward. 'The Myth of Nuclear Deterrence', *Nonproliferation Review*, 15:3, November 2008.

Windsor, Philip. 'IR: The State of the Art', in Mats Berdal (ed.), *Studies in International Relations: Essays by Philip Windsor*, Brighton: Sussex Academic Press, 2002.

Wright, Quincy. *A Study of War*, Chicago: Chicago University Press, 1942.

Wu Jianzhong and Robert Axelrod. 'Coping with Noise: How to Cope with Noise in the Iterated Prisoner's Dilemma', *Journal of Conflict Resolution*, 39, March 1995.

(iii) Selected Documents Cited.

'2005 World Summit Outcome Document', A/RES/60/1.

SELECT BIBLIOGRAPHY

'Authorization for Use of Military Force (2001 S.J.Res. 23), https://http://www.govtrack.us/congress/bills/107/sjres23.

'Ban Ki-moon Address to Sofia Platform', 12 May 2011.

'Efforts of the United Nations and the Organisation for the Prohibition of Chemical Weapons to Accomplish the Elimination of Syrian Chemical Weapons', http://www.state.gov/t/isn/rls/rm/2014/223973.htm.

Eliminating Nuclear Threats: A Practical Agenda for Global Policymakers, Report of the International Commission on Nuclear Non-Proliferation and Disarmament, Canberra and Tokyo, 2009.

International Commission on Intervention and State Sovereignty. *The Responsibility to Protect*, Ottawa: International Development Research Center, 2001.

Kosovo, Foreign Affairs Committee, 4th Report, Vol. 3, London: The Stationery Office, 2000.

Lord Hannay, House of Lords Debate on Libya, 1 April 2011, www.publications.parliament.uk/pa/ld201011/ldhansrd/text/110401-0001.htm.

Our Global Neighbourhood: Report of the Commission on Global Governance, Oxford: Oxford University Press, 1995.

'Reflections on Intervention', 26 June 1998, in Kofi Annan, *The Question of Intervention: Statements by the Secretary-General*, New York: United Nations Department of Public Information, 1999.

'Report of the Secretary-General's Internal Review Panel on United Nations Action in Sri Lanka', November 2012.

Statement by President Mahmoud Ahmadinejad to the 2010 Non-Proliferation Treaty Review Conference, New York, 3 May 2010.

'The Blair Doctrine', Transcript, 22 April 1999, *PBS Newshour*, http://www.pbs.org/newshour/bb/international-jan-june99-blair_doctrine4-23/.

'The Responsibility to Protect: Report of the International Commission on Intervention and State Sovereignty (ICISS)', Ottawa: IDRC, 2001.

The U.S. Army and Marine Corps Counterinsurgency Field Manual, U.S. Army Field Manual No. 3, Chicago: University of Chicago Press, 2007.

The White House, National Security Strategy, May 27, 2010, www.whitehouse.gov/sites/default/files/rss_viewer/national_security_strategy.pdf.

Treaty between the United States and Other Powers Providing for the Renunciation of War as an Instrument of National Policy. Signed at Paris, 27 August 1928; ratification advised by the Senate, 16 January 1929; ratified by the President, 17 January 1929.

'UK Paper on International Action in Response to Humanitarian Crises', *British Yearbook of International Law, 2001*.

UN Security Council Resolution UN doc. S/RES/1270, 22 October 1999.

UN Security Council Resolution UN doc. S/RES/1970 (2011), 26 March 2011.

SELECT BIBLIOGRAPHY

UN Security Council Resolution UN doc. S/RES/1973, 17 March 2011.

UN Security Council Resolution UN doc. S/RES/2149, 10 April 2014.

UN Security Council Resolution UN doc. S/RES/2150 (2014), 16 April 2014.

UN Security Council Statement UN doc. S/1999/957, 8 September 1999.

UNDP, *Human Development Report 1994*, New York: Oxford University Press, 1994.

INDEX

INDEX

INDEX